Anthony Barnett was the first Director of Charter 88, the campaign for constitutional reform, 1988–95. He co-founded *openDemocra* 2001, was its first Editor and writes regularly for it. He co-dire Convention on Modern Liberty in 2009. He is a Londoner

# THE LURE OF GREATNESS

England's Brexit & America's Trump

ANTHONY BARNETT

**Unbound**

This edition first published in 2017

Unbound
6th Floor Mutual House, 70 Conduit Street, London W1S 2GF
www.unbound.com
All rights reserved

Text Design by Ellipsis

A CIP record for this book is available from the British Library

ISBN 978-1-78352-453-2 (trade hbk)
ISBN 978-1-78352-454-9 (ebook)
ISBN 978-1-78352-452-5 (limited edition)

Printed in Great Britain by Clays Ltd, St Ives Plc

3 5 7 9 8 6 4 2

for
Henry Porter
Artist & Citizen

## England, 1830

These vague allusions to a country's wrongs,
Where one says 'Ay' and others answer 'No'
In contradiction from a thousand tongues,
Till like to prison-cells her freedoms grow
Becobwebbed with these oft-repeated songs
Of peace and plenty in the midst of woe –
And is it thus they mock her year by year,
Telling poor truth unto her face she lies,
Declaiming of her wealth with gibe severe,
So long as taxes drain their wished supplies?
And will these jailers rivet every chain
Anew, yet loudest in their mockery be,
To damn her into madness with disdain,
Forging new bonds and bidding her be free?

John Clare

Dear Reader,

The book you are holding came about in a rather different way to most others. It was funded directly by readers through a new website: Unbound. Unbound is the creation of three writers. We started the company because we believed there had to be a better deal for both writers and readers. On the Unbound website, authors share the ideas for the books they want to write directly with readers. If enough of you support the book by pledging for it in advance, we produce a beautifully bound special subscribers' edition and distribute a regular edition and e-book wherever books are sold, in shops and online.

This new way of publishing is actually a very old idea (Samuel Johnson funded his dictionary this way). We're just using the internet to build each writer a network of patrons. At the back of this book, you'll find the names of all the people who made it happen.

Publishing in this way means readers are no longer just passive consumers of the books they buy, and authors are free to write the books they really want. They get a much fairer return too – half the profits their books generate, rather than a tiny percentage of the cover price.

If you're not yet a subscriber, we hope that you'll want to join our publishing revolution and have your name listed in one of our books in the future. To get you started, here is a £5 discount on your first pledge. Just visit unbound.com, make your pledge and type **greatness5** in the promo code box when you check out.

Thank you for your support,

Dan, Justin and John
Founders, Unbound

# CONTENTS

# New Walls

If you are British, and especially if you are young and British, your right to move, live, love, work, research and settle in another country of our continent, may be taken away from you by Brexit, should it be implemented. The likelihood that the UK will leave the EU strikes at your freedom to be the European that you are. Equally important, it removes your ability to welcome Europeans to come and live with you. Instead they, and the millions of Europeans who have helped to make our country so much a better place to live in, face the threat of expulsion. Grief over the loss of a shared European future hurts the young especially, but not only. Scientists, artists, scholars, medical researchers, business people and engineers – all those engaged in creative work and cultures embedded in international collaboration that the EU has assisted so hugely – are torn inwardly as the UK is ripped out of their European networks.

If you are American, your right to exist without fear is in jeopardy. In a country of immigrants, to be an immigrant is to live in dread, if not for oneself, for relatives or visitors. Welcome to what it is like to be black, is one riposte, revealing what is at stake when contempt for due process, civilised government, honesty and every liberty except wealth rules in the White House. It was becoming possible to love, live and share life with others without regard to the colour of their skin, nationality or religion. This has been put at risk by the election of Trump.

Perhaps the expectations were unspoken and it was only after his election and the referendum that something precious was lost, that is akin to bereavement. In addition to personal fears a dangerous political poison is in the air. Many were elated at the prospect of

Trump and Brexit giving them voice and self-government, but in Washington and London authoritarian centralisers are bending the state to their will. These horrible developments are separated by the Atlantic but joined by more than the coincidence of taking place within months of each other.

Since the end of the Second World War, shared human rights have transformed the meaning of individual liberty across Europe. The German Chancellor Angela Merkel grew up in East Germany behind the wall that literally divided her country. No one could cross it without permission, or they put their life at risk. For her in an extreme form, but also for hundreds of millions of us, freedom to move across the EU means the end to a kind of imprisonment. Even if most of us decide to stay in our own country, this becomes a chosen destination when we have the right not just to travel but also to stay, temporarily or permanently, in any of the extraordinary range of settlements across the 4.3 million square kilometres of the Union. Suddenly a new wall has been thrown up across part of Europe. In 2017 the barrier of Brexit is just a declaration, all the more alarming because its meaning and consequences are still unclear.

The wall that Trump promises between the USA and Mexico is an expensive joke. Drugs fly. A significant barrier, often in fact a wall, exists. Millions of illegal immigrants are already caught and deported back. What is no joke is the symbolism of his proclamation: an internal wall is being driven into the heart of the country, separating Americans from one another. Legally nothing has so far been changed by Trump's election. In practice the dark history of vigilantism that harks back to the lynch mobs of the Jim Crow era has been fanned back into life. Instead of violent prejudice becoming marginalised and dying out, for the first time the Ku Klux Klan celebrated the election of a new president. A terrible permission has been let loose across the United States.

The paralegal enforcement of discrimination never stopped in the USA, but now we are witnessing its resurgence expressed by the intensification of widespread voter suppression.[1] A detailed report says 868 polling stations were closed between the 2012 election and 2016 at a time of population increase, hitting poorer voters especially and tilting outcomes to favour Republicans.[2] Because this is systematic it defines actually existing America. The elimination of blacks and other minorities as well as poor whites from the electoral roll in key states may even technically have won the election for Trump. Especially shocking is the acceptance of such suppression and its purposive racial bias – a collusion that makes the whole country complicit. Millions of Americans are not registered to vote even though they are entitled to, and millions are in effect prevented from doing so.

The United States barely qualifies as a democracy in this respect. No one with an interest in the election of the most powerful person on the planet could have failed to register the importance of 'the Second Amendment' in the presidential contest. It enshrines the right of American citizens to bear arms. Trump positioned himself as its defender and Clinton, falsely, as someone who would undo it, when she demanded fewer weapons of mass slaughter be sold to the mentally unsound. The National Rifle Association became Trump's number one lobbyist to defend the Second Amendment. Meanwhile the entire political system is in breach of the Fifteenth Amendment, about which nothing is heard:

> The right of citizens of the United States to vote shall not be denied or abridged by the United States or by any State on account of race, color, or previous condition of servitude. The Congress shall have power to enforce this article by appropriate legislation.

The election of Trump legitimates the deep springs of American racism, measured by its failure to defend the Fifteenth Amendment. A renewed separation, segmentation and walling up of the peoples of the United States has been endorsed if by an anti-democratic eighteenth-century electoral system. In a similar way, the touchpaper of racial and cultural divisions inside Britain has been lit by an arbitrary plebiscite called without a written constitutional framework, that tears us from our European neighbours and throws up a barrier between us.

However, this is not *why* 52 per cent of British voters plumped for Brexit; nor is it the intention of the 47 per cent of American voters who backed Trump to turn their country into a bastion of white supremacy. For some, yes. Both votes had a core of supporters who are plainly anti 'foreigners' – anti-Europeans, anti-Muslim and racist – but nothing like enough to deliver electoral success. Neither Trump supporters nor Brexit voters are single monolithic groups, indeed the impulse to stereotype them as such can draw on the same itch as racism. Brexit was presented as a campaign for democracy and national self-government, not intolerance. Nearly a quarter of Trump's supporters said he was not qualified and didn't have the temperament to be president, yet they voted for him.[3] A profound and multilayered process is under way concerning who has the right to rule, in what ways and how this relates to our neighbours and the world as a whole. It is political, economic, social, cultural, national, global and imaginative.

Imaginative because we look straight away to the tangible: shout out an unfairness, protest an injustice, mobilise to defend a specific right, point a finger at a lie. But we live in an age of the intangible: of hedge funds and derivatives, globalism and fundamentalism, carbon emissions and climate change; precariousness and longing; a desire for democracy locked in a system managed by the unaccountable. The intangible has physical consequences: houses are repossessed, heads literally roll, children go hungry, lungs get cancers, storms shatter communities, and some get yachts in warm waters. How this comes about is not straightforward. It is not just caused by globalisation – another intangible. There was globalisation in the nineteenth century and after the Second World War, both of very different kinds to today's. The 'globalist' system that Trump rails against and the Brexiteers want to join, where the market rules, is governed by world banks and international funds, yet presents itself as 'natural', seeking only to assist 'the market'. As for the market's responsibility, say with respect to the financial crash, Macavity, the master of concealment, is never there.

Only this time, in their millions, voters defied actually existing globalisation that pretends it is natural. They elected Trump and chose Brexit to end a 'rigged system' and 'take back control'. As they called out Macavity a double reversal took place. Those who believed that change is possible found themselves voting for the status quo, while those who thought the system is fixed voted for change and found it isn't fixed after all.

Or is it? We will see. For the achievement of the vote for Brexit and the election of Trump is that they show that we, the voters, can alter the system by voting. If this includes the opportunity for genuine democracy, we might even take control.

To understand what is happening is demanding. Brexit and Trump came about in a cataract of deceit, sound bites, evasions and demagogy on all sides. The agitation was shallow. Taking a measure of the causes has to run deep. The starting point, though, is simple and direct: the human affliction of Brexit and Trump. How is it possible that England, which is so accepting of immigrants it has mixed-race rioting and has looked outwards with its people emigrating everywhere, should come to regard freedom of movement as a one-way 'threat' of inward invasion – and risk turning itself into a closed, self-regarding society, prejudiced and divided, impoverished yet obsessed with moneymaking, separated from Europe's culture and leaving its immediate close neighbours – Ireland and Scotland – infuriated by our selfishness? Similarly, how can it possibly be that a country that elected Barack Hussein Obama twice running, and holds him in record esteem as an outgoing president, should choose a misogynist thug who plays the racecard to be his successor?

# PART I
# AFTER TRUST

Any attempt to hold ideologies accountable for the crimes committed by their followers must be approached with a great deal of caution.

Naomi Klein,
*The Shock Doctrine*, 2007

# 1

# Jailbreak

Everyone can sense that the Brexit vote and the election of Trump are about more than a mere referendum and election. I'm not talking about the facts, far-reaching though they are. Something irreversible has happened, which people feel in their bones: it is the end of an era, a truly historic moment: 2016 is a year 'like 1968', a year of 'revolution'. This was also the claim of Nigel Farage, the far-right bigot and England's downmarket version of Trump, who led UKIP, the United Kingdom Independence Party. A celebration was thrown for him in the Ritz in November 2016, to revel in his role in Brexit. Speaking from the gilded staircase of London's plush hotel, he leant over its banister in a posture that echoed Lenin addressing a crowd in Red Square. Farage predicted 'a bloody sight worse to come' as he hailed the past twelve months as 'the year of the big political revolution'.[1] The incongruity of the Ritz for a gathering of revolutionary triumphalism does not prevent it from being galling. Brian Eno summed it up for many of us:

> My feeling about Brexit was not anger at anybody else, it was anger at myself for not realising what was going on. I had thought that all those UKIP people and those National Fronty people were in a little bubble. Then I thought: 'Fuck, it was us, we were in the bubble, we didn't notice it.' There was a revolution brewing and we didn't spot it. Because we didn't make it. We expected *we* were going to be the revolution.[2]

In the speech to her first Conservative Party conference as the party's leader, the British prime minister, Theresa May, used the

R-word four times. She saluted the outcome of the referendum as 'the quiet revolution that took place in our country just three months ago'. It was revolution she went on to say with roots; 'roots', she added, 'that run deep'.[3] We should beware of Tories praising revolution. In May's case, she is trying to steal it. The aim of her phrase 'Brexit means Brexit' is to persuade us that it is over and there is no more room for argument. The decision has been taken, what follows is only the administration needed to implement it – her administration. She claims the Brexit revolution is in the past – it 'took place' in June 2016. Its roots may run deep but she has already cut off the flowers and put the quiet revolution into a vase. All that remains is for her to 'get on with the job'.

Perhaps unfortunately for her, Theresa May is astride the bow of a *Titanic* process, uncertain as to what is going on below deck and as clueless as anyone as to what will break through the fog in front. Britain, and in its own prodigious way America, has entered a period of transition. Unlike the British, Americans are used to thinking of their country as a revolutionary one. This is – or was – the case on the right, as well as the left. When Ronald Reagan came to give his final address to the nation on leaving the Oval Office, he said:

I've spoken of the shining city all my political life, a tall, proud city built on rocks stronger than oceans, wind-swept, God-blessed, and teeming with people of all kinds living in harmony and peace; a city with free ports that hummed with commerce and creativity. And if there had to be city walls, the walls had doors and the doors were open to anyone with the will and the heart to get here.[4]

Contrast this to the bleak, closed vision of Trump's inaugural address, where he declared that Americans were a 'righteous people':

We assembled here today are issuing a new decree to be heard in every city, in every foreign capital, and in every hall of power, from this day forward: a new vision will govern our land, from this day forward, it's going to be only America first ...

At the bedrock of our politics will be a total allegiance to the United States of America, and through our loyalty to our country, we will rediscover our loyalty to each other ... When America is united, America is totally unstoppable.

Under his presidency the doors will swing shut and the City on the Hill will become Trumpistan, a bleak, closed fortress. The rhetoric of openness that enchanted Americans right and left is to be pulverised by a siege mentality. Trump's repudiation of his country's expansionism made him the most unpopular president at his inauguration since polling started. It begins a historic disagreement over the nature of the United States. Also, the future of the world – do we want a planet where the most powerful countries put 'only' themselves first while demanding the 'total' allegiance of their people?

On both sides of the Atlantic, two hard-nosed governments are determined to stamp their vision on their societies. Trump and May have different world views but both seek to restore past grandeur and both claim an unprecedented popular legitimacy gained from upturning the once all-powerful, official order. Both in their different ways are closing their countries inwards – or trying to. Trump heads for protectionism while polarising domestically, which at least is having an argument of sorts. May wants free trade with Brexit but insists that the 'will of the people' has been heard and must now be implemented by her, and she will brook no opposition.

In contrast to their baleful visions, a different kind of unbounded energy propelled the extraordinary blows that struck both countries – and was the opposite of closure. John Berger suggested that if we are to look for a landmark to identify the nature of modern society, it would be a prison.[5] Not the old-fashioned prison of industrial capitalism, but the new open prison of finance capitalism. I will adapt, not reproduce, his argument. Here we are in a society of unparalleled wealth and productivity, where one report claims that 62 people own as much as the poorer half of the entire world population put together, while the top 1 per cent own as much as the remaining 99 per cent.[6] Furthermore, those at the top of politics proclaim they are working for the public good but pocket incredible sums when they retire or even before. If the results of being ruled by such a world were that we are free, safe, secure, honest, with our environment protected and our lives a decent challenge, people would cheer it on – despite the extreme inequity. Instead, for most people, the overwhelming experience of human life on this planet of unparalleled wealth is like being a prisoner, forced to labour under the confinement and insecurity of competition and precariousness – a world of debt and anxiety rather than the conviviality of shared wellbeing that is now a possibility thanks to human ingenuity and productivity.

The imprisonment takes different forms and seeks to penetrate our willpower. The weight of debt makes us passive. We are corralled by regulations of all kinds, which add up to a controlling framework in which we have no say. Insecurity is all pervasive and demotivates us, depriving us of the confidence to plan and even hope. Most of the time we are surveilled. This has always been the fate of the prisoner, but now with our phones we become our own guards. Unknown authorities access and can permanently store the history of our metadata, which records every web page we have visited in the past, every person we have linked to or communicated with on the internet, and all the locations we visit. The commercial websites that we interact with every day operate their algorithms to manipulate our desires and give us the pleasure of the choices they have pre-policed. We are free to speak, provided we are correct, but who decides this, and how? There is an obligation to ensure happiness that seems to be associated with the rise of new illnesses, physical and mental. Both 'happiness' and 'illness' threaten to become, some argue already are, forms of social control. The cost of seeking justice is beyond anything you can afford.

The most pervasive, intrusive and effective form of imprisonment is public and official language. This once mystified people with illusions as well as inspiring them to collective responses. Now it seems to mean nothing at all. The same words are used, but they sound like echoes. In the referendum campaign the then British Prime Minister David Cameron was told that voters doubted his sincerity and he needed to sound passionate. So he took off his jacket and told a hand-picked audience in front of television cameras how passionate he was. The context dissolved the content. The language of official, global power has ceased to mean anything that links us to real conditions and real choices. Instead, a seamless continuity exists, as exemplified by the transition from New Labour to the Conservatives in Britain or from Bush to Clinton in America, or was it from Clinton to Bush? This is not just the fault of politicians. Broadcasters who won't take time to listen. Journalists who only want to know if a story 'has legs', not whether it is true. Our media reproduce 'flat earth news' – press releases made up by PR companies whose staff outnumber the newsrooms of the major papers.[7] Politicians become the vacuum-sealed packaging of a corporate process that has hollowed out what used to be known as 'meaning'. 'Democracy' becomes a celebration of a system where differences between parties seem trivial and their fundamental agreement overwhelming, hence offering no real choice at all. 'Freedom', 'security', 'liberty', even 'the future', all become terms that taunt us with a reminder of what they once were.

What was the reality that everyone could feel behind the rhetoric? Since 1978, the income of the poorer 50 per cent of the American population has fallen by 1 per cent. At the same time the income of the top .001 per cent has risen by 685 per cent.[8] Pause and take that in. The annual income of the poorer *half* of the United States fell by 1 per cent over the last thirty years. At the same time it is often harder to secure good-quality jobs, pensions, houses, college education and health care. The flatlining of low and very low income in a society committed to growth is bad enough; it is much worse when accompanied by an intense deterioration of confidence in the future and a rise in precariousness. Meanwhile, at the very top, the wealthiest millionaires in America, who were already thriving by anyone's standards in 1978, have seen a near sevenfold increase in their annual fortune.

Under these incredible conditions, to exercise our actual liberty we are reduced to surreptitious conspiracy with each other using tricks and code and often song. As soon as we do so in ways that are measurable, companies move in to try and appropriate the authentic energy of the music to sell it on for their profit. One way that the more educated and wealthier exercise freedom is through travel. The poorer and less skilled do not have even this area of manoeuvre and are more confined.

Finally, everyone is trapped by the way voting and its outcomes are bought, corrupted, manipulated, spun by the public-relations industry and the calibrations of costly marketing analytics. In our celebrated democracy, choice becomes no choice at all. Elections are bought. It costs $10 million to win a seat in the US Senate. A few hundred families bankroll US politics. Those who make the better investment win. The way money works in the UK is less overt but just as cunning. People do not 'feel' their interests are represented because they are not. Trust has *not* been 'lost' by voters – it has been betrayed by their rulers. Voters are indeed being chained to a process that is stealing their freedom.

The European Union became the most highly organised example of making entire nation states powerless. Smaller governments could be reduced to becoming the prison officers enforcing the rules of imprisonment on their own people, with rules decided elsewhere in the corporate stratosphere of investment frameworks and the Eurozone. The treatment of Greece is the most glaring example. The impact is felt by everyone in all countries, everywhere – that this could be our fate. Then, in Britain and America, an opportunity arose.

Brexit and Trump are attempts at a mass breakout from the marketised incarceration of contemporary corporate democracy. Getaways, to be sure, led by mafias, crooks, would-be dictators, demagogues, and their shyster newspapers and websites. An escape likely to end in tears, therefore, and renewed confinement. But you can't understand either American or British politics without cheering on the desire to leave the open prison of the globalist order. Berger was asked why he had a 'hunch' that Trump would win and answered that if 'somebody who is actually saying something seems to suggest that there *may be* a connection between what he says and what he will do, such a person is a way out of a vacuous nightmare, even if the way out is dangerous or vicious'.[9]

The desire to escape from the open prison of manipulated politics is shared – often profoundly – by many who opposed Trump and Brexit. They saw in them not a route to freedom but a turning of the screw. You can be appalled by the undemocratic character of the EU and want to fight it rather than leave. You can be aghast at the Goldman Sachs compliance of Hillary Clinton yet regard her as the better president. Many were. I was. But the understandable reluctance to support Remain in the referendum as headed up by David Cameron, or to oppose Trump if that means being steered by Clinton, fatally weakened the general spirit and energy of the two campaigns, whereas the prospect of a jailbreak from the old order filled their opponents with energy and glee.

We face a contrast of enormous consequences. Widespread, resentful opposition to Trump and May is just getting organised but contains a momentous division – between those who regard the impulse of the 2016 revolt against undemocratic globalisation as justified, and those who want a counter-revolution to return London and Washington to the world order they helped create. Explosive uncertainty stalks both the United States and the United Kingdom as rejectionist energy creates deep shifts in the political culture and structure of feeling of both societies.

It can be seen most clearly in America, where millions supported Bernie Sanders in his bid to be the Democratic Party's candidate for the presidency. They opposed the corrupt system of Washington politics and at the same time supported modern progress, for all its insecurities, with its multicultural, internationally-minded tolerance. They wanted more of it, much more fairly shared. For them, divisive walls are being thrown up as bigotry and confrontation are discharged by Washington. Their dread is becoming prisoners of fear in their own country thanks to Trump's triumph. At the same time millions who already felt confined by static living standards, collapsing prospects and growing insecurity, while the rich, who got richer and showered them with globalist claptrap, are free! Well, let's see about that.

But what about those of us who saw through Trump, or suspected there will be no liberty in Brexit, and were also against the system? Do we have to be in conflict? Sam Altman, a Clinton voter, did the right thing when he went to talk to a hundred Trump supporters. One told him: 'I'm angry that they're so outraged now, but were never outraged over an existing terrible system.' Another: 'There's a lot I hate about Trump. But our lives are basically destroyed, and he was the first person to talk about fixing that.' A third: 'You all can defeat Trump next time, but not if you keep mocking us, refusing to listen to us, and cutting us out.'[10]

The Trump wars in America are more serious for the world and more immediately polarising than the long-term consequences of Brexit. But they are being expressed within the existing party system and may be contained by its still vigorous political institutions. The contradictions of the ogre president are clear enough. To put 'America First' has to mean jobs, raising living standards, investment in infrastructure and therefore, with its New Deal overtones, some kind of positive government. To 'deconstruct the administrative state', which Trump's strategist Steve Bannon says is their aim, means turning the USA into an open frontier for capitalism while engaging in 'existential' combat with enemies abroad. Opposing such a combination while distracted by canards and tweets, the Democratic Party leadership will prefer to restore an Obama-style presidency rather than address the systemic question Trump exploited. They will claim they have better policies on jobs, healthcare, immigration and national security. It is how they deliver on them and whose interests they are seen as serving that matter. The party's base, mobilised by the provocations of the White House, needs to learn the lesson and change the game now that the right has upstaged them.

In the United Kingdom, Theresa May's 'quiet revolution' will get noisy. With the main opposition party broken and a narrow referendum outcome being imposed as an irreversible fate, deep change is under way. For the first time in over 300 years, behind the traditional confidence of British government, the kingdom is splitting. Not into a class war, which the British always enjoy and the workers largely lose, but into a confrontation that runs through every class and nation and potentially divides society from top to bottom. What is most important at this early stage is to pull back from the immediate conflict to ask where it all went so wrong that millions thought the only answer was Brexit in the UK and Trump in the USA. Brian Eno's time of 'thinking hard, thinking out loud together' should begin, with emphasis on the word 'together'.[11]

# 2
# The Four Breaches of Trust

The history of the 2016 right-wing revolts that led to Brexit in Britain and the election of Trump in the USA begins fifteen years ago on 15 February 2003, when millions of us around the world marched and argued against the coming war on Iraq. It marked the first of four great breaches of trust that brought about a nativist downfall of the North Atlantic international system. Demonstrations can take the form of a potential uprising against a system of national or international power. Or they can be protests at the way government is carried out. Or they can express a movement demanding their rights. The enormous gatherings in the USA and UK, where a record one-and-a-half million gathered in London, were none of these. They were unique. They challenged the validity of a decision that had yet to be finalised. In this, the citizens who took to the streets in the Anglo-Saxon countries did something different from the demonstrators in other countries around the world who objected to Washington's belligerence. In Britain and in the United States the manifestations of 15 February were a many-brained objection in advance, warning against an action not yet confirmed. It was a clash of judgements. The crowds pitted their wisdom against the combined collective wisdom and acumen of their own leaders and institutions, over a decision to attack another country: a decision to go to war.

A month later, despite the unprecedented scale of the protests, the government of the United States, supported by the United Kingdom, defied the judgement of the streets and went to war on the barbarous dictatorship of Saddam Hussein. Weakened by years of sanctions, Hussein had long abandoned manufacturing his chemical armoury that supposedly justified the invasion. Iraq was conquered, not because it was a threat, but to avenge the terrorist crimes of 9/11. These had nothing to do with Iraq. But once avenged, the aim was to replace tyranny with democracy, conveniently installed over Iraq's extensive oil fields. Although its economy was weakening relative to China, then just acquiring full membership of the World Trade Organisation, as well as the European Union, American superiority, polished by alliance with a sycophantic, style-conscious Britain, would dazzle the nations of the planet with the reach and accuracy of the US armed forces. The attraction of Anglo-Saxon democracy and market freedoms meant an ideology of peace and profit, backed by unmatchable military might and strategic domination of the Middle East; it would open a new era, thanks to the mass-murdering provocation of a few bizarre fundamentalists. On May Day 2003, appropriating what was once the workers' festival, President George W. Bush announced 'Mission Accomplished'. In a pointed message to China, he did so from the flight deck of the nuclear-powered aircraft carrier named after an illustrious predecessor: the USS *Abraham Lincoln*. In a demonstration of planetary reach, it had just sailed halfway around the world from the Persian Gulf, through the South China Sea to the headquarters of the US Pacific Fleet in San Diego, after its strike forces had taken part in the launch of Operation Iraqi Freedom.

Wise heads had warned Bush and the UK's prime minister Tony Blair of the dangers. Three months after Bush's May Day triumphalism, the first major act of terrorist resistance blew up the UN headquarters in the Iraqi capital of Baghdad. Fifteen years on and the conflict has metastasised across the entire region and continues to this day. By chance, in the UN building there were two of my colleagues researching for *openDemocracy*: Arthur Helton, who was killed, and Gil Loescher, who was terribly wounded and lost both his lower legs.[1] Their fate personalises for me the experience of hundreds of thousands of Iraqis, Arabs, Kurds, Druzes, Christians, Americans, Brits and so many others, killed and badly wounded in numbers too considerable to count precisely, as well as their families devastated as much by the need to care for the traumatised and injured as to mourn the dead.[2]

Many were the warnings. Within two weeks of the invasion, on 3 April 2003, while US ground forces were still approaching Baghdad, Paul Rogers argued that the US showed 'no understanding whatsoever' of what it was doing and that unless it changed course, 'a thirty-year war is in prospect'.[3] John le Carré was more to the point; discarding his usual role as a cool observer he set out why Bush and Blair were 'mad'.[4] To no avail. In the two major English-speaking capitals that straddled the Atlantic, the ruling political-media castes (that is, the major parties, the 'intelligence' agencies, the Foreign Office and State Department, the press and media, above all Rupert Murdoch's) chorused their support, propagandised the assault and failed to question or expose its false and contrived claims. When the BBC attempted to do so after the invasion with a report about Blair's manipulation of public opinion, it was purged.

The failure of the two ruling establishments was complete on every level: military, economic, political and moral. Or rather, it was so great that it is still proceeding. The thirty-year war Rogers foresaw has only reached its halfway point with Trump and Brexit. They are part of the political blowback against an elite that, rightly, is no longer trusted. The military defeats were extraordinary and continue, as US surges and special forces try to limit the ongoing damage to its supremacy. (The UK was assigned two small battlegrounds, of Basra in Iraq and Helmand in southern Afghanistan; in both its army was humiliated and withdrew.) Economically, the waste of treasure, billions for Britain, trillions for America, fed the bubble of the financial crash. Morally, the invasion of Iraq launched 'post-truth' – which now stigmatises twenty-first-century political culture.

There has always been dishonesty in politics. In the summer of 2002, however, during the build-up to Iraq, a Bush political strategist, almost certainly Karl Rove, shared his knowledge of a step change (doing so, of course, off the record). He mocked 'the reality-based community', which he defined as people who 'believe that solutions emerge from your judicious study of discernible reality ... That's not the way the world really works anymore ... We're an empire now, and when we act, we create our own reality'.[5] Under New Labour the British echoed their master's voice. Not all of Blair's efforts were convincing, but even when his government's post-truth dossier of September 2002 that was supposed to set out the case for war proved to be 'dodgy', he was untouched.[6] In the USA a series of polls reported that nearly half the population believed that Saddam Hussein was directly involved in 9/11, although this was not the case.[7] This manipulation of public opinion stemmed from the Special Operations Unit set up in the Pentagon to generate apparently factual allegations.[8] None of the 'post-truth' falsehoods of 2016 came close to this.

Cheered on by the Murdoch-owned Fox News in the US and the *Sun* in the UK, the US and British governments defied the norms of old-fashioned honesty. Refusing to listen to 'experts', they poured gold and lives into the mountains of Afghanistan and the sands of Mesopotamia. Strategically inept, incredibly wasteful, they played Osama bin Laden's game. They undermined their own democracies, cynically manipulating consent, tearing out the heart of their norms and procedures, and debasing their historic institutions. The first great loss is symbolised by the false claim that Saddam Hussein was deploying weapons of mass destruction. The breach concerned far more than a terrible incident of dishonesty. An entire section of the public who believed in the fundamental political integrity, overall honesty and legality of their country's system of government lost their trust in it. Many clung to the hope that integrity would be restored. But their capacity to advocate its virtue, which is crucial to the reproduction of any system of authority, wilted in the scandal of mendacity for which no one was held to account.

At the turn of the century, the strategic question that most concerned the two capitals was how to consolidate American hegemony over the post-Cold War international system. This was the purpose behind the invasion of Iraq. Its humiliating failure leads directly to the meandering belligerence of President Trump. I am not exaggerating the global ambition of that moment. On 28 July 2002, well before the British Cabinet or Parliament had formed a view, Blair sent Bush a memo on the coming invasion, opening: 'I will be with you whatever' and ending: 'the crucial issue is not when, but how.' A week after the attack began, on 26 March 2003, Blair summarised their strategic purpose, writing to Bush: 'This is the moment when you can define international politics for the next generation: the true post-Cold War world order. Our ambition is big: to construct a global agenda around which we can unite the world, rather than dividing it into rival centres of power.' He proposes a six-part process as to how America should sort out global affairs.

At the same time, Blair continued, they both needed to overcome antagonistic public perception. He wrote:

> The problem is we're not communicating with the rest of the world in a way they understand. They get wholly warped views of the so-called right in American politics, played back through their media; until we end up with the fatuous irony of millions of liberal-minded people taking to the streets, effectively to defend the most illiberal regime on earth.[9]

Fatuous! Blair knew that the millions of protesters were not defending Saddam Hussein's regime. (Indeed some of us had opposed the British government arming him in the 1980s, but that's another story.) What we marched against was an ill-conceived illegal war of choice. A perceptive forecast of disaster was spelt out by one of the protestors, a rookie US senator for Illinois. He told a Chicago rally six months before the invasion, he knew that:

> Saddam poses no imminent and direct threat to the United States or to his neighbors, that the Iraqi economy is in shambles, that the Iraqi military is a fraction of its former strength, and that in concert with the international community he can be contained until, in the way of all petty dictators, he falls away into the dustbin of history. I know that even a successful war against Iraq will require a U.S. occupation of undetermined length, at undetermined cost, with undetermined consequences. I know that an invasion of

21

Iraq without a clear rationale and without strong international support will only fan the flames of the Middle East, and encourage the worst, rather than best, impulses of the Arab world, and strengthen the recruitment arm of al-Qaida. I am not opposed to all wars. I'm opposed to dumb wars.[10]

The speech was to make Barack Obama president. Pioneering the use of social media, a young generation mobilised to ensure that he and not Hillary Clinton got the Democratic nomination – that an anti-war candidate for change led the fight against the Republicans in 2008. A president who attempted healing, consensus and togetherness, even though a more far-reaching programme was necessary, Obama became a stopgap – although what seeded itself in his eight years may be decisive for future progress. He wound down US involvement in the wars of Arabia and prevented a rout. There was no unseemly overrunning of the American withdrawal, as there had been when the US was forced to evacuate Saigon in 1975. Instead, under cover of drones and smart combat, Americans were pulled away from the front lines of the fighting and their vast bases in the Iraq oil fields.

As a result there was no single moment that symbolises the second breach of trust in the North Atlantic system of authority. Had a Tory government overseen the military disasters the British armed forces suffered in Basra and Helmand, Labour would have demanded a full inquiry. Perhaps because Labour was in charge and the Tories were more easily persuaded not to embarrass the armed forces, defeat was spun as an honourable sacrifice and withdrawal ordered before the losses became too great. Also the UK contribution to the wars was more ornamental than strategic, and the commitment across British society far less than in the USA, although large enough to create widespread hostility and support for wounded veterans.

In the United States, a majority of the American public had supported the invasion of Iraq, many out of a desire for revenge on those who had inflicted the outrage and humiliation of 9/11. The penetration of the military in everyday American life is often missed by commentators who only experience the big cities. Around 1.5 million are in uniform and 800,000 in the active reserves. The number of veterans is hugely greater, and across the country families, especially in small towns, engage in a form of civic worship of the armed forces. They followed the wars of the early century directly and personally. Nearly 4,500 died in Iraq and over 2,000 in Afghanistan. Over 32,000 were wounded in Iraq and nearly 20,000 in Afghanistan. In the course of the two wars, more than 1.5 million served in Iraq and over 800,000 in Afghanistan. In total: 6,500 dead, 50,000 wounded, and over 2 million sent to the Middle East to fight or support the fighting – and this does not include the numbers deployed by the navy, air force and intelligence agencies in ongoing operations outside the immediate theatre for over a decade.

The two sets of citizens only partly overlap. Not all red-neck Americans who project their bigotry onto Arabs went to fight. By no means all the millions in the families who sent a member to fight are prejudiced. Amongst both communities a gradual realisation took place. In the dark of their nights, as one setback followed another, they realised that it was Mission Failure. The government of their nation, which they saluted from the bottom of their hearts, had called on them to do their sacred duty and then abused their loyalty by screwing up. This was the second breach of trust. It would take an 'outsider' to vent their feelings in 2016.

Obama cloaked the colossal, multi-trillion-dollar defeat in his careful dignity, helped by his raid on Abbottabad to kill bin Laden. Meanwhile, the Democratic Party machine turned into a holding operation for Hillary Clinton to reclaim the crown. Now apologising for her error in voting for the Iraq war, she nonetheless called for renewed escalation in the Middle East with a no-fly zone over Syria, illustrating a deafness to the need for change that would prove fatal for her.

She opened the way for Trump, the most appalling president imaginable. His triumph against extraordinary odds came in the wake of Brexit, which had ejected from office a Conservative regime led by David Cameron, who along with his financial chancellor,

George Osborne, referred to Tony Blair as 'the master'. It was a striking formulation, because Blair headed the opposing Labour Party. A similar cross-party liaison had flourished in America. When Bill Clinton congratulated his successor George W. Bush on the latter's father's memoir, Bush junior tweeted back his appreciation with the hashtag #BrotherByAnotherMother. The subsequent double acts of these brothers by different mothers are recorded on YouTube. They reek of chumminess. Their sense of entitlement is particularly stomach-turning when they josh with each other as George Bush's real brother and Bill Clinton's wife were both favourites to be selected as the next presidential candidate for their respective parties. An entire epoch seemed to be their plaything as they presumed their families had stitched up the selection and one of them would again enter the White House as kin.

The epoch was bookended by the Clintons. It started in 1992 when Clinton (Bill) took the presidency from Bush the father, and lasted until 2016 when Clinton (Hillary) was defeated. For shorthand, call it the era of the CBCs: Clinton (Bill), Blair, Bush, Brown, Cameron and Clinton (Hillary). In the UK, Brexit defenestrated Cameron. In America, Trump smashed both sides of their covenant; first by destroying Bush (Jeb) in the Republican primaries and then humiliating Clinton (Hillary) in what should have been her safe 'rust belt' states.

The CBCs were an Anglo-American project to oversee a post-Cold War global capitalism shaped by an American democracy itself captured by funders in a system that enriched all the CBCs personally. The market discounts tomorrow, has no interest in yesterday and is jealous of non-market influences – one of the most important of which is a sense of our history. Clinton (Bill) was elected president less than a year after the Soviet Union collapsed. Francis Fukuyama had just turned his famous article 'The End of History' into a book. Its title expressed the core conceit of the CBCs: that the past has become mere friction – out-of-date traditions that hold us back. They would be the makers of a fresh world order, the first of its kind. Blair addressed the jubilant joint houses of Congress in July 2003, in the glow of mission accomplished. 'Never', he told the assembled ranks of Washington, 'has there been a time when the power of America was so necessary or so misunderstood, or when, except in the most general sense, a study of history provides so little instruction for our present day.'

Those words defy belief. Perhaps when the world was in the grip of two nuclear enemies, each with an armoury capable of making the planet uninhabitable to humans, there was no historic precedent. To have just invaded Mesopotamia, home of Nebuchadnezzar and the legendary gardens of Babylon, and declare there was nothing concrete to learn from history is hubris unchecked. But, as Bush (George W.) put it in his droll fashion talking about himself, the CBCs did not 'do nuance'. Blair laid out their claim to command the world: 'There is no more dangerous theory in international politics than that we need to balance the power of America with other competitive powers'.[11]

Far from fearing that its dustbin awaited them, the masters of the new world order thought they had consigned history itself to the dustbin. Their post-Cold War, 'post-history' vision set out a global order with a single centre around which every nation gathered. From it would radiate an ever-growing one-world system of finance and trade that they called 'globalisation' as if it were a fact of nature. Only political parties that 'got it' could hope to enjoy power. All would play the same basic song: Republicans and Democrats, Labour and Conservative, their differences would melt in its rays. There was only one danger: the virus of terrorism. Apparently just as much without a territorial home as globalisation itself, its dangers vindicated the uniting of everything good to ensure its elimination. A war on terror provided the bracing discipline for a global melding, or what in Nazi Germany was called a *Gleichschaltung*. A privatising world market that rolled back the state everywhere would level trade barriers to create havens for corporations, bring hundreds of millions out of poverty – and feed the most incredible growth in inequality ever recorded.

The transformation of the world through the creation of an international trading system was an extraordinary improvement for humankind. But the gains were not shared. Domestically, in the US and UK, the globalisation of the CBCs undermined the inclusion and security that were the human achievements of the New Deal and the welfare state, to replace them with debt and insecurity. But who apart from marginal greens on the left and bigots on the right could object? Opposition would be dissolved in a world of democracy and freedom that was fit for only one political 'way'. For what was the point of alternatives? Militarism, financialisation, privatisation, surveillance and spin would weave an uncanny unity. As Blair put it to his Labour conference in 2005, 'I hear people say we have to stop and debate globalisation. You might as well debate whether autumn should follow summer.'[12]

High-energy consumerism and brand competition would be the new natural. Consumers would not want to challenge rule by glamour, celebrity and the super-rich, but instead would aspire to join their ranks. Public relations and advertising, now boosted by ever more sophisticated digital feedback, would shape desire to ensure this aspirational culture. A manipulated form of corporate populism would take over politics, with citizens reduced to customers, and political party manifestoes approved by marketing agencies. The CBC's model of globalisation (for there *are* others) hollowed out self-government and subordinated the law and living to the marketplace, which would then sell back what it had robbed us of: the spice of our lives.

It was not a plan, it was not a dictatorship. It was, as Blair might say, 'sincere' – for he used his gift for sincerity to put his case beyond argument. However, it also required military success and continued economic growth. Then, in a parallel, ongoing and even greater folly to the Iraq invasion, Washington and Westminster collaborated in 'post-truth' financial wizardry. Wall Street and the City of London were permitted to create a new monetary reality. In 2008, their pyramids of junk debt imploded. The financial crash destroyed the promise of a 'golden age', a 'new world order', one 'even greater than the industrial revolution' – the words were Gordon Brown's in a fevered speech to assembled bankers, on the eve of his replacing Tony Blair as British prime minister in 2007.[13]

The financial crash was the third great betrayal of the trust that regular people, middle- as well as working-class, had granted to the leaders of the post-Cold War system. It was supposed to be the best possible. In so far as it was not regulated, this was because their leaders assured them that all would benefit if the modern financial system was set free. The crash that reversed its growth was not due to trade union militancy, excessive wages or resistance to capitalism. On the contrary, following Bill Clinton's lead, parties of the left everywhere had rolled over to embrace the new world order.

The fourth breach of trust followed on directly. It was not a failure but a revelation. The justification of what was presented as the nature of globalisation was shown to be false, what Marxists call mystification and those who are on food stamps call bullshit. Because this falsity was a vital part of getting the public to accept the realities of economic life, its exposure may prove the most fatal to late capitalist economic system as a whole. 'The market knows best', 'Welfare is a burden that has to be diminished', 'Value only comes from moneymaking', 'State support must be minimised' – these are the slogans of a vast propaganda effort issued from every orifice of the media. Their mantra, that profit-making is the source of life and government, is at best a necessary evil.

In 2008 the financial system tottered as its reckless, but highly profitable creation of debt collapsed. In the UK, the Royal Bank of Scotland, one of the world's biggest, was within hours of going bust with its cashpoint ATMs freezing. The British government 'injected' £37 billion into failing banks. In the US, $700 billion was made available to 'troubled assets' from its banks. Men who were skimming millions in bonuses called politicians and demanded that they help them out to save the system. The banks and financial institutions were hosed down with 'quantitative easing', otherwise known as printing money, to revive them. They took billions from the government and ten years later the West's economy has still to recover. In an era of military reversal and economic stagnation, elites should share in the hardships they cause, alongside the publics who are the main victims. Instead of bankers being jailed, the rich gained even more in the post-Iraq, post-crash Anglo-Saxon system. Year after year they continued to enjoy a circus of a time. As average wages stagnated and the younger generation staggered into unprecedented indebtedness, top salaries leapt upwards and bonuses headed for the yachts. (To give two small economic measures of the way social and political as well as material life was coming apart: according to the Joseph Rowntree Foundation, while the British economy grew by 10 per cent between 2009 and 2014, real wages fell by 6 per cent; in the United States, in 2016, 95 per cent of households still had incomes below those in 2007.[14]) In both the US and the UK a palpable and historic breach of trust took place, enraging many as their prospects shrivelled while the wealthiest boomed thanks to government support not 'the market'. A widespread withdrawal of consent sowed the seeds that became the revolts of Brexit and Trump. It was not just the impoverishment or the downturn that did it. It was the growing inequity presented as being unavoidable and best for everyone while being fixed by those in power. It was the intensification of insecurity for millions who struggled while the very rich got mind-boggling salary increases and said it was all the work of 'the market system', for whose outcomes no one took responsibility.

Whatever your views of the US and the UK, both emerged from the Second World War with their states enjoying a profound loyalty across their societies. There were intense and ferocious disagreements over who should form the government. These were framed by a consensus of popular allegiance to the country's institutions. This invaluable and perhaps irreplaceable public culture was destroyed by the era of the CBCs and the accumulated impact of the four breaches of trust. In the wake of victory over Soviet communism, hubris led the CBCs to overreach – just as the protesters warned. Their political–military project of world rule failed and their economic leadership of global capitalism crumbled. These were not the only causes of the present consternation. The outcomes of Trump and Brexit were hardly intended; the CBCs wanted continued loyalty. But they embraced a form of capitalism that dissolved the institutions that threaded society together with forms of representation such as trade unions, political parties, local government and professional associations. Instead of working with them, the governments of the CBCs typecast them as 'vested interests' and 'restrictive practices' and they were pulverised by a right-wing media that glorified executive power and individual consumerism. A fascinating account by Matt Stoller of one moment of this process shows how the Clinton generation of left-of-centre American politicians undid the regulations of banking and finance and aided the concentration of corporate power that looped back to sever the relationship between citizens and government.[15]

In 2016 the CBCs got the hiding they deserved, delivered in the form of peaceful if shocking support for radical change in the ballot boxes of the referendum and the presidential election. An era that began with Clinton (Bill)'s renowned first law of politics, 'It's the economy, stupid', ended with voters saying: in the UK: 'No, it isn't'; and in the US: 'Then we will have a businessman', leaving his wife Hillary looking stupid. A quarter of a century after the Clintons first took the White House, we witnessed the consequence of the fourfold failure of the era of the CBCs: blatantly dishonest government; protracted military defeat; economic calamity generating widespread insecurity; and state-supported, elite hyper-wealth and corruption. Altogether the four breaches of trust led to loss of faith in the ruling order as a whole. In countries where popular loyalty draws on pride in their leading the world, no martial victory provided a political counterbalance to the social, cultural and economic decomposition of traditional authority in the wake of the crash in 2008. The American writer Stephen King observed that in 2016 there was 'a feeling that people were both frightened of the status quo and sick of it.'[16]

Rhetorically, the Trump and Brexit campaigns successfully assailed the corruption of an unaccountable, failing system. They proposed to revive greatness and prosperity by putting a protectionist America and a global Britain first. In his short, grotesque speech at his inauguration as president, Trump cashed in on the opportunity offered by the gap between politicians and people – a rupture he and his ilk had financed: 'Washington flourished, but the people did not share in its wealth ... The establishment protected itself, but not the citizens of our country. Their victories have not been your victories.'

Trump exploited the truth. He was right about the gap between rulers and ruled from which he himself profited. The CBCs broke the implicit covenant of twentieth-century democratic capitalism, that it would deliver overall fairness as well as improved lives and security for the working and middle classes, as they took it into the twenty-first-century. The same argument was set out in Prime Minister Theresa May's explanation of Brexit:

> The referendum was not just a vote to withdraw from the EU ... It was about a sense – deep, profound and let's face it often justified – that many people have today that the world works well for a privileged few, but not for them ... a call for a change in the way our country works – and the people for whom it works – forever ... And the roots of the revolution run deep. Because it wasn't the wealthy who made the biggest sacrifices after the financial crash, but ordinary, working class families.[17]

This confronts the millions who opposed the Iraq war with a complex, triple defeat. The anti-war movement was predominantly middle-class and educated – and was particularly enraged by the lie that Saddam Hussein posed a threat because he had weapons of mass destruction. (With Blair, this treacherous claim rested on a wilful refusal to assess the evidence, now well documented; while the Bush administration was more relaxed in admitting that it chose WMD to justify invasion as a matter of bureaucratic convenience.)[18] In both countries, however, many who came from the working classes that provide the bulk of the armed forces were less troubled by the illegality, provided the strategy worked. For them, what mattered was not lying but winning. From the point of view of the liberal opponents of the Iraq invasion three profound setbacks took place: they failed to stop the war, they lost trust in their government, they did not gain the support of the working class. I'm speculating, but to generalise it seems a division occurred within those who turned against the CBCs, that had a class basis. Middle-class progressives were appalled by their rulers' deceptions, the working-class pro-military by the fact that they were losers.

Public opposition to the CBCs never unified, and this is especially important in America. On the one hand, there were those who thought the wars were wrong and a product of blatant 'post-truth' deceit. On the other, there were those, indifferent to the 'correct' justification of war who were sold a certain victory. They too were betrayed. The two cultures are opposites. But unless the cultural 'left', with its embrace of feminism, human rights, multiculturalism, gay rights, environmental and planetary humanism also engages with and wins over the working classes, there will be no alliance to drive the Trumpists from power. The division reproduces the social conflict over the Vietnam war that rent apart American politics from the mid-sixties and is rooted in an imperial experience of international domination. One side wanted planetary responsibility, far-sighted norms and law-abiding enforcement that would isolate communism/fundamentalism. It was against the Iraq invasion but supported the continuity of the post-1945 international system now that it had broken the communist challenge. The other, wrongly regarding this as 'soft' and enraged by terrorist provocations, did not care about the trappings of a world order. It wanted and has now got a president who would substitute any appeal to long-winded values at his inauguration by saying: 'America will start winning again, winning like never before.'

This is why our present story begins with the scale, far-sightedness and frustration of popular opposition to the Iraq invasion of 2003. The 'big' ambition for world power that Blair articulated so shamelessly was dishonest and dumb. Even before war itself had been declared, the streets knew it was a folly. A transfer of practical wisdom from rulers to the ruled took place that humiliated the supposedly sophisticated leaders of the Anglo-Saxon world order. The upside: it established the precondition for genuine democracy. The downside: without the organised demand for such democracy gaining the support of the working classes whose young men and women flew to fight, the way was opened for demagogy to prevail in the wreckage.

We are now living in that wreckage. The verdict on the CBCs was not delivered by the millions who had objected vociferously to their illegal war. Nor by a successor generation of protesters inspired by the Occupy movement, with its demand for an end to the golden privileges of 'the one per cent' – even though they turbocharged the Bernie Sanders presidential campaign. Instead, a chauvinist element of the 1 per cent itself, resentful of cosmopolitanism, contemptuous of tradition, profiteers of shock and misrule, sensed the danger and the opportunity of a failing order. They took advantage of the withdrawal of support from the Clintons and the Camerons. They exploited growing popular discontent with privilege, corruption and a fixed system. They honed a cynical call and focused it using the latest digital analytics to tickle voters' personal fears and inclinations via the internet. Expel the Muslim other. Take back control. Summon back greatness. Fox TV and the *Sun*, which ten years previously had cashed in on the call to war, now cashed in again, to destroy those they had once cheered. Instead of expressing contrition for defeat, the tabloid and TV opinion-formers who, in the face of all the warnings, had backed sending the boys and girls to war as the century began, now endorsed Brexit and Trump, and helped bring the era of the CBCs to an end.

Trump and Brexit are thus part of a larger, ongoing tempest. A democratic warming that began on the left but only became a hurricane capable of taking power after picking up force from the warm waters of the right. It first struck down a government in India in 2014, when Narendra Modi won a surprising, decisive victory over the established Congress Party. For many Indians, Congress was an out-of-touch, globalised elite, ingrained with corruption behind its sophisticated veneer of entitlement. It looked to them much like the Clintons and the Westminster political elite would seem to their electorates two years later. As Pankaj Mishra writes, 'Like Donald Trump, Mr. Modi rose to power demonizing ethnic-religious minorities, immigrants and the establishment media, and boasting about the size of a body part.'[19]

Is it any comfort to know that we are not alone? I think it is. It helps to clarify how long-range historical forces are at work. While a close engagement with the British referendum may make only a modest contribution to understanding the American presidential election, the defeat of Hillary Clinton certainly helps to illuminate why the campaign for the UK to remain in the EU was beaten. From the start, behind the disastrous setbacks on the two sides of the Atlantic lurk the figures of Bill Clinton and Tony Blair, who together launched the malign and murderous epoch terminated in 2016. This is the story of a popular verdict on their joint enterprise.

# 3

# Roll the Dice

When 17.4 million people voted by a majority of one and a quarter million in June 2016 to take the United Kingdom of Great Britain and Northern Ireland out of the EU, they delivered a triple blow at three interlinked, once confident frameworks of power: the British state, the European Union and what used to be called the Washington consensus. Their vote repudiated their official governing class and the leaders of all the main British political parties; rejected the advice of the heads of all the major institutions of the land from the Bank of England to the Trades Union Congress; defied the oligarchy of the European Union as well as the wishes of every elected European leader, including those of France and Germany; and ignored the warnings of the presidents of the United States and China, along with the global organisations, such as the International Monetary Fund, who signalled the likely costs for both the UK and the world. All this was clear at the time and was in the news. Behind it, in the back of their minds, conscious or not, were the accumulated disappointments of the era of the CBCs. It was not that voters suddenly turned on their masters. From their point of view, their leaders had been turning on them, letting them down, lying, going to war, messing up the economy, for years. Many had simply withdrawn from voting as an expression of their disappointment and quiet rage. Now, across the country, voters – including nearly three million who had stopped voting in elections – considered the odds, heard the government's extreme warnings as to economic consequences and defied them.

This demanded courage. One measure of the audacity of the Brexit vote is the contrast with what normally happens in referendums. Voters stick with the status quo. While he noted warning signs and uncertainties, Peter Kellner of YouGov, with experience of decades of polling, wrote at the end of 2015 in the run-up to the referendum:

> My belief is that we are seeing something that so often happens in referendums round the world. Months before the vote, many people express their dislike of the current state of affairs and like the general idea of change. But as decision day draws close, more and more voters think about the alternative, and shy away. There are plenty of examples of the status quo gaining ground, especially in the final days of a referendum campaign.[1]

In England and Wales they did not shy away. If anything, in the final days, voters hardened their determination and even swung to change.

Another measure of how Leave voters held their nerve concerns the economic impact of their choice. The large Ashcroft exit poll showed a very high proportion of those who voted Remain saying they did so for fear of the economic consequences (43 per cent); another third (31 per cent) said it was because the UK would have the best of both worlds economically, which was the government's official view. Thus three-quarters of those who voted Remain cited economic reasons. It follows that most Leave voters heard the economic case as well.[2] The government won the argument, that leaving the EU was a big economic risk. Craig Oliver, the director of communications in 10 Downing Street, who was by the prime minister's side throughout the campaign, writes that on the economy: 'Our destruction of the Leave campaign was complete.' His rueful conclusion: 'The closest thing to a law in politics, "It's the economy, stupid!" turned out to be wrong.'[3] Despite the remain campaign's success in getting its economic case across to the public, a majority voted Leave. They decided that Britain 'could not afford' to stay because non-economic issues mattered more. According to Sky Data, 56 per cent of Leave voters *expected* short-term economic damage, although only 7 per cent thought it would be damaging in the long term.[4]

In the US, nearly 40 per cent of a large exit poll said what mattered to them most was a 'candidate who can bring change' – a staggering 83 per cent of whom then tagged the Republican candidate to bring it about. On both sides of the Atlantic, voters had had enough of the CBCs, especially the Clintons in America, whose rule stretched back twenty-four years since Bill Clinton was elected president in 1992. In one focus group in Wisconsin before the election, a voter said: 'We know we're not going to get any change with Hillary ... A lot of people feel like, *let's roll the dice*, and we're going to have to put up with a whole bunch of bad stuff, but maybe we'll get some things done with Trump.'[5]

Let's roll the dice! This captures the jailbreak sentiment on both sides of the Atlantic. Large numbers in all classes did not want continuity. The regime of duplicity had lost legitimacy in their eyes. If the left could not challenge this, what alternative was there but to gamble on the right, when unexpectedly offered a chance. Most voters in America, by a majority of nearly three million, decided against the risk of Trump, which suggests that the 60 million who backed the mogul knew he was a gamble. A majority in England felt the country should not carry on being governed in the way it was – it too was a wider decision than the choice on the ballot paper itself. They had had enough. They made a *judgement*: to roll the dice. One that was not about immediate policies, but reversing the direction of travel.

A year after the plebiscites of 2016, with president and prime minister acting in unprecedented circumstances, it is hard to recall how we got to this point. Voters rolled the dice in the hope of what? The ricocheting impacts of Theresa May's no-nonsense Brexit and Donald Trump's would-be dictatorship obstruct that most elusive of moments, the immediate past.

In Britain, some blame immigration, others claim a desire for self-government and escape from rule by Brussels caused Brexit. In America, there is a similar division between those who see Trump's victory as a revival of racism and those who see it as an attempt to escape from 'the swamp'. One of the most extraordinary things about many immediate post-traumatic analyses of 'why it happened' from distressed liberal scholars is what they manage to miss. Within six weeks of the UK referendum, Simon Wren-Lewis wrote a helpful overview of twelve sets of surveys and reports on Brexit that mushroomed in the shadow of the vote.[6] His conclusion is measured: 'taking all this evidence into account it seems that the Brexit vote was a protest vote against both the impact of globalisation and social liberalism. The two are connected by immigration ...' A frank, engaging and thorough examination of the US election, by David Roberts, has thirteen graphs and graphics as well as videos, pictures and tweets to illustrate his assessment. He covers turnout, regional differences, urban versus rural, age, demography, authoritarian personality correlations, racism, political messages, social media, the intensification of partisanship as parties weaken, economic populism, class, especially the white working class, and resentments of all kinds, especially white working-class resentment, in his quest to answer the question: 'What the fuck happened?' His answer: 'Everything mattered'.[7] Wren-Lewis is more professorial in his language but his exasperation is evident. Roberts's language expresses a wide-shared anger with himself, like Brian Eno's, and uses the same expletive.

Roberts's blog post was exceptionally clear, thorough and open-minded, which is why I quote it. Even he does not consider whether one of the things that happened was that millions of his compatriots voted for Trump because they wanted to 'Make America Great Again'. Had the message not chimed for them, far fewer would have voted for the man. The same principle applies to Brexit. I have yet to see a sociological analysis that considers if those who voted Leave did so because they wished to 'Take back control', the defining slogan of its campaign. After the referendum, I talked with a middle-class mother in her early thirties, not well off, and looking after young children. She was from the south of England and was living in the north, where her husband had a job in the charitable sector. She said she was not political and turned up her nose at words like 'sovereignty' when I asked if they mattered to her. She had no problem with immigrants coming here. She did not vote Tory and loathed Farage. Her view was: 'We do not need twenty-seven other countries to tell us what to do,' and so she cast her ballot for Brexit.

Exit polling reported that 49 per cent of those who voted Leave were like her, and said they were for Brexit so that decisions about the UK should be taken in the UK. A further 33 per cent said they voted so that the country would have control over its borders when it came to immigration.[8]

If we want to know why Americans voted for Trump, or Brits to take the UK out of the European Union, the place to start is with what was inscribed on the tin: 'Vote Leave, Take Back Control' and 'Make America Great Again!' (Trump's baseball cap omitted the exclamation mark). Voters chose to support what was proposed. Both battle cries combine a strong assertion about 'being in the world' with an appeal to resurrect an older history – a nationalist form of self-determination. Had the Leave campaign demanded 'Take Control!' it would have raised a question: How? Of what? It would feel like a threat to start a battle. Instead its call was, Take *Back* Control. Back has a double meaning, to take powers away from Brussels and to restore to us something we once had. Softened with nostalgia, its appeal was inspired by a past when, supposedly, we knew who we were and governed our own lives. It combines the thrill of being assertive and its unruly rejection of the boss class with reassuring restoration. It is radically defiant yet conservative. It also meant something specific. Dominic Cummings, who chose it, argues: 'Without fifteen years of out-of-control immigration, our message of "take back control" would not have had enough traction.'[9]

Trump's shout out to his compatriots was similar. If he had demanded 'Make America Great!' it would have raised the question of How, by making war? Or through yet more foreign adventures? Making America Great *Again* has a different connotation, of a return to a time when jobs were jobs and men were men and God's own country delivered a family home for everyone. It also gets around the question of what exactly does make America great (in case you think it could be its capacity to welcome immigrants and enjoy free speech, as Reagan seemed to, and he was not the only one). For it is embarrassing to ask in what way *was* America great, as this suggests you don't know your own country. We all do know, don't we, how great America was as the superpower that won the Cold War through its industrial and economic might. Trump's message too was that most seductive of mystifications: a call for change evoked by an appeal to the past. And when Hillary Clinton responded by asking when did America 'cease to be great', calculating this was a clever put-down that positioned her as the patriot, she accomplished what Trump's self-glorifying nonsense allowed him to evade: she posed an actual, practical question about an uncomfortable reality, while implying she would keep things as they were.

Both Trump's slogan and Leave's carried the subtext of the other. Unlike the United States, which is still the pre-eminent global power and only at the start of its loss of primacy, it is unrealistic for British politicians to call out loud for a return to 'greatness'. For this means empire. The Brexiteers' underlying desire is a return of *Great* Britain, but it is a sly, illicit longing for a mistress now well beyond their means. Also, the slogan 'Time to put the Great Back into Britain' has been worn out since the Falklands war, with repeated use by Murdoch's *Sun*. Instead, its motif, the appeal of planetary prestige, haunted Brexit's call through secondary arguments – most notably, that free from Europe's regulation the country will pioneer trade with the whole world and become, in a formula now adopted by Prime Minister Theresa May that echoes the longing for empire, 'Global Britain'.

The Trumpeteers did not lead with a slogan for control, as theirs was a less defensive campaign than Brexit. But they appealed to the identical psychic source of 'othering' foreigners, with a two-thousand-mile wall supposedly shutting off Mexico and super-vigilance of migrants, especially Muslims. These measures are more viscerally about 'taking control' than anything the Brexiteers have yet come up with. Trump's appeal strummed the same vile rhythms of victimhood that made Brexit appealing for many: regret for the loss of racial dominance expressed through attacks on the influence of 'political correctness' and foreigners, and stirring fear so as to make the country 'safe'.

Both campaigns linked the patriotic, the self-interested and the restorative. Both were belligerently nostalgic, and advocated a desire to take advantage of the world and fight back against the multiculturalism of globalisation. The appeal of Brexit and Trump was the lure of restoring greatness. Each had more than a touch of the supremacist, an element of revenge, a wounded pride and a desire to get even: get even with despised political elites who had abandoned their hard-working countrymen and women by stealing their votes through elections that offered no real choice and then serving up the country to Davos. Each also appeared to address people's actual circumstances.

Without the lure of restoration, the claim on the world made by Brexit and Trump would have been too radical for such right-wing causes and their leaderships. The battle cry of the victors of 2016 needed the flag of reaction to ensure control over the forces they might unleash. For curled within them is the still young python of democracy, capable of swallowing them whole. Brexit and Trump asserted two true and valid complaints against their country's government: that its existing, elitist system is rigged, corrupted and works against regular people, and that this can be changed.

They also insisted that they are change makers. Politicians from the tired elite always offered change but never meant it. A core promise of Brexit and Trump was that they were for real. Trump made it his calling card: I-am-a businessman-not-a-politician-so-I-mean-business. He had always been a politician running for his brand, just one who never bothered with being tied down by office, so the claim was one of his lesser half-lies. The differentiation was enough to assure his status as an outsider and his commitment to executive action. Many of his voters singled out his being a businessman as his qualification for getting America moving again.

In addition to having a strong, clear, defining message, the messenger had to be different and credible. For all the analysis of the causes of Brexit and Trump, their *leaders* made them happen.

Both Clinton and Cameron were terrible on the other side, as we will see, and lost their campaigns as a result. They were also the genuine products of the CBC world order, unable to commit to change because they wanted continuity. Given the resources and experience Clinton and Cameron commanded, and the risk of defying the system, their opponents had to be convincing individuals, especially because neither could count on traditional party machines. Brexit was a referendum that cut across traditional allegiances. Trump had never been elected to office before. In addition to the straplines that defined the two campaigns, voters backed a person – in the case of Brexit a double-headed person – who convinced them they *were* personally against the system and would deliver the upset as promised. Unsuitability for office became a qualification, guaranteeing outsider status; so too was daring to be 'incorrect', as it signalled a breakout from the confinement of hypocritical language and patronising social control that the tabloid media relished. Best of all, the appalled horror of liberals at the prospect of Brexit and Trump winning helped to convince the public that they were for real.

Boris Johnson and Nigel Farage provided the Brexit campaign's 'Trump effect'. Neither on his own would have done enough, but looking back they emerge as the double-headed hydra of the Brexit campaign: Johnson-Farage. It was Johnson-Farage who was the United Kingdom's equivalent of Donald Trump. Johnson brought television celebrity. He had not run a TV show like Trump, but he was a TV personality ruffling his blond hair, oozed uncontrollable narcissism, was nakedly power-hungry, said outrageous things and was relaxed with the fact that everyone could see through him. Despite being mayor of London for eight years and doing little that was memorable, he stamped himself and his image in the public mind. His weakness is that he is a cosmopolitan liberal and a product of the system. His joining the campaign at the last minute may have swung it, but he could not have won it on his own. Hence the importance of the other face of the hydra.

Farage had forced Brexit onto the agenda after years of UKIP campaigning. He liked to denounce weak-wristed members of 'the political elite' selling out the country to unelected bureaucrats. Unlike the physically imposing teetotaller Trump, Farage delights in an impish, alcoholic permissiveness. He earned his role through indefatigable local campaigning during which he honed his greatest skill: stirring racist prejudice and chauvinist hatred of the EU by making people feel good about their worst instincts, while not crossing the legal line into hate speech. Only a racist would call President Obama a 'disgusting creature' as Farage did,[10] or drop in a reference to how migration controls after Brexit will strengthen 'our proud ties to our kith and kin' in the *Telegraph* setting out his 'Vision for Britain'.[11] The prejudices of the UKIP voters he represented were concisely summarised after the referendum by a seventy-year-old supporter who told James Walsh of the *Guardian*:

> There are too many immigrants. UKIP will bring back the death penalty and we can get rid of the criminals in our community and end political correctness. The government must get on with leaving the EU more quickly. I want to live long enough to see Britain free of mass immigration and returned to greatness.[12]

This is the toxic stew that Farage stirred. He provided the hardcore that was built into the UK's Trump effect. At most 25–30 per cent of voters might have supported a campaign to exit the EU led by Farage alone. Combined into Johnson-Farage, bigotry embraced a politician who got up the noses of the political elite yet clearly had enough of the elite about him to know how the system works and make a credible pitch to lead the country.

There was a third aspect to the outstanding campaigns of Brexit and Trump that made millions decide to roll their dice: they inspired on-the-ground support. Johnson battle-bussed the kingdom from one end to another; Farage toured everywhere waving his European passport at the crowd and saying it should be British. They fought for their cause on the streets and in the squares and gained locality by locality by word of mouth. It also gave them grainy TV news with regular cheering people. Trump's effort was outstanding and overturned the massively greater spending on TV adverts by the Clinton campaign. He talked about what he would do, he told the crowds he loved them; they loved him back.

'Americanism not globalism, is my credo,' he proclaimed in his acceptance speech at the Republican convention, kicking off his campaign proper. He denounced the special interests that 'have rigged our political and economic system for their exclusive benefit ... My message is that things have to change – and they have to change right now.' With a plutocrat's audacity he claimed, 'Nobody knows the system better than me, which is why I alone can fix it. I have seen first-hand how the system is rigged against our citizens ...'[13] Would you really trust a top rigger to de-rig the system? By an overall majority of three million, American voters did not. But for the first time a presidential candidate called out the corruption and many rallied to this.

To give just one example of how Trump worked his cry, he took his message in a precisely targeted speech into western Pennsylvania at the end of June 2016:

> Pittsburgh played a central role in building our nation. The legacy of Pennsylvania steel workers lives in the bridges, railways and skyscrapers that make up our great American landscape. But our workers' loyalty was repaid with – you know it better than anybody – total betrayal. Our politicians have pursued a policy of globalization, moving our jobs and our wealth and our factories to Mexico and overseas. Globalization has made the financial elite who donate to politicians very, *very* wealthy. I used to be one of them ... but it has left millions of our workers with nothing but poverty and heartache.

I laughed when I read his claim that he 'used to be' one of them. And in the same speech: 'It does not have to be this way. We can turn it around. The people who rigged the system are supporting Hillary

Clinton. We can either give in to Hillary Clinton's campaign of fear or we can choose to believe again in America.'[14]

Many opponents of Trump were blindsided despite his blatant hypocrisy. Trump's demagogy appealed because America's political and economic system is 'rigged' and had never since the Second World War been subjected to such castigating language from a presidential candidate promising action. This fact is central to the story of what happened and links up the two core claims of the Leave and Trump campaigns, used to wrap their vile deceits. One: the political system is corrupted, wrong and unacceptable. This is so in the UK and the EU as well as the USA. Two: it can be changed. Knowing the first is true, and the second could be, turned the two campaigns into movements with energy and motivation that maximised their appeal and turnout.

I am not saying that the system is *only* or *nothing but* corrupt, and fixed by money and the machine. Were that the case it would not be possible to change it – and neither Trump or Brexit could have won. It is because the US and the UK are open, crudely democratic, law-based and free, that change is possible. Neither the USA nor Britain are totalitarian systems. Perhaps the best term to convey how the corruption is both systemic yet not all-encompassing is Trump's, as he found the language to mobilise support: the system is 'rigged'. Both Brexit and Trump's election were votes to dismantle the 'rigging'.

Some lumps of rigging fell off as a result. Much of it will stay: the rigging that matters in Britain is British, not the EU. In the USA, Trump has outsourced himself to Goldman Sachs. But the two campaigns were object lessons on achieving popular support for change from small beginnings over the course of a decade. 'A lot of people feel like, *let's roll the dice*, and we're going to have to put up with a whole bunch of bad stuff, but maybe we'll get some things done ...' The bad stuff is coming. But there is a positive lesson that won't be forgotten: willed change is possible, voters can take a risk.

# 4

# Explaining the Disruption

Across the world a new industry arose as political scientists, economists, advisers, think tanks and scholars and academics of all kinds got to work to try and explain what happened in 2016. Why Brexit and Trump? This book is but a drop in a tidal wave of websites and reports whose conclusions could be consequential for future politics. While many issues are unresolved and a lot more research is needed, an immediate division opened up – often not stated but stark for all that. Did the supporters of Trump and Brexit, to the best of their abilities, reflect upon the situation they found themselves in as well as the prospects before them, to come to their decision? In which case some analysis of whether they were right in the way they saw the system must be part of any explanation. Or were they the mere receptacles of prejudice and circumstances with their votes determined by factors such as lack of education or built-in character traits, such as dislike of strangers or support for the death sentence? A lot of research into voter behaviour is funded on the basis that it must be 'value neutral'. If one candidate says the system is rigged and the other does not, a methodology is permitted that allows the correlation of 'thinking the system is rigged' with other variables such as age or education. The issue of whether or not it is indeed rigged must not come into it. Thus academic research has a built-in bias against considering whether voter judgements are intrinsically justified. Instead, it prefers measuring whether they are externally correlated. This builds in an assumption that they are also externally determined, rather than being freely arrived at. This matters a lot with Brexit and Trump because, without having any evidence to 'prove' this, I think one of the attractions of voting for them was the sheer lure of agency. It was the jailbreak factor: the experience of democracy being so confining that any offer of escape was attractive.

The research and arguments about cause and effect are not only taking place in the relative calm of a seminar room, although these can be incredibly competitive. If there is no sustained recovery from the great financial crash, we may be in a situation of a potential widespread breakdown. This generates grisly and morbid manifestations of fakery, paranoia, real deceptions and mock objectivity made worse in the case of Trump and Brexit by massive efforts at denial by the losers, possibly motivated by the sinking feeling that there might have been good reasons for the outcome. Denial took three immediate forms: that the winners lied, that they cheated, and that they didn't really win. It is true that they lied, they cheated and in the United States in terms of the popular vote, Trump did not win. Does this undermine the authentic nature of the winners' support?

No single door opens the way to explain a narrow outcome. If an election is decided by one vote, you can single out any one person for blame, if you wish. In fact *every* single person has individual responsibility. Clinton's campaign manager 'blamed' the eighteen- to twenty-nine-year-old pro-Democratic millennials for 'underperforming' and losing the election.[1] Someone as inappropriate as Trump should never have been close enough to winning, for the low turnout of this category to make a decisive difference. 62,979,879 Americans voted for Trump. Why did they do so? This is the question. No one can be 'blamed' for this, except perhaps Clinton, who also attracted horrendous misogyny that she responded to with dignity and for which she should not be blamed.

It is harder to claim that Brexit did not win in the UK. This did not stop people trying. The philosopher A. C. Grayling wrote to the prime minister demanding that the UK stays in the EU. She asked one of her staff to reply, who wrote that the government had offered a referendum to the public saying the decision was for the voters.

Therefore the government would carry through their decision. Grayling would have none it, and responded:

> You write: 'On 23 June, the country voted to leave the European Union and it is the duty of the Government to make sure we do so.' You are wrong on both counts. Votes cast on the day, on a 72% turn-out, represent a Leave vote of 37% of the total electorate and 26% of the population of the UK. You cannot describe this as 'the country' nor claim that 'the country' voted to leave the EU ... On what conceivable grounds can you describe 37% of the total electorate and 26% of the population as 'the country'?[2]

On what conceivable grounds? Well, Brits dropped their ballot paper in the box knowing that whoever got the most votes would decide. And if the votes of 17.4 million are not sufficient, then, *mutatis mutandis*, as a philosopher might say, how much less so are the votes of 16.2 million? Would he have objected if the vote had gone the other way, that this was not sufficient to decide so grave a matter? It is also awkward because he has started a private, for-profit university that needs foreign students and he may have a vested interest. What he seems to claim is that he wants the country to revert back to how it was, without having to persuade a mere 26 per cent of the population or even a fraction of them to change their minds. Brexit supporters are right to feel disrespected and infuriated by such an attitude.

'They cheated and they lied!' Paul Krugman, a Nobel economist who writes for the *New York Times*, was angry about the way the vote was being 'rigged' against Clinton, including by the FBI – when he still thought she would win.[3] Clinton herself blamed the FBI for taking the wind out of her momentum in the final week by staging a phoney announcement that it was investigating her emails. With respect to lies, neither side was clean. Those who were against the system were especially exercised by the big dishonesty: the way the system has been run for decades. The four breaches of trust stacked up. Neither Clinton nor the Remain campaign acknowledged the scale of the systemic problem – how could they?

The biggest dishonesty of the EU referendum was plastered across the Leave campaign's battle bus: that leaving the EU would give us 'back' £350 million a week to spend on the NHS. It was a cynical deceit. The figure comes from a technical commitment to the EU of £350 million on which the UK gets an immediate rebate. It only pays in fact around £250 million a week. But it then benefits from EU grants and payments to the tune of at least £100 million a week. Thus the real figure for the UK's net contribution is £150 million a week not £350 million.[4] Nor would saving this by leaving the EU mean it would be spent on the NHS – the slogan assumes no overall loss of income to the exchequer from an EU exit, something that had no basis in reality. Michael Gove was the Cabinet member in charge of the British legal system and co-chair of the Leave campaign. Challenged on the figure during the referendum, he replied that the £350 million lie was justified because the EU 'could' demand that amount from the UK in the future. But he knew this depended on the UK's agreement. Had he been on the other side of the argument, the preposterous claim would not have withstood his forensic ability for a minute.

The deception worked: canvassers for Remain reported people on the doorsteps saying that they wanted £350 million a week for their NHS. Dominic Cummings, who ran the Leave campaign, says the slogan was central to its success (in a compelling report[5]). The question, then, is why was it not shot down? The answer is that the amount was an exaggeration with a core of truth: the UK makes a net payment of £150 million a week into the EU. To face down the enormous exaggeration of the Leave side still demanded justification of £150 million a week as excellent value. As the Remain campaign decided it would not put a positive case for being in the EU, it was unable to do this. It was therefore unable to expose the exaggeration. The deceit revealed a true weakness. In that sense it was on to something.

People know they are fed lies, they also, in Blake's unmatchable words know: 'A truth that's told with bad intent / Beats all the lies you can invent.' For many the intent of the Remain campaign was far more dodgy than that of the Brexiteers.

Speaking of the unsophisticated leads to another form of denying legitimacy to the votes for Brexit and Trump. Who *were* these people? It did not take long for surveys to conclude that it was thanks to relatively older, poorer and less-educated voters with more authoritarian personalities that Brexit and Trump triumphed.[6] Especially when it came to Trump: across all income strata it was the less well educated who voted in his favour.[7] The subtext is that the thick and stupid lack the necessary faculties to decide a country's future. But then, do the well educated have these faculties? Some of the best minds in Britain decided to call the campaign to remain in the EU, *Stronger In*. On the doorstep, an older lady worried that they were calling for the country to *join* the European Union. I'm assured, this is true. She was alarmed that if the country did join the EU, it would have to get rid of the Queen. You could despair that she is an ignorant fool not to *know* the UK is in the EU. But she had a point, or rather two. She spotted that *Stronger In* is ambiguous and can be read as an injunction, that we should join – something missed by some of the finest political minds in the country, fabled for their acumen. Also, in its heart Britain had never really joined. If it voted to Remain in 2016 it would be in for ever. Poverty and vulnerability can create a simplicity that leads to clarity. No one should patronise the underdog.

Because voting is the call of vulnerable humans it can be manipulated. Equally, once their manipulation becomes clear to them, the manipulated can change their behaviour. Elections are a reflexive learning process. George Soros makes this argument about markets and open societies. It means they can't be predicted. In elections the process is slower. But there was a growing frustration with the parties not offering alternatives. For decades the era of the CBCs had squeezed electoral choice – into the confines of their two-party 'post-democracy' duumvirate. The less educated are less able to change their lives. For them a vote for Brexit or Trump was attractive as a way of busting open the lack of choice. Each one of us is a grain of sand. This was a chance to come together and make an impact, for once. Were they wrong or stupid to feel this?

In the US, the poorest preferred Clinton. It was those with enough to be squeezed who voted for Trump, and many wealthy and middle-class voters backed right-wing change as well. But the marginal and excluded have been singled out: the more lumpen they are the less we need to regard them as agents. Two careful political scientists wrote on the London School of Economics blog:

> the vote for Brexit was delivered by the 'left behind' – social groups that are united by a general sense of insecurity, pessimism and marginalisation, who do not feel as though elites, whether in Brussels or Westminster, share their values, represent their interests and genuinely empathise with their intense angst about rapid change.[8]

This is academic pussyfooting. It is not that more marginal social groups 'feel' that the elites do not represent their interests, they *know* it. Almost overnight, an insidious social concept has appeared in our language. Stumbling out after a party, you might realise that you have 'left behind' your handbag or briefcase. When used about humans the term delivers a double passivity. In a well-known incident (which can happen to the best of us) David Cameron left behind one of his children in a pub. It was not the child's fault, obviously, while the father can be immediately forgiven for his embarrassing forgetfulness, as he had no intention of causing harm. The phrase 'left behind' thus extends two forgiving qualities when applied to humans and evaporates responsibility and agency on both sides. Groups across the US and the UK have apparently been 'left behind'. The term implies it was inadvertent. It is not their fault they have been forgotten. Nor, *of course*, did their governments and the ruling elites intend harm. It was just one of those things. Millions of families *left behind*.

Jean Seaton notes that there used to be a category of people called 'the poor'. George Orwell called them 'the common man'. We have learnt to call them (she was writing three years ago) 'the socially excluded'. Then she asks a shrewd question, 'What, one wonders, will another government call them?'⁹ Now we know. The objectification, the draining away of humanity continues. We are supposed to call them 'the left behind'. The loss of a sense of agency, both theirs and the ruling class's, is evident, as is the dehumanisation behind the apparently chatty terminology. Even if aging, uneducated and lacking in the 'values' of cosmopolitanism, the poor know. They know that the government is aware of their plight, as it calculates the value of their woeful benefit slips and reads reports on the poverty of their housing. The poor know that the same administration dishes out billions to help bankers. David Cameron called Coalville in West Leicestershire 'a dump'.¹⁰ The 'dump' voted 35,000 to 22,500 to leave the EU – its public housing council estates witnessing an 80 per cent turnout. The political parties, Labour, Liberal Democrat and Tory, did not 'leave the poor behind'. They dumped them and *let them rot*. This is why they did not come kindly to the gate and ask security if a message could be sent to the masters of the universe asking to please be remembered rather than 'left behind'. They kicked back when they could.

It was more complicated, obviously, but highlights the fundamental issue over how to understand what leads people to vote as they do. Never start with the presumption that they do not know what they are doing. In the UK, 16 million voted for Remain. Most said they did so for economic reasons. Where are the studies trying to 'explain' this? The academic community seems to assume that the reasons given by Remain voters explain their motives for their decision (perhaps many academics felt the same way). Why is a similar respect not extended to those who chose Leave? Does reason itself meet a cliff edge? Simon Wren-Lewis, an Oxford economist whose influential blog is very informative, can't get past the evident self-harm being inflicted by Brexit and therefore sees it as a pathology that needs diagnosis or a plot by callous tabloids to brainwash their readers. Will Davies spotted this element early as a possible attraction for voters, 'There is surely a faintly Trumpian psychoanalytic element to the "Brexit" campaign, in which supporters are quite excited by the dangers that leaving the EU poses, and unconsciously relish the economic uncertainty.[11] After the vote he ruefully contemplated that 'the self-harm inflicted by Brexit could potentially be part of its appeal'.[12] Also the excitement.

Both the excitement and the risk of harm are also true of war. Those who ready themselves for the fight to come have to prepare for pain, and one way to do this is to will the sacrifice. There was definitely a martial spirit in the lure of Brexit, while Trump proclaimed he wanted America to win. But not all wars are wrong. Some battles have to be fought. People may be mistaken in taking up arms, but as they prepare to be hurt they are not necessarily ill.

Many Trump and Brexit voters felt a long-term war was being waged on them and that they were striking back in self-defence. The chief executives of the top 100 companies listed on the UK stock exchange overwhelmingly supported staying in the EU. They earn an average of £5 million a year. It was announced shortly after the referendum that they had got an average pay rise in the past year of 10 per cent – £0.5 million.[13] UK average earnings are forecast to be no higher in 2022 than they were in 2007. What is this if not war, when nearly two-fifths of the population are very hard pressed to put their hands on £500 in an emergency? Nor is the inequity a matter of the poor. Millions of Conservative voters who made up the main body of Leave support are comfortable but still have to put children into debt for their university education. Meanwhile the ruling elite that once set an example has gone global and become obscenely wealthy. Many Conservatives also revolted against this.

The day after the vote, a sales assistant in the Manchester area told a reporter from the *Independent*:

> I would like to say on behalf of Leave we all know that there
> may be tough times ahead. In my 53 years I've had my fair
> share of them and they are not nice. Tough times make you
> unable to sleep, cry yourself to sleep, panic about everything
> – horrible. But tough times also mean coming out on the

other side – which we will – feeling stronger and able to deal with whatever life throws at us. We are a nation of strong hardworking and proud people. Do not call us morons or idiots. As a person who has nearly hit rock bottom but pulled myself up again I'm prepared to do it again for a better society.[14]

This statement was addressed to her country by a working woman. She registers the likely harm but does not relish it. A Trump supporter was more high-spirited, 'I want something new. I want the good old days back.'[15] A kind of madness gripped both the leaders of the Trump campaign, personalised in the narcissistic ogre himself, and Brexit's Johnson-Farage. The two countries were maddened by them in different ways, that fitted their contrasting national characteristics. In America the urge to self-determination and bring-back-greatness meant a gamble on Trump with the energies of Las Vegas. The Brits who took the risk on Brexit did so more in the spirit of the Blitz.

But they took an overview. They discounted the obvious lies of 2016 against decades of deceit, the financial costs of tomorrow against years of flat income, heightened insecurity and watching rulers get rich. They reacted to and reflected on the system and were willing to go through a barrier to get to something different. In this sense the voters for Trump and Brexit, less well-educated, less cosmopolitan, less tolerant, more desiring of a government that did what they wanted, acted like collective rulers. While the supporters of Remain and David Cameron, and Hillary Clinton for President, acted like people who had to do what they were told.

Another way to understand this is to think of it in terms of time. In Britain, the time frame that concerned most of those who backed Remain was the future, especially its economic prospects and how they might alter. The time frame that most concerned those who voted Leave was the past, and whether it should continue. That is why, to take the two top issues on each side recorded in the Ashcroft exit poll, 75 per cent of those who chose Remain cited economic prospects, whether of benefit or fear of loss, for their vote, whilst 80 per cent of those who chose Leave gave ending EU decision-making, whether in general or over immigration. The older you are, the more present the past is to you and the more you may want change. The younger you are, the more immediate are the future prospects of jobs and working and living in the European space and the less you may want to risk this.

Time frames illuminate how, on the issues of lies and truth, the two sides argued past each other. A Leave voter dismisses a lie from Johnson over Turks coming to the UK compared to the dishonesty of bailing out the bankers. But, says the Remain voter, this is not about the banking crash. Oh, yes it is, says the Leave voter. I don't want that 'system' any more. In a general election for a government that will last at most five years, people who support the same party have different time frames. The referendum gave their perspectives a novel context.

A similar division, although not as stark, afflicted America, precipitated by Trump's drive to become president no matter what. Trump promised jobs and walls and 4 per cent growth and deporting bad dudes. But perhaps above all his offer was to stop the future offered by Obama, which was being experienced most of all as culturally threatening as well as economically frightening. Those who voted for Trump wanted him to reverse the direction of change, even if it meant locking down Reagan's city on a hill.

Again, it is not that simple. There is one aspect of both votes that needs much more analysis. Since the Italian Marxist Gramsci argued that 'the masses' did not exist as political actors without mass political parties – and then developed his thinking about political change and the organisation of consent and domination – there has been an assumption that individuals on their own cannot alter the nature of their societies even in very large numbers. They need parties to achieve this. Part of the shock of Brexit was that it was not delivered by a party. This suggests a disintegration of the UK's politics. In the many hundreds of different interviews and quotations that I have read or seen over the past year, I do not recall one where someone has said: 'As a Conservative I voted for Brexit.' Two-thirds of Conservative supporters did so – out of individual choice, or choice experienced as an individual decision. Were the newspapers, TV stations and websites that excoriate political parties the alternative form of collective organisation? If so, how stable and lasting are they? In the US, the press focused on the importance of white working-class swing voters. These were a minor part of Trump's support, which was in the main traditional GOP voters who turned out for him if only to stop Hillary. Yet he ran as a businessman contemptuous of the Republican Party leadership. Mass anti-systemic movements no longer need parties in the traditional sense in order to come into existence. The question is whether they need them to have the all-important staying power.

Adam Tooze identifies 'Eight distinct sets of preoccupations ... swirling around the question of what caused Brexit and Trump. All are talking at once. Some are talking to each other. Others are not'.[16] He promptly added number 8½. I will return to the question of how best to understand change of this kind in a later chapter on combined development, when I have looked at the various causes – of Brexit especially. I want to emphasise that Brexit and Trump were conscious, deliberated choices finalised in the privacy of the voting booth. Tooze wrote an earlier post called 'Explaining Brexit and Trump: Search for a Method'. It refers to Jean-Paul Sartre's 1957 book *Questions de Méthode*. Sartre was attempting to unite his existentialism with its insistence on personal responsibility with Marxism, then locked into a communist determinism. His solution was that while individuals are formed by their class and social background, they are not determined by them. People with identical class origins can be very different people – what they are is decided by what they make of their specific material and social circumstances, their family especially. All humans are capable of being original. We are also historical animals born in one time, place and social and economic circumstance. What we learn to do is mediated through such circumstances but not controlled by them. All of us are capable of originality. We are now witnessing this on an unprecedented scale, the deliberate exercise of originality through the ballot box.

Enormous efforts will be made to tame, frustrate and leash this force which left Remain and Clinton floundering, because it is capable of being far more original than Brexit and Trump whose sails it filled in 2016.

# 5

# The Authenticity of Leave and Trump

There was no threat to capitalism. But there was a threat to the government of capitalism in the US and the UK. This was revolutionary enough. The threat broke through the established structures, taking the form of Trump and Brexit. The new administrations face novel issues as they seek to deliver on their pledge of change. I want to look at how they achieved their breakthrough in one respect only: by looking at the appeal to the authentic made by the two insurgencies (very different from an offer of genuine democratic reforms) and the official order's failure to respond. We have to be careful here as it means entering a hall of mirrors. Both Brexit and Trump addressed real issues. Yet both were brands, media constructs of the spectacle. With Trump this is blatant. Todd Gitlin lays down a coruscating indictment of America's inability to call a charlatan a charlatan, showing how:

> Donald Trump, toxic bullshitter, emerged from a whole zeitgeist of nihilistic attention-grabbing enterprises that we helplessly speak of as 'the media', that unprincipled, slithering, polymorphous process that observes only one logic: the making of fortunes ... The depraved persona of 'Trump' who has cast his malignant spell upon the world's oldest democracy, is a pure product of the American culture industry. He is not only a brand, licensing the use of his name; he has branded America, which has not yet grasped that the joke's on us.[1]

Brexit was not a brand like Trump. But 'Brussels' became a version of relentlessly negative branding that sold papers and stirred chauvinist contempt for Johnny Foreigner. For decade after decade, 'Brussels' was projected as a burlesque of malfunctioning busybodies, in an ongoing diversion from reporting on the realities of Britain's own government, to become the UK media's equivalent failure. Brexit's boastful postures were lit by its strobes.

In the election itself, Trump won America's electoral college thanks to a relatively traditional partisan battle. The surprising destruction of the US establishment's safety catches took place in the Republican primaries, when he destroyed a succession of the CBCs and evangelical candidates. In the campaign itself he held the allegiance of those who voted for Romney four years before, including women and the better-off, and added to them in some crucial states. He did so despite his repellent features for three reasons, in addition to his own considerable support. First, Hillary was such a polarising figure to Republicans, and brought so much of the past with her, and stirred so much misogyny, that anyone seemed preferable. Second, Trump's repellent features were an attraction for many, and it will take time to see if they just lent him the benefit of the doubt – the shallowest form of loyalty. Most important, Trump won over the evangelicals and religious right to back his candidacy after he marginalised their own Ted Cruz, and then promised to throw them the Supreme Court. This 'fusion of the two anti-Establishment Republican insurgencies was the crucial event', Mike Davis argues. It is represented in Trump's alliance with his likely successor and vice president, the smiling, born-again, Mike Pence.[2]

In the UK, the referendum and its outcome was without precedent. The Brexit vote cut across party lines. It was during the campaign itself that all the safety catches designed to prevent the destruction of the status quo failed. Leave was a predominantly white mobilisation drawing heavily on Tory support. Nearly 60 per cent of those who voted Conservative in 2015 (when they won the election) supported Brexit. Less than 40 per cent of the smaller number who voted Labour did so. Yet without the strong support of Labour towns, outside the big metropolises, especially those across the north of England, the vote would not have been for Leave. But they joined with the view held by smaller majorities across the more populous southern England where middle-class Conservatives were Brexit's centre of gravity. Thus a Tory-led campaign was dependent on Labour voters for its success. While the referendum divided voters across the UK, it allied them across party alignments. Decades of anti-European coverage in the tabloids laid the ground for this, as did the official stimulation of anti-immigrant sentiment by Cameron's government. As important, the Conservative Party itself was shrinking. Because figures may be retained locally, there are no definite numbers. Estimates by Tim Bale show a party that is small, old, male, middle-class and southern. Active membership is less than 130,000 and more than half are over sixty.[3] At some point between Cameron becoming party leader in 2005 and the election of 2010 when he became the coalition premier, Labour Party membership overtook the Tories for the first time in history.[4] Conservative membership was overwhelmingly hostile to the EU. Cameron and his largely pro-European Cabinet tuned into the networks of power and influence as you would expect. They did not have party support below them or a culture of influence and loyalty. They were running the government against the grain of what was left of their own party, modelling themselves on the Blair trajectory, lacking a political hinterland.

In a fatal miscalculation, David Cameron presumed that Nigel Farage would lead the referendum campaign to Leave the EU, which is why he was confident of success. But when he came back to Downing Street from Brussels with the terms for a new relationship with the EU to take to the country in the referendum, he was ambushed by a personal disaster from which the Remain campaign never recovered. One of his closest confidants and a family friend, Michael Gove, the then Lord Chancellor, with a reputation as an intellectual, decided he could not support continued membership now that the referendum forced him to choose. In a 1,500-word statement of his creed, Gove set out why, despite loyalty and friendship, he had to follow his conscience.[5] He had earlier spent the evening with Boris Johnson.

They had tried to formulate a 'sovereignty clause' – promised by Cameron – that would defend the UK's right to govern itself within the EU and discovered that there could only be one judicial master, the European Court. Without Gove's declaration, it is unlikely that Johnson would have followed suit. The double-act of Gove's willowy principle and Johnson's stout pragmatism might in other times have looked like Laurel and Hardy. Instead, Johnson too produced a statement in his *Telegraph* column, which like Gove fixated on sovereignty and self-government.[6] The other side never produced any equivalent overviews or statement of principle, written with their verve, passion and coherence.

As *The Times* noted, the Leave campaign was no longer led by 'fringe figures'; instead it was headed by Gove with his 'intellectual ballast' plus the 'political viagra' of Johnson, the country's 'most popular politician'.[7] What Cameron and his chancellor and strategist, George Osborne, had hoped would be a protest movement became an alternative direction for government, led by popular, experienced mainstream politicians. The cause of Brexit was transformed.

It is astonishing that Cameron went into such a historic confrontation without realising it would mean all-out battle with Gove rather than an easy campaign against the UKIP dog whistle. It was also surely a consequence of the weakness of his party's culture and inner life. He had personally persuaded Gove to leave journalism to be an MP. This was a fix. No mechanisms existed that obliged leading Conservatives to declare their positions on major issues to the party membership. Cameron was aware of his friend's opposition to the EU, but he assumed that Gove belonged to him and his circle, as there was no organised Tory Party tendency to claim him. In his account of this extraordinary moment in the country's history, Tim Shipman makes a revealing aside. Although they all admired Gove, Cameron's circle thought him 'a little bit funny because he believes things'.[8]

Anyone unfortunate enough to get within breathing distance of late-Britain's quasi-aristocrats will recognise the mocking conceit of this mix of commerce and snobbery, and the nullity of its values. Shipman provides a glimpse behind the app-controlled Venetian blinds of the well-heeled: for Cameron's circle, Remain was a matter of convenience. The Brexiteers *believed* in getting out.

Its belief and commitment gave Leave a moral edge, exhibited in the enthusiasm of its meetings. They had a jealous concern for British sovereignty. Immigration was more important as an issue, but sovereignty was needed to do anything about it. Four weeks before the vote, it was officially announced that net migration into the UK for 2015 had risen to a near-record 330,000 (with over 600,000 entering for more than a year and just under 300,000 leaving). 184,000 of the incomers were from the EU. The official Leave campaign had not led on migration until that point, and now pivoted. Cummings told Johnson and Gove: 'If you want to win this, you have to hit Cameron and Osborne over the head with a baseball bat with immigration written on it.'[9] They did. Cummings created a forceful, well-defined campaign with his battle cry 'Take Back Control' and linked it to the threat of uncontrolled immigration – symbolised by Turkey. They distributed a graphic map showed a huge arrow of Turkish hordes, assisted by Albanian and Macedonian outriders, pouring across Europe like locusts to strip a helpless United Kingdom of its child benefits. A 'threat' enhanced by the ongoing refugee crisis with its Syrian epicentre, which the map helpfully highlighted on Turkey's border.

The suggestion that Turkey might join the EU was a bigger lie than £350 million a week for the NHS. Obviously, it was ludicrous to suggest that the EU would allow Turkey to join and give unrestricted access to 75 million Muslims. But who knows? If those in Brussels did, then we in Britain would have no say. The Remain campaign virtually conceded the claim even though it was nonsense by refusing to talk about it. The sense of democracy and self-government contained in 'Take Back Control' appealed to voters who are not racists, because it emphasised borders as a positive rather than migrants as a negative. A Norfolk businesswoman who employs a workforce of around 125, a quarter from Eastern Europe, said on the BBC radio *Any Questions* that she welcomed migration and did not object to the year's 300,000 net entries. She voted for Brexit because she was frightened it could become a million. In this way even those who wanted high immigration voted Leave rather than be told the alternative was powerlessness.

Self-government was singled out as the reason for supporting Brexit by Thatcher's biographer Charles Moore in the *Telegraph*[10] and his anguished colleague Ambrose Evans-Pritchard, who was unflinching about the likely economic costs:

> Stripped of distractions, it comes down to an elemental choice: whether to restore the full self-government of this nation, or to continue living under a higher supranational regime, ruled by a European Council that we do not elect in any meaningful sense, and that the British people can never remove, even when it persists in error.[11]

The Harvard economist Dani Rodrik mapped out a now famous 'Trilemma' in 2001. This states that you can only have two out of any three of national sovereignty, democracy and globalisation. He gave Evans-Pritchard a sympathetic hearing for his choice of national sovereignty and democracy.[12] On the left, Olly Huitson quoted the EU Trade Commissioner saying: 'I do not take my mandate from the European people' and argued: 'The EU is not simply undemocratic, it is actively contemptuous of democracy. Better to fight our own battles here, under our own imperfect democracy.'[13] Boris Johnson said it was democracy that decided it for him, telling *The Times*: 'The fundamental issue is who runs this country.'[14] Michael Gove's 1,500-word apologia was an essay on this theme:

> I believe that the decisions which govern all our lives, the laws we must all obey and the taxes we must all pay should be decided by people we choose and who we can throw out if we want change.[15]

It was thanks to such arguments that Brexit attracted high-profile business support, such as the brilliant high-tech designer and manufacturer James Dyson, or Tim Martin, the owner of the

Wetherspoon chain of 1,000 pubs employing 35,000 people. Both strongly supported immigration for their businesses. Martin filled his bars and restaurants with Leave coasters and 16-page booklets of essays. Cheerfully apolitical, he told Decca Aitkenhead that he simply questioned 'the lack of democracy at the heart of the EU'.

He also thinks 'Britain has benefited enormously from EU migration, not just economically but socially and culturally'. The democratic deficit is Martin's sole objection to the EU project. 'The thing I cannot understand is that when I said I think democracy is crucial for the future of the world, I'd have thought people would pour out of the doors saying, "Yes! Tim is right!" But people on the remain side just don't seem to think like that.'[16]

Sovereignty was the starting point for the 'patriotic globalists' – Andrew Sparrow's description.[17] Daniel Hannan, an MEP and long-time critic of the EU's oligarchy and protectionism, used his influence to advance the idea of a trading network of the so-called Anglosphere as an alternative to the EU. It provided a framework for Leave to articulate hostility to 'rule from Brussels' without being protectionist or hostile to the City. Hannan's arguments have become more fanciful. He now celebrates Brexit as a rollback of the Norman yoke that crushed England after 1066.[18] But his confident arguments gave him a unique position, on the opposite pole to Farage, within the Brexit universe, and his argument shapes the thinking of the current UK government.

Vote Leave sold its message in full digital mode to stimulate support. In his account of the campaign Cummings emphasises the 11-point swing to strong support for Leave, from 33 per cent in September 2015 to 44 per cent in June 2016.[19] As he rightly says, their campaign could easily have been lost. At the end, Vote Leave clinched it with its marketing. Of its total budget of £13.5 million, it spent a quarter on social media advertising, mainly through Facebook and mostly 'persuading a group of about 9 million people defined as: between 35–55, outside London and Scotland, excluding UKIP supporters ...' to quote from an informative breakdown of its expenditure published by Cummings.[20] No serious news coverage or analysis of the digital campaign took place, as it remained outside the bubble of politicians and mainstream media, but it seems to have been a striking achievement:

> We squeezed every part of our £7m 'controlled' budget to enable us to focus as much as possible on digital marketing. We focused most of this money on the last 10 days and on about 9 million 'persuadables' – not our core voters – identified by the data science team from a variety of sources ... we discovered that essentially all relevant demographics responded best to £350m/NHS.

Compared to Leave's deadly combination of the tangible and intangible, of immigrants and sovereignty, the Remain campaign just sounded desperate. Although the issue of democracy did not enthral everyone. Just before the vote, I went to Doncaster, the heart of once working-class South Yorkshire, with my colleague Adam Ramsay. In 1980 it had ten deep coal mines employing 17,000: all gone. What struck us forcefully was the resignation of many of those who were going to vote Leave, convinced that nothing could alter things for them even if the vote was for Brexit. They were not talking about 'democracy'. Westminster had no presence for them, so they did not care if it 'took back control'. The prospect of Brexit triggering an economic downturn seemed irrelevant. From what? The possibility that house prices might fall, one of the dire consequences the chancellor had warned against, was a positive attraction.[21]

Yet Leave also challenged this widespread fatalism. In a Manchester speech, early in the campaign, Boris Johnson charged the prime minister and his coterie, whom he knew well, of having 'not a shred of idealism ... [they] keep saying ... we have no choice ... We agree with you about the democratic problem, they say – but it's the price we have to pay ... The EU, they say – it's crap but we have no alternative.'[22] Johnson turned the Cameron circle's idle contempt for Michael Gove against it. He held up their leader and denounced him as someone who did not believe in anything.

In a brilliant short book, *Exit, Voice and Loyalty*, Albert Hirschman applied the experience of corporate consumer marketing to politics. In the marketplace, if a buyer dislikes what they buy – for example a car – they can complain or take their business elsewhere: voice or exit. To prevent exit, firms build customer loyalty by making voice attractive. Apply this to politics and you can see how the narrowing of choice between the parties led to discontent and exit in terms of abstention and non-voting, as many became convinced that their voice or vote meant nothing. In 2016, both Trump and the Remain campaign surprised pollsters because many who had withdrawn and were therefore no longer surveyed for their opinions, went to the ballot box and 'gave voice'. Thanks to Trump's cunning, his speech writers grasped what was happening and exploited it outrageously. In his acceptance speech to the Republican convention, Trump addressed the American nation and especially the 'people who work hard but no longer have a voice'. He told them, the capital letters are in the official transcript, 'I AM YOUR VOICE'.

By claiming voice, Brexit and Trump offered exit from the status quo. The combination of positive and negative was intoxicating. As they mess up, whether you voted for them or not, the only legitimate form of resistance is one that welcomes the renewal of voice. The apparent authenticity of a demagogue like Trump is very different from integrity. I am not saying he should be copied. Nor Boris Johnson for Brexit, who opened his campaign for Leave by saying, 'We have become so used to Nanny in Brussels that we have become infantilised, incapable of imagining an independent future. We used to run the biggest empire the world has ever seen, and with a much smaller domestic population and a relatively tiny civil service. Are we really incapable of cutting trade deals?'[23] Both Trump and Johnson abused nostalgia to make a false claim of authenticity. They got away with it by speaking out for how their country should 'change'. They can only be exposed by an offer of better change.

# 6

# The Artificiality of Remain and Clinton

For those who opposed them, Brexit and Trump were tragedies in the original sense of the term. By tragedy, the ancient Greeks did not mean an accident, even with many victims, but the way well-intended actions may lead to a disaster that could have been avoided, had the protagonists not been in the grip of human ignorance, weakness and vanity. The actors who led Britain to Brexit and America to Trump did not want this to happen, they could have ensured it did not, yet were unable to change course. I have emphasised the energy and authenticity of the two incredible campaigns for Brexit and Trump. Without this they would not have won. But they did not deserve to win. Most voters were unconvinced. The messengers were obviously charlatans. They triumphed because the advocates of the status quo failed. In the UK the utterly pathetic set of arguments put forward by the Remain campaign lacked all positivity and self-belief. In the United States, Clinton's unresponsiveness to the content of Trump's themes and assertions opened his way to Washington.

Contrast the US candidates' two convention speeches. Here is Trump, whose official version has 282 footnotes: 'Big business, elite media and major donors are lining up behind the campaign of my opponent because they know she will keep our rigged system in place. We will build the roads, highways, bridges, tunnels, airports, and the railways of tomorrow. This, in turn, will create millions more jobs.'[1] Clinton's reply a week later: 'He [Trump] spoke for 70-odd minutes – and I do mean odd. And he offered zero solutions. But we already know he doesn't believe these things. No wonder he doesn't like talking about his plans. You might have noticed, I love talking about mine.'[2] It's too painful to continue. She refuses to register what he is doing. I can't put it better than Lawrence Lessig, furious that Americans never heard a counter-argument for dealing with a corrupt, rigged system because of a

> strategic decision by the Clinton campaign. Though pressed again and again by many to take up the issue ... and show America that only she had an actual plan that could fix the problem Trump so effectively targeted ... the Clinton campaign was resolute in either denying the charge, or ignoring the issue ... while Trump railed again and again against the 'insiders' and their 'corruption,' she acted as if she didn't even hear the question. The Clinton campaign decided that in the year of Brexit, in a moment of anti-establishment furore, they could simply ignore the issue and it would magically go away. That, I believe, was a mistake.[3]

It sure was. It made the presidential debates depressing and lowering to sit through. Clinton did not believe Trump could become president. She felt that answering him was a form of lending him her credibility. She exposed him as the misogynist bully he is, with consummate discipline. Her view was that he would then self-destruct. But everyone knew what he was like. Not believing a word he said, she never took what he said seriously.

An almost uncanny direct comparison between the referendum and the presidential election illustrates how Hillary Clinton's presidential campaign and David Cameron's Remain campaign locked themselves into their destiny, unable to respond to the popular, negative energies they stimulated.

In 2012, a week after Obama defeated Romney for the presidency and there was no longer an obvious front-runner for the Republican leadership, Trump trademarked 'Make America Great Again!' He didn't market-test it. He didn't need to. He was steeped in what would work for the publics he needed to arouse. It provided the defining campaign message that he wanted. In August 2015, Dominic Cummings, the

Leave campaign director, had a 'genius moment' when he decided on the slogan 'Take Control', which became, in an all-important twist, 'Take Back Control'.[4] An earlier three-person meeting planning the Leave campaign had decided on 'Vote Leave, Get Change'. The next day Cummings said he'd thought about it overnight and 'Vote Leave, Take Control' was much better.[5] He had worked with enough focus groups in the past to know what motivated voters. As with Trump, the instant decision was not market-tested. Like Trump, Cummings knew that his slogan allowed him to draw together the alliance he needed.

Also in 2012, Hillary knew she would be running in 2016. She had the learning experience of seeking the nomination in 2008, so you might think she would know her pitch. Instead, in sharp contrast to the way Trump formulated his slogan, it was farmed out. WikiLeaks released an email from her campaign team with a list of eighty-four different slogans they were considering in 2015.[6] These included Rise Up, Move Up, Family First, Making America Work For You, and No Quit, as well as A New Bargain We Can Count On. Many are quite ridiculous, such as Next Begins With You.[7] It's not clear she ever saw them all, but it was her process. They were drawn up by her strategy group BSG.

> BSG is a strategic research consultancy that marries language expertise with innovative research to frame choices so that your brand is the only answer. We advise global corporations, political leaders, and institutions in dynamic, competitive scenarios. We understand the rhythm and nuances of language and words. We give you the right words to use and much more. We map the competitive landscape so you know where to play and how to win. We give you the messaging framework and strategic roadmap so that everyone in your organization knows 'why' the messaging is powerful and how it will help you achieve the outcomes you want.[8]

BSG is a construction company for the language that John Berger perceived as a prison of meaninglessness, and that is how Clinton arrived at 'Stronger Together'.

An identical, if less expensive process was undertaken by Remain in the UK. They too were unable to find their own words. The full name of the official campaign was also professionally 'market-researched'. It became 'Britain Stronger in Europe' and the name for the campaign itself: 'Stronger In'. How about that? 'Stronger' is the product of identical processes, a sausage of branding that market research shows to be the best way to fend off a political challenge.

A better battle cry for Remain would have been 'Keep the best of both worlds', a phrase used by Cameron to commend his renegotiation. At least it would have been refreshing and more tangible. Had Hillary run on 'No Quit' it would have shown a sense of political humour. Instead, both Clinton and Cameron approached their campaigns as commodities, unable to see that it was precisely their way of doing politics that was under challenge.

The significance of the failure of their market-testing is hard to underestimate, because Clinton and Cameron were consummate, well-funded professionals who knew how to win. They represented the dominant form of politics, which regarded sincerity, independence, principle and real passion and *believing what you say*, as positively dangerous, because they risk 'message discipline' and threaten to distract attention from the centre ground where 'elections are won'. Tony Blair's imperative – that to be a leader like him you must 'appear to be natural while gripping your nature in a vice of care and caution. Don't let the mask slip' – was their imperative.[9] There is no clearer evidence that this form of politics has run its course than its inability to deliver what it was designed to do best: the well-marketed slogan – when up against opponents engaged in total war on both sides of the Atlantic.

Market research is a powerful means of shaping a message, provided you know what you believe in. Now, however, the CBCs had to justify themselves. Hitherto they had won by saying the forces of globalisation were for the best, and that they would oversee them and help spread the future benefits – without needing to be tied down by any promise as to what that future might be. After a quarter century of their real-world outcomes, in 2016 they had to justify themselves for what they were. They were unable to. All they could come up with was that America was 'Stronger Together' and the UK 'Stronger In'.

The legitimate heart of the cry for Brexit lay in the call for self-government against the encroachment of the European Union. The true kernel at the heart of Trump's shameless campaign was that the system is rigged. Faced with these claims, in both cases their opponents just tried to change the subject. They regarded the positive as too high-risk. The British prime minister and the Remain camp set out their case in terms of narrow, transactional advantage. Focus groups and market research told them that they would lose support if they engaged with issues like democracy, immigration and sovereignty, so mention of these issues was squashed. Claiming that the UK would be better off in and worse off out in terms of money was a visionless perspective even if true. It was echoed in the Labour campaign that the EU is on balance preferable for workers, in terms of their rights and the economy, without any larger sense of continental solidarity. Hillary Clinton was given every opportunity in her debates with Bernie Sanders, especially after she lost their primary in Michigan, to grasp that the corruption of the system was a real issue for her voters. Instead, she treated the need to compete with Sanders as equivalent to a ritual mortification of the flesh that would vindicate her professional approach – and declined to engage with arguments that America has a systemic problem and money had bought politics. She was raising hundreds of millions from the system. How could she denounce it?

In Britain the feebleness of the Remain campaign's slogans was exposed by its tabloid enemies. His spin doctors told the prime minister that being 'safer' in Europe was a strong theme. Cameron could have turned this into a positive pitch for solidarity with Britain's European neighbours. Instead, it was spun as part of project fear. Cameron gave a speech suggesting that Europeans could not be trusted without us and implied that a Leave vote could undo the peace that had held since the Second World War. It was coordinated with the former heads of MI5 and MI6, warning that to leave the EU would undermine the fight on terror. Scare operations were familiar fare to the tabloids during elections, which they played along with to support the Tories. They knew exactly what Cameron was up to: a PR operation, to position the Remain campaign over the British war graves across the continent. Mockery ensued. The *Sun*'s front page shouted that Cameron warned Brexit would lead to World War Three. The *Mail* headlined that the prime minister was so desperate he was warning that Brexit meant 'WAR AND GENOCIDE'. The nation scoffed. A Downing Street source said, 'This is what it must feel like to be the Labour Party during the general election.'[10] A week before the vote, women in at least one hairdressing salon just cracked up with contagious laughter as a new warning came up on their TV screen.[11]

On 10 June, two weeks before the vote, the government's campaign team assembled in 10 Downing Street. They felt things slipping away and debated what to do. Craig Oliver, who chaired it, describes how some of the participants wanted 'to make the positive case for being in the EU'. He was firm with them: 'Way back at the beginning of all this, we decided we needed to win over people who wanted to leave the EU in their hearts, but could be persuaded to stay when they realised it was a risk to their pocket and their future. That has been the core of our thinking and we need to hold our nerve.' George Osborne ended the meeting, concluding: 'Everyone slags off negative campaigning, but it is the only consistent message that's working for us.' As Osborne spoke, Oliver recalls, 'I look round the room and think several people look sick.'[12] As the ultra-capitalists behind Brexit pressed their opportunity, the guardians of the global order in David Cameron's Downing Street headquarters were lethargic and negative, living out the last cursed days of their existence as their staff wanted to throw up.

One person, above all, was responsible for the way the United Kingdom left the European Union. David Cameron himself. He has smoothly removed himself from politics, so that it seems as if he was never there, even after six years. Yet he inserted the Tories, the world's oldest political tradition, into the new global order to become himself one of the CBCs. Brexit cannot be understood without him. In the next two chapters I will look into how he brought about the referendum and what kind of political figure he is.

# PART II
# CAMERON

There is no science in the personal study of human nature.
Robert Louis Stevenson,
*The Story of a Lie*, 1879

# 7

# A Man of Means, Not Ends

It was David Cameron's EU referendum. He promised it in 2013, should he win the election in 2015. When he did, he set the terms of the negotiations for a new British relationship with the EU and the timing. He had the final word on the case for Remain that would be put to voters. He gave the last solo pitch on TV calling on the country to stay in. As the official instant history of his premiership recounts, the prime minister was 'clear that ... the strategic direction of the campaign will be set by his office in Number 10' and that he saw himself as 'the biggest asset that Remain have'.[1] He was the instigator, the strategist and the commanding general. Fought differently, Remain could have won. He lost. If any one person is answerable for what happened, he is. Much more than Farage or Johnson or Gove, in so far as any one man did, it was Cameron who led Britain to Brexit. What was wrong with his approach?

I'll start with one of the most disastrous evenings in the annals of British diplomacy. In 2012 Cameron decided the principles of his referendum strategy. He had to persuade anti-EU voters to back the Tories, not UKIP. Therefore he calculated that he would seek to win the coming election with a promise to renegotiate the UK's relationship with the EU before the end of 2017, then give voters the choice of whether to stay or go.

Before he could commit to this, however, he had to get the support of the German chancellor in advance of any speech that announced it. He believed: 'Merkel is the key. Without her support, the announcement could be a fiasco.' On 7 November 2012, Angela Merkel had a private dinner with him at 10 Downing Street. Cameron, 'using his full emotional force with her', explained: 'I need to make a pitch to the country. If there is no acceptable deal, it's not the end of the world; I'll walk away from the EU.' She tells him that Europe needs Britain – 'Without you, I don't know what is going to happen' – and asks him not to rush into saying: 'I'm leaving the ship.' Cameron tells her: 'This is our EU as much as anyone's ... I have to be pushy for our interests; but I don't want Britain to leave.' To prevent Britain's departure, he must 'listen to British public opinion' and get 'changes that will make it possible for Britain to stay in.' Merkel, who speaks English, tells him 'I do get it' and says she will try to help, but there are limits given Germany's obligations to her other European partners.

If you are confused, you are not the only one. Merkel, we are told, stares at him intently and tries to get inside his head to decide whether he is serious.[2] Alas, poor Angela, we know the feeling!

Cameron thought he had recruited the most powerful figure in Europe to his marketing strategy. To manage his party, he needed to retain the veneer of impartiality. His ploy would be to tell the voters that they could decide either way and that Britain would be fine outside the EU, although his preference was to stay. That way he would stop the downright anti-Europeans in his own party from splitting away. But Merkel should know that his real view and intention is that Britain must stay. No wonder she stared: he was going to tell the public he would walk away from the EU if the changes he got were not sufficient, while assuring her that he had no intention whatsoever of turning his back on Europe.

By so informing the German chancellor, he undermined his negotiating position over the changes he would ask for. That was stupid. By letting her in on the truth of his intention to manipulate opinion, he was revealing something worse. He intended to mislead his own party and the electorate as to the nature of his real views. The episode parallels Tony Blair telling the US president he was with him 'all the way' on an Iraq invasion but had to pretend to parliament that he was still assessing the evidence. Blair's murderous embrace of war was more grievous than Cameron's trickery, because staying in the EU was sane. But if the objectives were different the means were similar. There is a line of descent from the one to the other: contempt for the public, an entitlement to dishonesty, a British leader desiring to be strong on the 'world stage' crawling into the pocket of a major power.

In January 2013, Cameron gave his Bloomberg speech that announced his commitment to a referendum, saying: 'Of course Britain could make her own way in the world, outside the EU, if we chose to do so'. The thrust of his Euro-positioning was that it would advantage the country to remain in the EU provided he ended its commitment to ever closer union, obtained a return of powers to Britain and made the EU more accountable to national parliaments. On the surface, he was to achieve much of this after assiduous efforts of persuasion in his negotiations with the other twenty-seven members of the EU, including their agreement that 'ever closer union of the peoples of Europe' would not apply to the UK. But he already knew that he was not going to get them to agree to less Europe rather than more. Indeed, in the final version of the settlement that he recommended to the voters, he agreed that the UK should 'facilitate' further political union among EU members of the Eurozone in return for Britain's exclusion.

Within months of Bloomberg the dishonesty of his manoeuvre boomeranged. Douglas Carswell was a Tory backbench MP with a passion for direct democracy, and a critic of the EU. He was delighted by the prospect set out in the Bloomberg scenario. Then he was appalled to learn from members of Cameron's team at a private Königswinter conference and elsewhere that it was a façade.[3] Presumably they assumed no experienced MP could believe anything else and let him in on the strategy Cameron had plotted with Merkel. Carswell decided he had to resign from the party. He joined UKIP and forced a by-election. In a TV interview, he angrily denounced Cameron's approach as 'smoke and mirrors'. In his address to his constituents, he wrote:

No one cheered David Cameron more loudly at the time of his Bloomberg speech, when he finally accepted the case for a referendum. He would, he claimed, negotiate a fundamentally new relationship with the EU, and put it to the people ... But his advisers have made it clear that they seek a new deal that gives them just enough to persuade enough voters to vote to stay in. It's not about change in our national interest. It's all about not changing things. Once I realised that, my position in the Conservative party became untenable.[4]

Cameron's aim had been to use his referendum ploy to halt UKIP's rise and it seemed to be working. Instead, Carswell stormed to a by-election victory and boosted UKIP. It was a harbinger of Brexit, as the prime minister's duplicity gave the anti-European arguments credibility and UKIP its first MP.

There was a critical formulation in the long Bloomberg speech: 'For us, the European Union is a means to an end – prosperity, stability, the anchor of freedom and democracy both within Europe and beyond her shores – not an end in itself.' The admission was a calculated act of honesty. It was a true reflection of Cameron's attitude. But it took all passion out of the pro-European campaign. How could you support being part of something whose aim was peace and prosperity across your own continent if this was not, at least in part, an end in itself? However, the prime minister's key aim was his own personal success, which depended on his leadership of the Tory Party. And the party would rebel unless he made it clear that the sole end to which he was dedicated was British national interest – there could be no question of solidarity or sharing with the dreaded Europeans. He therefore defined the country's relationship to Europe as purely transactional, a matter of profit and loss. This then constricted all Cameron's efforts to keep the UK in the EU thereafter. 'Means not an end' was like a hangman's noose tied by the victim himself, to insist that there was nothing to gained from the EU but material advantage from what is a great cause and a continental identity. Yet again we see a politician confining his case to the tangible when what was at stake was intangible and determining.

Cameron made and then put his neck into the fatal loop, like an overconfident escape artist. He thought it would allow him to overcome the genuine weakness of his position. He had failed to beat Labour under Gordon Brown outright in 2010 and had created a coalition with the hated Liberal Democrats. In 2012 a hundred of his own backbench rank-and-file Tories MPs signed a letter demanding he commit to a referendum. In October 2012, fifty-three of them voted with the Labour Party to demand a cut on the EU budget, inflicting the most humiliating parliamentary defeat he had endured. Their rebellion was motivated in turn by the need of many of his MPs to respond to the rise of UKIP as an electoral threat. Neither the financial crash of 2008, with its bailing out of the bankers, or the MPs' expenses crisis of 2009, which implicated the whole of parliament in shady practices, had a direct impact on the outcome of the 2010 election. But indirectly the scandals undermined political loyalty to the established parties and even though UKIP's anti-elite message focused anger and blame on rule by unelected bureaucrats in Brussels, they gained hugely from the domestic scandals. In the European parliamentary election of 2014, admittedly on a pathetic turnout of 36 per cent, UKIP came first with 26 per cent of the vote, beating both Labour on 24 per cent and the Tories on 23 per cent. It was the first time that neither the Tories nor Labour had led a UK-wide election since 1906 over a century before. Cameron now feared for his parliamentary future. He had to prevent open division in Tory ranks and he did so by stealing UKIP's clothes. These were the self-interested calculations that led him to the speech that defines his life.

Cameron's weakness was what he thought was his commanding strength: his ability to take his distance from the EU and calculate 'the national interest'. In 2005, to get the votes he needed to win the party leadership, he declared he was a Eurosceptic and pledged to take the Conservatives out of the European People's Party – an alliance of the European centre-right, mainly Christian Democrats, in the EU parliament. Cameron's culture and instincts were at best indifferent to European culture and hostile to sharing sovereignty with the EU. However, at that point public support for the EU was high and sustained. It had become associated with the upside of New Labour, the expansion of rights, social liberalism and improved economic conditions. Cameron therefore triangulated his party's antagonism towards the EU with its then popularity among voters. To achieve this, he decided to depoliticise it as an issue and make the EU disappear into the background. He opened his first party conference as its leader, in 2006, with a short welcome in which he told them they must stop 'banging on about Europe' while 'parents worried about childcare'. 'Let us', he concluded, 'show clearly which side we are on. Let optimism beat pessimism. Let sunshine win the day.'[5] Accordingly, in his main set-piece speech that concluded the conference, he did not mention the European Union at all.

It was the high point of Cameron's support for Europe. When he later made the case for membership of the EU, the sunshine was beginning to pale. He never spoke positively about Europe itself without adding criticism of it. He could not present himself as being a European – as well as being a true Brit. Before he entered the final round of his negotiations with the leaders of the EU in November 2015, he repeatedly set out his distance from it by proposing a banal caricature of the contrast between his own national identity and European sentiment:

I come to this question with a frame of mind that is practical, not emotional. Head, not heart. I know some of our European partners may find that disappointing about Britain. But that is who we are. That is how we have always been as a nation. We are rigorously practical. We are obstinately down to earth. We are natural debunkers. We see the European Union as a means to an end, not an end in itself.[6]

Supposedly, it was Napoleon not the prime minister who taunted the British with being a nation of shopkeepers. Indeed, since Margaret Thatcher declared that 'The lesson of the Falklands is that Britain has not changed', Cameron's Conservative Party has delighted in an emotional, Powellite self-belief in 'who we are'. The key phrase is the Blairite, verbless sentence: 'Head, not heart'. Cameron's pollsters had already identified the 'Hearts versus Heads' constituency as a crucial swing sector of the population; meaning those whose desire was to leave the EU but were willing to be ruled by the better judgement of their pockets. The prime minister's later private poll calculated this group as about 14 per cent of the electorate.[7] Now he projected 'head not heart' as representing the national essence. Certainly it summed up his own heartlessness.

Cameron set up the referendum as a contest between those who were willing to fight for their country as an end in itself, with all the crude passion and prejudice this inspires, and those like him who took a 'rigorously practical' approach. From the referendum's outset Cameron got Britain wrong in terms of what it had become 'as a nation'. Yet this was actually the central issue of the referendum. He even said so himself. When he finally announced the date in Downing Street on 20 February, Cameron's speech writers were right to state: 'We are approaching one of the biggest decisions this country will face in our lifetimes. Whether to remain in a reformed European Union – or to leave. The choice goes to the heart of the kind of country we want to be.'

Naturally, many voters responded by following their heart.

# 8

# Words Pop Out of His Mouth

What kind of person carries the responsibility for the referendum and its outcome under whose influence all in Britain now live; what were David Cameron's political qualities and flaws, and how could someone like him come to run the government in the first place? No exercise in asking why Brexit happened can avoid the unpleasant task of delving into these questions, as he came to personify the country's forty-year relationship with the EU and thereby contributed to its rejection. Before he announced the referendum, Cameron informed his then coalition deputy, the Liberal Democrat Nick Clegg, of his intention. Clegg challenged him on the risks and recounts how: 'I was breezily told that all would be well, of course it would be won.'[1] To call a referendum is one thing – the long-standing heavy weather system of British politics pushed persistently in its direction. The breezy casualness of Cameron is something else. That he could even pretend to face down the storm he would unleash with his light-hearted windiness points to the question that matters. It does not concern the 'real' David Cameron, which is a distraction of celebrity individualism; it covers the source and nature of his political judgement. Where did his calamitously superficial self-assurance come from?

For it is not the case that because Cameron is superficial he is insignificant. His single-minded personal ambition and well-manicured slipperiness may make him a lightweight in the story of the CBCs compared to the big narrative figures like the UK's Blair and Brown, or Bush and the Clintons (Bill and Hillary) in the USA.

But the man without baggage was the perfect traveller. He took the capacity for self-interested adaptation for which the English ruling class is famous to a new pitch of rootlessness and distilled the era's deceitful spirit of government to perfection.

Westminster's culture is short-term: it judges by outcomes and forgives wrongdoing if it succeeds. It is all very well to show, as I have just done, that Cameron was wretchedly instrumental in his approach to the defining issue of national identity, saying that the EU was merely a means to an end. But the referendum was close. He nearly pulled it off. To accuse him of being opportunist, even on an issue as important as EU policy, invites the reply that it might have worked, in which case he would be admired for his mastery of the moment. But I believe the failure of Cameron's referendum stems from his entire approach to power, and that this was bound up with the intrinsic duplicity of his politics. Furthermore, his manipulative approach linked the referendum to a chain of political and financial scandals, the sleaze, corruptions, duplicities and unearned privileges that defined the way all three main parties, Labour and Lib Dem and Tory, had governed Britain since the downfall of Thatcher.

Indeed, even as Thatcher swept away 'old-boy' privileges, she prepared the way for the new corruption with her sale of arms to Iraq, the Pergau Dam scandal that the senior civil servant Tim Lancaster refused to sign off, and the Al-Yamamah arms deal that benefited her son Mark, just to name three instances. As a consequence, the passion of those who supported Brexit drew strength from widespread anger with the rotten, selfish way the country is governed, and Cameron's leadership tempted voters to use the referendum to reject the way Westminster politics has been conducted.

Cameron is one of those politicians who enjoy unlimited personal ambition untroubled by the burden of larger purpose. He was shameless in his desire to counterfeit himself as a courteous one-nation leader who loves his country. A telling incident reveals his desolate professionalism. In the run-up to the 2015 election, he was sent a private poll that showed only one voter in three thought he was in touch with ordinary people. He circulated it to his team with a note at the top: 'Please, operational grid, give me the right language and speaking and physically attack me with the right words before an interview. I will do whatever I am told.'[2] Can you imagine a May, a Trump, a Farage, a Johnson, a Corbyn or a Sturgeon requiring their aides to 'attack' them with 'the right words'? In certain narrow circumstances, perhaps, if asking for a better way to present a given argument that they believe in, or to improve the way to strengthen a case. But they would never promise to do 'whatever' they are told to say in general. Whereas, after five years as prime minister, Cameron tells his team he'll say anything to make it appear that he is in touch, and instructs them to devise the language. The note reveals both his unrestrained ambition and lack of larger purpose.

Another incident, telling because apparently trivial, reveals the scale of his inner abyss: he forgot the name of his football team. As a man's identification with his football team is made early and for life, it is a form of destiny harder to forget than the name of your partner, should you have one. Yet Cameron, giving a speech in praise of Britain's ethnic diversity, told his audience he supported West Ham. He had to correct the record by comparing himself to the leader of the Green Party: 'I had what Natalie Bennett described as a brain fade. I'm a Villa fan … I must have been overcome by something.' Quizzed about it on Sky News, Cameron said: 'By the time you have made as many speeches as I have on this campaign all sorts of funny things start popping out of your mouth.'[3] If his opponent, the Labour leader Ed Miliband, had told a TV interviewer that funny things popped out of his mouth, the *Mail*, *Telegraph* and *Sun* would have rubbed it into public consciousness. As this was an election in which Cameron was their candidate, his embarrassment was conveniently forgotten. We too can ignore the gaffe. What is revealing is his justification. Anyone can make a slip of the tongue, but nobody who cares about what they say would tell a broadcaster that all sorts of things pop out of their mouth. The reason why an election campaign puts you under such pressure is because everything you say counts.

Sometimes Cameron's words were remembered. If rarely by the London media, in one case at least by Barack Obama. In 2011

Britain joined France in attacking the Libyan dictator Gaddafi after he threatened to wipe out, street by street, those who opposed him in his country's second city, Benghazi. The US eliminated Gaddafi's air defences, then the British and French air forces successfully supported the dictator's overthrow. The UK spent £320 million on the bombing. With fewer than 10 million people, plentiful oil and no threatening neighbours, Libya offered a chance to show how Western military intervention could lead to constructive outcome for local people. David Cameron flew into Benghazi in triumph and pledged passionately to the crowd, with his words broadcast by the BBC, that Britain 'will stand with you as you build your country and build your democracy for the future'.[4] A mere £25 million in aid followed, less than 8 per cent of what the UK spent on bombing. The country fell apart. The betrayal enraged the American president, who broke diplomatic convention to publicly rebuke the UK's premier, telling Jeffrey Goldberg of *Atlantic* magazine: 'When I go back and I ask myself what went wrong, ... there's room for criticism.' He accepted some of the fault was his and then singled out Cameron who, in Obama's words, stopped paying attention as he became 'distracted by a range of other things'.[5]

It was criminal negligence, but it concerned a foreign country. The British prime minister's indifference turned to dishonesty at home when it concerned the central platform of his economic policy. In a 2014 party conference speech, Cameron described Britain as 'a country that is paying down its debts'. This was false. More important, Andrew Dilnot, chair of the UK Statistics Authority, officially confirmed that it was false. The annual additional amount the government was borrowing, known as the deficit, was in decline, but total debt was rising.[6] It was an extraordinary falsehood because Cameron had already been officially rebuked for making the same claim the year before, this time in a party-political broadcast. Cameron claimed: 'We're paying down Britain's debts.' It prompted fury from Andreas Whittam Smith, founder of the *Independent*. He pointed out that as prime minister he could not but have known that while he had been in office 'public sector net debt has expanded from £811.3bn (55.3 per cent of GDP) to £1,111.4bn (70.7 per cent of GDP)'.

> A party-political broadcast is a deliberate act, not something said on the spur of the moment. Every word and every image is carefully considered. The deceit about paying down the debt will have been in the script for days or even weeks. The Prime Minister is better placed than almost anyone to know what the truth actually is ... Has it really come to this? Has the Prime Minister of the day solemnly addressed the British people and deliberately, coldly, with aforethought, told them a downright lie? If so, what scorn for the electorate that implies. What insufferable arrogance.[7]

Scorn for voters helped win Cameron the premiership. In January 2010, in the run-up to that year's election, he said: 'We've looked at educational maintenance allowances and we haven't announced any plan to get rid of them. We don't have any plans to get rid of them' – only for them to be scrapped five months after he won. In March 2010, Cameron made a promise: 'I wouldn't change child benefit, I wouldn't means-test it, I don't think that is a good idea.' Within three years, means testing was introduced. In April 2010, on the eve of the election, Cameron said: 'We have absolutely no plans to raise VAT.' Two months later, it was raised from 17.5 per cent to 20 per cent. (The previous year, Cameron had argued that VAT is 'very regressive, it hits the poorest hardest'.)[8]

In 2006, Cameron repositioned the entire Tory Party to make it environmentalist, even rebranding the party's logo to a tree. He made 'Vote Blue, Go Green' one of his election slogans. In 2013, he told aides working on energy legislation: 'Get rid of all the green crap.'[9]

His most pitiless dishonesty concerned the NHS, the institution British voters care about more than any other. In a 2009 speech to the Royal College of Pathologists, Cameron pledged: 'There will be no more of the tiresome, meddlesome, top-down restructures that have dominated the last decade of the NHS.'[10] It was a promise he repeated: the NHS would be safe in his hands. If any single commitment swung him the election in 2010, this was the one. As he was repeating his pledges, his team were preparing the Lansley reforms to marketise the NHS, a top-down reorganisation that was to be described by the chief executive of the NHS as a restructuring 'so big you can see it from space'.[11] To convince voters of his sincerity, Cameron deployed the experience of his badly disabled son: 'For me, it is not just a question of saying the NHS is safe in my hands – of course it will be. My family is so often in the hands of the NHS, so I want them to be safe there.' In the same fraudulent speech he promised 'no more pointless and disruptive reorganisations'.[12] As for being safe in his hands, in 2010 when he won office figures for NHS England show a total of 144,000 beds. As the population rose this number fell to 130,000. He inherited from Blair spending on the NHS of 8.8 per cent of the country's gross domestic product and a New Labour commitment that it would rise to equal EU averages, then 10.5 per cent. Instead, it has fallen back to 6.6 per cent and 'the gap between us and our European neighbours' is 'growing'.[13]

The pitiless nature of Cameron's politics is most starkly revealed by the way he manipulated voters' hopes and desires with respect to the NHS. Often, people cannot believe that powerful politicians are wicked humans because policies seem impersonal. A vignette of a face-to-face encounter brings home the awfulness of Cameron's moral vacuum more powerfully than even the Libyan betrayal.

Jamie Reed was the Labour MP for Copeland in Cumbria from 2005 to 2017 and recently resigned. He published a brief reflection of his highs and lows in parliament. Cameron was the low point:

> For most people, politicians exist on the edge of their peripheral vision. But there are times of crisis when this vision is shattered and politicians are brought into sharp focus. This focus rests upon the character, wisdom and judgement of the politician in question ... the lowest point of my political career took place on 2nd June 2010 when a gunman killed 12 people and shot and injured a further 11 in my constituency.

In 2005, I ran on a promise of building a new hospital. The following five years saw the last Labour government provide the money and begin the foundations of the new hospital and the demolition of the old hospital was under way before the coalition came into power in 2010. On entering office, Cameron and Osborne scrapped the new hospital building in my constituency, despite the hospital being half knocked down ... In the midst of the shootings, I invited David Cameron to the hospital, to see how effectively it had operated in response to events, but also to convince him to reinstate the money for the new hospital project.

I sat by the bed of a constituent, a gunshot victim, as she spoke with the prime minister and pleaded with him to return the funding and to safeguard local hospital services. He promised to do that ... How I wish Cameron had honoured his promise. How I regret giving him the benefit of the doubt. How sad I was, over the following months and years, to be constantly reminded of the way in which the prime minister had revealed his character during the time at which my community needed its prime minister the most.

Today, I remain furious at the way in which, when character, integrity, honesty and compassion were called for, the prime minister filled this void with a calculated deception told to a gunshot victim in a hospital bed. Not simply the low point of my parliamentary career, this episode remains one of the low points of my life.[14]

Sometimes people get what they deserve. The most fateful of all David Cameron's dishonesties delivered the justice of expelling him from office. It was the pledge, set out in the Tory Party's 2010 election manifesto, to 'take steps to take net migration back to the levels of the 1990s – tens of thousands a year, not hundreds of thousands'. Five years later, admitting that it had not worked, the 2015 manifesto pledged: 'We will keep our ambition of delivering annual net migration in the tens of thousands, not the hundreds of thousands.' Cameron knew it was not in his power to achieve such low figures. He signed off on the words because they would help him win. Race relations in Britain have been poisoned ever since.

Melissa Kite published a mocking diary about Cameron's Notting Hill set for the right-wing weekly *Spectator*. She knew him well. After he resigned she wrote:

> In office, Cameron abandoned so many commitments it became impossible to chart the U-turns. My own personal favourite ... was his supposedly heartfelt declaration on the BBC's Countryfile that he would no more ruin the countryside by building on it than put at risk his own family.[15] Months later, rural communities were complaining about government-backed attempts to build on the green belt ... he would say one thing and the result would be the exact opposite.[16]

In the summer of 2015, John Sewel was deputy speaker of the House of Lords and chairman of the Lords' Privileges and Conduct Committee – the body that upholds standards of behaviour among peers, for which he was paid £120,000 a year. This allowed him to discuss the qualities of the country's political leaders while snorting hard drugs in the company of two prostitutes. He also invited them to join him later in the autumn for dinner in the House of Lords, where he would doubtless have continued with his sharp insights on the denizens of Westminster, had the pair not recorded the episode and sold it to Murdoch's *Sun*.[17] The video of the occasion is online, viewed over 1.7 million times, and it was given front-page treatment in the tabloid.[18] Such is elite political life in Britain. Sewel's insider view of Cameron was as succinct as his line of cocaine: 'He's the most facile, superficial prime minister there has ever been ... he just shoots from the hip and makes one-off commitments he cannot deliver on.'[19]

Yet for six years he was regarded as a successful premier. He made people think he was born to lead and usually appeared to know how to strike the 'right note'. The clichéd explanation of this facility reinforced by Britain's class-obsessed media is that it comes from Cameron's privileged, upper-class origins in Eton and Oxford. He is a toff. His breezy complacency comes from his elite presumption of superiority. In the end, it was his sense of entitlement that distanced him from reality – and meant he could be laid low in the referendum by horny-handed ex-workers and frustrated petty-bourgeois. That such a view is fashionable signals the superficiality of a London milieu that Cameron himself is part of, one which has wiped history from its memory card. For the British ruling class was always extremely wary of the danger to its supremacy posed by the lowest and middling classes. Through war, religion, manufacturing, monarchy and trade, generations of Etonians and Oxford alumni, by hard work as well as instinct, were trained to protect themselves and the country they commanded from the populace. After enormous demonstrations, Disraeli gave the franchise to the male heads of skilled working-class households in 1867. Almost immediately a permanent civil service was installed. It was designed to ensure that the machinery of the state remains in the hands of trustworthy mandarins from good schools, should government ever fall into the hands of an unschooled working-class party. The device became one of the most lasting checks against popular dictatorship built into the UK's informal constitution. I mention it only to illustrate the long-standing nature and seriousness of upper-class Britain. When it comes to permitting the exercise of power by the subordinate classes, not only do you take action to prevent it, you pre-empt even the possibility by thinking decades ahead, just as you landscape your estates for future generations.

Cameron's blithe upturning of this long tradition was not a sign of his toffness but of his failure to absorb the practical wisdom of his class. When tradition mattered, he embraced trendiness; instead of imperial substance, he embraced commercial messaging. His modern style, superficiality and ultimate catastrophic failure come from his having *abandoned* Establishment politics and the traditions of Eton, in favour of a global corporate culture, with its single-minded dedication to marketing, public relations and immediate returns.

Cameron became an MP at the age of thirty-six. After five post-Oxford years in the Conservative Party research department, aged twenty-seven he joined Carlton Communications, which he left to enter parliament seven years later in 2001. Within four years he was his party's leader and five years after that, aged forty-three, prime minister. In this short time, his most formative experience was working as director of corporate communications at Carlton for its then ferocious boss Michael Green, variously described as 'vile' and 'a horror'. Green was building his media empire, where Cameron himself was remembered as 'a PR man capable of dissembling and doling out disinformation'.[20] Over the turn of the century, the Cameron who was to lead Britain had himself reforged by the pressures of London's and possibly the world's most brutal, short-term, commercial environment, as it chased the fortunes of an exploding mass media.

Cameron certainly enjoyed the advantages of his privileged schooling and stockbroker background. But the seven biblical years he was trained as a corporate, media and public-relations operator were more important than five years at Eton for turning his inheritance into a political career. He is the product of his shameful profession much more than of his once arguably honourable background. Like so many of us, Cameron is a modern migrant, not a stay-at-home. Most politicians are. The snobbish hypostatisation of a person's origin as being their identity, as if we lived in a Hindu caste system, blights public perception in England. The example of Margaret Thatcher is a good illustration. Once again thanks to Britain's obsession with class, she is seen as being what she was born as: a provincial grocer's daughter. That, however, was when she was Margaret Roberts. Dennis Thatcher was a very successful, hard-working businessman who became a millionaire and then a director of Burma Oil. She took his name, lived with his cheerful racism, and part of her confidence and approach to the economy were rooted in becoming his wife. It was not without personal anxiety, but as a young woman she married into wealth, security and a business perspective that were far from those of a small-town grocer – and more important for her politics.

Like her, Cameron's approach to politics was shaped not by what he was but by what he became in his twenties. He too was someone who wanted to slip the coils of his family, not represent it. But whereas the Thatchers, politician and businessman, fought to break out of the disastrous situation Britain faced in the late 1960s, suffocated by a consensus that embraced decline and protected vested interests, Cameron and his wife hit London when the town was on a roll. Their early adulthood was marked by expansion, not calamity, as London became the playground of globalisation, where those with money could hardly avoid making shedloads more. One example is Cameron's mother-in-law, Lady Astor, who moved from retail jewellery to co-found OKA in 1999, the global luxury home-furnishing chain. A better one is her daughter and his wife, Samantha Cameron. She joined Smythsons, the exclusive Bond Street stationery outlet, as its product development director in 1996, aged twenty-five, and took part in a management buyout two years later. In 2005 it was sold on to a consortium for £15.5 million.[21] The question for the young Tory David Cameron, with his ambition in politics, was not how to save his country, in this case from the glaring corruption, lack of democracy and the unfairness of globalisation – which would have been the project of a true Conservative. It was how to shake off his roots in his country's past to ride the 'new future' for all it was worth.

Carlton Television under Michael Green was, I've been told, among the worst of London's media companies. The year Cameron joined to become Green's senior communications executive, it was officially censured for its 'glib and superficial' output by the broadcasting standards regulator. At one point, the London *Evening Standard*'s television critic wrote about what was then the future prime minister's home from home: 'What is the difference between Carlton TV and a bucket of shit? Answer: The bucket.' Cameron's job was to deal with financial journalists, reporting on Carlton's fate in the media marketplace. One of them, Jeff Randall, who served on the *Telegraph* when it was a serious broadsheet, was appalled to see him bid for the Conservative leadership and wrote: 'In my experience, Cameron never gave a straight answer when dissemblance was a plausible alternative, which probably makes him perfectly suited for the role he now seeks: the next Tony Blair.' Another, Ian King, the *Sun's* business editor in 2005, told his readers that Cameron 'would not cut it' as party leader:

> Along with other financial journalists, I was unfortunate enough to have dealings with Cameron during the 1990s when he was PR man for Carlton, the world's worst television company. And a poisonous, slippery individual he was, too. Back then, Cameron was far from the smoothie he pretends to be now. He was a smarmy bully ... he loved humiliating people ...

The consensus is that Michael Green was a monstrous figure at Carlton TV. After he left and started his political career, Cameron told an interviewer how Green was an 'inspirational, swashbuckling entrepreneur ... I learned from him how to get things done, how to lead with conviction.'[22]

There was a real transformation taking place within the golden bubble of London's expansion. Those who were building businesses, developing policies, creating programmes, making works of art, even starting websites, were genuine entrepreneurs in their efforts, as the first wave of the digital transformation swept the analogue world. But this hard work was represented, in the best and worst senses of that word, by the black arts of PR. Since the crash of 2008, we may have gained some understanding of the parasitic character of the financial sector. The nature of the cultural bubble that accompanied the lopsided growth of financial capitalism is less well understood: the growth of junk messaging, junk art and junk television that accompanied junk bonds. This was Cameron's cultural milieu.

The development of modern advertising and marketing in the 1920s preceded the first great crash. In the 1990s marketing became globalised. Its images and messages floated, digitised and dissociated even further from historic notions of reality, as people's image became more important to them than themselves. The first principle in the politics of this meta-defining universe was not to 'mean' what you say in the old-fashioned way. In its space, what a message says lies in the external impact, not its content. Success is truth. Language must be lubricated to escape the friction of boring accountability that might interrupt its intended impression. So if a journalist asks a politician or business person about something that went wrong, the best response is not to feel accountable but to be able to say with all sincerity that the story 'no longer has legs'. The objective is always tomorrow's perceptions, to keep 'the narrative' on the move, deploying misleading sincerity and 'unintended' lying. The master was Tony Blair, who showed that only those with unhinged self-belief can thrive in such an airless environment. Step forward David Cameron.

In the 2001 election, two wealthy, well-educated young MPs were elected to the Conservative benches. While most of the Tory Party was thrashing around with impotent anti-European spasms and homophobic nostalgia for the era of Thatcherite sadomasochism, they grasped that the Labour premier was showing the way out of their impasse. His example offered a path for the right: socially tolerant, at ease with the world of money, confidently dismissive of the restraints of convention and ruthlessly focused on the exercise of power. These two were David Cameron and George Osborne.

On the eve of his bid for the leadership in 2005, after a mere four years on the opposition benches, Cameron said one true thing: 'I am the heir to Blair'. It was the evening before the leadership contest at the Conservatives' 2005 conference. The party had just lost its third election in a row and there were five candidates in contention. David Cameron and his collaborator George Osborne attended a *Daily Telegraph*-hosted 'dinner with newspaper executives'. Cameron told them he was 'the heir to Blair'. Andrew Pierce of *The Times*, reported: 'if his hosts were in any doubt about what they had heard, Mr Cameron repeated the mantra'. In addition, 'Mr Osborne, defending the heir to Blair boast, said: "we have nothing to be ashamed of in saying it".'[23] Cameron and Osborne wanted the people who mattered to know that their objective was to steer Britain's most ancient political party into the tailwind of Blair's Labour government, so as to inherit the mantle of his manipulative corporate populism.

Cameron then gave a speech of pitch-perfect Blairism in his bid for the leadership:

> I want people to feel good about being a Conservative again ...
>
> That's what I mean by change: we've got to change our culture so we look, feel, think and behave like a completely new organisation.
>
> By changing our culture we can change politics, too. When I meet young people, they tell me how sick they are of the whole political system – the shouting, finger-pointing, backbiting and point-scoring in the House of Commons. That's all got to go.
>
> So let's build together a new generation of Conservatives. Let's switch a new generation on to Conservative ideas. Let's dream a new generation of Conservative dreams ... We can lead that new generation. We can be that new generation, changing our party to change our country. It will be an incredible journey. I want you to come with me.

Only someone as limitlessly ambitious but completely lacking in originality as Cameron could have so perfectly adapted himself to the Blairite project. His public-relations expertise allowed him to internalise the Blair approach so flawlessly that he prefigured the master's own language. Six years later, Blair titled his account of his politics *A Journey*. Movement without a principled objective, with all the excitement of novelty and, most important, a single leader who pointed 'the way', became the prospectus offered the country by Cameron, just as it had been by Blair. It would become the Tories' turn to switch on a new generation with their 'ideas'. As a political vision it was not so much a journey as a trip: a hallucination of frictionless futurism, a free-market high. The unstated implication is that those who do not 'get' the incredible transformation are lethargic spoilers – old or old before their time. None more so than those who resist globalisation, including Britain's membership of the European Union. In this feel-good political culture, tangible choices were dissolved by post-honest language. Many railed against the false radicalism and injustice it perpetrated and permitted, especially on the left. When the response finally exploded it came not from that flank, where Blairism and Cameron had invested most of their protective armour, but from the right, after the financial crash exposed their illusions.

# PART III
# BREXITANNIA

Those states like the UK, which have the least social solidarity, the least commitment to major interests, to 'national' goals, the weakest institutions of informal economic co-ordination, and the least developed local and regional structures of economic governance, will tend to fail.

Paul Hirst,
*From Statism to Pluralism*, 1997

# 9

# Short Preface to Brexitannia

Every single person who voted for Brexit or opposed it – or abstained because unconvinced by the whole lot of them – made a judgement. By a slim majority, voters across the United Kingdom decided it was best to leave the EU. If history and circumstances had been different, so could have been the outcome. What, then, were the larger circumstances that led to their call?

There were four historic forces that forged the conjuncture of Brexit and one excuse that became the headline cause. The four were: the unhappy nature of England; the market-driven form taken by globalisation whose name is neoliberalism, with its inequity and undermining of democracy; the direction of the European Union; and the absence of any convincing left-wing vision of the future. The excuse, which worked its way into all four, was immigration.

All four causes and the excuse were necessary to make the mix explosive. Neoliberalism has priority as it shaped the failures of Labour and the European Union that Brexit protested against. The impact of all three – the global, the EU and the left – as well as the movement of people they encouraged, then had to find expression in national politics. In Scotland, their combination led voters to crush the country's Labour Party, which had been its historic ruler. This satisfactory revenge led to overwhelming support for remaining in the EU. In England, where the historic ruling party is Conservative, the mix exploded into Brexit.

This part is the heart of the book and focuses only on why British politics ended up with Brexit. The other three causes are widely debated. I will look at them in the next part briefly. But the way Brexit is a full-blown crisis of the UK as a country, and within this of England, has not been analysed. I have emphasised that, like the election of Trump, Brexit must be respected as a conscious judgement by people of the way they are governed and not 'explained' as if it was a mental disturbance. Any judgement made on the fate and future of one's own society and its government will be rooted in its history – for we are historical animals.

# 10

# It Was England's Brexit

It was England's Brexit. Up until now I have written about how 'the country' voted, treating Britain as a single entity, and the Leave and Remain campaigns as single arguments. But the call for sovereignty had different impacts in the distinct parts of Britain. The United Kingdom of Great Britain and Northern Ireland is a multinational state in the process of reconfiguration. Think of it as a lopsided pentagon, only one part of which – England – voted decisively for Brexit.

In her first major speech as prime minister, Theresa May claimed:

> Because we voted in the referendum as one United Kingdom, we will negotiate as one United Kingdom, and we will leave the European Union as one United Kingdom. There is no opt-out from Brexit. And I will never allow divisive nationalists to undermine the precious Union between the four nations of our United Kingdom.

The premise of her approach is flawed. Had Britain genuinely voted 'as one United Kingdom', this would have needed no emphasis. Technically, the referendum was a single vote counted on the same day. But by saying how they wished to relate to their European continent, voters in the UK's nations also passed a judgement on how they related to each other. Precious or not, the union was not unanimous. Starkly different answers show that 'we' did not vote as 'one United Kingdom'. The opening claim of May's premiership is a falsehood: not a description of what happened, but an English claim of right over the other countries.

There are five parts to the UK: Scotland, Northern Ireland, Wales, London and England-without-London. Scotland, a self-conscious country with its own parliament, voted to remain in the EU by 62 per cent to 38 per cent, a hugely impressive majority of 24 per cent. Northern Ireland, a province with an electorate of only 1.25 million, whose domestic government is now established by international treaty, known as the Good Friday agreement, voted on a low turnout of 62 per cent for Remain by 55.8 per cent to 44.2 per cent, a comfortable majority of 12 per cent. Wales, a small, long-colonised and linguistically divided country, voted Leave by 52.5 per cent to 47.5 per cent, a narrow majority of 5 per cent, and the only part to return a close result, well below double figures. London, a global city bursting at the seams, populated by 8.5 million, of whom 3 million are foreign-born, with an electorate of 5.5 million, voted Remain by 59.9 per cent to 40.1 per cent, an overwhelming 20 per cent majority. England-without-London, by far the largest of the five, with 46 million inhabitants, and with the highest turnout, voted Leave by 55.4 per cent to 44.6 per cent, a decisive majority of close on 11 per cent. By doing so, England-without-London swung the outcome. It voted by a majority of well over 2½ million for Leave, the other four parts of the Kingdom combined voted by just under 1½ for Remain.

Added together, the UK voted for Leave by only a small majority of 4 per cent. But the largest, determining part, England-without-London, was clear and definite in its judgement. Any attempt to demand a return to a shared political relationship with the EU must confront the undeniable reality of England's desire.

This reality does not completely exclude London. Due to its size, while only a 40 per cent minority of Londoners voted for Brexit, they numbered 1.5 million. This is larger than the total, overall UK majority for Leave of only 1.25 million. If every single voting Londoner had cast their ballot for Remain, Britain would still be part of the European Union. But the Londoners who voted for exit echoed the sentiments of England-without-London, and it was this England that carried the day.

Some of its other great cities, such as Bristol, Liverpool and Manchester, voted Remain. A similar pattern to the London versus rest-of-England divide can be seen *within* England-without-London. Thus, Liverpool with its international connections especially to Ireland, voted strongly to remain by 58 per cent to 42 per cent but around it, St Helens, Halton, Warrington, Knowsley, Cheshire all voted Leave and took the region with them. English towns like Brighton, Cambridge, Reading and Oxford, connected by culture, commuter lines and universities to the greater London megalopolis, backed Remain as strongly as the capital itself. Nonetheless, even including this urban desire to stay in the EU, every single region of England-without-London voted to exit the European Union. Across the different Norths, the Midlands, the coasts of the East, the South and West, counties of wealth and counties of deprivation, each with intense, often competing histories, England-without-London turned its back on the continental union, from David Cameron's wealthy Cotswold constituency of Witney to Ed Miliband's deprived one in Doncaster.

One way to measure the strikingly English nature of the Brexit vote is by comparing the 2016 referendum with the UK's first referendum on Europe in 1975. Then, the Scots voted to stay in Europe by 58 per cent and the English by nearly 69 per cent. Forty years later the Scottish vote to stay rose slightly by 4 per cent, while the English one dived by over 20 per cent. In 1975, 6.8 million of the English (including Londoners) voted to leave; four decades later over 15 million did so.

Viewed from Westminster, the Scots with their parliament are often seen as uppity and peculiar, intent on stepping out of line with the realities of the world. But from a more generous perspective the English are the odd ones out, intent on a perverse form of change. The desire to break out of the border-less jail of neoliberalism, to shake off the EU's lack of democracy, and the impact of the failure of the left, were felt across all parts of Britain, and contributed to the Brexit vote everywhere. But it was in England-without-London that their combination was transformed and swept the board, creating a cross-class, cross-party movement that overwhelmed regional differences. Most of the bigger cities, except narrowly Birmingham, voted Remain, but were trumped by the surrounding towns and boroughs. Lisa Nandy, Labour MP for Wigan, a town of 100,000 outside Manchester, gives an eloquent account in *Huffington Post*, that she aptly titled 'The England That Lies Beneath the Surface'.[1] Something has happened in England-without-London that made it receptive to the anti-EU forces, something that knitted the arguments together and amplified them. Something national.

Suddenly aware that they were out of touch, the London media rushed to the North of England, to see if Brexit could be blamed on the lumpen working class missing out on the benefits of economic growth. A convenient presumption of economic determinism was built into this territorial manoeuvre. It sidestepped the national question and placed all the weight of reporting onto a mythological 'real country' with authentically poor health. To grasp what is happening we need analysis as well as journalism, but we do also need reporting of lived realities to break away from metropolitan stereotypes of small-town backwardness. To explore what happened with a sense of where it happened, I have chosen three places, starting with the modest southern county of Wiltshire. It is not coastal or removed to the edge, nor is it central, being just outside of London's commuter belt. England is impure, but Wiltshire could claim to be its heartland, the middle of the old kingdom of Wessex and site of the battle of Edington where King Alfred defeated the Danes in AD 878.

There are seven parliamentary constituencies, all of them currently Conservative, four returning massive majorities averaging 20,000. Across southern Wiltshire run the beautiful chalk downs, much of them owned and controlled by the army for military exercises, which employs around 30,000 in the county. Across the north runs the M4 corridor, which links London to Bristol and Cardiff. On the London side the M4 passes through Swindon, a town of over 200,000 people with the Intel corporation and the UK's Honda factory (which employs 3,600 and has just had £200 million of Japanese investment in its Civic range) and W. H. Smith's headquarters. Swindon used to be the major junction of the Great Western Railway, and now houses a museum to its heyday. The M4 then passes close by Malmesbury, with the HQ and research laboratories of Dyson, a rare home-grown global manufacturing company of hi-tech appliances. Between the M4 corridor and the south downs, across Wiltshire's wealthy farmland, are the world-heritage tourist sites of Stonehenge and the ancient Avebury stone circles; monuments to the profound antiquity of the country's pre-Christian settlement, both are actively promoted to the tourist industry. They make the medieval splendour of the cathedral town of Salisbury, Wiltshire's second town, look almost modern. Then there is Marlborough, with its nineteenth-century public school, charging over £30,000 a year per pupil, that went co-educational and had Kate Middleton as a border. Near Swindon, on a road between RAF Lyneham and the M4, is the village of Wooten Bassett, made famous by the way its inhabitants spontaneously started to salute the coffins of the dead, as they were driven through after being flown back from Afghanistan and Iraq, in what threatened to become a reproach.[2]

The county's population is approximately 700,000, of whom 200,000 live in Swindon. There are pockets of high deprivation where 40 per cent of children are in poverty. But its overall unemployment rate is very low at 2 per cent. Weekly earnings are high in Swindon but low across the county, perhaps helping its ranking as the fifth-most attractive place to invest in the UK. The rural areas are very white, Swindon is below average in terms of ethnic groups making their home there.[3]

At the centre of the county is the small market town of Devizes, once a hub of the wool trade, now with a population of 11,000; 'Wiltshire's hidden gem' it calls itself on its website, adding: 'Today Devizes can boast nearly 500 listed buildings, probably the highest concentration anywhere in England.'[4] Just four miles south of the M4 and on the London to Bristol Great Western Railway is the much larger market town of Chippenham, headquarters of the growing Good Energy company supplying carbon-neutral power across the country.

Thus, Wiltshire is a contemporary European place. From Umbria to the Danube, Andalusía to the Haute-Savoie, the continent's distinctive micro-regions are packed with long local histories, tourist sites, modern manufacturing, the remains of ancient and recent wars, religious monuments and logistic centres. All of them are largely prosperous with some pockets of poverty. It being in the heart of wealthy southern England, Wiltshire's pockets of misery and ill-fed, badly educated children are somewhat larger. Otherwise, just like its continental counterparts, Wiltshire evolves but has not been 'left behind'. It may resist the fashionably cosmopolitan, but it has witnessed far-reaching change, from canals to railways to motorways. In easy reach of London, Southampton and Bristol, it is well connected to the wider world. Many an EU subsidy has been ploughed into its landscape. From well-heeled Salisbury to suburban Swindon, there was a 79 per cent turnout of registered voters in the referendum. By 151,637 votes to 137,258, Wiltshire voted Leave, with Swindon supporting Brexit by 54 per cent.

If you want to give Brexit its true home, think of conservative Wiltshire. Here is the heart of England's anti-European sentiment. It suffers from no excuse that makes it marginal. It does not host the retired in cheap seaside settlements, who have fled from the multicultural cities. It is not the site of traumatic deindustrialisation leaving its landscape blighted. It isn't removed from London, or isolated like Cornwall. There is nothing that permits us to sneer or belittle it, to explain away its determination to leave the EU. It does not have a university town, but that is because it is modest, not marginal. It may feel pinched rather than prosperous and laced through with deprivation, but this is true across the UK.

These days, after Brexit, it is not calm. Late on Saturday evening, in fact in the small hours of Sunday morning, on 12 February 2017, there was an incident in Trowbridge. Trowbridge is a village on the west of Wiltshire, close to Bath in neighbouring Somerset. Two of my in-laws went to retire on its outskirts, to a quiet place they liked, after he had taught classics in a public school, having fought in Italy as a young man in the war. Army families live there.

It has a Wetherspoon pub, the Albany. A fight broke out between three young men. Within seconds over a hundred men and women were brawling, punching and bottling each other, for no apparent reason, as the entire pub became a seething punch-up. A clip on Facebook was viewed over half a million times. A spokesman for Wetherspoon said: 'The pub has never encountered an incident like this.'[5]

Maybe a clue as to why Brexit flourished in Wiltshire can be found in the village of Pewsey, south of Marlborough. A historic settlement, where myth has it King Arthur housed his wife while he fought the Danes, its population has risen from less than a 100 recorded in the Domesday Book to around 3,500, thanks to the railway line. It can be very tough if you have to live there as a single mother, as you can see from a *Wiltshire Voices* film that lets the inhabitants speak for themselves.[6] It was the home of the builder who inspired Mark Rylance's performance as Johnny 'Rooster' Byron in Jez Butterworth's *Jerusalem*. A hugely successful play in London and on Broadway, *Jerusalem* anticipated the fantastic longing of Brexit. Its central character around which the entire play revolves is Johnny Byron, living in a caravan, a wild outsider who attracts local youth and introduces them to drugs and permissiveness, not so much an outlaw as someone whose spirit is lawless. The play takes place on St George's Day, when he has been served with his final eviction notice. Johnny 'Rooster' Byron does not personify the ambitious impulse to embark on global trade with the Anglophone world, nor a desire to re-establish posh sovereignty in parliament, nor the lure for imperial superiority, and certainly not bigotry, as he welcomes everyone for what they are, fellow travellers and migrants. Instead, he represents an ancient desire for freedom in the modern world, to tell the present social order with its town councils, rules and diets to 'fuck off'. Far from seeking control, he is bursting with the subversion of control. 'Rooster' is part hooligan, part descendant from English pagan gods, part seer offering teenagers a passage from suburban rectitude into the sublime, part a demand for purpose, not corporate calculation. Tremendous debates about England and Englishness were galvanised by the play and by Rylance's performance as Rooster.

One aspect was little noted. Johnny 'Rooster' Byron himself does not mention England or make any ideological statement whatsoever. He revels in everything that is projected onto him, while his pure Englishness is free from any responsibility or claims about 'who we are'. He would be horrified by the strictures of Theresa May. Had Johnny Byron dragged himself out of his stupor to the polling station, which he would never have done, as he had no legal address, I'd like to think that as a true contrarian he would have voted in the same way as the notoriously politically incorrect Jeremy Clarkson and supported Remain.[7] Perhaps he'd have realised that the bureaucrats of the European Union would be more likely to protect his human rights than the brutally indifferent centralisers of Whitehall, eager to see the end to riff-raff so that the Russians can buy woodland estates in Wiltshire untroubled by caravans. But the audiences that cheered him on and gave him a standing ovation, the Tory anarchists, romantic urbanites and frustrated suburbanites, who identified with the spirit of a man who recklessly defied faceless authority in the name of Gog and Magog and King Arthur – many of *them* voted Brexit. As did the sullen suburban inhabitants of Pewsey and the tight towns and villages of Wiltshire, resentful of their children's emancipation under the influence of the sex, drugs and drinks of today's world, for Rooster also represented the unmooring spirit of globalisation at the same time being English. The *Guardian*'s theatre critic thought it was a knockout and captured the play's communication of a life force our society hungers for:

Rylance described Jerusalem as 'satisfying a hunger in audiences for wildness and defiance. There's a feeling that they've eaten something they haven't eaten for years – something they'd forgotten, that's really needed for their health.' And certainly, to watch this play is to experience a kind of reawakening: a rekindling, if not of nationalism, then certainly of a sense of belonging; to see it, to understand it, feels as if Butterworth has struck the core of our national identity.[8]

Let's head north, to the emblematic story of a building. It is in Knutsford, Cheshire, south of Manchester, in the constituency of Tatton. This is one of the wealthiest parts of England, with many footballers' mansions. George Osborne, Cameron's chancellor of the Exchequer, became the local MP after 2001, and built up a majority of over 18,000. The building is at a key spot on the roundabout near the centre of Knutsford, the constituency's small main town with a population of 13,000. A splendid, listed Edwardian structure, it housed the Conservative Club from when it was built in 1912. As a spokesman told the *Knutsford Guardian*, 'In the olden days these clubs were at the centre of the community.' That was when, in the 1950s, the Conservative Party across Britain had over two million members. Today, the party's membership is aging and hardly more than 130,000. In 2012 it had to move out of its splendid Knutsford home. 'It is sad, but to be honest the number of people who used it didn't make it viable.'[9] Four years later, and OKA, the high-end global furnishing company, moved in.

Co-founded by David Cameron's mother-in-law, the formidable businesswoman Annabel Jones, also known as Lady Astor, OKA began as she and her two colleagues realised there was a niche market fitting out holiday homes for people like themselves who buy them in Florida.[10] They called their company OKA, as the letters are computer-friendly, good for any language, and mean nothing except in Samoan, where it is the word for surprise. Today, she and her colleagues spend months scouring Southeast Asia for materials to source well-made, contemporary but not modern tables, chairs, textiles, fittings and baubles. Her aim is to build it into a £100 million company.[11] OKA needed an outlet to expand into the rich countryside of England's north-west and selected Knutsford's finest building, with its high ceilings and car park. When it opened, they naturally hoisted the company's logo up the rooftop flagpole where, for a hundred years from 1912 to 2012, Tories had flown the flag through wars, jubilees and coronations. To some of the locals, OKA might just as well have run up the skull and crossbones. A website was set up, inviting comment. Trevor Jones of Princess Street wrote to the *Knutsford Guardian* and summed up local reaction, in what we can now see as a Trump-like tweet before its time: 'Why has our patriotic Union Jack flag that flies over the conservative office been taken down for a black OKA flag, disgraceful.'[12]

Until recently, the English landed nobility gained the allegiance of every stratum of British society through their place in the hierarchy of imperial loyalty, their Christianity, their military experience and their shared wartime effort and sacrifice. The Astors, being blow-ins from America, were outsiders; today their roots in global capitalism are no longer exceptional. Their kind of aristocracy is now displacing the traditional value system. As they sell their retro-chic interior range to the top of the world's housing bubble, no equivalent loyalties are being created by the ultra-wealthy to bridge the growing divide at home. While the staff at OKA may have dutifully voted Remain, despite all its wealthy inhabitants the people of Tatton discarded any remaining deference and voted Leave by 2 per cent, choosing the Union Jack over the black flag of globalisation.

The third visit is to where our civilisation began. In the Midlands, to the west of Birmingham, which became in the eighteenth century 'the most heavily industrialised few square miles on the planet'. To get inside the experience of what happened I'm quoting the novelist Anthony Cartwright, who has kindly given me permission to extract some passages from a fine essay he published in *Granta* immediately after the referendum in July 2016.[13] He has his own interpretation; these paragraphs are just drawn from his description.

When I ring my dad on the day of the referendum he tells me that he has seen people queuing off the Rowley Road to vote. The hills fall away south below the line of voters, past the blackened brick of the air shaft that comes from the tunnel bored through the land below, past the shell of Cobb's Engine

House which used to pump water from the nearby mines into the canal, past Clent and Walton and the woods that once belonged to King Offa and Saint Kenelm, webbed with lanes where they say Harry Ca Nab, the leader of the devil's hunt, still sometimes rides on his wild bull. He will surely be out tonight; Lord of Misrule. Those queuing can see all the way to Malvern, always blue in the distance, under the Severn Jacks, soft clouds that come from the west. This is an old country, layered, like the coal and limestone and ancient seabed buried within it ...

My great-great-grandad settled his family here, in a hollow of the hill near the tunnel mouth, in one of the cottages covered by the engine house's shadow in the late afternoons. Llewellyn Williams: Grandad Williams, remembering the sun's glitter on the River Dee fading in a soft rain come from Wales. My dad's Uncle Sam told us how he could hear the thud of the engine as it pumped through the dark nights and shook the land around it.

The family moved on some time after, down the hill again into Cradley Heath, eventually to the chainyard where my dad was born years later, the same year as the NHS. They banged chain: men, women, children. Almost all the world's chain, the cables and anchors of Empire, came from five towns visible from this hillside. A study in 1897 called the chainmakers 'the white slaves of England', making reference to an outbreak of typhoid in the notorious Anvil Yard a decade before. These were skilled workers kept in squalor, holding their heads high and proud. When the women led a strike in 1910 to secure the country's first ever minimum wage and won, John Galsworthy called them 'the chief guardians of the inherent dignity of man'.

The flags will be out soon for 14 July, Black Country Day. Red, white and black tricolours, links of chain emblazoned across them. The flag of the Black Country is a recent invention, created this century by a schoolgirl called Gracie Sheppard for a competition. The region was 'Black by day, red by night', according to Elihu Burritt, Abraham Lincoln's consul to the industrial midlands and the man credited with first using the term Black Country. The pattern of the flag is shaped like the Red House Cone in Wordsley, where they used to blow glass. So much of the Black Country is in the past tense.

14 July 1712 was the day Thomas Newcomen fired up the world's first working steam engine to pump water from the Earl of Dudley's mines. This is the machine that James Watt later adapted, and which shapes the world we live in today, for better or worse. Newcomen had come to the Black Country from elsewhere, like so many of the others that came afterwards, from Devon in his case. It was one of his engines that pumped in Cobb's Engine House. Henry Ford bought the engine in the 1920s, took it to Detroit as a holy relic. Cobb was the farmer whose fields they undermined. Anyone trying to understand what has happened to England, what happened on 23 June's referendum, and in the many years before, might do well to visit the silent engine house ruin in its green field with black crows, and ponder ...

'No one's queued to vote round here since the days of Attlee', my dad says ...

More than two to one voted in favour of Leave across the Black Country, with over double the turnout of the local elections held just a month before. The West Midlands as a whole returned a 59 per cent leave vote, the highest of all the country's regions.

I have quoted Cartwright's passage at length for its qualities and because he does four things: he takes us into the Brexit vote within a family; he takes us to the birthplace of the industrial revolution and how those now living there are aware of this and proud of it; he shows the deliberation of those voting against their rulers in a determined condemnation (not a 'protest'); and he lets us experience their profoundly good reasons for condemning a form of government that spends tens of millions restoring and maintaining its country houses and is not investing here. But then the great estates were based on ruthless clearances.

From the origins of industrialism to the most ancient stone circles of Europe, from the research laboratory designing today's leading domestic devices to the showroom of home-grown globalist furnishers, a clear, cross-class majority of people in England made a statement about how they are governed. That puts it too politely. In their hearts and often in the pub they said it in Anglo-Saxon: they echoed Johnny Rooster and told the smooth salesmen of Westminster and their EU to 'Fuck off'. Similar accounts could be drawn, each with their specific history and tone: from Cornwall, remote and stubborn; to Kent, proud and defiant; to the North East, ironic and self-regarding, and the many other regions with their Shakespearean echoes – York and Lancaster, Northumberland, Buckingham, Warwick and Norfolk. A complete anthropology of the regional nuances and twists of Brexit, for and against, would be well worth writing. My purpose here is different and simple: to signal that across all of England-without-London the undeniable range, scale and rootedness of the desire for Brexit was national.

National, because England's historic neighbour, Scotland, with its own long history and 'Braveheart' tradition, responded quite differently. They are just as capable of telling the governing classes to 'Get it right fucking up ye'. But Scotland's self-confidence had a positive twist, and led a large majority to want to participate in the European Union, rather than embracing England's negative courage of choosing to withdraw.

The denialist claims that the referendum was not valid, because it was based on deception or ignorance or lies and cheating, are not worth the sand that they run into. A nation spoke. Not the United Kingdom of Great Britain and Northern Ireland, but the England within it. England defended its identity in the only way that was allowed. Its decision must be challenged, there is a better way to be England; its genuineness cannot be denied.

Many who are English, should they read this, will revile inwardly. A private voice will protest that while I may have captured something of the spirit of Wiltshire, and Cartwright takes us beautifully to the experience of the Black Country, the Scottish are nationalists and we are not. If you in any way share this feeling, a sense of resistance to the idea that Brexit is the expression of English nationalism that you should share in any way, I'd ask you to just hold it in suspense rather than denial.

When the voters of the UK were asked if they wanted to renew their membership of the European Union, it became a vote on how the country is governed. Different forces, tangible and intangible, were at work. These included immigration, the refugee emergency, the effects of austerity, the outrageous rip-off of the financial crash, the loosening of loyalties thanks to the internet, the undemocratic nature of the EU, the implosion of social democracy. The majority response to these forces in Scotland and Northern Ireland, the second- and third-largest nations of the UK, was to seek closer relations with the EU, with more and better continental solidarity. A similar response came from London, the global city. But across England-without-London, the comeback was the opposite. This is the central fact of the referendum's outcome. All the wider influences were concentrated into the force field of the English spirit. There, they reinforced each other in the prejudices, longings and judgement of English voters across their land to create a decisive majority for Brexit, one that overwhelmed the proportionally larger majorities for Remain in the cities and less numerous parts of the United Kingdom's pentagon. It was undeniably England's Brexit. To understand why this was so, is to understand why it happened.

# 11

# Anglo-Britain, the Hybrid Nationalism

In January 2017, Theresa May told an American audience that by leaving the European Union the United Kingdom had taken a decision to restore our 'national self-determination'.[1] Even Scots, and Welsh who voted for Brexit, will wince at the claim. She was speaking for England. In October 2016, in her set-piece speech to her own party, she spoke of the 'divisive nationalists' of Scotland, Wales and Northern Ireland. At the same time, throughout the speech she refers repeatedly to Britain as a 'nation' – and how she intends to build a 'new united Britain'.[2] Apparently, her English nationalism is not divisive. It is unifying. It is British.

The *Daily Mail* provides a dramatic example of this sleight of hand, amusing if you are from south of the Scottish border, infuriating if you are to its north. In February 2016, when it was clear that a referendum was coming soon but had not yet been announced, it seemed that Cameron might stitch up the entire Cabinet behind his deal to stay in the EU. Deprived of a unifying leader with traditional Conservative appeal and reduced to the leadership of Farage and UKIP, Brexit would be lost. The *Mail*'s editor, Paul Dacre, ran a pained, ferocious editorial. It was headlined in huge bold capital letters, that occupied most of the paper's front page: **WHO WILL SPEAK FOR ENGLAND?** Its opening words (the italics are mine) went: 'Today the Mail asks a question of profound significance to our destiny *as a sovereign nation* and the fate of our children and grandchildren. Who will speak for England?' The editorial continued on an inside page. Buried there it adds in a parenthesis: 'and, of course, by "England" ... we mean the whole of the United Kingdom.'[3] The *Daily Mail* prints a separate Scottish edition. Its editors replaced the front page.

'By England ... we mean the whole of the United Kingdom'. This admission lies at the heart of Theresa May's project for Brexit Britain. As her government seeks to pull the UK away from Europe and gain trade with the rest of the world to compensate, the Westminster state must impose unity at home, especially on the smaller nations. To make the form of Brexit that she has chosen work, the prime minister of England, for that is what she is, must discipline Scotland, Wales, Northern Ireland, as well as London.

How was Brexit driven by England, and how did this lead to the form it has taken under May's premiership? My plan in answering this double question is to start with the unique hybrid nature of Anglo-British self-consciousness. This has gone unchallenged because what can be called England's 'defining classes' (those who define 'who we are') have, with the exception of Billy Bragg, adamantly refused to be English, or 'merely English' as many put it. At this point most discussions of nationalism go deeper into sources of its values and cultural expressions and compare the English with the Welsh, Scots and Irish. I originally planned to visit, research and write about these nations because Brexit belongs just as much to them as to the metropolis. The race to publish ruled this out in terms of time, but also my priority is to delve deeper into the causes that lie in Anglo-Britain. This must not be taken to suggest that the other nations do not matter as much. The different consequences between the four nations will grow in importance under the stresses of May's strategy and may subvert, indeed should subvert, the ambition of the Brexiteers.

There is no question that nations and nationalism are a shaping force in our contemporary history, not mere superstructures or false consciousness, but they are not defined by their froth. What matters are their institutions, which include their constitutions and their governing principles as well as their media, military, financial, educational and industrial complexes; their cities, suburbs and countryside. I focus on Britain's governing institutions, their political culture and how they organise self-belief in the country's political system, something that is especially important in a democracy that does not have a written constitution.

A proud, imperial set-up with its institutions and codes has been trashed over the last thirty years. People cast their eyes away, which only preserves the discomfort. I will take a look. Tony Blair played a significant role due to his form of high-energy ambition, originally developed to escape Labour's long tradition of losing. More than anything, his politics and Cameron's inheritance of them undermined the legitimacy of Westminster government, that in turn led to Brexit. How could such a disastrous approach have been permitted? In this part of the story, the media and Rupert Murdoch play a key role, for without the tabloids we would still be in the European Union. Not because they imposed themselves, for they stir and follow sentiment as much as lead it, but because they would not challenge sentiment and indulged prejudice. Now, they are the most influential set of institutions in the land. To understand how we arrived at this unacceptable situation, I swoop into the country's post-war past to retrieve a sense of who has governed Britain and how they have done so.

Think of it as the people living in the debris of their land, watching on their screens the new skyscrapers of London rise and shine. The debris is not poverty or lack of money but something intangible and inescapable: the end of Great Britain. They'd love to have it back but know they cannot and should not. Theresa May has pitched them her Global Britain in its place, to feed their ambivalent desire. In doing so this most English of premiers, a vicar's daughter from rural Oxfordshire, drives straight to the heart of their longing. England–Britain is a post-empire hybrid. It has generated a special nationalism, a two-sided entity: English within and British without. The English aspect of this identity is more often personal, even whimsical, and has a romance as well as a Rooster hooligan element. It is the English countryside, the English rose, the English sense of humour. Whereas Britishness is exterior-facing and imposing, it is the British navy and

Britain's government in Whitehall that carries the lure of greatness. The sweet and the violent are attached. When Argentina occupied the Falkland Islands, it was as if 'the Nazis invaded Ambridge'.[4] The *people* – the 800 families of the barren islands of the South Atlantic – became the personification of pastoral *England*. The islands were *British* (as, today, is Gibraltar). Parliament rallied every sinew to support a *British* task force, sent to liberate the innocent English on the other side of the globe.

In a period when the UK's global influence was rapidly diminishing, the Falklands episode was a high point. Since then the institutions of Britishness have lost their capacity to hold the country in their thrall. The Monarchy, the Cabinet, the House of Lords, MPs, the civil service and now the judiciary have come under assault, as being out of touch or corrupt, or both. But Britishness is an old ruling culture, it does not give up easily and clings to its English roots. Reciprocally, the political expression of English nationalism is trapped in its diminishing Britishness until, like the grin on the Cheshire cat, not much more is left than shouts of 'sovereignty'.

This creates an extraordinary anomaly when it comes to the representation of English interests. Thanks to devolution and the creation of national governments in Scotland, Wales and Northern Ireland, there is an Arts Council England, English Heritage and NHS England. Huge sums of money and cultural influence are at stake. But there is not a single major English organisation or think tank that sees its role as representing English concerns, opinion and interests as such. England has no civic institutions, no parliament or assembly, no body of its own, to give it voice. After stepping down as an MP, John Denham founded the Centre for English Identity and Politics at Winchester University, to study this lack, which underlines the reality of it. The Church of England is a British institution supporting the Crown that referees Anglicanism internationally. The Bank of England is Britain's bank. The Conservative Party is now just called the Conservative Party. The Labour movement too is a British formation. There is a TUC Scotland, the Trades Union Congress in London speaks for Britain – there is no English TUC. Although there are Scottish and Welsh Labour parties, *the* Labour Party has no English section. The Greens have a separate party in Scotland, but it is the Green Party of England and Wales. Only the Lib Dems have a formally federal structure with an English section, but you would not know it. There is the BBC, the British Broadcasting Corporation, with a BBC Scotland, a BBC Wales, a BBC Northern Ireland and ... the BBC. There is the British Council, which exists to project the UK's culture and language around the world. There is no English Council.

English votes for English laws, known as EVEL, was introduced in October 2015, but this was far from a measure that gave English people voice. It dealt with the anomaly of Scottish MPs being able to vote on legislation that effects only England, and it was only a change to the standing orders of the House of Commons.[5] If the speaker certifies that proposed legislation affects England alone, it must go through a grand committee of exclusively English MPs. This may protect England from unfair attention of Scottish MPs in Westminster, it does nothing to express or enhance England in any sense comprehensible to the English public. MPs, concerned at the loss of legitimacy thanks to the lopsided nature of devolution, sucked the issue into the protocols of the House of Commons and turned it into a problem of their own procedure.

A House of Commons backbench debate about parliamentary sovereignty on 4 February 2016 had a classic example connected to Brexit. Bill Cash, a famous anti-EU obsessive, quoted G. K. Chesterton to his fellow MPs: 'Smile at us, pay us, pass us; but do not quite forget, For we are the people of England, that never have spoken yet.' No one said: 'Shame, this is a British parliament!' Peter Grant of the Scottish Nationalists, a lonely pro-EU speaker, responded: 'But we are not the people of England; we are the people of Scotland.'[6] The English ignored him.

An undeniable reason for this state of affairs is that there is no popular demand for distinct English political representation. The Campaign for an English Parliament does its best, but the unassailable logic of its arguments falls on deaf ears. There is not the concern or desire amongst the English to insist on what is condemned as 'another layer of government'. The idea is seen as stifling not enhancing representation. The Scottish parliament may be resented by the English, but there is no wish to copy it. On the contrary, the House of Commons, which was England's parliament in another time and a previous building, is still regarded as England's representative body by the English, even though it is British. English presumption is being reproduced there every day, as Cash showed.

English people, however, are losing their belief in Westminster and its self-important debates. They always enjoyed being rude about it, very rude, in the way that comedians and satire express a form of love. Gradually, the whole thing has gone sour. It is no longer funny that MPs fiddle their expenses. The Lords is ridiculous, a crony-filled chamber that does not even have any decent aristocrats to speak of. Hideous over-centralisation makes local government pitiful. The result is a displacement of English exasperation with the whole damn lot of them ... onto Brussels. Somehow or other, even though we won the war, Europe seems to know what it is about and we do not.

Thus the English enjoy a high degree of self-belief inside a shell that does not belong to just them. As Michael Kenny shows in his fully researched study, the English have 'a hybrid form of self-understanding' thanks to their Britishness. Writing before Brexit he argues that a struggle for 'the soul of Englishness' is emerging, but does not foresee it being resolved by a traditional call for a civic English nationhood.[7]

This strange state of affairs is underlined by the 2011 Census which introduced a question on national identity for the first time. It allowed people to tick more than one national identity. English identity, either on its own or combined with other identities, was the most common in Britain: 37.6 million people (67.1 per cent of the UK population). Of these, 32.4 million people (57.7 per cent) chose English as a sole identity. This compares with 10.7 million, a third of the number, who chose a British identity only. Among people residing in England, 70.1 per cent associated themselves with an English identity, either combined or on its own.[8]

In 2014, a *Future of England* survey, initiated by IPPR and edited by Richard Wyn Jones, tracked the rising numbers identifying themselves as being English. In the process, it asked people which levels of government they thought had 'most influence' over them. In Scotland 4 per cent of respondents thought the EU had the most influence; in Wales this rose to 6 per cent. In England an astonishing 26 per cent thought the EU had 'the most influence'. In an earlier survey, they had asked this question across the EU, where the highest results outside England were 9 per cent in three peripheral areas: Brittany, Upper Austria and Galicia. In that survey 31 per cent, that is, nearly a third rather than just over a quarter of the English, thought that Brussels had the greatest government impact on their lives.[9] It is bizarre that between a quarter and a third of a major nation should believe something that is plain wrong. For a start, it means they think their own government is not just misguided but useless (perhaps that is not so wrong). Belief in the scale of its impact correlates with antagonism towards the EU. English hostility to the European Union is based on a delusion of its influence, linked to a nihilistic sense of the futility of Westminster.

Unlike all other parts of the UK and the EU, England has no government of its own. The researchers surmised that there was a causal relationship: being deprived of a credible, representative power that clearly belongs to you, leads to anger with the most remote authority of all, which is blamed as the source of your powerlessness. Or to put it the other way around, you only feel comfortable within as large an international association as the EU if you feel directly represented by a government formed around your primary identity. Within England this seems to be confirmed, as London with its mayor has lower levels of euro-resentment.

Born out of imperialism, in its heyday England's Britishness was a wonderful nationalism if you were part of it, tolerant and respectable at home and gung-ho abroad. Gradually it has been compressed. First the Irish and now the Scots want to escape. The English still want to be represented by Britain – it remains the other side of their singular coin. But they also feel ill-treated by the class system that lies at the heart of Britishness; a feeling of grievance that is justified. Especially when it comes to public education for those from families unable to pay for it privately, i.e. a large majority – because public education is poor and confining.

A recent, little-noticed clash vividly illustrates what might otherwise seem elusive about the way this feels and how explosive it can be. Jonathan Portes is an Anglo-American expert on migration, who was chief economist to the Cabinet from 2008 to 2011. In 2013 he co-authored an op-ed in *The Times* with Gus O'Donnell, the ex-secretary to the Cabinet and head of the civil service, who had been his boss in the Cabinet Office. They wrote: 'Immigrants don't just fill specific short-term gaps in the labour market, they bring new skills and aptitudes. And by making the job market more competitive they increase the incentive for natives to acquire new skills.'[10] Later, Portes advocated the advantages of immigration in the *Observer*, writing: 'Immigrants have different skills and experiences to native workers, so they complement rather than substitute for natives, helping raise wages and productivity for everybody.' He quoted a government paper that refers to 'native employment outcomes.'[11]

The article that was co-authored with the ex-Cabinet secretary was singled out in a righteous, scathing and brilliant polemic by one Nick, the son of a Birmingham steelworker, aroused by the use of the word natives: 'The alternative for the "natives" – being forced into lower-paid jobs or thrown prematurely onto the scrapheap – was clear enough, but left unsaid,' he wrote. It was part of a wider criticism of Janan Ganesh, who writes for the *Financial Times* and is the biographer of the then chancellor George Osborne. Nick was so enraged by Ganesh that he literally shouted at his copy of the *FT*, he tells us, when he read that those forced out of work or who find their wages undercut should simply be ignored by the government. 'Rich democracies,' Ganesh pronounced, 'may have to live with a caucus of permanently aggrieved voters amounting to a quarter or a third of the whole ... A seething minority is still a minority.' With more than a touch of bitterness, Nick conceded that at least it was a rare, honest expression of the brutal view held by the international elite. They are willing to condemn the 'working class' to empty servitude, because they are a mere outnumbered caucus of the aggrieved, a permanently powerless 'quarter or third'.[12]

In normal times, Janan and Sir Gus might laugh at the chippy frustration of Nick and those like him educated in Sheffield. But these are not normal times. Their critic is Nicholas Timothy, now joint chief-of-staff to the prime minister and one of her speech writers. Timothy does not agree that immigrants always have a positive economic impact. In addition to challenging the argument of Portes and O'Donnell, he repudiates any treatment of working people as 'natives'. Portes is a social scientist not a politician, and believes he uses the term in a neutral fashion to mean the locally resident workforce. But that someone who was the country's most senior mandarin should adopt the description shows a staggering indifference and contempt: a complacency as to how vulnerable the elite are and a lack of respect for those who do the heavy lifting. More significant in terms of the wider political culture, there is good reason for Timothy's justified sensitivity. The English lower classes, which is most of us, have an anxiety that comes from not being real citizens with constitutional ownership of our country. It makes us even more stroppy, while inducing a sense of insecurity. At the back of the mind of every English person who has not been to public school, and feels shut out of the networks of access and privilege, is the fear that they are indeed a mere native, subject to the whim of blundering masters. Brexit was not a revolt of the natives. The British are not natives. It was a revolt of the English against being treated as if they are natives – and against a feeling of helplessness that they cannot prevent this. The anxiety is justified because the exposure is real, if your sense of national identity is a hybrid Anglo-British one. The English are increasingly disenchanted with those who seem to rule us but who deny responsibility for the outcomes. Given all we have been through together, are 'they' still treating us like 'natives'?

Anglo-Britain is a crustacean of a country. It has a soft English interior and a hard British exoskeleton. From the point of view of the English inside the beast, the relationship between inside and outside is indeed under threat. The Scots, Northern Irish and Welsh cohabit it, because the whole point of the shell is to enclose a multinational greatness, or else it ceases to be British. A point Theresa May makes emphatically. The smaller nations threaten the shell from within by trying to leave. The European Union, which the British crab itself partly inhabits, challenges its shell from without. It is an even larger and more dynamic crustacean actively defining itself as a future project. Sharing the sea, patrolling the ocean bed for sustenance in such circumstances, became nerve-racking for the English within their increasingly ill-fitting old British exoskeleton. For as well as the Scots hammering at it from within and the EU pressing on it from without, the great British crab's once magnificent shell is in structural disrepair in terms of its own mechanics. No wonder the English felt angry and anxious. They seized the opportunity of Brexit as the offer of a wonderful solution: England can be once more an 'independent' British crab. A liberated, self-determining decapod, free at last to be a Global Crab and grab trade deals at will from the ocean floor with its own sovereign claws.

Provided the Scots and the Irish come along, that is, and can you really trust the Welsh? By being committed to the *British* Westminster and Whitehall, the English deprive themselves of their own political self-determination. This is the irony. The real foreign threat comes from their British masters. Their attachment to Britain prevents the English from realising themselves. Unable to exit Britain, the English did the next-best thing and told the EU to 'fuck off'. It was a displacement of feelings for their own elite. English attachment to the British state is the problem. A cruel master, it gave them a choice: the English could abandon Europe, or carry on as before, feeling threatened and vulnerable, under Cameron the heir to Blair. Understandably, the English refused to carry on. But their chosen alternative will trap them even more deeply into the source of their misery: the British state. It needs to go. It is the deep cause of Brexit.

There is a simple way for the English to be free. Just ask the Scots, the Welsh and the Northern Irish to take their fate into their own hands. In a cooperative spirit, the English should request them to be independent. In this way, the English too will emancipate themselves from the integument of the British system. English government can then be transformed into a democracy by the English. England will then have its own parliament, the house of the common people, preferably elected on a practical but proportional basis like any modern democracy.

Britishness will not disappear. The opposite is likely. Its historic legacy and ongoing influence has never belonged exclusively to the English. Relieved of its political confinement in Whitehall, Britishness will flourish in the many sites and sources of British identity including outside the British Isles – and doubtless in shared institutions as well.

If this suggestion seems incredible, it is not because the Irish, the Welsh and the Scots would be tremendously opposed to their own independence in Europe, but because it seems unthinkable for the English to be on their own. To step out of the clothes of the past should not be that hard for a country with a spirit of adventure. But it is. We need to understand why.

# 12

# I'm Not English. Oh Yes You Are!

'As an English person, I would like to declare up front: I do not want to be English.' In a sentence, this tells you why the UK is no longer in the European Union. The author Paul Mason is a scathing critic of Brexit; I respect him a lot. In no way is it his intention to support the cause of leaving Europe – whether under the banner of Farage and his backers, Gove and Murdoch, or Boris Johnson and Theresa May. I am not blaming Mason for something he passionately opposes. But from his egalitarian, internationalist perspective, he expresses with exceptional clarity an educated English repugnance for their nation. One that has deprived the English of a country they can believe in politically. The contradiction here is very powerful. The English have an immense cultural self-awareness of being English, with deep and varied historic and regional roots, that creates a fearlessness. But it is coated with a defensive armour of Britain's one-time imperial class system, which subordinated yet employed them. The popular fascination with the servant and striving classes, who in endless ways juggle defiance and deference in television costume dramas and soap operas, reflects this strong and persistent tension. To spring the trap, the English need England to become itself. With a healthy patriotism and self-belief, it will then become possible to be at ease with being European as well. An enormous resistance needs to be overcome. I'm going to use Mason's article to address it.

Mason is not denying that he is English: he just refuses to let this define his political status. Instead, he cloaks what it means to be a native of England with a globalist sentiment, which he does by appealing to the planetary reach of the English language. He thereby joins most of his country's cultural intelligentsia, right and left, whether filmmakers, television pundits, artists, columnists, actors, directors and playwrights, poets, novelists, scientists or academics, in refusing to come to the help of their English nation. Without them, it will remain trapped for ever within a Britannic integument that is incompatible – institutionally and emotionally – with membership of the EU.

Mason's stark declaration followed the Conservative election victory of 2015 and their promise of EVEL, to ensure 'English Votes for English Laws'. He wrote a column in the *Guardian* headlined 'I do not want to be English'.[1] His writing is distinguished by his trenchant thinking and grasp of political economy. His book *Post-Capitalism* is a sweeping contribution to a much-needed development of a strategy to replace market fundamentalism. In it, he shows that a confrontation is under way, rooted in the economy. Networks are replacing the hierarchies of the forces and relations of production. The challenge to control the networks is now the struggle of our time, he argues. It means that the most hierarchical area of all, politics itself, will be upturned. It is a compelling analysis.

Mason is the opposite of a narrow or nostalgic critic. That he too feels a shudder of revulsion at the thought of England as the definition of his citizenship confirms the strength and penetration of this negative culture of feeling. At least he does so fearlessly. A less brazen attitude is widespread across England's educated classes of all political persuasions. Many a time have I heard people – whether from the nether reaches of the House of Lords, the residues of New Labour, or sympathetic and scrupulous friends, say: 'I don't really feel English', or 'I'm not interested in being nationalist', or 'I'm a northerner and a European', or 'I'm a Londoner and then international', or 'Unfortunately I'm English', which at least is a recognition. The exception to this pervasive miasma is Billy Bragg, wrongly belittled as a mere bard, whose passionate argument for a progressive English patriotism was accorded 'a certain charm' by the *Guardian*'s Decca Aitkenhead, when all seemed well in 2006.[2]

Her kind of patronising superiority provoked the grim Anglo-Saxon defiance of 2016. But, and here is the rub, until the English can accept that they are English, there is no way back to Europe. This won't happen unless those like Paul Mason check into reality. Strange as it may seem, the only road back to Europe for those that wish this, as Mason does, is via England.

Mason observes that, thanks to the Scottish Nationalists' domination of Scottish politics, English issues will become more important. His response is: 'as an English person I would like to declare up front: I do not want to be English'. He does not object to the cross of St George — he accepts that football has taken back the English flag from the racists. But, 'If I examine my own gut feelings', he writes, he finds he has more in common with his class and Celtic cultures than any Englishness which he defines as meaning, 'public schools and the officer class' (although these are *British* institutions which recruit across the UK and were integral to the creation of the Empire). His concern is that because new 'English institutions' are coming, 'sooner or later someone is going to try and foist an English narrative on us'. It will fail, he predicts, because 'at the centre of English culture lies neither institutions, nor customs, nor sports teams, but a global language'.

'English national identity' will not emerge, 'Because of the class and cultural divides within England, and because our linguistic identity is so full of free gifts from the rest of the world. Sure, this is a legacy of empire, but the empire itself was born out of trade and sailing, two activities whose identities are central to English identity, which explains why it is so difficult to pin down.' Mason concludes: 'Please don't try to burden me with yet another layer of bogus identity politics. The only identity I need can be created by speaking and writing in the most malleable language on earth.'

The assumption here is that we need only one identity. If so, it can be international. From financiers to globe-trotting academics, it's a familiar song of those who benefit from globalisation's ability to abstract them from everyday life. It should not seduce such a grounded observer as Mason. Working for Channel 4 and *Newsnight*, he reported memorably and sympathetically on the new generation of protests. He went to Wall Street to film the Occupy movement in their encampment at Zuccotti Park, where they flew the American flag quite naturally. They could do so in part because it symbolises a republican and revolutionary patriotism, one with which they were quite at ease.

Before that, Mason covered at length the development of the Greek crisis, and the country's fight against German-imposed austerity. It was impossible to share any sympathy with the Syriza government's election and initial defiance of Eurozone austerity, as he did, without experiencing its Greek patriotic distinctiveness. On the warm evening when young crowds gathered to celebrate the *Oxi* referendum – when the Greeks voted No to the terms being imposed on them by the EU – they sang wartime songs of resistance to Germany's occupation. In Scotland, Mason was one of the few contemporary analysts to recognise that the impulse of youthful support for Scottish independence during the referendum of 2014 was linked to the same international insurgency of opposition to the existing world order that drove the young Greeks and the Wall Street occupiers. I met him in Glasgow when he was with his team, filming during the final hours of the referendum itself.

None of the protesters would have regarded themselves as being *only* Scottish, *only* Greek or *only* American. They were also part of an inchoate movement seeking global solidarities, as well as local loyalties and decentralisation – a tolerant civic nationalism opposed to both exclusivist chauvinism and indifferent globalism. Yet Mason regards his own country and himself as being in no need of similar open-minded civic patriotism. He extends his solidarity to them but recoils at the prospect of becoming like them. As they reframe their national identities in a democratic fashion, he insists he has no need for national identity at all.

The young who identify themselves as Americans in Occupy Wall Street, or as Greeks in Syntagma Square, or as Scots in calling for independence, are part of a forward-looking defiance of an unequal world order, not a regressive attempt to 'foist identity politics' onto all and sundry. Civic nationalism is not about fusing your politics with a signifier buried in your background or DNA. Identity in its emancipating sense is part of the relationships to be found in the movement outside of yourself, for example, by liking not hating other countries. How you carry and share your national identity matters. Denial is disabling. If the English were to embrace the truth of their existence, it would be an act of modesty, equalising matters. Its repression is a neo-imperial indulgence – an arrogant refusal to be like other people.

When it comes to the spontaneity in the marketplace, Mason sees how larger forces are at work that manipulate economic subjectivity in terms of choice and consumer fashion. With national identity too, gut feelings are never just the outcome of one's own experience, even though they are stronger. They are also formed by social forces, if slower historical ones that shape us. Nationalism developed alongside industrialisation. The nation that initiated this was 'God's firstborn: England', in Liah Greenfeld's terms. This is an exceptionally important insight. In the modern jargon of internet startups, England had the first-mover advantage. Being the first nation to industrialise gave it a near monopoly advantage. Thanks to its legal structures and naval power, England precipitated the industrial revolution that transformed humankind. All other societies had to mobilise their resources to resist being subordinated by the impact of the 'first nation'. They had to catch up and industrialise themselves – from America to France, Germany to China. It was this material 'nationalisation', as Ernest Gellner argued, that brought pre-industrial societies into the modern world via nation states. They did so culturally too, with print culture generating the extraordinary identification of oneself with many others, so powerful that, as Ben Anderson sets out in *Imagined Communities*, we are willing to die for our nation.[3]

As the first modern nation, the English enjoyed an enormous advantage. They did not need to rebel against others. They had no need to internally forge their nationalism to defend themselves, *they* were the threat for others from the start. Their immediate island neighbours were recruited into what became a joint project: the British, not the English Empire. This applied to the working classes as well. In the early 1970s, Tom Nairn wrote *The Left Against Europe* to explore why the Labour movement and the British left felt no need to be European and overwhelmingly resisted becoming part of the European Union:

> British imperialists were not simply the first, the biggest, and the most successful plunderers on the international scene; they were also the best at pretending that their empire was really something else. It was this 'liberal imperialism' which the British workers' movements grew up within. From the outset therefore, nationalism was to assume for them this distinctive and tenacious colouring. Their 'living community', their 'participant democracy' was not that of a mere battling nation-state: it merged into a greater, spiritual, multi-racial, inter-continental and realistically heterogeneous something-or-other.[4]

Today, it remains excruciatingly painful for many on the left, who are the inheritors of the workers' movement, to abandon their special something-or-other for, well, for Englishness. Instead, in the Labour Party, Britishness has been embraced with even greater resilience than on the Tory right. But Scottish nationalism has not just become an indelible part of the UK. Its political expression, the SNP, has expelled Labour from its Scottish redoubts. While Scottish Toryism was an addition to the English Tories, the Labour Party was co-created by Scottish and Welsh leaders alongside English ones. Labourism was British from its conception as the island's working class was formed by Clydeside and the Welsh valleys as much as by the Black Country and the London docks. The profound grip of this experience means that even after the end of New Labour, when the SNP has clearly displaced their party in Scotland, Labour leaders such as Ed Miliband and Jeremy Corbyn, both Londoners, found the idea of Labour becoming an English party unimaginable. A visceral shudder went through them and their supporters at the thought. To become what they clearly and obviously are remains intolerable.

There are political reasons for Labour's resistance to recognising itself as an English party. It points towards abandoning an absolute commitment to governing alone, that is built into winner-takes-all Westminster politics. Labour is very tribal and party members hate the idea of electoral alliances. There is also a cultural imaginary getting in the way. A good look in the mirror without their British make-up would tell them they are English, but they fear the perception that they will be seen as narrow, Farage-like, bigoted and altogether dreadful – 'bogus' is Mason's word – and go to the most extraordinary contortions to deny it. One being a direct escape into internationalism.

Paul Mason attempts a genial variation of this. He knows he must have an identity, so he makes it linguistic: 'The only identity I need can be created by speaking and writing in the most malleable language on earth.' Such an argument, however, must apply equally to everyone brought up with English in their mouths. Would an American, a Jamaican, a middle-class Indian or Pakistani, or a Canadian *deny* their national identity in the way that Mason does? Of course not. Yet they have the same access to English as he does. Speaking English may enhance their national identity, it does not replace it. Suppose that the world language Mason enjoys was not called English, but instead its name was Jamaican. Would Mason argue that he has no need at all to regard himself as English because he speaks the world language of Jamaican?

His claim only appears to be plausible because his native language and his nation have the same name. Thanks to England being the first nation and creating the largest empire of the early industrial period, its tongue has become a world language. Mason uses this to deny his need for a mere nationality. In so doing he expresses a presumption that is quintessentially English. Unlike everyone else around the world who include attachment to their country among their identities, the English felt no such need. Their nationalism expressed their unselfconscious superiority, of having no need to be nationalist like other, lesser, peoples. Mason is *being* an English nationalist when he reproduces this denial.

Mason is right in one vital respect. He, and millions like him, will refuse to embrace the creation of an English identity within Britain. They are not going to support a movement to create an English parliament underneath the existing British-Westminster system. After all, they are 80 per cent of the British and Northern Irish population. For the Scots, having their own new parliament is a way of growing as a people, of becoming more themselves in both Britain and Europe. For the English, to set up an assembly of the English in addition to the House of Commons, when this is already England's parliament, represents no such emancipation. Powerful regional assemblies are essential, as Westminster is far too centralised. But these do not address the national question. Nor will an additional parliament that is perceived as adding 'another layer' of oppression and a further grinding down. Also, to call for an 'English parliament' would not appeal to many inhabitants from Scotland, Ireland, Wales and many other nations, in what is a mongrel country. The solution is just what Mason so far at least, objects to. Ask the other nations to be independent and the parliament of England will be the House of Commons.

Today, Europeans describe themselves as being civic nationalists to distinguish their form of patriotism from exclusivist, chauvinist mobilisations of the past. Open and tolerant both internally and externally, nationalism in Europe has become pluralist and lawful, rather than bullying, monomaniac and demagogic. There are new fascistic nationalists around, but the scale of the resistance to them shows a new civic normal is being created. A further twist is how this will be challenged by the fifth, digital, element that is adding itself to the dimensions of land, sea, air and outer space that form the environment for our species and our planet. As well as being civic, nationalism is now becoming networked. Networked nationalisms will play an essential part in public identities this century. In this context to say that one's own distinctiveness is *only* national is to defy the nature of modern life. To deny that one's identity is *also* national is to deny that one lives amongst present-day humanity. Those of us who are 'English persons', to use Paul Mason's description, should embrace reality: we are English Europeans.

# 13

# Big Britishness

For the peoples of the UK, the only alternative to putting aside Britishness and becoming English-Europeans, Scottish-Europeans, Irish-Europeans and Welsh-Europeans is to be Brexit-British. There used to be another alternative, a civic British Europeanism. Britain is not a nation, but as a country it generated a multinational nationalism with enormous loyalty. Danny Boyle's projection of Britishness in the opening ceremony of the 2012 Olympics showed how it too can be civic, multicultural, humane, witty, egalitarian and pluralist. The hybrid potential of much Anglo-Britishness is part of its long tradition of energy and adaptation, which includes the Scots, Welsh and Irish for whom Britishness is a vital part of their identity too.

The flame of Olympic Britishness was extinguished in the EU referendum. It can live again culturally but it was smothered politically. The country was presented with a choice between two powerful but regressive forms of right-wing Brexit-Britishness. A positive, pro-European Britishness was rejected by the official Remain campaign led David Cameron along with Peter Mandelson, Tony Blair's colleague. They wanted the UK to stay in the EU as a platform to project their desire for hard-edged global leadership. Against them were Boris Johnson and Nigel Farage, who headed the two Leave campaigns. They both wanted a 'Global Britain' independent of European interference. Labour proved incapable of offering an attractive international vision of its own, trapped between its leader's view of the EU (that it was good for tangible benefits, such as rights at work) and Mandelson's concern not to rock Cameron's boat. The delusion generated by the British state, that the country has no need for solidarity and only acts in its own separate interest, gripped the leaderships of *both* the Leave and Remain campaigns.

This is obvious in terms of the Union Jack-waving, anti-European appeal of Brexit. It was less obvious in the Remain campaign, but more damaging in that it undermined its own case. It is important to examine this shameful aspect of the attempt to persuade the country to stay in the EU, because it shows why those who wish to change the minds of English voters cannot do so by reverting to the case made in 2016.

Boris Johnson was right: David Cameron thought the EU was 'crap'. The then prime minister wanted the influence, the network, the world standing and the financial gains of membership. As for the European Union itself – its ways, languages, parliament, flag, cultures and solidarity – he had no time for them. Cameron insisted that the Remain campaign's appeal to stay in the EU had to be based on his calculated Euroscepticism. He told voters he did not 'love Brussels', told his staff that he wanted 'less Europe not more Europe'.[1] As for what he told his children ... At the start of the campaign he gave an interview to the *Independent* and said that he was 'teaching his own children that Britain is "special" and should belong to international organisations in order to "*shape the world's future* as well as its past"' (my italics). He continued: 'the world I want my children to grow up in is [one] where there's a big, bold, brave Britain at the heart of these institutions trying to deliver a world based on the values we care about – democracy, freedom, rights ...' Cameron uses the same hyperventilating greatness rhetoric the Brexiteers adopted when they advocated a global Britain forging a new Anglosphere. The prime minister continued in the same vein, saying he wanted Britain to be 'a swashbuckling, trading, successful, buccaneer nation of the 21st century'. The newspaper's interviewer adds 'within the EU'.[2] The European Union was only a prompted afterthought. It played no emotional part in the prime minister's vision for his children. Instead, he wants them to believe their country's future is a scrubbed-up planetary Anglo-Britishness, flashing its Francis Drake as it shapes the world.

Before the official campaign began, Cameron exploited the chance to send an official booklet to every single household in the UK saying why the government believed voting Remain was best for Britain – without having to offer the Brexiteers an equal right of reply. The government spent £9 million of public money setting out the official case for staying in Europe. It was a massive opportunity to establish the terms of the debate with a serious case. Instead, the booklet was patronising, simplistic and padded with dull photographs. Worst of all it revealed that the government's case was based on a dislike of Europe. It opened with five negative points about the EU, to prove how the UK had 'secured a special status' in the larger Union and had kept its distance from it, among them: 'The UK will not be part of further European political integration'. It could have opened with pride in Europe's achievements, in which the UK had played an active part, from the single market to expanding Western freedom to the ex-Soviet satellite countries of Eastern Europe. But EU membership was not presented as a matter of solidarity for Britain. The government launched the campaign to Remain by saying in effect: 'We too are against the EU, but think it is in Britain's selfish interests to remain'. The rest of the booklet set out the advantages the UK could extract from membership while not being exposed to the risks of full-blooded engagement. In this way, the public was offered a choice between two varieties of hostility to Europe. A majority found the stronger brew more attractive. The UK walked out of Europe on two Big-British Eurosceptic legs. One was called Leave, the other Remain.

The outstanding exception on the Remain side in England is Caroline Lucas, the unique Green MP. She called on her supporters to commit to a shared Europe that we would change from within, saying: 'Another Europe is Possible'. She worked with that campaign within the UK and with the cross-European campaign, Diem25. She was largely ignored. The British media showed no interest in serious European ideas, but it cannot be blamed for failing to report people who were, as they did not exist in the mainstream. The official 'Stronger In' campaign directed by Downing Street asphyxiated any independent cultural mobilisation for Europe. To be positive about Europe would have disrupted its Project Fear, whose positive premise was that to Leave the EU would threaten Britain's global interests.

Towards the end of the campaign, on 8 June, George Osborne, Cameron's closest ally and then chancellor of the Exchequer, was subjected to a vigorous half-hour interview by the BBC's Andrew Neil. Osborne told viewers: 'Let me be clear. This is a battle for the soul of the country.' Then he used the identical language Cameron deployed when he told the *Independent* that he wanted his children to believe in a Britain that will 'shape the world's future'. Osborne said he wanted a Britain that 'shapes the world – not one shaped by the world'.[3]

How can it be the objective of the British government to 'shape the world'? If the phrase was uttered by a leader of China, or India, or President Trump, we would be angry or anxious. Similarly, if it had been Palmerston in the nineteenth or even Churchill speaking in the mid-twentieth century, the world would have listened and been afraid. But today, this is not a role for a country with a chronic 5 per cent trade deficit and less than 1 per cent of the planet's human population. If, however, Osborne had said he wanted a country that 'shapes Europe', or Cameron had said that he wanted his children to be part of a Britain that 'shapes the future of Europe', the leaders of Europe would have raised their heads with interest and respect. But a deep groan would have emanated from London's media-political caste. What dullness, what a dim horizon of policy details, what loss of sovereignty! Think about it, however. England has no chance whatsoever to 'shape the world' any longer, but it *could* have helped shape Europe and can do again.

The Brexiteers have abandoned a very ambitious but achievable aim of growing like Germany within the EU, for the fantastical ambition of growing even faster while outside it. Their Big British ambition was *shared* by Remainers like Cameron and Osborne, only they wanted the UK half-outside the EU. The referendum debate was a clash between Tory factions who shared a similar pretention. Those for Leave were for 'Global Britain'. Those for Remain for a 'World Britain'. Both were Big British, neither was pro-European.

Along with the fantasy, there is a reality to it: the luscious underbelly of their Britishness. Take the example of George Osborne. When he was deposed from being chancellor of the Exchequer by Theresa May to become a mere backbench MP on £70,000 a year, he took to the international circuit of banks and hedge funds. Between July 2016 and February 2017, he cashed £786,450 for giving fifteen speeches and then took a job for one day a week for £650,000 a year with BlackRock, the world's biggest asset manager.[4] Now he also has a niche as editor of the *Evening Standard* but it won't pay so well. As chancellor, his pension reforms had released huge funds, which were welcomed by BlackRock president Robert Kapito. He claimed: 'up to $25bn of UK pension savings annually was now "money in motion"'. Thanks to Osborne's decision, 'BlackRock is uniquely positioned ... We intend to put a lot of effort into putting together more retirement products to capitalise on this market.' Osborne himself, as chancellor, had met with BlackRock five times between October 2014 and July 2016, the last time just before he was sacked. We know this thanks to a furious investigation by the *Daily Mail*.[5] A follow-up report revealed that Osborne's former chief of staff, Rupert Harrison, now works full time for BlackRock. Formally head boy at Eton, Harrison, according to another report in the *Mail*, 'has been credited as the "architect" of the pension fund changes. After recruiting Mr Harrison, BlackRock boasted: "Given his experience shaping the recent pensions reforms in the UK, he is uniquely placed to help develop our retirement proposition."'[6]

Osborne defended his payments saying: 'It's not different from what previous chancellors have done, Labour and Conservative.'[7] This is only too true. His immediate predecessor, Labour's Alistair Darling is now on the board of Morgan Stanley – although his speeches earn less than Osborne's at a mere £10,000 average.[8] Gordon Brown, who preceded Darling and became Labour prime minister, declared more than £3.6 million of payments from outside interests between losing the 2010 general election and stepping down as an MP in 2015.[9] He now works for Pimco, another huge global asset-managing company. Blair's staggeringly lucrative gold-digging is notorious. Less well known, his predecessor, John Major, Tory prime minister from 1990 to 1997, is a multi-millionaire having worked for the secretive Carlisle Group.

All of these figures advocated that the UK remain in the EU. The one-time leaders of Britain have personally exploited the legacy of British public office to profit from it in a striking American-global framework. When Osborne says he is battling for 'the soul of this country' and wants it to 'shape the world', he is in effect looking forward to advising the American world of high finance. Others too are part of this American system and look forward to its fruits. The Churchillist Boris Johnson, the Murdoch employee Michael Gove, as much as Cameron and Osborne, not forgetting the latters' referendum co-conspirator Peter Mandelson, who now runs an international consultancy called Global Counsel. The British political elite do not shape the *American* world order but they make a pretty penny assisting it.

Nor is it merely personal. While the country's political leaders and editors talk about sovereignty, 54 per cent of the UK stock market is owned by the rest of the world (according to the Office for National Statistics).[10] Whether it is ARM, the country's leading chip developer, London's tallest skyscrapers, its main financial paper, its car manufacturers or its railways, the UK seems to have lost ownership over much of its substance. As the *Daily Mail*'s Alex Brummer, one of the few financial journalists to be concerned about the implications, noted, 'Over the past two decades, everything in Britain has been up for sale ... four of the big six energy companies, major port operators P&O and Associated British Ports, most of our airports, nuclear power generator British Energy, nuclear contractor Westinghouse, Thames Water and much else.'[11] It gives the whole argument about self-government, taking back control and sovereignty a strange sense of unreality.

As a Remainer who is now leading Brexit, Theresa May is seeking to bring together both wings of Big Britishness, Global Britain and World Britain, into her Brexitannia. David Cameron's swashbuckling world-shaping claptrap and Boris Johnson's Empire-aping Churchillising farrago will be melded under her command into a single Brexit Britishness. To unify the Tory Party when it was on the edge of disintegration was an extraordinary achievement. She did it by playing the Big British card.

Even if May had been minded to become a democratic reformer, the need to bring the different sides of her party together would have prevented this. Brexit under her leadership is a form of closure. She has to keep her party united, the kingdom united, the press on board and immigrants out. The government cannot now permit an open, Olympic option of a human-friendly, tolerant Britishness based on solidarity and pluralism. May has closed down a progressive version of Britishness that was always Labour's dream. The Union is hers and she will insist on defining it. Britishness is now Brexitness. If you want to resist Brexit, you will need a patriotism. If you are English, your own wonderful country is available. Why spurn it, when there is no other option?

# 14

# English European, a Modern Nationalism

Because Brexit has triggered an English nationalism, I find myself writing for three different readerships, two facing in opposite directions. Those who are English and who voted for Brexit have different assumptions to those who voted Remain. Although a remainer I respect the audacity of those I know who voted to Leave. They are not racists, they are democrats – and I take my hat off to you as we all head for the cliff. If you are Brexit English, happy to see our Celtic cousins peel away if that is what they wish, then you have no problem with your national identity. But if you are Brexit *British* like the prime minister and don't want to lose Northern Ireland and Scotland, then you do. On the other side are those who voted Remain, most of whom, according to surveys, are likely to feel British not English, or British first. For us, leaving the EU explodes our identity. Some felt being in Europe relieved them of the need for nationalism, in a way that parallels Paul Mason. Yet here we are caught in a movement of repudiation of our continent's government, driven by English nationalism. Under Theresa May as Big Britain threatens political solidarity with our neighbours, it actively defines Britishness in a combative fashion.

The third group is made up of those who are not English, from Scots to South Africans, who may or may not live in the UK, curious or concerned about the fate of the UK. In this chapter I want to address, briefly, fellow Remainers nervous of our nationalism.

We have a problem, especially if we are determined to ensure that at some point we rejoin the EU (provided it survives). It is a new problem. I'd identify it as this: any return to Europe involves abandoning the British state and therefore political Britishness as an organising distinction (not a cultural one). To join the battles of our home continent over its future, we need to recognise ourselves as English Europeans becoming politically English by helping to ensure the independence of Scotland and the unification of Ireland (as stipulated in the Good Friday Agreement). Hopefully, Wales too. This will then give us the opportunity to create a new form of nationalism.

Such a claim may sound surprising. Is not nationalism inherently fixed in its form and regressive in its ideology? To think this is to be taken in by nationalism's self-presentation. To become an English citizen in the land of Shakespeare does not mean adopting the quivering shrillness of a ghost of England's past. It is true that every classic nationalism presents itself as unchanging – as expressing the essence of being French / Russian / Vietnamese / American / Greek / fill-in-as-appropriate. Because all are conservative in the sense of managing change by providing continuity. Nationalism projects itself as representing all that is upright in what we are, because all of us, in our different nations, are part of the human condition, at present undergoing the transformation from a rural to an urban species We need something to hold on to and help us make the best of this. Nationalism provides a means of doing so – claiming to be unchanging so as to aid societies to manage and handle their transformation.

Which is why the great explosion of nations coincides with the century of transformation from 1870 to 1970. This is the hundred years identified by Robert Gordon as witnessing an unparalleled and, he argues, unrepeatable increase in productivity and alteration of the nature of human life on Earth. Towards the beginning of that century, in 1879, 'the electric light, the internal combustion engine and wireless transmission were all invented within ten weeks of each other'.[1] Nationalism as we know it is inconceivable without these extraordinary advances, especially the development of radio.

What this means is that all nationalisms also alter, often profoundly. They too are part of the human condition. They are not unchanging after all. Nationalism is not a fixed form of identification that shuts you into a little box. It is an ongoing part of the argument about what it means to be human in a changing world. Other nationalities understand this because they experience it. The English don't yet because, mostly, they do not think of themselves as being English in a national sense, as we have seen. England too has changed a great deal even over the last fifty years. The alteration now is that we have come face to face with the need to rid ourselves of the British state.

It will mean becoming what we are. But this is not a static, fixed essence. Perhaps it is better to say that we need to become like other peoples, all of whom have a national identity. In a wonderful, heart-felt essay on 'the biggest defeat of my life', written the day after the referendum, Tim Garton Ash went out of his way to say he is an English European, although he also hoped to keep Scotland on board.[2] He understood the need to be English, in order to be the European that he is. Reeling at the prospect of Brexit, he did not yet take up the challenge to the British state this now demands. Each European nation is different. What would be specific about being English European?

Three things for a start. First, the timing. In *Imagined Communities*, Ben Anderson shows that newspapers were critical in the creation and development of early nationalism, organising communities of national identity among people who had never met or known each other. Newspapers had a fixed territorial reach and language. Today, many people, especially the under-35s, do not read newspapers any longer. They get their information from Facebook channels or Twitter or traditional newspaper apps. These platforms may in turn soon seem archaic as new networks replace them. How we read, watch and share what matters to us has gone irreversibly global. This is bound to have a profound long-term effect, as a generation that has never known analogue media takes command over the coming decades. Nationalism will become networked. This is likely to mean it will be multilayered and people will be much more at home in giving themselves combinations of identity. The sense of nationalism as fate will diminish. Its insistence on difference will be less chiliastic. The need for a national identity will remain as a fulcrum of sharing change rather than as an expression of existential threat. In their own ways, Islamic fundamentalists, Trump-style America-firsters and *Daily Mail* Britishness are part of the resistance to this change – angry protests against it, seeking out enemies, breakers not makers of new shared entities, trying to polarise us back into the strongholds of the past.

Second, England was the first mover of modern nationalism. This gave a geographically small island the power to create a planetary empire, and England will never be threatened by the disappearance of its national identity in the way many nationalisms feel they are. Paul Mason was on to something about the English language giving him something special. Englishness has achieved an evanescent presence that makes us natural citizens of the world. At the heart of any nation are its core institutions, but cultural limbs stretch far with issues of identity. Provided we do not let this go to our heads, or use it as an excuse to escape the need to be normal, it is an enviable legacy. We will be English Europeans foremost, but not just English Europeans, given the exceptionally long and intimate history with the rest of the world.

Finally, there is the advantage of not having to name the new parliament. There will be no obligation on those living here – who become citizens of England for administrative purposes – to feel they need to identify with 'an English parliament'. We will be represented in the plain House of Commoners. This pre-nationalist term for England's parliament can then become the centre for a European-networked nationalism with an international twist.

# 15

# Why the Right Wins and the Left Loses

Brexit is embedded in at least three decades of British history and will take years to implement – or reverse. The force that will stick with it or change its course is the English nation. If a historical account of the roots of Brexit is essential, its central theme is what has happened to the government of England. But, as we have seen, England is trapped within the shell of British government, once an immensely successful form of ruling others. Today, it prevents England from being European. The British state comes between England and Europe and – because it absorbs their identification – stands in the way of the English engaging in the fight for democracy in Europe. The loss is not just England's but also the continent's, which needs the energy, self-confidence and democratic spirit of the unconquered island.

A three-centuries-old Methuselah – the British regime with its unwritten constitution and supposed parliamentary sovereignty – is now being backed to the hilt by Theresa May's premiership. Her Brexit Britishness is based on a presumption that Brexit will restore the British constitution. For she has to draw on all the absolutist resources of that constitution to impose what she claims is 'the will of the people'. This is ironic, because the constitution has developed since 1688 to ensure that the people are kept at arm's length from direct influence. Indeed, May's Brexit can be seen as an attempt to bury the people as an active force by restoring what she thinks was the old form of authority. After a decade and a half of democratic reforms that she describes as 'drift', the prime minister seeks a return to traditional elective dictatorship and the Union. She is not building on the democratic upsurge of the referendum vote to ensure more and better public involvement. Her aim is to close down 'the people' as an active force. 'No second referendum' was a pledge in May's personal manifesto when she put herself forward to be the new leader of her party, just days after the referendum result, which she accepted. She offers the old normal: government by an honest elite that the people can now trust. However, the constitutional foundations on which she is building her strategy are unlikely to take the strain.

The Scots as well as the once-dominant Protestant community in Northern Ireland were conscious allies with the English in a joint British empire. Its expansive influence and opportunities allowed the smaller nations to breathe for themselves because the Britain they shared was never on its own – was never just Britain. To preserve the British state in isolation and make a virtue of it, which is what 'Brexit means Brexit' means, if it means anything, is hardly a return to the old normal.

This takes us to a hard but essential part of the argument. It is difficult because Brexit poses difficult issues, and we must shake off the jocular, philistine, public-relations superficiality of a ruling political-media caste that thinks winging it is a sign of being smart. Theresa May is right in one respect: this is 'serious'. In this respect if no other she has raised the bar. To get serious means to get a grip on the constitution.

Here I want to address one paragraph to those on the left. Why is it that the left always loses and the right wins? Because the left is not interested in constitutions. The left generally prefers the tangible to the intangible; it thinks that policy outcomes matter more than what it regards as abstract, fancy talk. In this fundamental way, the left is wrong. The intangible shapes the world and persists, and meanwhile the left loses. Of course, feudalism has feudal kingdoms and industrial capitalism, bourgeois regimes. In this sense, the mode of production determines the political and constitutional form. Capitalism needs property rights, and once it gets going it will destroy feudal restraints.

But we live out our lives within a mode of production – our lives do not stretch across epochal transitions. Even then the outcome takes a legal form. Those who set the rules win the day, and tomorrow as well. This is something that ruling classes understand. Wake up and smell the constitutional coffee!

Indeed, the whole of English society needs to reawaken a passion for constitutional culture. One of the shocking aspects of the referendum was the absence of serious public engagement with the great issues that were bandied around, such as parliamentary sovereignty, the European Court of Justice or human rights, let alone taking back control. The reason was embarrassment. We no longer know how to talk about these questions in public, or what level of understanding can be assumed. Yet from the Levellers to the late Victorians the constitution was a matter of intense debate, concern and relevance. It was a measure of England's self-belief – while Scotland had its own tradition going back to the 1320 declaration of Arbroath. The constitution mattered and was considered by many as the reason for England's imperial supremacy. Coleridge wrote an influential book about it, *On the Constitution of the Church and State*, in 1830. He gave Hegelian depth to Burke's notion that to conserve itself a state needs the means to change, and he set out an influential argument for the balance of harmony, alteration and cultivation.[1] Can you imagine an English poet today writing a full-length volume on the constitution? In 1864 Gladstone shocked the Victorian public when he announced his conversion to voting reform. He did so by telling the House of Commons: 'every man who is not presumably incapacitated … is morally entitled to come within the pale of the constitution.'[2] It was regarded as an important declaration. No Victorian would have dreamt of saying, 'We don't have a constitution', a phrase you can often see in newspapers today. Patently the country had and still has a very distinct one. Our predecessors were fully alert to the fact that the country's constitution was an active force in and on their society. They well understood that they lived within its pale.

In the last century, this active culture shrivelled. Ferdinand Mount points a finger at Ivor Jennings, whose influential *The Law and the Constitution* of 1933 turned the whole thing into a machinery of Fabian administration. A view adopted by Labour intellectuals like Harold Laski, who advocated the constitution's capacity to impose working-class interests through administrative means, and therefore opposed codification.[3] This Fabian vision of government as administration extinguished popular interest, as it was virtually designed to do. And Britain's constitutional culture withered.

So we need to start with first principles to establish why our constitution matters to all of us and is not a Fabian plaything. In a sentence, a constitution sets out the rules for how a society's rules are made or changed. Every country has one, whether it is written down in one place, or many, or not at all. And all constitutions do three things.

First, they establish the authority that different centres of power have, including with respect to each other. Can the upper chamber frustrate the lower? What is local government permitted to do? What authority do judges have over the legislature? This is where the famous separation of powers comes in, or, in the case of the UK, does not come in because they are fused: between the executive (the government and civil service), the legislature (that makes laws but does not administer them) and the judiciary (which adjudicates what is lawful when this is disputed). The constitutional definition of powers includes how the constitution itself can be changed and therefore how flexible it is.

Second, all constitutions define the powers and rights of citizens, in the UK's case, citizen-subjects. Do individuals have the right to vote, to assemble, to free speech, to property, to equal treatment? How are such rights protected? Can the executive imprison us or invade our liberty through surveillance without cause? If not, how must it establish due cause? Crucially, how do citizens give their consent to such changes in the constitution?

In addition to rights and powers, all constitutions express the aspirations of their society: their sense of purpose or direction. This might be to be non-racist (South Africa), to be Islamic (Iran), or to be liberal and not fascist (Germany), or universal (France). Aspiration need not be part of the main constitutional text, thus 'Life, Liberty and the pursuit of Happiness', the aspiration of the US constitution, is in the Declaration of Independence. Historically, England–Britain, felt it had no need of vulgar aspiration when, after all, everyone else aspired to be like us.

You can see immediately that because constitutions are about the way a whole society relates to itself in terms of aspiration, powers, rights, obligations and citizenship, they are living things. How a constitution is lived is *always* more important than what is written down. A constitution can be a defining, codified document; but the way people, and especially people with power, define their constitution is always more important than the way the constitution defines the country. We can see this in the United States today. Every child pledges allegiance to its constitution. Nonetheless, as Mark Danner writes, 'Ours is famously said to be a government of laws, not of men, and yet we find in the Age of Trump that the laws depend on men and women …'[4] The crucial point, however, about moving to a written constitution is that it enables citizens to engage with how their country is run.

The arbitrary nature of the referendum seems to be shifting opinion in favour of finally writing down our own. But the classic British response to having a written constitution has been either it won't make any difference, or we don't want to be like the USA. The latter illustrates a long-standing ignorance of the issue combined with awareness of America. This leads people to think that if Britain adopts a written constitution it will be like America's, which is not the case at all. The US has one of the oldest, most rigid constitutions, and is in effect racist in the composition of the Senate. It has politicised the Supreme Court, which in turn has ruled that money is voice and therefore no limitation can be placed on indirect financial donations for politicians, reinforcing the corruption of the political system by big money. The American example is not what it means to have a written constitution. On the contrary, there are over 150 constitutions in the world, including the Swedish constitution that dates to 1810 and is admirably flexible, or the German Basic Law that British lawyers helped to draft. An attractive, bespoke constitution right for our time, with built-in flexibility, is easy to imagine. But not easy to achieve.

The heart of the issue is the need for a spirit of citizenship and its claim of ownership: of being able to say with confidence and politically: 'This is my country'. Once, when a group of students were being taken round the Cabinet offices, one asked: 'What is our constitution?' The reply was: 'It's something we make up as we go along.' No doubt meant with a touch of flippancy, it was also revealing. The mandarin 'we' was not the 'we' of 'We, the people'. Until England has a democratic constitution grounding sovereignty in its citizens, we will live within one owned and controlled by the elite. A shift in ownership in terms of the legal piece of paper may be a mere beginning of taking possession, but such a claim to ownership is essential.

The English vote for Brexit rejected a system that closed them out, misgoverned and took advantage of them, which they mistakenly blamed on the EU. It also sent a message that many voters want democracy as well as economic justice. The Leave campaign locked onto this with its slogan 'Take back control'. How can you be in control if there is no document of ownership for the house you live in? Brexit was a displaced demand for our own constitution.

From the late 1980s, when I argued with politicians and political journalists about the need for a democratic constitution, the old saw was wheeled out: 'If it ain't broke, don't fix it.' New Labour came along and really did break it – with extraordinary negligence – and declined to fix it. An unwinding of the constitution has followed, a breakdown that resulted in Brexit.

If this is the case, however, it should not be just me who is saying so. Britain's rulers have shown exceptional foresight in sensing the need to pre-empt change that might overthrow their interests, especially since the Great Reform Act of 1832, which was explicitly and successfully passed as a preventative measure. The UK's elites are deeply committed to a united Britain and its world standing. If I am right about its breakdown, some of them would have sensed this too. At least one of them has. Just as CERN's identification of a Higgs boson confirmed the latest theory of particle physics, so Robert Michael James Gascoyne-Cecil, 7th Marquess of Salisbury, corroborates my analysis from his distinguished, different, point of view.

Many of Robert Salisbury's forebears have played a role in high politics since the sixteenth century, when his family's founder, William Cecil, was adviser to Elizabeth I, and his son to both Elizabeth and then James I. The 3rd Marquess of Salisbury was prime minister three times between 1885 and 1902. Robert Salisbury himself was Conservative leader of the Lords until 2001. Dedicated to the Union and with strong links to Scotland, after the 2014 referendum he took the long view and concluded Scottish independence is inevitable unless pre-emptive action gains the positive commitment of a clear majority of the Scottish people to a British union. On 1 March 2015, he wrote in the *Sunday Times*: 'we Tories believe only in necessary evolutionary change. However, once in several centuries, the true Tory must accept that the nation demands more radical solutions if it is to survive. This is one of those times'.[5] Few, if any, have the family lineage to crack a joke involving several centuries, but he is shrewd as well as good-humoured. He announced the creation of a cross-party Constitutional Reform Group, which has drafted a fully worked out new Act of Union.[6] Its core proposal is that a parliament of England replaces the House of Commons and an all-British elected chamber replaces the House of Lords, to become the House of the Union. Once passed, the Act would only come into force if endorsed by all four nations in their own referendums. The outcome would be a positive expression of a United Kingdom identity, within the framework of a shared union, legitimised by popular consent. Salisbury sees how England must discard Anglo-Britain and become itself, for its union to survive, now that Scotland has a parliament. Coming from a family that benefited from Henry VIII's break from Europe, he naturally opposed membership of the EU and argues that:

> Brexit is an opportunity for the country to renew itself.
> For such a renewal to have a chance of working, we need a
> constitution that works.[7]

Salisbury's excellent judgement shows why the right wins. He does
not flinch from the new national forces resurgent across the UK.
He sees they must be expressed not suppressed for the preservation
of the ruling order. He grasps why this means they must have their
own *constitutional* form, for the national question is a constitutional
question. He sees, therefore, that far-reaching reform is essential to
ensure his cause: the class-rule of conservatives. He describes this
as the country renewing itself thanks to Brexit. I want a different
renewal: an England in which the heirs to the Levellers can succeed.
Being pre-socialist, they fully understood the need to express their
politics in a constitutional form. Where Salisbury and I agree is that
the current constitution no longer works. Theresa May says it must
be made to work, as she intensifies her autocratic deployment of its
centralised powers. This is likely to fail within a decade. Already,
Salisbury has put in place his plan-B. Can the left do the same? To
see why it should, I will prove the constitution is broken, and look at
who broke it and how. Brexit can be seen as the wrong answer to the
right question that follows from this breakdown – namely: how can
England be governed differently?

# 16

# The Discombobulated Constitution

When it comes to the constitution, I must declare an interest. I coordinated the Charter 88 campaign for a democratic written constitution that influenced New Labour's thinking. This culminated in a Charter 88 lecture given by the then Labour leader John Smith, who had succeeded Neil Kinnock after Labour lost the 1992 election. Smith was to die of a heart attack two years later. In his lecture, he committed Labour to the reform agenda that was implemented at the end of the decade. Tony Blair, who was Smith's shadow home secretary at the time, participated in the drafting. In addition, Smith also unified the reforms he promised and proposed a 'new constitutional settlement'. This was a cautious refusal to commit to the written constitution that Charter 88 campaigned for, but the direction was clear: changes of such a far-reaching nature needed to be integrated into a purposive, coherent programme that would put parliament on a new democratic footing.

At the beginning of 2017 I attended the launch party for *openDemocracy*'s new openJustice section and found myself next to Charlie Falconer, who became Blair's lord chancellor in 2005. He asked me what I thought now. I said that if New Labour had delivered the new constitutional settlement that John Smith proposed, instead of the country having to endure its current fragmentation and a half-reformed House of Lords, we would have a Britain we could believe in and would not have voted for Brexit. He responded, with the full force of New Labour's intellectual and political aptitude: 'Bollocks.' I don't give up easily. Falconer would be a valuable ally. We exchanged emails. I wrote in a friendly way saying:

> The contrast with Scotland shows what I mean. It did have a new settlement, reinforced, indeed, by the later independence referendum. They are confident that their sovereignty resides in the people not 'the Crown in Parliament' and this self-belief meant they were far more willing and able to share powers with Europe without feeling unduly threatened.

I did not hear back.

I'll expand the discussion I did not have with Falconer to summarise what has now gone wrong. After 1997, there was a historic opportunity to reform the UK's constitution as a whole, when New Labour came to power. The party's manifesto committed it to a raft of significant changes: a Scottish parliament, a Welsh assembly and a London mayor, all reliant on referendums to approve them; a Human Rights Act, freedom of information and ridding the Lords of hereditary peers. These went ahead and were far-reaching: the territorial integrity, the legal culture, the claims of citizens, the accountability of the civil service were all challenged in fundamental ways. Together, the New Labour package broke the *coherence* of the ancient, informal constitution. But despite strong arguments, no new settlement was proposed to replace it. Crucially, Blair refused to back a proportional voting system for the House of Commons, necessary for a European-style polity when this could have been achieved.

The opportunity for a new settlement that would have associated the new national parliaments with the British constitution was lost. Of course, it would have constrained Blair's power as premier. That was the point. Since then, the administration continues, taxes are raised, government proceeds and the security services are well funded. But the system of British government, once famous for its supreme self-confidence, has become a zone of fragmenting reforms. This contributed to the conditions for Brexit because it reinforced the country's underlying insecurity. As a multinational entity, Britain cannot but be threatened by the EU, an even larger one, if Britain is seeking to preserve its constitution, while the bigger European Union is extending its. Had New Labour adopted a written constitution that empowered a UK constitutional court, which like Germany's could rule on the democratic validity of the EU's policies, British voters would not have felt so threatened by sharing sovereignty within the EU.

Instead, the incoherence of the British constitution generated a sense of vulnerability and defensiveness, especially for the English who had seen the old one dismantled around them as Scotland, Wales and London gained their own institutions, and even the once violent backwater of Northern Ireland got its Good Friday Agreement and visits from Bill Clinton.

What could have taken place with democratic leadership at the cusp of the new century, when the economy was growing, the Tories were disabled, there was energy for change, and Labour's reforms were fresh and needed a coherent destination, cannot be achieved now by a central initiative in the way Robert Salisbury advocates. The UK is too divided territorially, the economy is on a knife-edge, inequality is explosive. Brexit did not just emerge from a crisis of identity across the UK. The crisis of identity is also a crisis in reality: the character of British rule laid down in 1688 and 1707, and the commanding institutions it created, are approaching termination. I will now look at three of these: the Cabinet, the Commons and the Lords, and then some of the institutional detritus such as the Privy Council. Out of their weakness springs an increasingly unharnessed executive power permitting the premier to become presidential in all but name.

## Cabinet government

In the opening chapter of Walter Bagehot's *The English Constitution*, published in 1867, he makes his famous distinction between the dignified and the efficient parts of the way the country is governed. The chapter is devoted to the Cabinet, which, Bagehot argues, is the heart of the efficient machine of the country's unique system of government. The monarchy and public flimflam are merely a decorative curtain behind which the real business of government is conducted. For him, the English constitution's uniqueness lies in 'the nearly complete fusion of executive and legislative powers ... The connecting link is *the cabinet*. By that new word we mean a committee of the legislative body selected to be the executive body'.[1]

A hundred and thirty years later, in 1997, Tony Blair implemented a reform as radical and far-reaching as any of his other changes to the way Britain is run. In his first Cabinet meeting, two ministers posed questions they thought relevant for the new government. Afterwards, an angry Blair demanded an explanation. 'We have cabinet government,' he was told. But his instructions were: 'From now on I want to know in advance about anything Ministers want to bring up.'[2] Every department of state was informed that henceforth no minister could raise or introduce a topic in a Cabinet meeting without the prior agreement of the prime minister's office. This decision 'brought effective Cabinet government to an end', Robin Butler explained to me. From that point on, Cabinet meetings became gatherings for the mere presentation of decisions, not the making of them. The Cabinet ceased to be a committee with collective responsibility for the final determination of policy to be submitted to parliament, or even a check on the executive.

There has not been any serious discussion or analysis of this historic episode that I know of, except in Tom Bower's biography of Blair.[3] He underplays its constitutional significance, since his focus is on Blair's centralisation of power as he swept aside the old order. Robin Butler, who was the Cabinet secretary and head of the civil service at the time, was aware of its consequences when he later, after his retirement, wrote an important report into the decision-making that led to the Iraqi war.[4] Responding to it, Peter Hennessy was appalled: 'If the full cabinet will not take on a dominant prime minister in full cry, there is no other part of the system of government that can compensate for such supineness.'[5] The Cabinet could not have done this because it had already been severed at the knees. With its members banned from raising anything that was not already permitted, there is nothing to stop a dominant prime minister. As an authoritative summary of the New Labour period put it, the 'fiction' is maintained but 'there is no longer any real attempt to achieve collective responsibility'.[6]

The centralisation was deliberate. In 1997, Jonathan Powell, Blair's chief of staff, had warned before they got to office that: 'You may see a change from a feudal system of barons to a more Napoleonic system'.[7] The informal ministerial culture of collective responsibility was late nineteenth-century but it was not feudal. It developed as a way of preventing dictatorship and all the arbitrary disasters that accompany it. Then, after the 2001 election, Blair implemented a 'formalised destruction of the Cabinet system' and brought the 'key officials and their staff on foreign affairs, defence and the European Union' into 10 Downing Street so that they ceased to 'serve the Cabinet as a whole'. These changes, hugely important, were introduced without any parliamentary authority or assessment. I'm quoting from an angry analysis by David Owen, who had been foreign secretary in the previous Labour government. Drawing on the Chilcot Report, he concludes that the Iraq war would not have happened if the traditional circulation of papers had taken place. A system built to stop Napoleons was dismantled. Parliament did not protest. The Iraq war followed and became a variation of the march on Moscow. Owen considers that Blair should be impeached.[8]

Cabinet government had turned into prime ministerial government after 1945, as the party system professionalised politics. Even so, it remained a weighty body capable, even under Mrs Thatcher, of stormy debates and argument – despite her authoritarian style and wilfulness. It was only dispatched by Blair with such ease and finality because new forms of political machine had arisen, based on public relations and media messaging, to develop policy and command the public's vote.

Perhaps the final blow was David Cameron's creation of the coalition government with the Lib Dems headed by Nick Clegg. They and their two deputies formed the Quad that decided 'all major matters of policy'.[9] The *coup de grâce*, which told us that the Cabinet itself has now become part of the decorative arrangements of the British constitution, came in December 2012. The Queen was invited to attend. 'Cameron opened the meeting by saying it was the first time a monarch had attended a full cabinet since George III in 1781.'

There were good reasons for that monarch's expulsion. George III had insisted on a disastrous war against the American colonies. The monarch was henceforth excluded from direct political influence. Instead, as the personal popularity of the monarchy grew, it became a popular, protective shield for the British state. It may have been dignified rather than efficient, but it gained and retained the public loyalty vital for an elite system. To preserve this gift, the monarchy had in turn to be shielded from party politics. It became essential to ensure that the Crown was not openly associated with decision-making, to keep it above the fray. To suggest that the monarch attend the Cabinet itself would have been shocking. Now, however, the Cabinet is so harmless it can do the Queen no harm. Apparently, she was interested in a presentation on the war in Afghanistan. But as Patrick Wintour shrewdly noted in the *Guardian*, 'In a sign that cabinet is no longer the true epicentre of decision-making it was not until a meeting in the afternoon of the national security council that ministers agreed a 4,000-troop drawdown next year in Afghanistan.'[10]

What was once the effective core of the British constitution – which defined the collective nature of its executive power – has been taken over by the prime minister's office, serviced by the security state. Britain now suffers from a form of presidential rule without effective checks. The culmination of Blair's hijacking of the Cabinet came with the composition of the letter to trigger Article 50. A discussion about whether to include a reference to Britain's military contribution to European security and implicitly threaten its withdrawal if the EU failed to agree terms was discussed in a Cabinet committee. It agreed that on this front Britain had 'a strong hand.'[11] The letter itself, the most important and much planned communication about the country's future – its tone, balance and detail – was then decided in private. The Chancellor of the Exchequer was asked the humiliating question on the BBC's morning *Today* programme as to whether he had been shown the letter before it went to the President of the EU's Council of Ministers. The Cabinet was gathered on the morning of Wednesday 29 April 2017, to receive a report on its contents before it was delivered by hand in Brussels. But the letter itself had already been signed and dispatched.

The image of the signing was presidential. Theresa May sat at the Cabinet table alone. In place of the Cabinet Ministers who once represented the collective wisdom and foolishness of British rule, but at least did so together to show that we did not suffer dictators or autocrats like lesser nations, there was a flag. Flags are for display! Now one stood hanging sinister and still in the Cabinet room itself when the country had always been above that sort of thing – and for · a very good reason. It was not just the end of Cabinet government, Great Britain had become Freedonia.

## Commons and Lords

Now that the Cabinet has bitten the dust, what about parliament? Three judges dissented from the majority of their colleagues in the Supreme Court case which ruled that parliament must decide if the government can trigger Article 50 to start the UK's formal exit from the EU. Their minority argument can be crudely summed up as follows. Parliament is sovereign, and therefore it is not for us judges to tell it what to do; if it wants to vote on triggering Article 50, then parliament has the power to insist on this and order the government to propose the necessary legislation. The three judges did not persuade their colleagues. In one way, it is a pity that the Supreme Court did not rule that it was *up to parliament itself* to decide whether triggering Article 50 was a matter for parliament. Then we would have seen what MPs are made of. Except that we know. The prime minister had made it clear that if a motion had proposed an act of parliament was necessary, the government whips would have ensured it was defeated. The House of Commons is now a plaything of the executive.

The derisory role of the Commons needs to be distinguished from MPs personally, who are often even more despairing of it than members of the public, as they must live with it every day. One of them, Caroline Lucas, published a book on becoming an MP and her strategy for change. She experienced the collapse in public trust in the Commons and understood why – 'The culture of Parliament is decrepit.'[12] When the UK was about to enter the then Common Market in 1972, there were six days of debate in the Commons. Before John Major set out for EU Maastricht Treaty negotiations in 1992, where he got an opt-out for the UK from the single currency, there were two days of debate in the Commons. But there was no debate at all in 2016 before Cameron set off on his negotiations.

When he came back there was just a short question-and-answer session that he managed quite easily. The Scottish parliament both debated and then voted on the agreement Cameron made in Brussels in which the other twenty-seven member states agreed that 'ever closer union of the peoples of Europe' would not apply to the UK. The Westminster parliament did not. There was a short backbenchers' debate on sovereignty and, the year before, on 9 June 2015, a one-day debate on the EU Referendum Bill, much of which concerned whether sixteen-year-olds should have the right to vote and other matters of its procedures. The decision to have a referendum was taken as a matter of party policy and did not go to the coalition Cabinet. When the voters decided to leave the EU, the government decided that parliament should not be asked to authorise the implementation of the referendum. Only when the courts ruled that this was illegal, and the government had to get parliament's agreement, there was a debate and a vote. If this is the restoration of democracy, give me the EU!

The reputation of the Commons had anyway been permanently damaged by the expenses scandal of 2009 – when the Freedom of Information Act led to the sale of an unredacted disk of all MPs' claims. Many were grotesque – David Cameron had charged the nation for planting wisteria against his new constituency home, and was made to pay the money back – some were criminal. Many MPs had flipped their homes, legally, to take advantage of expenses. The public was aghast. Politics was dirtied, thanks to the *Daily Telegraph*, which acquired the disk. Its owners are the reclusive Barclay brothers, who live in the tax-light Channel Islands, make full use of tax havens and made part of their initial fortune from casinos.

The damage was twofold. Public service itself was caricatured as a racket. This reinforced the dominant and corrupting argument of the age of globalisation, that there is no escape from market greed. I believe it is possible to reverse this. In addition, the central political institution representing democratic Britain, the Commons itself, was detached from public allegiance and loyalty – to the delight of media moguls and all those whose aim is to promote competitive individualism, otherwise known as rule by the few. This loss is irreparable. 'I have always thought that to sit in the British parliament should be the highest object of ambition ... To serve one's country without pay is the grandest work a man can do,' Trollope wrote, explaining why he tried to become an MP in 1868 (he failed).[13] Accompanying the wealth and ruthlessness of the imperial kingdom was a strong sense of civic virtue and the public good. This culture has now been trashed. David Marquand has set down a sustained, scholarly account of the villainy in *Mammon's Kingdom*.[14] For this broken elite system to return to public values is impossible. There could be a revival of what Trollope called his 'conservative-liberalism', but no value system will be created by his beloved British parliament, which has surrendered itself to the party system and the executive.

Proof lies in the red as opposed to green leather half of the Houses of Parliament, the Lords. Or rather, the so-called Lords. For, apart from ninety-two peers who are its only elected members – as they are voted for by the wider aristocracy – it no longer contains hereditary aristocrats. In February 2015, the Channel 4 programme *Dispatches* reported on a sting operation carried out on the Tory MP Malcolm Rifkind and the Labour MP Jack Straw. Both expressed interest in becoming well-paid consultants. Straw, who had worked for Blair as home secretary and then foreign secretary, and for Gordon Brown as lord chancellor, was hoping to become a member of the House of Lords. If he did, he explained, it would be easier: 'The rules there are different and plenty of people have commercial interests there ... I'll be able to help you more.'[15] The rules say that peers should not seek to profit from their role, but membership pays an attendance fee of just £300 a day. Straw said his commercial rate is £5,000 a day. His fellow MPs found he had done nothing wrong. What he said about the Lords is true. In effect, with respect to commercial legislation it is for sale.

At least one half of parliament is a scam. The 2012 Health and Social Care Bill opened up the NHS to commercial companies, as a step towards its marketisation. The Social Investigations team, headed by Andrew Robertson, calculated that, '1 in 4 Conservative Peers have financial interests in companies involved in private healthcare. 1 in 6 Labour Peers. 1 in 6 Crossbench Peers and 1 in 10 Liberal Democratic Peers.'[16] What would received opinion be about a developing country that filled one half of its legislature with business friends and political cronies of the ruling parties and had them dress up in tribal costume once a year, while the rest of the time they gave warm welcome to laws that opened up the state to the businesses and consultancies that pay them? Welcome to late Britain.

There have been many promises to 'reform the Lords' over the last thirty years. Doing so looks easy. The problem is that it is not a ludicrous appendage that can be easily altered. It is one half of parliament. It initiates a lot of legislation and must pass everything. Its reform means either it is replaced by an elected upper chamber, that becomes a rival to the Commons, or it is recreated in some other way to do a different kind of job. In which case the Commons will have to take on the detail of legislation much more seriously. This would then strengthen MPs vis-à-vis the executive and make government harder. No prime minister will endorse it. The executive benefits from the corrupt weakness of the set-up. The government can whip and control the Commons, leaving the hard graft of legislative scrutiny to the Lords. Should they want to change something, it is less of an embarrassment if done by expert peers. If they want to ram it through, they have the democratic high ground and can ignore the Lords. With the Commons and Lords twinned together in this way, the executive exercises its 'elected dictatorship' and the undemocratic mixture taints all politics and politicians, contributing to the contempt for 'the lot of them' expressed in the vote for Brexit.

This contempt is not an ignorant prejudice. Parliament institutionalises the corruption of politics and its subordination to financial interests. The latest, most systematic analysis is Martin Williams's 300-page account of his research into *Parliament Ltd.*[17] He even shows how MPs can cover up their smaller investments (you cannot publish in a book or newspaper the names of shareholders because to request the information from companies for this supposedly publicly listed information – which anyone can do – you must provide the name *and address* of anyone you intend to disclose it to. As you cannot know this of your readers, publishing them means you can be sent to jail for two years). Peerages are sold. Banks and the arms industry have acquired direct and indirect influence in the Commons and the Lords. Cosy business links are covered up systematically by MPs and Peers keen to insist on their right to govern themselves as a sign of their integrity and importance. Through a wealth of examples focused on parliament, Williams's confirms its role in a wider system of graft described in studies by Richard Brooks, Owen Jones, David Whyte, James Meek and others.[18] It is not that all MPs are corrupt, many are not. Some like Margaret Hodge try to scourge malfeasance. The scandal is that the frequent scandals concerning both houses of parliament are not scandals at all, they are normal, and they function to weaken the peoples' representatives and strengthen the executive.

## From the Privy Council to local power

Other institutions are losing their resonance too. The briefest survey of some illustrates the incoherence. For example, the Privy Council is, 'The oldest institution of government in the world'.[19] It is the Queen's secret council that meets every month and holds the elite's reserve power. In an extreme emergency, those who rule the United *Kingdom* can fall back on the absolutism preserved by it. Technically the Cabinet is merely an executive subcommittee of the Privy Council. You cannot be leader of the opposition without being recruited, which demands that you kneel and brush the Queen's hand with your lips. Labour's stubborn Jeremy Corbyn is a republican and it is not clear if he submitted to this ritual humiliation. To that extent, it still retains its privacy. All Cabinet ministers are made members and become 'Right Honourable' for life. But it is the opposite of a collective body. No one has the right to attend meetings, or even to know if they are taking place. The quorum is three. Yet it issues the orders of the realm. How handy is that? Seeking a way to regulate the press while bypassing parliament, Cameron turned to the Privy Council. Perhaps this will drag a pre-democratic institution into the light.

The best defence against crumbing institutions at the centre is to have confident decentralised ones that know their own minds and can raise their own revenues. Instead:

> England is very unusual ... in having become one of the biggest centralised administrative units in the world, and managing this is a perennial, and perhaps insoluble, contemporary political problem ... our public spending controlled from the centre is roughly twice that in France, Japan and Italy, and more than three times that in Germany.

Robert Tombs makes this point in the conclusion to his encyclopedic history of the English.[20] His observation quantifies an enduring weakness in English politics. The air is filled with issues and problems that remote ministers cannot resolve, while funding does not go to those who could solve them. The British state learned to privatise. It sold houses and shares to individuals and the country's utilities to foreign buyers. French and German nationalised providers acquired power and train services, a process now expanded in 2016 by the sale of most of the national grid of gas pipelines to China and Qatar. But the state has not learnt how to democratise control over budgets to England's local government and bitterly resents having done so to Scotland and Wales. The absence of credible and effective intermediate government leaves a country exposed to demagogic populism.

One way of witnessing the strain within the UK's unresolved democratisation is the Oath or Affirmation of Allegiance and Pledge of Loyalty for those becoming British.[21]

I swear by almighty God (or, I sincerely and truly declare and affirm) that on becoming a British citizen, I will be faithful and bear true allegiance to Her Majesty Queen Elizabeth the Second, her Heirs and Successors, according to law.

Is this citizenship or is it subjecthood – an oath to join a democracy or an absolutist state? The answer is both. Traditionally the oath was sworn in private to a solicitor. Labour introduced public ceremonies in 2004. I do not scorn the holding of a ceremony: to bring someone into a political community is an important moment both for them and for those they join. But the idea of the ceremony was taken from the United States and, typically, New Labour was seeking the emotion of democratic fealty without the substance of codified checks and balances that, based on popular sovereignty, make a citizen a citizen.

The UK's constitution is not working as a whole. This is different from, if linked to, examples of failure, corruption, stupidity or very bad government. Since 1996, initially under Stuart Weir and David Beetham and now under the direction of the LSE's Patrick Dunleavy, *The Democratic Audit* has been tracking democracy and government in Britain and comparing it with international norms.[22] Overall, it is an unhappy record. But it does not follow *necessarily* that the system is failing. All kinds of crimes, violations and inequities can occur within a society that is basically healthy.

What *is* breaking down in Britain is the constitution as a system of representation that generates loyalty and belief and provides effective voice for its citizens, including oppositional voices. The Commons was once virtually worshipped as the British nation at prayer. The Cabinet was lauded as the centre where executive and legislative power fused. The prime minister was the leading source of power in the land, but never a dictator, always at the head of a mighty troika of Commons, Lords and Cabinet, which directed an independent civil service who did the heavy lifting of the state. Today, the disintegration of the parts mean each starts to work against the other. A House of Lords that does not even have the legitimacy of the accident of birth objects not to the Commons but to an unchecked Downing Street that has turned the Cabinet into little more than a classroom. Democratic identification with such a farrago is impossible.

Brexit cannot be understood without taking a measure of England's discontent with the way it is governed. But even more important in deciding the referendum's outcome was the feebleness of the Remain campaign, its shallowness and inability to advocate a positive relationship to the EU. This weakness was rooted in its inability to summon up confident belief in the strength of Britain's own institutions – to show how they could hold their own by joining in continental collaboration. London by contrast has a powerful image of a mayor who naturally voiced exactly the kind of positive vibe for the EU that should have marked the whole Remain campaign. The combination of crumbling central institutions and a calamitous absence of any regional ones outside of London meant there were no public forums in England able to inspire a European future for the country. Meanwhile the Leave campaign appealed to save British sovereignty.

# 17

# The Sovereignty of Parliament

If the defining institutions of the United Kingdom's government now seem corrupted and aimless, how about that crucial and distinctive *principle* that distinguishes British rule, the sovereignty of parliament? In the absence of strong institutions, this has become a disguise for elected dictatorship. For decades, many who opposed British membership in the EU talked about 'the loss of sovereignty', often making it sound like a vital fluid. Its origins go back to the absolutist, pre-democratic character of the British state. If it means anything it means the opposite of people taking control, as it stands for a sovereign in control of subjects. Yet it has come to represent the right of British voters to control their own destiny. It is necessary to take it seriously, as the main conceptual justification for Brexit.

As a concept, sovereignty is more fraught than democracy, and the idea of it being 'shared' with the other EU countries is alarming if sovereignty is central to the definition of your state and the legitimacy of your parliament, as it is with the UK. The United Kingdom – the royal moniker is significant – is characterised by 'The absolute sovereignty of the Crown in Parliament'. This was not an abstract idea when the Victorians formulated it in the late nineteenth century. A. V. Dicey's *Law of the Constitution* spelt it out with an authority that was immediately recognised: 'The one fundamental dogma of English constitutional law is the absolute legislative sovereignty or despotism of the King in Parliament.'[1]

The Victorians wanted to clarify how the country's influence actually worked at the high point of its imperial reach, when the

Commons and Lords were referred to as the Imperial Parliament (a term that came into use around 1800 and dropped away after India and Pakistan gained their independence in 1947). Although Great Britain enjoyed a separate legislature, executive and legal system, it never had a formal separation of powers or a paper constitution. Instead, the Imperial Parliament could draw any boundary it decided on the face of the planet or pass any law to which the Queen gave her assent. To be sovereign means to have the final power to decide something. To have absolute sovereignty means the power to decide everything, with no higher authority over you whatsoever. At that point the British ruled most of the world.

The origins of their parliamentary despotism – a collective Leviathan – go back to the seventeenth century. In the civil war, the Levellers argued that a nation should be governed by a republican code – the first time such a proposal was formulated. They were defeated. The victors were property owners who secured their predominance in arrangements that gave them a form of royal power. This was achieved with force. It was neither tolerant nor democratic. But it was comparatively open, flexible and intelligent. Over the next three centuries it retained a shape-shifting energy as it joined together monarchical absolutism, aristocratic privilege and capitalist energy in a new form of rule developed over time: Cabinet government accountable to a parliament of Commons and Lords under the Crown. It created an engine of global conquest that was centralised yet flexible, with informal built-in checks that protected the kingdom from both would-be dictators and, especially, direct democracy. No effort or skill was spared to ensure domestic consent. But this was – and was seen as being – the opposite of popular sovereignty or 'government by the people'.

When, with the 1972 European Community Act, the British parliament agreed that the authority of what was becoming the European Union could legislate, regulate and adjudicate its law across Britain, this was a definite, if partial, historic loss of sovereignty. It will be reversed if Theresa May's version of Brexit is completed. The prime minister has emphasised her aim: 'we will take back control of our laws and bring an end to the jurisdiction of the European Court of Justice in Britain ... Because we will not have truly left the European Union if we are not in control of our own laws.'[2]

Will the cardinal principle of the absolute sovereignty of parliament come back and the British constitution be made intact once more, restored to its pre-1972 condition, as the prime minister believes? The answer is no. Since 1972, in at least three significant ways, thanks to the referendum itself, parliament's own commitment to be lawful and the rise of Scotland, Dicey's organising principle of the British constitution, that parliament has absolute sovereign sway, has been undone. The UK's government still has power; it no longer has principle.

## The Brexit referendum is constitutional dynamite

Cameron assumed that the result would confirm the status quo, and this was what most MPs believed too when they voted to have a referendum – that it would renew public consent to elite rule. Instead, it didn't. After she took over and promised to implement the instruction of the people, Theresa May decided she would proceed to trigger Article 50 using the power of the Royal Prerogative. This is the right of the executive to make international treaties without the involvement of parliament. As accession to the EU was an international treaty, the prime minister claimed she could proceed to undo it by Royal Prerogative. The High Court ruled that because the 1972 Act affected people's domestic rights (for example, with respect to EU laws against discrimination or for safety at work), it could not be regarded as a purely foreign relationship, it was also a matter of domestic law. Therefore it could only be undone by another act of parliament.[3] In response, the minister for Brexit, David Davis, was unusually incoherent, saying: 'Parliament is sovereign, has been sovereign, but of course the people are sovereign.' And the government appealed to the Supreme Court, which ruled by eight to three that the High Court was right. An Act was necessary. This was then passed by the House of Commons, giving the government the go-ahead to activate Article 50. Members from each of the two biggest parties gave remarkably similar justifications for their vote. They had voted Remain in the referendum; they thought it was wrong to Leave; but felt they must accept the outcome of the referendum.

These MPs argued that they had to subordinate their judgement on this vital matter to the majority view in the referendum's ballot. The plebiscite's undoubted democratic nature meant it had a greater authority than their own. The result is that a new sovereign, 'The People', has arisen and is now regarded as senior to the old one: Parliament. Unless 'The People' changes its mind, the Commons and Lords – both with Remain majorities – must obey and vote to leave the EU. In fact and in spirit the referendum drove a stake through the heart of parliament's absolute sovereignty. Technically, this has been the case since the first use of a referendum in 1975. But 2016 was the first time this was put to the test, when the outcome was the opposite to the declared views of a majority of MPs. The obvious danger is that the new sovereign can be summoned up in an ad hoc way to decide arbitrary issues. What if a referendum was held on whether or not to expel immigrants after a party won a majority with this commitment? A codified constitution is now needed to secure some principles and set down the nature and basis of popular sovereignty, now its reality exists.

The issue is not about MPs failing to act in the spirit of Edmund Burke, who claimed members of parliament should decide issues for themselves and not according to the views of their electors. The party system has long put paid to that notion of MPs following their personal judgement of the merit of an issue. Rather, the referendum ended the historic representative character of parliamentary politics as a whole. The Commons became a mere vehicle for a direct decision of the public.

The people are not yet sovereign. Britain is not a modern democracy. But the people now *can be* sovereign and impose their will, and in the case of Brexit are apparently doing so. The country is no longer ruled by the exclusive might of parliamentary absolutism.

Parliament's sovereignty has now been shared in a way that cannot be reversed.

## The primacy of the rule of law

This story is entertaining if technical and shows what a mess the constitution is in. In 2005 the Blair government passed the Constitutional Reform Act. It removed the law lords from the House of Lords and created the Supreme Court and altered the role of the lord chancellor. Apparently under pressure from the judiciary, which disliked and perhaps feared Blair's arbitrary methods, the Act opens with: '1. The Rule of Law. This Act does not adversely affect— (a) the existing constitutional principle of the rule of law'.[4] It follows that parliament has put itself under the *constitutional principle* of the rule of law. Therefore, if parliament does something unlawful, the courts can strike it down. For example, if parliament approves secret courts where the accused cannot hear the evidence against them, or seeks to deprive, say, asylum seekers of the right to appeal against an arbitrary process, then depending how it is done this could breach fundamental Magna Carta rights that none can be detained without due process. Such rights are the foundation of the rule of law and such legislation could be found unconstitutional. A parallel example is the case brought by John Jackson on behalf of the Countryside Alliance against the Hunting Act, saying that the Parliament Act of 1949 on which it is based was invalid. The claim was rejected, but probably 'the very fact that the law lords adjudicated on the validity of the Hunting Act establishes their jurisdiction'.[5]

The issue greatly agitated the late Tom Bingham, a senior law lord, whose book published in 2010, *The Rule of Law*, ends by rebuking one judge in the Hunting Act case for claiming that judges can qualify the supremacy of parliament if they so decide. Bingham feared that parliament might indeed 'infringe the rule of law'. Not least because 'our constitutional settlement has become unbalanced', exacerbated by the way 'the last ten or twelve years have seen a degree of constitutional change not experienced for centuries'. However, in Bingham's view, only 'the British people, properly informed' should rectify matters, not 'unelected judges'.[6]

As it is, the contradiction remains unrectified. The judges can now decide to overrule parliament, if parliament acts in a way judges deem unlawful, because parliament itself has passed into legislation the fact that there is a second constitutional principle superior to that of the supremacy of parliament. The degeneration of the UK's constitutional culture means that most of those who are supposedly politically literate, many MPs for example, are unaware of this contradiction, even though it lies at the heart of their legitimacy. Those who are aware just hope it will not become an issue. Some say it does not really undermine parliament's supremacy as it could revoke this part of the 2005 Act, although it is hard to imagine parliament explicitly giving itself the power to act unlawfully (and if it did, this would itself be tested in the Supreme Court). The unease among authoritative experts seeps into the wider consciousness. Without realising quite why, many feel that something fishy is going on behind all the fine talk of the sovereignty of parliament. They are right.

## Scotland

The Scotland Act of 2016 opens by stating:

> The Scottish Parliament and the Scottish Government are a permanent part of the United Kingdom's constitutional arrangements ... it is declared that the Scottish Parliament and the Scottish Government are not to be abolished except on the basis of a decision of the people of Scotland voting in a referendum.

This strange piece of legislation came about thanks to the 'Vow' that the three main Westminster party leaders made to ensure the Scots did not vote for independence in the 2014 Scottish referendum. The House of Lords Constitution Committee strongly objected to the wording:

> It is a fundamental principle of the UK constitution that Parliament is sovereign and that no Parliament may bind its successors ... we are concerned that these provisions, as

currently worded, risk introducing uncertainty concerning
the absolute nature of parliamentary sovereignty where there
should be none.[7]

The committee's objection was ignored. The 'uncertainty' has been
built into law. That is to say, it is no longer certain that Parliament
applies its absolute sovereignty in this instance. The right of prior
popular consent to fundamental change in Scotland is now part of
the British constitution.

Something more important has taken place in Scotland than the
bleak prose of legislation about a possible future. The Victorians
who developed the concept of sovereignty wanted to know how
the world *actually worked*. It might be possible for parliament to
abolish, say, the office of the mayor of London, in the way that
Thatcher abolished the Greater London Council when it was led
by Ken Livingstone in the 1980s. But Scotland is not a municipal
authority, it is a country. It can gather its own taxes and administer
its affairs. If the British government attempted to abolish Scotland's
government, as it well might wish to do, then whatever the new Act
says it might indeed get parliament to agree. But if most Scottish
people wanted to retain their parliament, Westminster would
be unable to impose its will, short of an inconceivable invasion
that would anyway be defeated. The Scotland Act *pretends* that
Westminster has a power to abolish the Scottish parliament and
then generously legislates to constrain this power by saying if it
is to be exercised it must have the consent of the Scottish people.
Meanwhile it has no such power. North of the border, sovereignty
*already* rests with the people. Not as an abstract formulation,
but as fact. Geographically, as well as legally, the writ of the
absolute sovereignty of parliament was already broken before the
referendum. The absolute sovereignty of parliament that Brexit
claims to restore is legally, nationally and in terms of referendums
already a chimera.

# 18
## The Monarchy and 'The People'

The one exception to the story of degeneration and loss of belief of the central, defining institutions is the monarchy. However galling for republicans, the monarchy played a long game helped by the Queen's personal longevity, and has saved itself. With the next three kings lined up, it is already projecting its claim into the twenty-second century. How it achieved this and at what price helps to demonstrate my argument. For the monarchy went through its own equivalent of a Brexit shock with Princess Diana. It then found a way back, after discarding its precious freight of untouchability.

Three key moments were 1992, when Andrew Morton's revealing book on the marriage of Diana and Charles was published and they separated; 1995, when Diana gave her *Panorama* interview setting out her claims directly; and 1997, when she died. The Queen publicly described 1992 as her Annus Horribilis – a horrible year. She had good reason to. As well as the open conflict between the heir to the throne and Diana, with lurid personal tapes of conversations between them and their lovers filling the tabloids, two of her other children ended their marriages and Windsor Castle caught fire. Her acknowledgement shared the crisis of the royal family with the public, an unheard-of breach in protocol. It was a permission to debate the nature and role of the monarchy and its future in a potentially influential fashion.[1] It is hard to convey the force of the post-war taboo preventing such discussion. The monarch had been satirised from the sixties, and derided by the Sex Pistols on her Silver Jubilee in 1977. But the unwritten prohibition of serious discussion only began to erode in the 1980s. After 1992, the Crown was still worshipped, but it became an institution that could be publicly criticised without the critic being pilloried.

Three years later Diana gave her extraordinary interview. Looking back, it is easy to see why Donald Trump, as well as talking about how he wanted to 'nail' her in his usual disgusting way, virtually stalked her after the break-up with Charles. Apparently, 'He bombarded Diana at Kensington Palace with massive bouquets of flowers, each worth hundreds of pounds ... Trump clearly saw Diana as the ultimate trophy wife,' while Diana commented: 'He gives me the creeps.' Trump, inevitably, reported that they had 'a great relationship'.[2]

During an extraordinary hour-long interview, watched by over 20 million, Diana said:

> I think the British people need someone in public life to give affection, to make them feel important, to support them, to give them light in their dark tunnels ... I would like a monarchy that has more contact with its people – and I don't mean by riding round on bicycles and things like that ... I'd like to be a queen of people's hearts, in people's hearts ... I don't think many people will want me to be Queen. Actually, when I say many people I mean the establishment that I married into, because they have decided that I'm a non-starter ... because I lead from the heart, not the head ... I think every strong woman in history has had to walk down a similar path, and I think it's the strength that causes the confusion and the fear. Why is she strong? Where does she get it from? Where is she taking it? Where is she going to use it? Why do the public still support her? When I say public, you go and do an engagement and there's a great many people there ... And I want to reassure all those people who have loved me and supported me throughout the last 15 years that I'd never let them down.[3]

The main elements of what we can now recognise as *celebrity populism* are in play. An attack on a cold-hearted Establishment for its calculated indifference to regular people. The attack being made by a member of the Establishment, with all the authority of knowing it at first hand, who has gone rogue. A position of being truly on the side of the public and understanding their pain, along with a liberal use of the word love and sharing one's love (something Trump now does a lot). Measuring 'the people' by the size of the crowds and media attention. And at the same time, at length in other sections of the interview, attacking the media for its destructiveness while using the media to broadcast this attack.

When Diana died two years later, Blair declared she was 'The People's Princess'. The use of 'The People' entered British political vocabulary with a new meaning, perhaps for the first time. Not because of the prime minister but because 'The People' occupied the huge spaces of the royal Mall in an enormous, spontaneous mobilisation. Quite unlike official events, such as celebration of royal marriages, the crowd was completely outside of official control. It also stayed with a sense of resolve. The People would not have the princess scorned. In her Balmoral Scottish fastness, the Queen declined to have the royal flag flown at half-mast over Buckingham Palace. She and her family responded just like the cold, heartless, oppressive 'Establishment' that Diana had warned about. Had this standoff continued, the Palace and the royals could have been overwhelmed. Elizabeth conceded to the prime minister's unequivocal advice, flew to London, made a TV address and briefly joined the crowds to examine the myriad of bouquets. The day was saved. It was a harbinger of Brexit, of the public willing to separate itself, calmly and deliberately, from a distrusted, traditional authority; with quiet resolve, to borrow a phrase from Theresa May.

It transformed the relationship of the Crown to the public for ever. Millions continue to love the Queen and remain attached to the monarchy as an institution. But its sanctity has gone – destroyed by Diana's attempt to modernise it. Absurd as it might seem, Diana, like Charles and the rest of the royal family, believed in divine right. This is what she signals when she says she is against them 'riding round on bicycles and things like that', as immensely wealthy Dutch and

Scandinavian royals do, acting as if they are normal. They may be privileged but they do not pretend to be different. It was the opposite for Diana. She was more royalist than the royals and believed in reviving the curing royal touch. The interview was her call for them: to up their game, reach out and provide 'heart' to the people. It was an attempt to revamp the royal family. She sets out her aim in the last part of the interview, clearly prepared in advance: to get Charles to stand down as being unfit to be king so that the succession goes straight to William, divine right having made its way to him through her loins.

The ridiculous scenario of Diana orchestrating the succession as queen of people's hearts shows she was partly deranged by the adulation she so skilfully encouraged. Her death saved the royals from an internal civil war. The people would have been persuaded not to follow Diana, but she would have retained a noisy, devoted following obsessed with the injustice she had suffered. When she died, however, 'The People' came together as one and obliged the sovereign to bow her head and salute the Princess in her catafalque. A shift of influence took place, a kind of democratisation, if the word can be used in this context.

The royal family, which has a small committee to consider its plans and prospects, learnt how celebrity populism that lionised their esteem was a fatal temptation. They organised a careful, managed retreat which included minimising media intrusion. A form of normalisation was adopted. William was sent to university at St Andrews – small, traditional, good quality, isolated, and as far away from London as it is possible to be. He was allowed to marry a commoner whom he met there. Security will keep him from bicycles, but he has been given the ambition of appearing to be ordinary and becoming human. This is the price the monarchy is paying for its institutional survival. If a written constitution comes their way, as it should, he will not have a problem swearing a coronation oath to uphold it. It will then define his role, and divine right will come to an end.

The larger issue is one of identification. The Queen is already seen as embodying the past. For the opening of the Olympic games, she was used in a James Bond sequence and a stand-in dressed as her parachuted into the arena in a stunt. This gave her the common touch but also put her in her place. At her coronation in 1953, she was heralded as the face of a 'New Elizabethan age'. Then, the monarchy was at the centre of imaging the country's future. Still flushed by emerging intact from the war, at the height of Churchillism, with the great man himself as her prime minister, the Queen could take the weight of representing the country's aspirations. She was surrounded by supporting institutions that she personally headed and which defined us: the armed forces (she took their salute on horseback), the Church of England, the civil service and indeed the hereditary House of Lords, not to speak of debutantes coming out in their annual ball at Buckingham Palace and round-the-clock deference. In his wonderful account of the web spun by the monarchy and its grip on the British mentality, *The Enchanted Glass*, Tom Nairn has a hilarious but also troubling discussion of how the Queen was adored and entered people's dreams, thoughts and imagination. The monarchy with its associated glamour of backwardness was central, he argues, to multinational British nationalism. It was a relationship willed by people who wished to remain subjects. He quotes John Buchan writing in 1935: 'The essence of the British Monarchy is that the King, while lifted far above the nation, should also be the nation itself in its most characteristic form'. The royals carried this essence through the war and Queen Elizabeth took it to new heights.

Forty years later, after a slow deflation, Diana bid to rekindle a new version of Buchan's essence: as the Queen of people's hearts, the light in their dark tunnels. She saw that only a populist monarchy could be the personification of today's cruder, grasping nation. Diana's was a loathsome, patronising pitch. The car crash saved the day. But the response that followed as the people occupied the Mall and clapped the coffin taught the royal family never again to put themselves forward for such a role. The route to normalisation is much safer, if this is the choice a demotic age imposes on them. They have survived – but no one would now describe Britain's story as the 'second Elizabethan age'.

Thanks to Rupert Murdoch we know that the Queen supported Brexit. The Palace promptly denied the report, as the issue is too divisive. With a form of civil war stretching ahead, they cannot allow themselves to be the focus of massive public ire by either side. It is a long way from 1953. Also, there is something healthy about Brexit that harmonises with the republican spirit, in its anti-elitism and demand to 'take back control' rather than be controlled. This too is dangerous for them. Looking back, the millions who lined the streets to applaud Diana's shattered body can be seen as the people mourning the end of their hope – a hope of renewing a Britishness they could enjoy by dreaming of her. If so, there is no longer the same urge, looking past Elizabeth, to dream of Britain. The Family continues. But a peculiarity of Great British nationalism was that it needed a pre-modern personification, because of its primitive, seventeenth-century formation. Without an adored monarch to define it, Britishness and the monarchy may live on, but Britain as a state may not long survive.

# 19

# The Blair Coup

To understand the causes behind the calamity afflicting British institutions, that led to Brexit, it is vitally important to see them as a consequence of failed renewal. This is very different from a story of mere decline. Back in the 1960s, the Establishment saw the need to 'manage decline'. It did not want the way society was run to change, believed in Britain's great-power status, but could see that in world terms it was being gradually overtaken. It saw no way out of this except membership of what would become the EU. Later Margaret Thatcher and her team set about reversing decline in a different way with robust conviction. Then New Labour built on Thatcherism. This is a story of renewal and energy, not passivity. Renewal that does not work, however, can lead to breakdown. In Britain's case, Brexit.

Like the royal family, the UK is not a slowly decomposing Miss Havisham, frozen in time, jilted, living in mourning, longing for what might have been. It had many successful and fulfilling relationships, including illicit ones, and a life blessed with far more good fortune than bad. Most of all, since 1688, for all its conservative philistinism, it has ruled a country of science and invention, unleashed the industrial revolution, and persistently adapted and modernised when necessary. Its neighbours had a worse time and the EU can be seen as an attempt by Europe's other historic empires (the Dutch, Portuguese, French, German, Italian, Spanish, Austrian, Belgian and Swedish) to find a new place for themselves as nations, in a world where conquest should no longer be acceptable.

The question for Britain was whether it could find its future in the EU's daring collective enterprise, even at arm's-length, while retaining the pound as its currency. The answer in 2016 was no –

from England-without-London, where a large majority narrowly carried the day across the UK as a whole. The roots of this English repudiation lie in the *failure* to renew the institutions of Britain coherently. This does not mean that no renewal was attempted. On the contrary. Nor does it mean that Brexit was conservative either. It was not a rejection of change but an understandable expression of extreme exasperation at the disappointment of botched renewal and a willingness to bet on a different form of change. The gamble was mistaken and won't work. Instead, it will deepen the breakdown in the long run, as it cannot carry Scotland and Northern Ireland with it, not to speak of London. The only way forward for the nations of Britain is separately, at the political level – when each with its own voice will co-create cultural rather than imperial Britishness.

If there is one person who could have avoided this by putting in place a renewed British state and constitution that would have flourished within the European Union, it was Tony Blair. Instead, he laid down the basis of the present calamity when he insisted that the 'young country' he became premier of in 1997 embark on a disastrous course of incoherent reform. In the process, aided by his serpentine consigliere Peter Mandelson, he wrecked an irreplaceable 300-year legacy of consent.

To understand this difficult, for many tragic, and explosive inheritance, consider the impact of the New Labour reforms that brought about what Lord Bingham rightly described as 'constitutional change not experienced for centuries'. Each one was refreshing in its impact, though all had been long demanded and campaigned for. Every one of them worked on its own terms, which shows that constitutional reform succeeds in Britain if people gain real powers they can use for themselves, as opposed to symbolic forms of consultation that offer mere participation without responsibility.

Very briefly, the Scottish government was meant to satisfy hunger for devolution, dish the nationalists and integrate that nation into the UK. Instead, it took off under its own steam to give the nationalists power and pointed Scotland towards independence. The Welsh assembly was approved in the 1997 referendum by a whisker: 50.3 per cent to 49.7 per cent, a majority of fewer than 7,000 votes, with a turnout of barely 50 per cent of a total registered electorate of 2.2 million. Yet, as a result, within a decade Wales is creating its own law for the first time for almost five hundred years. The mayor of London is now elected by the largest direct mandate in Europe, after the president of France. The city's growth and character would be inconceivable without this, and it now has the first Muslim mayor of any major city in the West. Dislike this if you will, but it works and generates self-belief. The most original and popular politicians of the last twenty years in Britain include Ken Livingstone, Alex Salmond, Boris Johnson and Nicola Sturgeon. Two have been mayor of London, the other two, Scotland's first minister. Blair aside, they were the most recognisable figures in UK politics until Theresa May joined them. All four would have been throttled by the deadly culture of Westminster, and reduced to marginal mavericks if their political careers had been confined to the House of Commons. They personify the effectiveness and success of devolution and reform – it releases democratic energy.

The Freedom of Information Act passed in 2000 has pried open a highly secretive political culture and is now used regularly, locally and nationally, by the media and citizens. Without it, the corruption of parliamentary expenses would still be in place. Its effectiveness can be measured by the constant attempts to roll it back and make requests more costly. The Human Rights Act has ensured that rights are now a political norm. This is an enormous cultural shift. When I first campaigned for human rights legislation in the 1980s, the prevailing view, Labour as much as Tory, was that rights give power to judges, undermine our democracy and do not belong here. Today, Theresa May wishes to repatriate all adjudication of rights to British courts. But no one would conceive of abolishing human rights legislation altogether; it is understood to be an essential protection for both minorities and individuals against corporate and state power.

A further success was the transfer of authority to set interest rates from the Chancellor of the Exchequer to the Bank of England.

This too was a considerable constitutional reform introduced by New Labour in 1997. Today the Bank publishes the minutes of its meetings to share its thinking, removing monetary policy from the short-term party-political manipulations of an over-powerful executive.

In addition – outside the Westminster system but of extra-ordinary historical importance – the Good Friday Agreement between all the political parties of the province and both the UK and the Irish governments, brought peace to Northern Ireland. It ensured that the historically Protestant and Catholic communities were to be co-represented in its government, human rights were built into its processes – and that if a majority vote to leave the UK and join Ireland, the British government is bound to accept this. It brought an end to a protracted civil war with significant terrorist attacks on the mainland.

The new political institutions and processes were, except for Northern Ireland, legislated in as grudging and limited fashion as possible. Yet all of them have expanded their influence and power and are continuing to do so. Why is it then that if you add up all these pluses you get a minus? Because in their different ways each reform broke part of the binding narrative of unified sovereignty. The nations now have their own parliaments. London has a direct, presidential-style vote for its mayor, unprecedented in UK history. The secrecy of the uncodified way of doing things has been abolished. Human rights and judges with their own supreme court have transformed the standing and role of the judiciary. Booting out hereditary peers ended the entrenched, conservative weight of the old Lords. From the point of view of preserving the British polity, it was madness to do all this and not put in place an overall reform – a new settlement to bind them together. Blair refused. Instead, at the start of the reforms the Scottish parliament was treated with contempt in public (Blair compared it to a parish council), while in private every administrative effort was made to control and limit its significance (with Blair instructing there be a unified civil service over Scotland, Wales and England and concordats to bind each department of the newly devolved administrations). In Wales,

Blair even tried to personally select his own candidate to be the new first minister.

But what was legislated democratically in the open could not be undone by underhand bureaucratic fiats. Each new institution established its own momentum around its own *raison d'être*, and got going. As they did so, their culminative forces became centrifugal. In less than a decade they started to strip the United Kingdom of coherent democratic meaning as the old regime was pulled apart. People embraced them, and as each reform worked on its own terms, together they threatened rather than renewed the British constitution as a whole.

In case it should be thought that all this is easy to argue now, and that I'm reading back onto earnest and well-meaning reformers limitations that could not have been understood at the time, it needs to be said those involved did know what was stake. I had a direct confrontation with Blair in 1999, that I've written about elsewhere. His chief of staff, Jonathan Powell, summed up my argument for me as 'after us the deluge'.[1] Much more important, the reforms were indeed originally conceived as a coherent democratic package by one participant in their conception: Gordon Brown. He argued in 1998, after New Labour took office, 'we must move from an old, centralised uniform state – the Britain of subjects – to a modern, pluralist democracy – the Britain of citizens ... Britain will need not only unifying ideas of citizenship, but the new constitution we propose.' The agreement he and Blair made, however, when Brown agreed that Blair should be the leader, gave Brown control over economic policy but not the constitution. Instead, shortly after, the lord chancellor, Derry Irvine, doubtless at Blair's direction, denied any such suggestion: 'We have embarked on a major programme of constitutional change realigning the most fundamental relationships between the state and the individual ... We are not, however, hunting the chimera of constitutional master plans, nor ultimate outcomes.'[2]

The civil service drafted a speech for Blair that set out an overview of the reforms. He turned it away. His contempt for the old, binding, British narrative with its procedural pomposities was refreshing; he rightly scorned it as a brake on progress. But he had no intention of replacing it with anything that would have held him in check or made him accountable.

Instead, he turned to the executive powers preserved by the empire state. Blair pushed aside the worm-eaten bulwarks of informal checks and balances, the advice of Sir Humphrey, the raised eyebrow of how we did things, the party conference or the trade union bloc vote. Just as each New Labour reform took on a life of its own, so did his summary abolition of Cabinet government to replace it with unminuted rule from the sofa: cutting across procedures, doing away with written records that might hold him to account.

This was the tragedy of Blairism. Alongside much needed social reform and public investment, two opposing sets of far-reaching change rent apart the way the United Kingdom was governed. In a short time New Labour oversaw the greatest set of democratic reforms in 300 years, an astonishing advance that received no single accolade or recognition from the master communicator. He hated them, as his memoir makes clear, freedom of information above all. At the same time he exploited the weakness of the traditional state to break the cabinet and rule by himself, initiating the most undemocratic centralisation of prime ministerial power ever seen. Out of it came the Iraq war.

# 20

# Manipulative Corporate Populism

To implement legislation that swept aside so much of the past and at the same time centralise control in a way that tore down old restraints demanded more than personal self-belief. Blair headed a team which had worked intensively for a decade to find a way forward that would make Labour able to govern. With the unions and Labour's working-class base in secular decline, Clinton's triangulation offered a way to win. In place of internationalism, there was globalisation – creating jobs, generating tax revenues. Instead of the old left–right politics, a new arc to office based on market research. As social democrats, Blair and Brown aimed to improve, not replace, capitalism, and here was a better form of capitalism itself, planetary, socially emancipating and hi-tech, whose tax revenues could fund essential welfare and positive reforms. This was the New Labour project. It was with an impatience to achieve delivery that Blair asked himself how is such an approach best run? His answer was to apply the model of corporate power to government. Like a corporation, the state will sell its services to the public, who are treated as consumers, not citizens.

Take the way a large company works today and compare it to a government department. In the company there would be a continuous reassessment, from first principles, of what the company is trying to do and how it is doing it. In particular there would be a relentless focus on system improvement through use of technology, perpetual analysis of the customer base and how its habits and wishes were changing; and a comparative study of what the competition is up to.[1]

Blair's needs include values that are 'dynamic' and change that 'works'. They explain the refreshing can-do nature of New Labour – in sharp contrast to the aimless drift of the Wilson and Callaghan Labour administrations of the 1960s and 70s and the baffling, indecisive humanism of later Labour leaders like Ed Miliband and Jeremy Corbyn. But the state is not a company, the public are not customers, and the product for a political party is obtaining power. In adapting Clinton's techniques, Blair developed what I call manipulative corporate populism.

This adapted the classless appeal of the large corporation, constantly investing in its brands and marketing, as much as its products, seeking to manipulate public demand in a growing global marketplace. It became Blair's ideal for the conduct of power that made a left/right distinction redundant, replacing it by the need to be tough rather than weak, clear not confused, modern not old, and above all 'strong' by leading, not following.

In Blair's hands, corporate populism displaced and sought to eliminate two long-standing British traditions. Most obviously, it displaced the political inheritance of the Labour Party. Clause 4 of the old Labour Party's constitution was vaporised, with its commitment to public ownership. Fabianism and Labourism, the defensive, collectivist trade-union protection of working-class interests by seeking improvement through the routines of the British state was defined as 'old' and abandoned. The process was loudly supported by the press and media, who replaced the relationship between the party and the people, helping to both atomise and organise the public. Socialism was replaced by Blair's 'Third Way' as he attempted, briefly, to present himself as a thinker with a philosophy. It was much derided, best of all when Francis Wheen said it was somewhere between the second coming and the fourth dimension.

But traditional Labour politics was replaced by a much more creative effort at reform and improvement, in response to the enormous changes going on across the world economy. For Blair it was *The* Third Way: the 'the' was the most significant of the three words. For the concept that reform lay somewhere 'between' communist state control of everything and untrammelled capitalism was hardly original. Within the enormous space opened up between these two extremes, Blair's claim was that there is *only one* route. Given the possibilities, a guide is essential to *the way*, and this can only be the leader. While it announced itself as an all-encompassing approach, 'The Third Way' was also a control mechanism. Because the notion was a ploy it did not take long for it to be forgotten, but the driving ambition for control that it revealed never faltered.

It was not just the British who attempted to reconceive their country as a global business, the same process was also taking place across Europe in Christian democratic parties of the right as well as social democratic ones. In *Ruling the Void*, Peter Mair showed how publics and elites were disengaging from each other, leaving a 'governing class' dangerously remote from voters, who were fleeing political parties, as were their members across all European countries. The media reinforced this atomisation. The corporatisation of politics under the influence of global marketisation created what Colin Crouch termed post-democracy.[2] The UK witnessed an extreme version.

Blair's destruction of the traditional routines of British government and its institutional culture was more important for Britain than his discarding Clause 4 Labour politics. The UK's regime was never democratic. Blair took it from pre-democracy to post-democracy and on the way abandoned its organisation of consent. With his corporate populism, Blair finished the job begun by Margaret Thatcher when she broke the influence of the civil service and its non-market procedures. The high point was winning his first election as prime minister in June 2001. On the surface little changed from his 1997 victory, with Labour losing five seats and the Tories gaining one, so that Labour retained its huge parliamentary majority. But turnout fell below 60 per cent – a historic post-war low. Labour lost nearly three million votes and the Tories nearly one-and-a-half million. After the most radical set of constitutional reforms the country had ever known, there was no general country-wide burst of energy, no sense that anything transformative had occurred. And that was because Blair and company did not believe in the constitutional reforms or wish to align themselves as architects of a new settlement that would empower citizens. Instead, theirs was a stealth revolution of closure, spin, sofas and message control to lock in corporate populism. It did not need to be popular in any dangerous democratic sense. On the contrary, manipulation and marketing aimed at gaining brand loyalty, not active consent of the historic kind that bound British institutions to the people.

Three months after the 2001 election, al-Qaida's hijackers struck. Global influence beckoned through the smoking wreckage of the Twin Towers. Blair had already tested out a military alliance with the United States with Bill Clinton in the Balkans, when he persuaded a reluctant president to commit ground forces in Kosovo to oust the Serbian overlord, Milošević. Now, all the major powers agreed to support US action in Afghanistan to winkle out the mass-murderer bin Laden. It was when attention switched to Iraq that Blair saw his chance. He had to ensure the Americans kept the British in their battle plans. Putting all his considerable persuasion to work, he bent the military, the secret services, the Cabinet, the Commons and the media to his desire.

I noted in the opening section how the enormous scale of opposition *in advance* of the final decision to invade Iraq meant that a transfer of practical wisdom from rulers to the ruled took place, as it became clear that Britain was led by dangerous fools. We can now see the full consequence of this for the rapidly weakening constitutional order of Britain. The people who took to the streets in unmatched numbers to oppose the war assessed reality with more foresight than their masters – the UK's political class, its so-called 'intelligence' services, the Labour government and the Tory opposition, the Foreign Office, the Murdoch-inspired press, and most of their crony lordships. This turned upside-down the core assumption of the UK's informal constitution: that the people cannot be trusted and the ruling class knows best.

The absolute sovereignty of parliament was never exercised as a dictatorship over the people of mainland Britain. It was always lawful in its way and it also always sought to establish consent. Consent is very different from democracy. The fundamental assumption of the UK's unwritten operating system was that those who rule will get it right and the populace will accept that those who govern them know best. If they get it wrong, as they did with appeasement most notably in 1938, they will provide the men with the courage to correct matters.

With the invasion of Iraq, in unprecedented numbers members of the public made the right judgement and demonstrated a greater democratic intelligence. The British, who take pride in knowing how to fight a necessary war, saw that this was not the case with Iraq. Their genuine wisdom torpedoed the legitimacy of Britain's ruling elite below the waterline. On a matter of war and peace – the highest calling of the state – the people were right and the Westminster political elite were wrong. The voters were wiser, more restrained and made better judgement than their collective masters. The fundamental principle of the unwritten order of British government was upturned. With it went any justification for corporate populism there might have been. Paramount among all Blair's acts of constitutional vandalism is his responsibility for destroying trust in the ultimate wisdom of those who govern. Fifteen years later, it birthed Brexit.

The argument against this interpretation is that it overstates the opposition to war. After all, Blair won the election two years later. The anti-war movement, so the objection goes, was just an episode that shows that however conspicuous, mere protest is impotent and changes nothing. My response is, first, that a breach of this kind runs deep and its implications grow as they sink in. The reason that the Chilcot Inquiry into the war took so long and only reported in 2016 was that the perpetrators were desperate to postpone it, in the hope that it would become irrelevant and all would be 'forgiven'. Which suggests that what happened to the way the country is governed remains unresolved even now. Second, Blair and his New Labour government only won the 2005 election numerically. It should have been a walkover. There had been eight continuous years of economic growth between 1997 and 2005, a unique achievement. The NHS and schools were at last getting the funding they needed, and it was showing. The Tories had lost their way and were the 'nasty party'. Desperate, they fell back on the most racist billboard slogan possible this side of hate speech: 'Are you thinking what I'm thinking?' Wow, it should have been a confrontation to remember. Instead, Labour got just over 35 per cent of the vote, an absolute historic low. Turnout was reluctant at 61 per cent: in no other country of the democratic world would Labour have been able to form the administration on its own. But thanks to a grotesquely unfair electoral system, Labour got 55 per cent of the seats, a comfortable 66-seat majority in parliament, down from their previous majority in 2001 of 160.

The election of 2005 acted to deepen that separation of the public from 'the political system' which has brought such fatal consequences. This is what you would expect if the Iraq invasion undermined the constitution as I have described. In a very significant development, Labour lost the popular vote in England. Across the country, Tories got 72,000 more English votes in total than Labour – but 90 fewer seats.[3] It was a democratic scandal. Faced with it, Blair and New Labour had a final opportunity to address the United Kingdom's main national question and bring England in from the cold. They ignored it. The alienation from politics accelerated by the constitutional outrage of the Iraq decision was expressed in the separation of England from the Westminster system. Ignored, the English waited for their moment.

# 21

# From Churchillism to Thatcherism

I have looked at the way Brexit was a national vote of England. Then at how England's nationalism is locked within Britain, a union now challenged by Scotland, and how their unhappiness drove the English to blame Brussels for their discontent. The Brexit that resulted has been defined by Prime Minister May. She seeks to unify the spirit of both the Leave and Remain campaigns in a Big Britishness that is improbable internationally and unsustainable internally – because its constitutional claims seek to roll back time itself. The national question is framed by the constitution and in Britain's case its 300-year settlement is broken across its parts – the Cabinet, the Commons, the Lords, the civil service, local government – as well as between the nations of the Union. Today, its different nations are now on separate paths, while its exaggerated claims of absolute sovereignty no longer outshine the attraction of a democratic citizens' constitution. The cause of this undoing was political: New Labour radically decentralising the ramparts of the British state while turning the central turret into an autocracy. From the centre Blair took the country into an illicit, unwanted and stupid war which it lost, in the process undermining the consent that was fundamental to the entire edifice.

How could such a story have come about? Only if we can answer this, can we be confident of the need to close the book of the British state and open a new and better relationship to a now networked world. The answer runs through Britain's post-war history and goes back to May 1940, when Churchill took office after Labour called for him to lead the war against Nazism. The Labour Party's leader Clement Attlee told his supporters: 'Life without liberty is not worth living. Let us go forward and win', as he took them into the wartime coalition. He himself became Churchill's deputy. Significantly, 'liberty' is no longer a word familiar to the lips of Labour leaders. After the war, Attlee won the 1945 election, to lose to Churchill in 1951. Churchill left office only in 1955, aged eighty. It was a joint fifteen years, dominated by the two of them. To give you an idea of the cross-class nature of the coalition period, the head of the country's largest trade union, the Transport and General Workers, Ernest Bevin, became minister of labour from 1940 to 1945, to oversee the conscription of the workforce into the war effort. He then became foreign secretary until 1950, aiding the creation of NATO and insisting that Britain make its own atomic bomb – 'We've got to have the bloody Union Jack flying on top of it' – which was done in secret from parliament but not from Churchill.

In 1939, Great Britain went into the war as a self-confident *empire*, in alliance with France and with far greater resources than Nazi Germany. It emerged as a proud but impoverished *country*.[1] The compression of this gigantic moment turned an imperial regime into a society that was neither empire or nation. The colonies would gain their independence over the next fifteen years. But for most voters their loss was less important than a gain. The effort of war had stripped down the ruling class and created the chance to bury the inequities of the thirties and the stark divisions that led to British appeasement of fascism and then the conflict in the first place. When the crowds celebrated victory, it was not just because the country (as opposed to the empire) had not been invaded or occupied. In addition, they cheered the coming defeat of the pre-war past and its 'five evils' of poverty, ignorance, squalor, disease and unemployment, set out in the Beveridge Report in 1942 and embraced as war aims from then on. Which is why they voted for Attlee to secure the implementation of the welfare state. There followed a wartime peace, after 1945, that was austere, rationed, shared and run from above, within the American alliance. For all the ferocious disagreements, it was a collective attainment politically. It was not the case that the Tories ran the war and subsequently Labour the welfare state. *Both* were a joint, all-party achievement. After initial Conservative resistance to the welfare state in 1945, they embraced it and its Keynesian commitment to full employment which allowed them to return to office in 1951 committed to its continuation.

The mental and social force that held this Great British world together was Churchillism. The immense pressure that followed May 1940, of being defeated but defiant and then of total war, created a common mentality. Churchillism was forced on the man himself, who was conscripted into it reluctantly. Rather than being a spokesman for it, it was projected onto him. It was much more than a mere coalition of old Tory imperialists and younger Labour men. The pressure created a profound alliance across every class, nation and political tradition. It was not a fusion – each component retained its individuality – but a political amalgam which transformed everyone inwardly as the country faced its 'finest hour'. It induced in each their own variety of Churchillism, while making them all feel essential for the whole. It embraced Tory imperialists, Whig internationalists, Labour reformers, trade unionists, antifascist socialists (such as George Orwell), communists, Quaker pacifists, Liberals (including Keynes, the theorist of full employment, and Beveridge), the American alliance, the press and the BBC.[2] After the war it won the peace, creating the NHS, nationalising basic industries and dismantling the heart of the empire as India and Pakistan won independence. So far as its role in the world was concerned, a key text defined this: *Britain and the Tide of World Affairs*, the 1954 Reith Lectures given by Lord Franks when he returned from being the UK's ambassador in Washington. He described the 'consensus' of all parties to NATO, the 'Sterling Area', the nuclear deterrent and stationing troops in Germany, for all agreed, 'Britain is going to continue to be what she has been, a Great Power'. Emphasising 'the necessity of the Commonwealth to Britain's continuing greatness', he asked, 'What is this small island with its 50,000,000 inhabitants if it has to go it alone?'[3] A good question for today.

This domestic and international mindset was not a mere ideology – there was far too much disagreement and conflict of interests within it for that. Churchillism was a structure of feeling that was everywhere. This is why its name is unfamiliar: no one opposed it, no one fought for it, it was simply inescapable. It was being British. In its time, that is, but we Brits still live within its shadow and it vibrated through the halls of Brexit. While anti-socialist and very anti-communist with Stalin as the external enemy, Churchillism was broadly collectivist in the wartime, not the democratic, fashion (neither the NHS nor the nationalised industries had workers on their boards, for example). This collectivist approach produced what became known as consensus politics. (The term 'Butskellism' was coined because the economic policies of Rab Butler and Hugh Gaitskell, Tory and Labour chancellors respectively, were indistinguishable.) A shared Keynesianism embraced the state's responsibility to ensure full employment, but with an attitude that remained paternalist.

If citizenship is one form of agreed universalism, Churchillism was another, opposite, kind of consensus. Because it was shared, the society it held together was strong enough for the old tribalisms to continue. The social divisions of pre-war Britain were largely retained. Churchillism granted no dissolving rights. Instead, there was a clubland character to its collectivism: trade unions kept their immunity, the class system was preserved, the City was a world to itself, the BBC was run like the army, Oxbridge remained unchanged, each was in his or her place. Nowhere was this sense of being together but separate, defensive but defiant, truer than with respect to Europe. On 9 May 1950, the Schuman Declaration called for the creation of a supranational authority over French and German Iron and Steel production to prevent any recurrence of Franco-German hostility.[4] Churchill responded:

> We help, we dedicate, we play a part, but we are not merged and do not forfeit our insular or Commonwealth-wide character. I should resist any American pressure to treat

Britain on the same footing as the European states, none of whom have the advantages of the Channel and who were consequently conquered.[5]

This insularity was *internalised* into everyday life in Churchillist Britain. All the institutions, from the Trade Union Congress to the BBC and the banks, stubbornly stuck to their own ways. The spirit of Churchillism inoculated every sector from any desire to change 'the way we are governed' or 'the kind of country we are'.

Quite rapidly it induced a reluctant fatalism. The passion for greatness stayed but the reality saw global power slip away. Churchillism became a culture of managed decline. Having scorned participation in the creation of what would become the EU as beneath its standing – for Great Britain was one of the world's 'Big Three' (the other two were the USA and the then Soviet Union) – the consensus developed that Britain had to join to preserve its influence.

The agency that reached this view of what was best for the country was 'the Establishment'. Anthony Sampson mapped it, in a once famous book that became a best-seller when it was published in 1962, *Anatomy of Britain*. Sampson was an exemplary reporter – and a wonderful gossip – but not a thinker. He charted how British life was run by overlapping circles of acquaintances, predominantly from public schools and Oxbridge, linked together in a clubland of mainly old boys. He did not conceptualise it historically. The ease with which this connected world of very different views shared in the government of the country was not just down to their class or education but also to the common experience of total war.

The reorientation into Europe failed to reverse Britain's relative decline, and the seventies were marked by incoherent decomposition, especially within the Labour Party. Unlike the United States, France and Germany (where the post-war generation confronted their parents' collaboration with Nazism), Britain in the late sixties only experienced a small wave of political radicalism. But England generated an exceptionally influential and creative musical and commercial rebellion, which had absorbed American music, television and sexual liberty – and a social revolt against status and exclusion. A generation gap opened between it and stuffy wartime Establishment paternalists. Because England's sixties were commercial as well as libertarian, they pulsated into the Conservative Party. While iconically retro in her cultural appeal, Margaret Thatcher first made her mark in October 1968, criticising the oppressive role of the state. She was to become the prime minister who broke the taboos and restrictions protecting consensus and released England's pent-up energies.

Just as Churchillism was pressed onto Churchill so, in a narrower way, Thatcherism happened to Thatcher. She was not an ideologist, but she had the will, personality and instinct to orchestrate and drive forward a radical turn after she won office – aided by her cold-blooded willingness to say:

> people are really rather afraid that this country might be rather swamped by people with a different culture and, you know, the British character has done so much for democracy, for law and done so much throughout the world that if there is any fear that it might be swamped people are going to react and be rather hostile to those coming in.[6]

Thatcher led a transformation of British society. She scorned 'consensus politics', having concluded that it was essential to break the stultifying (as she saw it) collaboration between the trade unions, the state and industry. Thanks to the Falklands war, she seized the banner of Churchillism and turned it into a combative anti-working-class patriotism, tagging the trade unions as 'the enemy within', leaving Labour flabbergasted and undoing its legacy of British unity. It gave her the electoral victory and enough support to break the miners, the Labour movement's praetorian guard. After which she proceeded to open the City of London up to the world, by smashing its closed shops and tribal complacency and deregulating finance with the 'big bang' in 1986, arguably the most radical measure of all.

A deep change was taking place. Stuart Hall, who first coined the term Thatcherism – presciently, before she came to power – described it as 'reactionary modernisation'. He meant by this that while in terms of conviction, collective fantasy, Victorian values, English masochism, feeling 'swamped' and greatness, Thatcher's appeal was reactionary, her commitment to reversing British decline and installing a modern, global capitalism driven by market values was oriented to the future. Hers was a contradictory, complex project. She was not just a reactionary, she was also a deadly serious moderniser and the left, he argued, needed to wake up to this and respond creatively.[7]

While Thatcher carried the trappings of Churchillism with her, she abandoned its spirit to turn against its wartime ethos. The nature of the change that Thatcher oversaw can be described simply as replacing post-war collectivism with market individualism. As she explained in 1980:

> What's irritated me about the whole direction of politics in the last 30 years is that it's always been towards the collectivist society. People have forgotten about the personal society. And they say: do I count, do I matter? To which the short answer is, yes. And therefore, it isn't that I set out on economic policies; it's that I set out really to change the approach, and changing the economics is the means of changing that approach. If you change the approach you really are after the heart and soul of the nation. Economics are the method; the object is to change the heart and soul.[8]

It took a decade. Forty years on, a new contest is shaping up for the hearts and souls of people across the United Kingdom. Thatcher's individualist approach opened the way for the marketisation of society. It became, what Hall recognised, a genuine modernisation – adapting the UK, and especially the south of England, to global capitalism as privatisation and deregulation pioneered neoliberalism to replace Keynesian liberalism. Thatcher's lasting appeal springs from her Janus-faced combination of reaction and modernity. Its legacy can be felt still in the adoration Brexiteers have of her memory. The tabloids and some of her followers have attempted to drape the former prime minister's clothes on Theresa May. But they also have a toxic legacy of division and polarisation, whereas May has explicitly understood the Brexit vote to be a rejection of heartless financial engineering. She has proposed instead a consensual vision where the Conservative state once again takes up the duty of care. To answer Lord Frank's challenge of 1954, 'What is this small island with its 50,000,000 inhabitants if it has to go it alone?' she needs the unity of everyone as well as a competitive spirit with the rest of the world as she confronts rather than collaborates with Europe. The moment of Thatcherism is indelibly etched in the mental perspective of Brexit. But its 'enemy within' is not a cussed, collectivist, defensive working class or a closed world of privileged restrictions and poorly managed nationalised industries. Instead, it is the sophisticated, the open-minded and the foreign investors who resist the coherent application of Brexit, while May herself desires a domestic social conservatism modelled on the 1950s. It is a stew of contradictions. World politics might come to its rescue and offer a resolution, but how could such nostalgia for the period of nostalgia come to pass? The answer lies in the shattering failure of the Blair solution and the looming power of the tabloids, as Britain was taken over by a political-media caste who then went to war with each other.

# 22

# From the Establishment to the Political-Media Caste

The measure of Margaret Thatcher's achievement was New Labour. Its project was to naturalise the triumph of her individualism by expelling collectivism from its political home, the Labour Party. Corporate populism modernised the reactionary aspect of Thatcher's reactionary modernisation. That sounds a mouthful, doesn't it, but each part has a clear meaning as I have shown. Thatcher modernised the UK economy by opening it up, from selling council houses, to breaking the miners, to the big bang of City restrictions. She covered her radicalism in a reactionary cultural narrowness and propriety. Blair modernised this cultural aspect of Thatcherism, liberalising life and society. He did so by adopting a centralised corporate model for running the state, ensuring its popularity through the use of marketing and positioning at the same time as preserving and consolidating Thatcher's marketisation. In this way Blair expanded her economic individualism into political and social individualism. In the process he transformed the ideology of individualism from being solely aspirational to becoming rights-based as well. Thus, as Thatcher's Victorian values lost their appeal, New Labour kept her embrace of the free market but added a welcoming face. As well as human rights: sexual tolerance, permissiveness, freedom of information, devolution, inward migration, rejection of chauvinism and pro-Europeanism.

Britain was linked to a further level of globalisation: the international circuit of human rights law. Tragically, Blair used the embrace of human rights to justify military intervention. He went to Chicago in 1999, and in what he thought would be a historic speech, declared: 'We cannot turn our backs on conflicts and the violation of human rights within other countries if we want still to be secure', which meant the world needed, 'a new doctrine of international community'.[1] If instead Blair had worked with Brown to shape a new doctrine for British democracy, they would have achieved something lasting. The country was ready for a genuine replacement of the Establishment and its Churchillist mentality.

In blasting apart the vested interests, closed shops and clubland culture of post-war consensus politics, Thatcherism had confounded the old order. To pull this off she remained a genuine stickler for its institutional conventions and procedures. Those seeking advancement in the old ways still conspired, but they lost their moorings. The painful disorientation that resulted could be seen in the John Major premiership after Thatcher's fall in 1990. For the next seven years, the snake was sloughing off its skin. A much shinier serpent took over from the Establishment with Blair's arrival in Downing Street in 1997: the political-media caste. A venal, professional fusion of centralised high politics, market relations and policy-making, supported by big funders, took over the country's government.

Manipulative corporate populism was only their method of rule. What mattered as much was who they were. They were not a mere 'political elite' or 'political class'. They could never have survived without media support, and the relationship between media, politicians and public relations became a mutually beneficial symbiosis. Murdoch's papers were so much part of it that they began to operate as if they had impunity from the law – not understanding that the introduction of human rights was transforming resistance to their methods. Much the best account of the transformation so far is Peter Oborne's trilogy, written as it was under way between 1999 and 2007: *Alastair Campbell: New Labour and the Rise of the Media Class*; *The Rise of Political Lying*; and *The Triumph of the Political Class*. The books develop an angry critique of the men and mendacity of the new political-media caste and their corporate populism. Oborne's term 'political class' has since been misused to deride politicians alone. It has even fed the fake populism of tabloids pillorying all politicians as a group. In fact, as his arguments lay bare, a relatively small number of journalists, TV and radio presenters, editors and public-relations consultancies, all far better paid than MPs, were essential participants in the governing London-based network – while most MPs were excluded from it. Hence my tweaking the concept to make clear that it refers not to politicians as a group (many are honest and marginal), but to a governing caste forged out of an alloy of leading politicians, PR fixers, journalists, editors and media proprietors.

It was a transition from the government of a whole society by a traditional, widely connected Establishment that had paternalistic, public-service values to the government of the state by a modern, narrow political-media caste with populist, market values. Thatcher was its initiator, Blair its maestro, Cameron its result – and Rupert Murdoch was its god, the aging deity who presided over and outlasted them all.

An enormously significant change took place. It was not a revolution in which one class displaced another; instead a transformation occurred within a ruling class. The long lines of privilege endured as the UK power network was reconfigured. Perhaps a big part of this was due to a change in how they got their money. The Establishment's wealth was indigenous, sourced in British holdings and traditional imperial ones. The political-media caste cashed in on American and global corporate money and by servicing Middle Eastern oligarchs (the 1973 crash that transferred vast sums to OPEC producers was a trigger date). Its rulers got richer but separated themselves from the country at large. Instead of politicians and top mandarins sharing weekends at country houses with judges, soldiers and British bankers who may have been paternalist but had fingers on the pulse, they had weekends away with fund-managers and talked about *The West Wing*. For women, family relationships, children and sexuality, the progress was significant, but in terms of being implanted in and identifying with the country, it was a damaging withdrawal.

Most studies of British politics, as opposed to social histories of different periods, are about either the Conservative Party or the Labour Party, or focus on other smaller parties. Such monographs never capture the dynamics of what is happening politically because the transitions that matter are all-party. Both Labour and Conservatives were fully part of the same Establishment in the 1950s and 60s – they co-founded it in the wartime alliance. The governments of both parties were likewise integrated into the same much tighter political-media caste that started with Thatcher, reached its apogee with Blair and concluded with Cameron. A changeover took place of supreme significance in the bipartisan exercise of power, as it went from the broad Establishment to a narrow caste, as individualism replaced collectivism across the land. The cultural contrasts may seem superficial but they reveal how far-reaching it was: from the stiff upper lip to passion and tears; from being consensual to being obsessed with strong leaders.

Why it took the narrow, philistine and dishonest form that it did is in large part thanks to Murdoch's cold disinterest. An Oxford-educated Australian who transplanted himself to the United States helped by the cash flow of the *Sun*, Murdoch dismissed the offer of a peerage and regarded becoming a mere media baron as contemptible. Nor was he alone. He may have been a Darth Vader to Britain's kindly Jedi kingdom, but he should not be over-demonised; the Maxwells and Rothermeres and other players (including Michael Green, Cameron's boss) emulated him. However, in terms of media power he was first among equals, and a key moment was his buying the *Sunday Times* and *The Times*. Already the owner of the *Sun* and the *News of the World* – the most brutal, sexist and best-selling tabloids – he took over what was once known as 'The Thunderer', *The Times*, the voice of the Establishment itself.

At Murdoch's request, Thatcher had him to a private lunch at Chequers, her official country home, on 4 January 1981. The meeting was kept secret by the prime minister and denied by Murdoch. The strictly confidential minute of the event by Thatcher's press secretary, Bernard Ingham, the third person who was present, only became public thirty years later.[2] Murdoch opened by praising the newly elected Ronald Reagan and offering to facilitate meetings between Thatcher and the president's advisers. Having proposed himself as a player capable of improving relations with Washington, he explained his bid for the *Sunday Times*, in whose profitability he was confident, and how his expanding it would hurt the *Observer* – the Sunday paper opposed to Thatcher. He promised to keep *The Times* open despite its losses. He also shared his early plans to reduce manning and break the hold of the print unions. She thanked him.

Shortly after, when his bid came up in the Cabinet committee that had to decide whether to refer it, 'Thatcher opened the discussion by highlighting the exemption under the Fair Trading Act 1973 that would allow Murdoch's bid to avoid a referral.'[3] Murdoch got 37 per cent of Fleet Street as the deal was given the all-clear. A direct, undercover, as well as open alliance unfolded between the media mogul and the premier. Neither could have imagined the payback for Thatcher a year later in the 1982 Falklands War, when the *Sun* led the pack. They became each other's fans. The role of the British media was transformed – not overnight, but from that point on. Under Thatcher – and with Murdoch in the lead – as James Curran has rightly put it, there was a shift from the press barons of old who merely supported or opposed with all their might whoever was in power. Now, they 'went into coalition with the government'.[4]

In 1983, thanks to blunder and greed rather than design, a notorious episode confirmed the subordination of the traditional, Establishment code of standards to new, vulgar, populist ones. Rupert Murdoch bought what were said to be Hitler's diaries from *Stern* and had the historian Hugh Trevor-Roper authenticate them. As the *Sunday Times* was about to go to press with their 'historic scoop', it became clear that they were a complete forgery. Murdoch ordered the presses to roll, saying: 'After all, we are in the entertainment business.' He then waved aside the concerns of his journalists, saying that the paper had gained and kept 60,000 sales.

His words were a death sentence on the journalistic and reporting standards of the Establishment's broadsheet press. Its serious papers could no longer be trusted. Whether a story sold papers mattered more than whether it was true: revenues now trumped integrity.

No idealisation of the previous press barons is necessary to see that a crucial standard had been broken. The popular press had always been partisan, campaigning and occasionally outrageous. A famous episode was the fabricated Zinoviev letter the *Daily Mail* published in 1924, four days before a general election, which declared that the Communist International looked forward to a Labour victory. The letter, however, was forged by Britain's own intelligence services and planted by them – a fabrication made by the British state with intent.[5] The allegation was widely believed. It reinforced the concept that newspapers revealed the truth, even when it did not. By contrast, Murdoch cashed in by publishing what he knew was a forgery, refused to stop the presses and showed no remorse at the time. The owner of *The Times*, the historic representative of the larger interests of British rule since the Napoleonic wars, told the journalists of the *Sunday Times* their role was show business; and through them all his employees. *The Times* itself should have thundered at its fellow broadsheet that there are fundamental professional standards which must not be surrendered for want of long-term damage to the honour of the country's way of life – and the standing of its media and governing class in the eyes of the public. It could not do so: it had lost its independence.

Since this story of the Hitler diaries is well known, indeed legendary, why set out a potted history of the UK since 1940 in order to arrive at it? Because Murdoch's response is usually recounted as a joke, and with a shake of the head, to show what a card he is. Whereas what I want to identify is the loss of authority by the country's historic Establishment. I don't mean its specific institutions – Eton, the clubs, Oxford and Cambridge – which still exist. The UK is a much richer society in the twenty-first century than it was in the 1960s and 70s, and even more unequal. The historic institutions have got in on the act, especially thanks to Middle Eastern money.

What has been displaced is the Establishment as a network of influence that self-consciously defined British society and through it the country and its place in the world. Cameron was an Etonian but in order to become a member of the political-media caste, he had to be reprogrammed for seven years in public relations. In the process, as we have seen, he lost the capacity to mean what he said. Chomsky once argued that however atrocious the ruling class were in propagating dishonesty, they needed their own, smaller-circulation, elite papers to be relatively truthful, so that they themselves could know what was going on. This assumes a ruling class that believes in itself. Britain's no longer did.

One consequence in terms of British government was an increased permission of corruption. Thanks to its Insight team, the *Sunday Times* had been the UK's and perhaps the world's greatest investigative paper. Given Insight's size, quality and experience, it is unlikely that Thatcher would have survived all the scandals of her affairs through the 1980s: Death on the Rock, the Pergau Dam, the Westland Affair, the al-Yamamah warplane sale to the Saudis, arms to Iraq – one of them would have brought her down if Insight had thrived. She survived them all, as Murdoch protected his hero.

The 'coalition' of media tycoons and Downing Street faltered when John Major succeeded Thatcher in 1990. Murdoch and Major met only three times in seven years, with Murdoch supporting the Eurosceptics in their disputes with Major's government. In 1997 Murdoch prepared to support Blair, who had courted him, but was also not anti-EU. As it became credible for him to switch to Labour, three months before the election Murdoch had dinner with the Conservative prime minister to give him one last chance to bend. In his evidence to the Leveson Inquiry into phone hacking, Major recalled:

> Mr Murdoch said he really didn't like our European policies ...
> If we couldn't change our European policies his papers could
> not and would not support the Conservative government ...
> It is not often someone sits in front of a prime minister and

says to a prime minister 'I would like you to change your policy or my organisation cannot support you.'[6]

During the UK's referendum, the *Evening Standard*'s Anthony Hilton reported: 'I once asked Rupert Murdoch why he was so opposed to the European Union. "That's easy," he replied. "When I go into Downing Street they do what I say; when I go to Brussels they take no notice."'[7] To his credit, Major showed Murdoch the door and he duly switched to Blair. 'The coalition' of media and government was renewed. It came into its own with the Iraq war. Murdoch had learnt from the Falklands how battle cries sell papers and earn long-term loyalty with paybacks from the government. By now a US-based global proprietor, his Fox News channel gained hugely from its bellicose encouragement of Bush's Iraq invasion. All 175 of his titles (selling 40 million in three continents by one count) arrived at the view that the controversial invasion was correct.[8] In Britain, Paul Dacre told Leveson: 'I'm not sure that the Blair government – or Tony Blair – would have been able to take the British people to war if it hadn't been for the implacable support provided by the Murdoch papers. There's no doubt that came from Mr Murdoch himself.'[9]

This introduces another major player in the story of Brexit. Dacre was the editor of the *Daily Mail*. In July 2016, after their success in the referendum, the Tory supporters of Brexit started to fight amongst themselves over the leadership of the party. Boris Johnson was the front-runner but notoriously unreliable. Michael Gove bid to be in control of the exit negotiations in return for his support. Gove's wife, Sarah Vine, emailed him, and in the excitement sent it to the wrong person and her message was leaked. 'Crucially', she wrote to her husband, to stiffen his resolve, 'the membership [meaning the membership of the Tory Party who vote for the new leader] will not have the necessary reassurance to back Boris, neither will Dacre/Murdoch, who instinctively dislike Boris but trust your ability enough to support a Boris–Gove ticket. Do not concede any ground. Be your stubborn best.'[10] Three things are remarkable about this message. First, Vine was a columnist for the *Daily Mail*, while

Gove had worked for Murdoch. The couple went to the wedding celebrations of the mogul's fourth marriage. As a couple they are an emblem of the political-media caste. Second, Vine regards two men, Dacre/Murdoch, as being of equal importance to the entire Tory Party membership. Third, she puts Dacre ahead of Murdoch.

Dacre worked at the *Daily Mail* from the early 80s and became its editor in 1992. Uniquely, for such a powerful newspaper impresario, he is not the proprietor. His focus is on his readership and his country. His success has been impressive, catching the aspirations and fears of middle England. He understands in a way that most editors do not that a paper is the spaces between its articles, the pacing and contrasts of its stories and headlines, the balance between familiarity and novelty of its coverage, all of which make it, for its regular readers, a home from home. In 2017 the *Mail* sells over 1.5 million copies a day, only 100,000 less than the down-market *Sun*, twice that of the old working-class *Mirror*, nearly four times the sales of the conservative *Telegraph* and *Times* and nearly ten times the sales of the left-of-centre *Guardian*. The *Mail* is well down from its peak of 2.5 million in 2003, but the others have declined more: the *Sun* was then selling 3.5 million, the *Mirror* over 2 million, the *Telegraph* nearly a million. A family paper enjoying a high multiple readership, in 2014, 'Its 4.3 million daily readers include more from the top three social classes (A, B and C1) than the *Times*, *Guardian*, *Independent* and *Financial Times* combined.'[11] If Britain today has a 'Thunderer', it is the *Daily Mail*.

Like Murdoch, Dacre is strongly Eurosceptic and supported Brexit. But they came to a shared view from different routes. Murdoch's hostility is not rooted in a British patriotism, but the cold self-interest of a global mogul. His dislike of Brussels is external: Murdoch prefers the *weakness* of Westminster to the growing strength of the EU, as this makes the UK more pliable to his wishes. If the European Commission had offered to work with his media interests, the *Sun* would have bellowed for Europe and scorned the wretches who wanted Leave as little Englanders. By contrast, Dacre wants a strong, self-confident British government, not a corrupt and manipulative one. His opposition to the EU comes from a domestic concern: that subordination to Brussels undermines belief in the UK and leads to a loss of self-confidence and a weaker democracy.

For example, Dacre surprised many when he backed the notorious pro-European Ken Clarke for Tory leader in 2001 and 2005. The *Mail*'s 2005 editorial is a gem of far-sightedness. It applauded David Davis (the current minister for Brexit) as tough but 'surrounded by some pretty dubious figures'. Cameron was regarded as 'attractive', but 'insubstantial ... too obsessed with aping Mr Blair'. Clarke, while pro-European, now accepted that the UK would not join the euro. It's worth a long quote to see how Dacre thinks:

> This paper was mocked when it backed Mr Clarke for the leadership in 2001 – only for it to emerge afterwards that he was the candidate Labour really feared ... We know his strengths – he's fearless ... this paper, which has been consistently Eurosceptic, has long argued that the debate over the euro has, for the foreseeable future, been overtaken by events. So isn't Mr Clarke showing precisely the kind of astute pragmatism that has been in such short supply in the Tory Party? But his greatest appeal, as Labour's third term degenerates into a Blair/Brown power struggle, is that he has two invaluable aces up his sleeve. Firstly, as the economy falters and tax rises look inevitable, no one in his party is better placed to attack the Government's economic record ... Secondly, on Iraq Mr Clarke is uniquely qualified to start a long overdue demolition job on this Government's shameful war record and to restore Britain's integrity on the international stage. The ineluctable truth is that Mr Blair led Britain into an illegal war on the coat-tails of the Americans, lying to the country as he did so – and has disgracefully got away with it ... Mr Clarke has none of that baggage. He bravely spoke out against the war – and no one has dared accuse him of not being a patriot.[12]

Rupert Murdoch would never have endorsed the pro-European Clarke and could not have denounced the Iraq war in these terms; he was a virtual perpetrator of it and cared nothing for legality. Dacre, by contrast, wanted a prime minister of and from middle England who could secure its interests. That was in 2005 when economic growth was running high, before the Treaty of Lisbon upped the EU's claim on member states, and the crash led to the savage punishment of the Eurozone's southern members.

Dacre's *Mail* dreamt of the marriage of Thatcher's conviction with the inclusiveness of Churchillism long before Brexit. As a guideline for appealing to middle-class readers nostalgic for the lost world of post-war greatness, yet fearful of anything that smacks of the collectivism of those years, who relished the individualism and dominatrix sexuality of the Falklands afterglow, but disapproved of the corruption and permissiveness of the globalisation it heralded, Dacre's dream became an astonishingly powerful formula for readers and advertisers.

Perhaps that 2005 election, when Labour won 90 more seats than the Tories in England but lost the popular vote to them, was the submerged turning point – the election that corporate populism lost by every measure except the electoral outcome – with no one really noticing. Newspapers selling millions must retain a *daily* attachment to their readers, however. Westminster politicians, locked into an undemocratic winner-takes-all election system that spits out unfair results every four or five years, have a different take. Cameron and Osborne, as we have seen, embraced Blair and announced themselves as his 'heir' soon after the 2005 result, at the very point that the ground beneath his feet had shifted. Dacre especially felt things going wrong.

A double movement was taking place within the political-media caste that believed its supremacy was untouchable. A civil war began between the politicians and the press in which the media gained the upper hand in a division that would lead to Brexit. A big, perhaps decisive factor in this shift of power was the erosion of the cultural strength of political parties as both membership and identification with them slumped – a process intensified by the media's war on politics and politicians as such. Party leaders came to be dependent on the media they used. In a reflection on 'public life' in June 2007 as he was about to step down, Blair argued in a thoughtful speech that changes in the media were destructive. He analysed a desperate and wrong-headed search for 'impact' rather than reporting on content – and blamed the press! The master of 'impact publicity', he could not resist his old habits and gave them the dramatic headline they needed as he accused the tabloids of being a 'feral beast, just tearing people and reputations to bits.'[13] In fact the parties, first Labour then the Tories under Cameron, were slain by the sword their own leaders wielded, as their supporters, members and non-members alike, slunk away despised and ashamed.

It took four years before there was a full-scale showdown. The tabloids were right to regard the political elite as unrepresentative. After 2010, all three of the main Westminster political leaders, David Cameron, Ed Miliband and Nick Clegg, had been political advisers in their twenties (Clegg in the EU), and known no other life than conspiracy and political positioning. All moved within Oxbridge-dominated networks of politics, public relations and the media. So privileged was their pole that for them hardly any grease impeded their climbing it. It was a form of insider trading. Murdoch especially took advantage of their weakness, treated them with contempt and crucified whoever got in his way. Finally, the Oxbridge chaps snapped. The incident is revealing. Even if much remains hidden, we can see in it the dangerously riven nature of the British polity, and the deep veins of its instability – its leaders slip and slide as their footholds crumble. Soon after this spasm of disintegration, sometimes known as the phone-hacking scandal, Cameron latched onto the idea of a referendum.

Andy Coulson became deputy editor of the *News of the World* in 2000 under Rebekah Brooks, who was a Murdoch favourite. He became editor in 2003 when she moved to take over the *Sun*, but had to resign in 2007 when his royal correspondent was found guilty of phone hacking. Coulson claimed he knew nothing about it and that it was an isolated case. Six months later David Cameron, now leader of the opposition, hired Coulson to oversee his communications, allegedly urged by Brooks to do so.

Over time another issue emerged that for legal reasons never became an open scandal. A deliberate hint is in the title of *Dial M for Murdoch* by Tom Watson MP and Martin Hickman. It involves Coulson, when he was at the *News of the World*, rehiring Jonathan Rees after Rees had served five years in jail and was under suspicion of killing his partner Daniel Morgan. The police charged Rees with the murder in 2008 but it did not go to court until 2011, when the trial collapsed. In the meantime, Cameron became prime minister. Serious private warnings were sent to Cameron and at least one cryptic public one by Peter Oborne, for the issue was *sub judice*. Its headline was the point they all put: 'Does David Cameron really need this tainted man beside him?' Oborne also accused Coulson of running 'a large private intelligence service, using some of the same highly intrusive techniques as MI5. This illegal surveillance was targeted at the most famous and most powerful men and women in Britain.'[14] He was not sued. In effect, the entire political-media caste, the whole of Westminster, asked itself a question: Is Cameron's debt to, and need for, Murdoch and Rebekah so great, and is he himself so malevolent, as to take such a man and his methods into the heart of government? He was. Cameron appointed Coulson and put him in charge of government communications, even though – which was shocking enough for some – he could not get full security clearance.[15] Westminster shuddered.[16]

Then, the determined investigations by the *Guardian*'s Nick Davies led to an article saying that the *Sun* had hacked the phone of a young murder victim, Milly Dowler. Suddenly, the public shuddered too. It seemed that nothing was sacred. The Murdoch machine would treat ordinary working-class people as if they were scum, just like celebrities. There is a delicious aspect to this. In the days of the Establishment, the *News of the World* would ruin the lives of ordinary people at will to gain a lurid story, but fought shy of exposing the great and the good. Now tabloid anti-elitism reversed the terms. Anyone posh or famous could be worked over, and the nicer and more decent a celebrity, the more their private life was the target for intrusion. Regular, 'ordinary', folk, on the other hand were revered and became sacrosanct. Now, the tabloids' populism boomeranged on them. It was a hack too far, when it could have been you or me.

Murdoch usually rations himself to one malpractice at a time, which he gets away with. This time he overstretched. He had bid to expand his influence even more by acquiring the whole of BSkyB satellite television. On top of that, he joined in a fight over the Labour Party, because after the 2010 election the wrong Miliband brother had won the leadership thanks to trade union support. The plan was to oust 'Red Ed' within the year and the *Sun*, which Murdoch takes the closest interest in, published an attack by Tony Blair on Labour's still fresh leader. The media scented blood. Ed Miliband and his team concluded they had nothing to lose. In what they afterwards called the 'sod it' meeting, Miliband decided to do what none had dared before. He counter-attacked the man who had ruled the UK roost since 1981, and went for Murdoch by calling for the resignation of his head of operations, Rebekah Brooks.

The match lit the tinder. Within the week, on 13 July 2011, David Cameron announced what would become the Leveson Inquiry, a state-sanctioned investigation to put on trial the behaviour of the UK's press. Referring three times to the 'firestorm' in his short speech, the prime minister told the House of Commons:

> There is a firestorm, if you like, that is engulfing parts of the media, parts of the police and, indeed, our political system's ability to respond. What we must do in the coming days and weeks is think above all of the victims, such as the Dowler family, who are watching this today, and make doubly sure that we get to the bottom of what happened and prosecute those who are guilty.[17]

To launch a huge official inquiry into the role of the press and to promise regulation if necessary was a colossal step, driven by rage and anxiety that went much deeper than just a response to the

Dowler phone tap. Looking back, it can be seen – just like the response to the death of Diana – as a Brexit pre-shock. The tectonic plates of public consent were moving. Apparently, Paul Dacre could hardly bear to speak to Cameron again, regarding himself as entirely innocent. But Dacre too would have to undergo the public humiliation of answering for himself before Leveson. The BSkyB deal was frozen. Coulson went (and was later sent to jail), the *News of the World* was closed. The Oxbridge boys had tamed the moguls.

There are opponents you should never leave to live another day. But neither Cameron or Miliband had sought to overturn the 'free press' of corporate power, just to clip their wings. They are not the kind of enemies to appreciate restraint. Revenge, as the saying goes, is a dish best served cold. The moguls had the means to prepare their breakfast. Miliband was shredded relentlessly and without mercy (also his father was monstered as press regulation became likely[18]) until he was destroyed in 2015. Clegg too was dismissed into the phantom zone. Finally, adding an extra rictus to their smiles on referendum morning ... finally, Cameron was rubbed out.

In the referendum, the tabloids functioned as conscious political agents bending their coverage to drive home their desire, which, except for the *Mirror* and a hesitant *Mail on Sunday,* was for Brexit. Hardly bothering to cover up their role with occasional touches of semi-objective reporting, the Brexit papers shaped and strategised their coverage to defeat those whom they opposed. A quantitative analysis of 2,378 articles on the referendum by the Reuters Institute concluded that the press was skewed, highly partisan, treated the vote as a game or contest, and marginalised voices outside politics, ensuring that the undecided were uninformed.[19]

A destructive feedback loop developed as the coalition of the government and media barons turned against itself. The papers undermined the public's belief in the political system. Then they attacked the politicians for overseeing a system that undermined people's belief. Then the politicians attacked the press for undermining them. Then the press assaulted the politicians for being obsessed with the press. All the while, the public voted less and bought fewer papers, generating the 'void' below the exercise of government.[20] Then, the whole lot of them fell apart as the EU referendum turned into a war. The tabloid media lined up against not just the government but the entire political wing of the ruling arc that they were part of. As we have seen, the *Mail* thundered for politicians to 'speak for England'. Two who mattered were bold enough to do so, and stepped forward: an adopted Scot (Michael Gove) and the great-grandson of a Turk born in New York (Boris Johnson). Both were journalists – in fact, better journalists than politicians. Some denounced them for being 'mere hacks', as if their profession lacked gravitas. Perhaps so, but it also meant they were embedded in a network of allegiances and knowledge that needed to sell papers every day. They and their proprietors and editors were closer to public opinion, and in this sense, back-handed compliment though it may be, the better democrats – and the press prevailed.

Brexit has created a new stage in the coalition of government and press. Only this time, primacy has passed to the tabloids. In a thoughtful analysis of the nature of May's government after her Copeland by-election success in February 2017, Tim Montgomerie observed: 'From day one she's been determined to build relations with the *Mail* and *Sun*, and through them with their swing-voting readers.'[21] Indeed. This is a dependency relationship. Of the two, it is the *Mail* that matters most – Dacre's swingers are Theresa's people. For within what became the winning alliance over Brexit lies the difference between a Dacre perspective that wants Brexit to rebuild a strong, clean Britain that enjoys peace and fair government, and Murdoch's desires for Trumpite shocks, division, belligerency and high-tension deals. At the moment of their joint triumph, the two tabloid autocrats have begun to move apart.

However, in the coming civil war over the nature of Britain that Brexit has initiated, the tabloids dominate the field. Politics and politicians alone will be unable to reverse the result. It will also be a fight for our lives against much (not all) of the parliament of toads and weasels sometimes dignified with the name of the mainstream media. Only one force can dominate them now – democracy. Maybe, just maybe, provided the internet really can dissolve their corporate monopoly without creating new ones, democracy has a chance.

It would be wrong to blame the *Mail* for this. On the contrary it is a rare case where everyone else got it wrong. Despite the wicked monstering of its opponents, alone among the major institutions of public life the *Mail* has been consistent in regarding the integrity of British institutions as of crucial importance – and their loss of it with alarm. The *Independent* tried, but the economics of broadsheet publishing, and the indifference to their own country of Britain's very wealthy capitalist class, sank the paper. The *Guardian* has played a heroic role in trying to support a virtuous world, from cutting down Murdoch to exposing surveillance and spelling out climate change, and under Alan Rusbridger it altered American history. But flummoxed by Scotland, nervous of England, it has lectured or teased but not engaged effectively with British democracy or – a crucial part of the *Mail*'s success – family life. All the other titles have submitted to foreign or flawed ownership, from casinos to pornography. Except for the *Mirror*, which speaks for a declining class and has not been able to escape its defensive role to call out to the country as a whole. All through the twenty-first century, as the constitution has crumbled around him, Dacre has demanded politicians and causes fit for the country he believes in. He thinks he has found them in Brexit and May. But they belong to him more than they do to the United Kingdom. Understandably. For there is only one remaining institution in which people believe that boldly claims to stand for Britain. Only one left with the vigour and self-belief, the declarations of decency, the curtain-twitching prurience, lust for discrimination and feverish energy to sustain the desire for the unmanageable fusion of Churchillism with its comforting tribal consensus, and Thatcherism with its thrilling individualist conviction. That institution is the *Daily Mail*.

# 23

# The *Daily Mail* Takes Power

The referendum's outcome caught everyone unprepared. Michael Gove, whose forceful decision to support Leave turned the campaign, was fast asleep. He had gone to bed confident that he had made his stand and the country would continue as before. He and his wife Sarah Vine were woken by a call at 4.45, as she recounted in her column. "'Michael?' a voice said. "Michael, guess what? We've won!" There was a short pause while he put on his glasses. "Gosh," he said. "I suppose I had better get up.'"[1] The government too was taken by surprise. Cameron simply resigned. Only the Bank of England had a contingency plan, to provide extra credit to steady the markets. This was hardly long-term.

One single figure with any standing had thought about implementation. He had long abandoned his one-time ambition to become Conservative prime minister. Instead, from the back benches he became his own government's – and especially Theresa May's – leading critic of their assault on liberty. In February David Davis published a lengthy paper in *Conservative Home* filled with graphs that detailed and advocated the golden promises of Brexit.[2] Immediately after the referendum he set out how best to negotiate them.[3] He was as surprised as anyone to be given the job, as Secretary of State for Brexit, to deliver what he suggested. May turned to her bête noire with instructions that he become her white knight. There was no one else.

Following Cameron's resignation, the Brexiteers had fallen out amongst themselves in farcical confusion, and May emerged as the only disciplined and serious politician in contention. Far from being prepared herself, she had supported Remain. The way she backed the

Cameron government had been low-key, reflecting her loathing of his and Osborne's methods. But in a private, off-the-record discussion at Goldman Sachs on 26 May 2016, a month before the vote, she told its financial specialists: 'I think the economic arguments are clear … I think being part of a 500-million trading bloc is significant for us. I think … a lot of people will invest here in the UK because it is the UK in Europe,' and: 'one of my messages in terms of the issue of the referendum, actually we shouldn't be voting to try to recreate the past, we should be voting for what is right for the future.'[4]

The country voted the other way. Cameron was decapitated. The Tory Party leadership contest was announced on the evening of 29 June, May declared her bid to be prime minister next morning – and set out what has now become the UK's policy on Brexit. She decided she was the best person to 'recreate the past'. At least she understood what she was doing as she put herself forward to be the party's and the country's leader. This is how she explained her change of mind:

> We've just emerged from a bruising and often divisive campaign. Throughout, I made clear that on balance I favoured staying inside the EU – because of the economic risk of leaving, the importance of cooperation on security matters, and the threat to the Union between England and Scotland – but I also said that the sky would not fall in if we left … now the decision has been made, let's make the most of the opportunities … the task in front of us is no longer about deciding whether we should leave or remain. The country has spoken, and the United Kingdom will leave the EU. The job now is about uniting the Party, uniting the country – securing the Union – and negotiating the best possible deal for Britain.

The sense of the vulnerability of the Union as her priority is present from the start:

> The process of withdrawal will be complex, and it will require hard work, serious work, and detailed work. And it means we

need a Prime Minister who is a tough negotiator, and ready to do the job from day one.

And Brexit itself? A famous phrase was born.

> First, Brexit means Brexit. The campaign was fought, the vote was held, turnout was high, and the public gave their verdict. There must be no attempts to remain inside the EU, no attempts to re-join it through the back door, and no second referendum. The country voted to leave the European Union, and it is the duty of the Government and of Parliament to make sure we do just that. Second, there should be no general election until 2020.
>
> There should be a normal Autumn Statement, held in the normal way at the normal time, and no emergency Budget.

She then developed an unequivocal statement that promised a government that works for everyone; to alleviate the injustices of life for blacks, for women and for white working-class men. It was said to have been drafted for her by Nick Timothy, who had immediately joined her campaign team having, significantly, worked for Leave. He is now her joint chief-of-staff. They added this barb for Cameron and Osborne:

> Frankly, not everybody in Westminster understands what it's like to live like this, and some need to be told that what the government does isn't a game. It's a serious business that has real consequences for people's lives.

May had met with Dacre before she made this leadership announcement and knew his concerns . The same evening 'it must be Theresa' was emblazoned across the *Mail*'s front page. Readers were directed to the editorial, which bears Dacre's hallmarks. Normally, it said, the *Mail* 'would not show its hand until the end of a contest'. But with the Tories disintegrating before the public's eyes, 'what the country needs most is a solid and steady hand on the tiller'. It added that May should bring senior Brexiteers into the government with her. Which she duly did. 'The need for a new era of cleaner, more honest, gimmick-free politics has never been greater'.[5]

The next day the *Mail* ran a profile of May that dug out everything positive that could be found.[6] Its headline in bold was: 'The vicar's daughter who met her husband at a Conservative disco: Deadly serious. Utterly steely. After all those Etonians, could this grammar school girl, whose grandmothers were in service, be just what Britain needs?' A question so loaded it fell off the page. Buried in the profile, a reader could discern reports suggesting she had a chronic inability to delegate.

In the short time span between the referendum and her standing for leader, Theresa May did not so much win over the *Daily Mail*, as the *Daily Mail*, its voice, views and priorities, recruited her. With no record of originality, her version of profound reflection is to declare that she 'gets things done'. After twenty-five years in politics, Theresa May has no obvious connections to any think tank. Although she works with Nick Timothy, who has a considerable grasp of Conservative history and policy, she herself shows no interest in ideas, saying only that in order to conserve you must change. As the country faces an unprecedented concatenation of economic, strategic, diplomatic and constitutional uncertainty, and needs a leader with imagination, it has got one who prides herself in getting on with the job, not rethinking what the job is. Serious and determined, May is a first-rate second-rank politician. Beggars can't be choosers, Dacre must have decided, and did his best to project her as the new Thatcher, full of strength and inner conviction.

Every holder of her office is now haunted by the way Margaret Thatcher reshaped the country. But Thatcher's conviction was harnessed to a formidable programme of domestic transformation and a new culture of government, whether you liked it or not. During her four years leading her party in opposition, Thatcher and her team prepared for power, spending meeting after meeting analysing the nature of British decline and trying to understand how to confront it. John Hoskyns, who became her head of policy in Downing Street, 'spent a year preparing a huge diagram showing how all aspects of decline were connected'.[7] Not only was Thatcher the candidate of a significant network of strategists, supported by think tanks, she carried Hayek in her handbag and generated what her official biographer calls 'wonderment at the phenomenon of a party leader in search of ideas'.[8]

The contrast with May could not be greater. Despite this there was a striking and formidable coherence to the general direction set by the new prime minister as soon as she formed her government. Overnight, all her ministers were singing from the same song-sheet, and doing so comfortably. She turned the party's face against the city slickers of globalisation and positioned its social and economic aims to support the 'just about managing', the very people Labour's Ed Miliband had been scorned for identifying as the 'squeezed middle' in 2010 – and was greeted as if she were extraordinarily far-sighted. In all this, she adopted a formed ideology and set of attitudes: she embraced the perspective of the *Daily Mail*. She spoke like its editorials: in short, clear, purposive sentences that left you in no doubt what to think. Across her party everyone grasped the culture and its pitch – they had been reading it year in and year out: 'The British people have spoken'; 'Brexit means Brexit'; 'hard work'; 'serious business'; 'no backsliding on Brexit', 'no second referendum'. Above all, Theresa May shared the *Mail*'s sense of England's grievances, especially with migrants – and England's desire to be British.

These are circulation-building stances for a newspaper. They offer the clarity, spirit and alarmism readers enjoy. But not the politics for a situation as grave as Brexit. In her first speech to her party conference as leader, in October 2015, the prime minister announced she would activate Article 50 in March 2017. It was a moment of utmost gravity. She should have – but did not – recognise, measure and reach out to the immense divisions that Brexit could open within the country. She could have – but did not – consider the implications for the entire continent that Britain once helped liberate from fascism. Instead, her tone, brevity and practical approach were identical to a *Daily Mail* editorial. There was no offer of an open process to explore how best to proceed that might muddy the water. It was not inclusive, it was directive. The *Financial Times* reports that at 'the heart of her new administration is a coterie of loyal and long-serving advisers'. Two exceptions: her private secretary, inherited from Cameron – 'It may be no coincidence that he came from a security background'[9] – and her new official spokesperson ... the former political editor of the *Daily Mail*.[10]

She took ihto Downing Street a tight team drawn from her six years in the Home Office. Its bleak culture at the coalface of immigration, border control, surveillance and what America calls homeland security reinforced an approach that fits with the *Mail* and has a specific government culture of surveillance and selection behind it. Will Davies calls it the 'protective state' that is 'ready to discriminate, and won't be ashamed to admit it. It will discriminate regarding good and bad economic activity; it will discriminate between good and bad migrants; it will discriminate between good and bad ways of life'[11] – and it will introduce grammar schools to discriminate between children. To fulfil this you need to know who is good and bad, and May's most lasting legislative achievement before she became premier was the Investigatory Powers Act that became law at the end of 2016.[12] This legalised all the illegal bugging and snooping that the UK's deep state had been undertaking. The Act is the most intrusive authorisation of powers of surveillance in the West, permitting police and a wide range of officials the right to monitor metadata without a warrant.

Theresa May has become already a historic figure in the way her labile predecessor Cameron was not. She may be limited but she has integrity. Even though she supported Remain, she is now genuine in her commitment. We have seen that Cameron's team identified those who wanted to leave the EU in their 'hearts' but were willing to follow the wisdom of their 'heads' and pockets and vote for Europe, to be the key constituency they had to convince. Theresa May shows every sign that she was one of them, willing to support remain pragmatically but longing to sign up to Leave in her heart. One public emblem of this is the 40-page pamphlet she co-authored with Nick Timothy in 2007, on how to restore parliament's sovereignty over EU legislation. It expresses frustration with the failure of the UK system to get a grip on EU legislation that is regarded as an intrusion.[13]

When England's voters defied the pragmatic argument about the economic benefits of EU membership and Cameron resigned, they gave May a once-in-a-lifetime opportunity to become prime minister. Her heart leapt at the chance. She has embraced what she is doing. She is not being hypocritical or lying. Her heartbeat is synchronised with each edition of the *Daily Mail*. It provided the no-nonsense, Brexit-means-Brexit headline approach she embraced. It set cutting back on immigrants – which is different from being in control of how many come – as a top objective, along with removing the UK from the orbit of the European Court of Justice (which adjudicates the EU's single market). Both these now count for more than economic growth. This means the real Brexit.

At first, no one in the UK's business circles and across Europe was sure what would happen. There were many options, many ways to Brexit. It dawned on them that what May stated when she announced her candidacy, and then in her October 2016 speech to the Tory conference, she meant. More than that, she was relishing the challenge. She is enjoying her role, as the woman who will deliver Brexit. She *wants* to put immigration control and removing the UK from the jurisdiction of the European Court of Justice, before the economy. For her, it is about self-government and taking back control. *Her control.* Not the people's: they have spoken, and that is enough.

May's problem, and more important, her country's, is that such an approach is not going to work. To embark on any considerable public enterprise you need three things. First, you need the ambition to really want the objective. It might change its final shape as other forces impinge, but you must fully will the end in its broad dimensions. Second, you must will the means: the effort, the daily discipline, the demands on others, the focus, determination and, when necessary, patience. With respect to Brexit, Theresa May has these two aspects in full degree. She really wants Brexit as she conceives it. She is really determined to achieve it by every means at her disposal.

But there is a third aspect as well, that is out of your control. There need to be the resources to carry you through. These are not just money, time and skills. They include, above all else, other people ready to join you, who want to make your aims their own, who release energy and invention and solve problems and think like you while thinking for themselves. The greater the aim, the more you need others acting independently to achieve the goal. If it is transformative, as Brexit is, it needs to become a movement. If it cannot create popularity, the effort will fail.

Theresa May does not have the capacity to appeal to a movement across all Britain that can make a success of Brexit in this way. She needs people and the country to come together, but her approach is sundering the nations and fragmenting the English. Yet she can steer no other course. Without the ability to orchestrate, which involves trusting others to play well, she cannot mobilise the unified support she needs and already claims as fact. On 17 January, the prime minister set out her *Plan for Britain* not to the House of Commons but to the ambassadors from the EU, assembled in Lancaster House. 'After all the division and discord,' she told them, 'the country is coming together.' Clearly, it is not. The words felt more like an instruction.[14]

The rigidity to her approach stems from the trap she finds herself in, of Britishness and Brexit. As we have seen, it fell to her to fuse together the Cameron Remain campaign vision of a World Britain and the Leave campaign's Global Britain into her own Big Britishness. She has borrowed the Leave campaign's slogan. But for her it necessitates a domestic programme of social intervention and equalisation not a bonfire of regulations. To deliver her Brexit means mobilising the public to 'come together'. This needs a big, open democratic process, and something else too. For as May warned before the referendum, there will be serious costs and losses for the British economy. She needs to level with the people, raise their morale with inspiring defiance, to prepare the country for a five- to ten-year turnaround if all goes well. But how can she do this when the promise of Brexit was a treasure chest of free trade? She herself did not make this claim and has been careful not to repeat it. Her colleagues did. But she failed to repudiate their optimism at the start. By implication, the public is looking for hundreds of millions for the NHS, oodles of business from global expansion and a great spurt of growth as the country is 'liberated' from Euro-restrictions.

Managing this expectation will be hard enough. She carries an even larger constraint around her neck. Retaining 'our precious Union' is her stated priority. What she regards as the glittering necklace of Britishness is becoming her noose. It prevents any frank and democratic process that would, for example, be a space where the Scots and Northern Irish could work for their own relationship with the EU. For her, a child of Churchillism, their leaving and thereby ending Britain is unimaginable.

There is only one route to May's Brexit, therefore. It has to be imposed: 'There must be no attempts to remain inside the EU, no attempts to re-join it through the back door, and no second referendum.' The word 'must' is stamped on the whole thing from the start, in her election address, before she even was prime minister. It defines her approach in the language of the *Mail*. 'The country' will not be allowed to change its mind so far as she is concerned.

This is hardly the best way to bring people together. At the beginning of her *Plan for Britain*, the prime minister said Brexit 'means taking the opportunity of this great moment of national change to step back and ask ourselves what kind of country we want to be'. But she was not *asking* that all-important question, she was answering it – and cutting off any further debate. Her conclusion: 'I want us to be a truly Global Britain.' She mentioned 'Global Britain' eleven times and the phrase is capitalised in the official text of the speech on the Downing Street website; the harmonics with Great Britain, the lure of the time we shaped the world, is inescapable.[15]

Imperial greatness was a joint project and to have a chance of working 'going global' must be too. At one point May asserts: 'A stronger Britain demands that we do something else – strengthen the precious union between the four nations of the United Kingdom', but later, 'one of the reasons that Britain's democracy has been such a success for so many years is the strength of our identity as one nation'. Is it four nations or is it one nation? To the Europeans she explained that Brexit is an attempt 'to restore, as we see it ... national self-determination ...' But if the Scots ask for national self-determination, they are sharply condemned as divisive. The prime minister is not being muddled: she is having it both ways. The English have done this for far too long. As I showed earlier, to the world the English see themselves as one nation: Britain. Amongst ourselves, we can talk of our four different nations. As she put it to the Scots, speaking in Glasgow, the government is determined that there will be no new barriers 'within our own union'. The words 'our own' reveal what is taking place. What is projected by her as a British voice is heard in Scotland as the cold command of England claiming possession.

The prime minister has succumbed to a most human, and in a leader the most dangerous, of pressures. She is projecting her desire as reality. 'After all the division and discord, the country is coming together' when it isn't. 'The referendum was divisive at times. And those divisions have taken time to heal' – as if they have healed. What we are witnessing in Theresa May is an English voice, in charge of its 'precious union', determined to bend Britain, and therefore in the first place Scotland, to its will. Already, her insistence is tying her in knots. Writing in the magazine of the Holyrood parliament, she told Scots to behave, saying:

> When we take decisions on a UK-basis, whether in a referendum or a general election, every individual has an equal voice. So, in June last year, when the UK as a whole was asked if we should leave or remain in the European Union, every voter had an equal say and the collective answer was final.[16]

The logic seems impeccable until you examine it. If every individual had an *equal* voice in general elections, we would have proportional representation and coalition government. More important, *who* asked 'the UK as a whole'? The prime minister identifies herself with this question. It *presumes* the 'collective answer' that she claims was demonstrated by its answer. Any doubts about the centrality and force of May's determination with respect to Scotland were blown away by her extraordinary speech in Glasgow to the Scottish Conservatives, which included:

> I wanted to make clear that strengthening and sustaining the bonds that unite us is a personal priority for me ... the fundamental unity of the British people which underwrites our whole existence as a United Kingdom ... We need to build a new 'collective responsibility' across the United Kingdom, which unites all layers of government ... I am determined to ensure that as we leave the EU, we do so as one United Kingdom ... a unique responsibility to preserve the integrity and future viability of the United Kingdom, which we will not shirk ... at the heart of the United Kingdom is the unity of our people: a unity of interests, outlook and principles. This transcends politics and institutions, the constitution and the economy ... We are four nations, but at heart we are one people. That solidarity is the essence of our United Kingdom ... [17]

A unity that 'transcends' even the constitution. In the age of Brexit and Trump, when rebellion against traditional authority is the spirit of the time, I'd think twice about laying down the law in such terms, that insist on her personal priority as a matter of fate.

She claims she has *answered* the question 'What kind of country are we?' It is Global Britain with our Parliamentary Sovereignty. When she explained this to Europe's ambassadors, she added:

> Our political traditions are different. Unlike other European countries, we have no written constitution, but the principle of Parliamentary Sovereignty is the basis of our unwritten

constitutional settlement. We have only a recent history of devolved governance – though it has rapidly embedded itself – and we have little history of coalition government. The public expect to be able to hold their governments to account very directly, and as a result supranational institutions as strong as those created by the European Union sit very uneasily in relation to our political history and way of life.

As I argued above, there is an incompatibility between absolutist Britain and the EU. But you can see here how the residues of Churchillist defiance and Thatcherite conviction have fused into a toxic stubbornness. May assumes that her holy trinity of the Union, the unwritten constitution and Parliamentary Sovereignty are in fine fettle. She has to. But they are not. They are fundamentally weakened and incoherent. The EU ambassadors to the Court of St James have their advisers and consult widely. They are aware of the ailing nature of the UK constitution. They will not be taken in, even if they are impressed by the inflexibility of May's personal determination.

May is a grammar-school traditionalist. Her chosen method for delivery is a return to Whitehall Knows Best – which at its frequent worst is secretive, even despotic. In this way she has set her face *against* the energy and originality of the vote to Leave. By describing the arrival of Scottish, Welsh and Northern Irish parliaments as merely a peculiar 'devolved governance', she hints at a famous (for those in the know) dismissive phrase of Enoch Powell: 'Power devolved is power retained'. As for coalition, we will have no more of such 'little histories'! She is taking the UK out of the EU to preserve the Westminster system, with national parliaments reduced to local government, human rights removed from being constitutional claims, less freedom of information, the Lords put back in their place – this is Britain in 1972 when Theresa May was sixteen, and the British were good subjects who still admired our leaders.

May's close advisers describe their approach as a 'new model conservatism', with overtones of Oliver Cromwell's New Model Army.[18] But he led a civil war that oversaw a regicide – not just the summary firing of a chancellor of the exchequer out of the back door of Downing Street. If Brexit was an uprising against the governing 'political elite' and their international friends, it was also a challenge to the way policies are imposed. 'Take back control' has thrilling, democratic implications if it means that people themselves start to take control. Brexit was not just about unfair policies, it was also directed at *who* made decisions and *how* policy is decided. Freedom from the European Union should have delivered the country on a more democratic course, replacing the hyper-centralisation of Whitehall and winner-takes-all elected dictatorship as well. Instead, reimposing them will crush the vitality and democracy out of Brexit.

The positive energy of the Leave campaign was rooted in a spirit of rebellion that goes back to the seventeenth century. For the most part deeply comatose, it was always latent – and has been awakened. This time a modern Cromwell, even in the guise of Theresa Britannia, is unlikely to triumph.

For three reasons. First, Brexit is just beginning. After the Welsh assembly was endorsed by its sliver of a majority, Ron Davies, the then Welsh Labour leader, said 'devolution is a process not an event'.[19] What was true for Wales is far more so for Brexit. There is nothing 'final' about it, nor should there be. Brexit demands, as May herself says, people 'coming together' and the 'country uniting'. This won't happen when people are told they *must* unite and are given ultimatums about what is final. For Brexit to work as a process, it needs to grow and gather support, not be dictated. The example of Thatcher's firmness and success fills the air thanks to the tabloids. Thatcher's belligerent leadership worked only when she also released individual capacities, opened markets whether for houses or on the trading floors, and empowered individualism. When she sought to insist on an unfair poll tax designed to drive voters from the electoral register, and began to regiment the population, she was broken.

Second, Brexit is an old people's home. What does trading as 'Global Britain' mean to a young person who wants to live in Berlin, Paris, Rome, Madrid or Lisbon? The YouGov survey of 5,500 voters on the day of the referendum shows the 18–24 age group backing Remain by 71 per cent. It was pensioners over sixty-five who supported Leave by 64 per cent, and won the day. Among the under-25s, young women voted by an overwhelming 80 per cent to 20 per cent for Europe.[20] The future is becoming more feminine, more open and cooperative with other peoples and cultures, less obsessed with absolute sovereignty. The ineluctable demography of the new networked nationalism will undo Brexit absolutism.

Third, the force of Brexit is nativist and the natives who voted for it are the English, in rebellion against being treated as natives in the only way they can rebel – so far. The UK referendum on membership of the EU was not about the economics, as the Remain side ruefully acknowledged after the vote. It was about what kind of country we want to be. Does England therefore have the right to decide what kind of countries Scotland and Ireland want to be?.

The prime minister is caught up in a profound, unstoppable, reimagining of what the United Kingdom means, even as she insists that she will not accept such reimagining. Her idea of a Global Britain more interested in trade with Uruguay than with Umbria is a spectral hope in the swirling fortunes of a world on fire, while young women across all of Britain's nations look the other way.

In the first part of this book, I showed how Brexit and Trump were driven by a desire to make a jailbreak out of the prison of meaningless language, elite gobbledegook and an imposed power-lessness and inequity while those in charge do marvellously well. The breakout was overdue. The tragedy of the mass escapes of 2016 is that they were led by political mafiosi and scoundrels cashing in on the discontent. Apply this rough-and-ready description of the positive spirit of Brexit Britain today, as May pipes the UK out of the EU. Unlike Trump, who is an experienced godfather and campaigned single-mindedly, the Brexit Cosa Nostra are all over the place. Boris Johnson, Andrea Leadsom, Nigel Farage, Daniel Hannan, Michael Gove – this is a hopeless bunch of ne'er-do-wells who can barely shoot straight even when they aim at each other. Thanks to their incitement, the English breached the walls of elite language, unaccountable Euro-sovereignty and the unctuous hypocrisy of globalist regulation – only to find themselves without a reliable guide to sustain their liberation.

Then, striding purposefully from the home office of the prison itself, came sub-commander May. She told them: I understand you. You are right. The conditions were atrocious. The people in charge claimed to belong to the whole world and belonged nowhere. I applaud your resolve to be rid of them. Also, there has been discrimination. Relations with other prisons have been conducted only to the benefit of the owner (for the prison is privatised). From now on I am your commander. I will speak in plain language. We will take back control, with myself in charge. Close the gates and get back to your cells, or we will lose our precious union. No one can escape to declare their national cell-block independent. We are one prison again.

The United Kingdom as a prison of nations? I think not.

# 24

# The BBC

If, in England's Britain, the *Daily Mail* is the last institution standing with the self-belief to speak out for 'the nation', what about the BBC? It continues – like a familiar motorway that most of the public travels on, rather than somewhere they go to. The BBC was viewed with suspicion by the Brexiteers as the voice of an 'elite' stitch-up, and the tabloids bad-mouthed it whenever they could. After the vote many on the Remain side thought it biased the other way and complained that the BBC gave too much coverage of UKIP and failed to transmit positive views of Europe.

A fragmentation is taking place across the UK, often very lively and now energised by the Brexit verdict. Far from an arid political desert, the landscape has cacti blooming everywhere. Especially, as we have seen, the new parliaments and mayors given institutional form by Labour's reforms in the last years of the twentieth century, from Edinburgh to London. Had the BBC been able to renew itself along with them and shared their energy and self-confidence, it might have conceived of interesting in-depth ways of covering the issues raised by the referendum, that would have deepened understanding of the issues and their consequences – features that the referendum campaign so badly lacked.

One relevant contrast is with the new Supreme Court, created by Labour's 2005 Constitutional Reform Act. It only began to sit in 2009 (previously it was part of the House of Lords). The case that challenged the government's right to trigger Article 50 and allow the UK leave the EU without parliament's approval threw the court into the limelight, and all eleven justices participated. Suddenly, a bunch of judges most people barely knew existed were being live-streamed.

Interest was much heightened by the *Mail*. The High Court was the first to hear the case, brought by pro-Europeans, and it ordered the government to get parliament's agreement to proceed. The *Daily Mail* denounced the three High Court judges as 'Enemies of the People'. It splashed their faces across the top of its front page and exposed their private lives and views. This was disgraceful, as the judges had made a call about the law, not the pros and cons of Brexit. They had, however, frustrated the wishes of Theresa May. She was getting on with the job and wanted no further argument.

In the dust-up that followed, the paper was widely reprimanded and the judges defended. Generally, the most important point was missed: the *Mail* had not spoken on behalf of its readers – in the way the tabloids pride themselves on. It claimed that it and the prime minister are now the voice of 'The People'. But at the end of the episode a new, measured and thoughtful voice was speaking to the country in a way the BBC could not – the Supreme Court judges.

The BBC could never have made an overt claim to be the voice of 'The People'. Once, it *was* their guardian, in the days when the Establishment ruled. It had the integrity and influence of a trusted limb of the larger state, dedicated to 'educate, inform and entertain' without any further need to define its aims. As the Establishment and its paternalist culture went into decline, it needed to renew itself. Greg Dyke, who had made a considerable impact in popular, commercial television and was an early down-to-earth supporter of Tony Blair, became the director general in 2000. His business experience in the media world gave Dyke a rare grasp of the need for political reform, which New Labour circles, obsessed with control, mostly lacked. Had the Blair government committed itself to rebuilding democracy in the UK, instead of trying to impose it by force on Iraq, it would have had a shrewd and fearless supporter in a Dyke BBC, capable of popular engagement.

Instead, although the Corporation reported the build-up to the Iraq war faithfully enough, as the conflict unfolded an early-morning BBC radio broadcast reported that the government had deliberately 'sexed up' a 2002 Iraq dossier that justified a case for war. Clearly, it had. Technically, however, the BBC's reporter was sloppy. To claim that Downing Street was involved in deliberate deceit needed two sources when he only had one, and anyway Blair's people knew better than to leave fingerprints. The prime minister's press secretary, Alastair Campbell, complained vociferously. Fed up with the constant bullying, Dyke defended his team. When, later, David Miliband got his seat in parliament, Blair advised him: 'Go around smiling at everyone and get other people to shoot them.'[1] Seizing the chance, Blair gave Campbell the go-ahead to shoot and wing the Corporation. Without going into further details of the massive inquiry that followed, the BBC Board caved in and Dyke was – in effect – purged. Thousands of BBC staff signed and published an open statement:

> Greg Dyke stood for brave, independent and rigorous BBC journalism that was fearless in its search for the truth. We are resolute that the BBC should not step back from its determination to investigate the facts in pursuit of the truth.[2]

The BBC was fearless no more. Just as Blair's Iraq invasion undermined the public's historic trust in its government, so after his gunmen raked the Corporation, it has never been sure of itself since. Tessa Jowell claims that when the BBC's 2007 Charter renewal came up and she was secretary of state for culture, Blair told her he didn't see the need for the BBC and she saved its existence. I suspect he was just testing the waters. By then, he did not need to bother with the huge antagonism such a step would provoke. Its new director general was overpaid and understanding.

Dyke had started to give the BBC something of the free spirit that Scotland's parliament and London's mayor achieved. Much more was needed. And possible. *openDemocracy*'s OurBeeb ran a feature asking 100 people across the spectrum for one idea for a better BBC.[3] It became a vivid illustration of the extraordinary belief in the BBC and desire for it to do more, from programme ideas to a digital public space, to opening its government to the public – a Dan

Hind suggestion.[4] The BBC could have become a democratic public broadcaster without being populist and gaining in quality. It was, alas, a constitutional reform too far. The BBC remains the overwhelming source of news and television in Britain, with its 74 per cent share of the TV news audience, over 70 per cent of the radio news and 40–50 per cent of online news. If you include print journalism, then more than half of all the news reports people listen to, watch or read online in Britain is originated by the BBC. Murdoch's group is next with an estimated 9 per cent, just ahead of the Mail group.[5] Nothing touches it so far as the public is concerned. It is far from broken, therefore, but its spirit has been bowed.

The night and morning of the referendum result showed how the BBC merely rehearses the order of things rather than encourages public self-confidence. A historic referendum is a festival of democracy. It was treated as routine. There was an amusing moment just after 4 a.m. on referendum morning. David Dimbleby, who was the single anchor for the evening, had just called the outcome. There to discuss it with him were – in the name of balance – a Remainer and a Leaver: Hilary Benn MP, a Labour Remainer, and Jacob Rees-Mogg MP, a Tory Leaver. These three were on the cusp of history, the first to assess the significance of a transformative outcome for the country, for Europe and arguably for the world.

It was a trio of the sons of the living dead. David Dimbleby's father, Richard Dimbleby, had been the dominant BBC public affairs broadcaster, from the coronation of 1953 to Churchill's funeral in 1965. A careful interviewer of the Establishment, he was a master of making the public feel respectfully safe in live broadcasts. Jacob Rees-Mogg's dad had been the editor of *The Times* from 1967 to 1981, until Murdoch took it over (he later praised him for his beneficial influence), headed the Arts Council, which he cut back, and was made a baron. He was an ideologist of the Establishment's embrace of Thatcher. His son Jacob is a fund-manager and MP who affects theatrical double-breasted suits and a plummy voice. A thoroughly right-wing Brexiteer, worth around £50–100 million, he personifies the mental shrinkage of the transition from the Establishment to the political-media caste that accompanied the ballooning of legal but ill-gotten gains.[6] Finally, Hilary Benn's father, Tony Benn, was the grand old man of the Establishment Labour left, and its most eloquent anti-European. Hilary Benn personifies the long, slow parricide and accompanying guilty feeling that haunts his generation of the Labour Party, as it abandoned Labour's loyalty to Great Britain and shifted to a staid embrace of Europe without the zest and the excitement of cosmopolitanism.

Who could possibly doubt that these children of three of the country's formative father-figures were there on merit? I apologise for the ironic question. Nobody who was still awake at 4 o'clock that morning could possibly have thought this was the best trinity the country could provide. The BBC was carrying on as people expected it would, being as safe as possible, just like a reliable motorway. Each one of them had enjoyed a privileged start in life and together they formed a picture of continuity. So that there was a grimly comic aspect to their contemplation of a revolution directed against themselves. Benn expressed his personal sorrow at the vote. Dimbleby asked whether Brexit would now happen. Rees-Mogg, its double-breasted Robespierre, thought it would because, he solemnly declared, 'power flows from the people'. His father, and what is left of Edmund Burke, would have been whizzing in their graves had they been able to tune in. Almost carelessly, Rees-Mogg discarded the fundamental principle of British sovereignty, which is that power does *not* flow from the people. Neither Dimbleby *fils* nor Benn *fils* raised any objection, or indeed showed any awareness, that Rees-Mogg's observation turned British history upside down. A political system that had lived by its passion for parliamentary sovereignty had just been knifed in the heart. They chatted on: three sons of a once mighty order, in the early morning of a BBC studio.

Evidence that a wing of the corporation was indeed pro-government as the Brexiteers alleged came in an appalling hour-long documentary at the end of August 2016, two months after the referendum. It was an overview of why it turned out the way it did, presented by Laura Kuenssberg, the BBC's political editor.[7] Her view was that Cameron was complacent when he committed the Tories to a referendum to stop the rise of UKIP. After he won the 2015 election, Cameron did not get much of a reform deal from the EU, although she felt he did his best. Meanwhile, those who wanted Brexit were planning and focused. When Cameron set the referendum date, two of his close mates, Gove and Johnson, betrayed him. They supported Leave and deserved to be mocked. But the Brexit campaign had devised a cunning slogan, 'Take back control'. Lies were told on both sides – only the Leave side's lies were smarter.

Meanwhile, Peter Mandelson was in control of the Remain campaign. Why this throwback to the past was its spokesman we were not told. A young Will Straw was its chief executive. His father, Jack Straw, did time in Mandelson's New Labour project, as home and foreign secretary. In their interviews Mandelson and Straw both blamed everyone else, especially Jeremy Corbyn, for it all going wrong, and they felt 'let down'. The fact that it was Labour that lost it was confirmed by four old, northern, white, working-class men with bad teeth, who said this was so in a pub. No wealthier home county Leavers or Conservative voters came into the picture, even though they were more numerous supporters of Brexit. The Remain campaign meanwhile stuck to fear of the financial costs to persuade people to stay in the EU. They won this argument. But then the Leave campaign pressed the immigration button. Immigration was decisive according to Nigel Farage. The decent Remain side had no comeback against the horrible racism he aroused.

That was it, folks. The 'inside story'. All is explained. In her summing-up, Kuenssberg concluded that it had been 'two fingers up' at parliament and described the Leave campaign as 'a coup'.

So according to the BBC's flagship political reporter, when the opposition wins 17.4 million votes and frustrates the prime minister, the government and world officialdom in open combat in a contest called by the government itself, it is a coup. For that, all UK households are owed a rebate on the licence fee. The gravitational influence of the Cameron government ruled her presentation. It also showed how the official culture of the BBC is inimical to discussions of democracy, because if it was not democracy that overturned the government, then it had to be conspiracy.

The perspective did not go unchallenged. Kuenssberg's predecessor, Nick Robinson, became a presenter on the Radio 4 *Today* programme and three weeks later gave a different report from the Suffolk coast in which he said:

> It has become something of a cliché hasn't it, that the country voted to leave the EU thanks to a revolt of northern working-class former Labour voters. That is, of course, a vast oversimplification. Here in Suffolk on the east coast almost six in ten people voted to Leave, this in a county which has only Conservative MPs, all of whom incidentally voted to Remain. This is an area whose prosperity depends on trade, on tourism, on farming and fishing ... Come here to Felixstowe and you are reminded that the golden rule of politics, of every election campaign and every referendum turned out to be fool's gold. It was *not* the economy stupid. It was instead concerns about democracy, sovereignty, control, that triumphed.

Robinson interviewed a fisherman who said: 'in terms of the fishing it's about accountability to me'. Also, a businessman who services the container port and employs a lot of east European drivers, 'I should have voted to remain but as a citizen I voted out.' 'Anyone who voted Leave like you in the hope that drivers would be Brits in the future, are they kidding themselves?' Robinson asked. 'Absolutely. This vote had nothing to do with immigration,' he replied.[8]

The BBC did not debate the enormous clash of perspectives. Bound by the obligation of neutrality, it would have needed courage. *openDemocracy*'s OurBeeb made a stalwart case that the country should be better informed,[9] but the major political parties did not set out lively arguments for Europe that it could report. Caroline Lucas, the sole Green MP, had a justified grievance in not getting coverage of her eloquent case that the EU needing to be improved through the UK remaining part of it. But the lack of belief in Britain being European reflected England's prejudice when this needed to be challenged. However, the BBC is at ease with populism. It gave UKIP airtime beyond its relevance, perhaps with a special reason in mind. Drawing attention to the barbarians at the gate, and how awful a threat they are to British civilisation, must surely reinforce demand for a well-funded gatekeeper. Who else can that be but the Corporation? It may not be able to stand for Britain but it is prepared to be its own last defence.

# 25

# What Kind of Country Do We Want to Be?

As he announced the date of the referendum from the steps of Downing Street, the then prime minister, David Cameron, told voters that the issue of EU membership 'goes to the heart of the kind of country we want to be'.[1] Four months later they rejected his advice as to the kind of country we are. After Theresa May moved into Downing Street to replace him, she used his same words. She told voters that the outcome was 'a turning point for our country. A once-in-a-generation chance to change the direction of our nation for good. To step back and ask ourselves what kind of country we want to be'.[2]

Traditionally, Britain's ruling classes have distinguished themselves by never asking such a question and scorning those who wished to. They took pride in not bothering to write down a constitution, let alone drone on like lesser countries about who 'we want to be'. The English especially have taken themselves for granted without what they regard as the nonsense of identity politics. This is one of the ways that other peoples were made to feel small or at least not quite so significant. As I have described above, scholarship on nationalism has explained why: it is because the English were 'first born' as a nation at the start of modern industrial history, giving them the advantage over everyone else.

It is quite exceptional, therefore, for two prime ministers in succession to raise the issue so directly and in such an open fashion. In both cases, however, their motive was to preserve what they could of Westminster's exceptionalism. They posed the issue

239

of what kind of country we are, not to start a debate but to impose their own solution. The question in both cases was rhetorical. For all that, the obligation they felt to put it clearly was a step towards a much-needed political normalisation and even the possibility of real change.

It was to the credit of the right that they insisted on keeping the question alive in the first place. The kind of country we want is the starting point of self-determination, it is central to political life, and therefore to what it means to be human in our present epoch. One reason why the right won such dramatic successes in 2016 in England is that their opponents on the left fled the field of meaning and identity. In Scotland, where this was not so, the governing Scottish Nationalist Party showed that asking 'what kind of country we are' can assist the influence of a party of the centre-left. It gave their First Minister Nicola Sturgeon the confidence to stand up to May when no one else dared. But in Westminster, the British parties of the left, above all the Labour Party, in its benighted obsession with the tangible, talked only of what they perceived as practical, economic matters, and were unable even to have a wholehearted row about what kind of Europe they wanted, let alone what kind of Britain. I am not talking here about formulaic gestures but real engagement with the unhappiness and insecurity of the UK's place in the world and the growing national movements within it, as well as its multicultural identities.

It's a paradox, because you might expect the left to query the country's nature and destiny and the right to resist such questioning. At the end of the 1990s, with the rise of New Labour, this was the case, with Labour saying we should be a 'young country' and 'seize the future' and proposing a lot of far-reaching constitutional reforms, while the Tories were passing anti-gay legislation until they were thrown out of office.

I have gone through some of the fundamental issues and post-war history to show why this situation was reversed. The older uncodified multinational United Kingdom does not fit easily with the larger constitutionalising multinational European Union. New

Labour had the opportunity to confront this but preferred, in Blair's words, to 'overcome the greatness of our history to discover the full potential of our future'.[3]

New Labour did good things. Admittedly at the top of a boom, it saved the NHS, invested heavily in schools, passed historic constitutional reforms. It should be seen as a renewal that failed – a failure that was continued by Cameron's Conservative version of the project until 23 June 2016. Then, rather than lead the country into the difficult exercise of taking a step back to ask itself where it goes from here, in a continuation of the democracy of the referendum, May has done the opposite. She has decided to squelch the divisions and furies aroused by the June vote, especially the stark national differences revealed between Scotland and England. There is one country, in her view, and it has made up its mind 'for ever'.

In the name of change she intends to return Britain, as she keeps on repeating, to its 'Precious, precious union'. Her answer to the question, What kind of country are we?, is set out in a special Brexit website, *A Plan for Britain*.[4] As it was launched she explained:

the referendum last summer was not just a vote to leave the EU but an instruction to change the way our whole country works – and the people for whom it works – for ever.

Her goal is 'a great United Kingdom a country that works for everyone, not just the privileged few'.

That is what our *Plan for Britain* will do. We will forge a more global Britain, securing a new partnership with Europe and reaching out to old friends and new allies alike. We will help to build a stronger economy where everyone plays by the same rules. We will support a fairer society where success is based on merit, not privilege.

This is the overarching goal of our *Plan for Britain*, because nothing is more important to me than seeing this United Kingdom thrive. This precious union of nations, joined together for over 300 years, is the most successful the world has known.[5]

To achieve this outside of the EU she will have to defy a form of Dani Rodrik's trilemma. She wants lots of free trade with the entire world. She wants the UK to be unpenetrated by the laws of others. She wants very little immigration. Any two of these are possible, if hard enough, without the third. Can a country have all three? The stress of trying to achieve the impossible makes her relationship with the other, non-English nations very rigid. The country is on the edge of a breakdown.

Britain has been here before, since 1945, seeking to preserve its historic 300-year success when under tremendous internal strain. It has resolved the crisis by external measures. One of these was to join what would become the EU. But usually it is the special relationship with America that has rescued the country and ensured continuity. May went to visit President Trump as soon as she could, and delivered a classic pitch for the revival of the special relationship to a gathering of the US Republicans before meeting Trump the next day:

> The United Kingdom is by instinct and history a great, global nation that recognises its responsibilities to the world ... as we rediscover our confidence together, as you renew your nation just as we renew ours, we have the opportunity – indeed the responsibility – to renew the special relationship for this new age. We have the opportunity to lead, together, again.[6]

With *Donald Trump*? He is for protectionism, unenthusiastic about NATO, wants trade deals of a kind that will damage the UK's surplus with the US, does not – cannot – shake hands with Angela Merkel and even attacks a chimeric GCHQ. He is putting the entire alliance at risk.

There can be good breakdowns, that lead to a necessary resolution of a crisis. There is no need to be frightened of this one, given the vitality and wealth of England, the resources it can draw upon. What even its exceptional legacy cannot do is make the impossible possible.

I have worked through the state of the UK's constitutional nations, structures and principles to test their resilience and see where the spirit of modernisation, built into them since 1688, is heading. Crucial in all this are the twists and turns of the ruling elite over the last seventy years, since the Churchillist post-war settlement. The Establishment gave way to manipulative populism – sold out, is probably how Theresa May and the *Daily Mail* see it, with justification. The City of London has become the greatest money-laundering machine in the world and draws on a unique global network. Otherwise, culturally, socially, politically and militarily, as well as economically, the UK is part of Europe. Can the country pull out of its homeland continent, while cutting away the huge economic gift of immigration, and yet still prosper? This is the gamble Theresa May and the *Daily Mail* have taken as they attempt to beam Brexitannia back into the twentieth century, somewhere between the advent of the Beatles and Punk.

# PART IV
# FROM GLOBALISATION
# TO IMMIGRATION

Elites have failed and, as a result, elite-run politics are in trouble. Throughout the high-income countries one sees the emergence of populist political – xenophobic populists of the right and egalitarian populists of the left. What these share is an ability to muster the inchoate anger of the disenchanted and the enraged who feel, understandably, that the system is rigged against ordinary people. History suggests that such anger will not end well. Often it has ended up with authoritarian rule, civil war or external war. Elites frequently attempt to exploit or indeed to exacerbate such populism for their own ends. But this, too, tends to end badly, even for themselves.

Martin Wolf,
*The Shifts and the Shocks*, 2015

# 26

# Neoliberalism: Just Say the Word

If there was a single puff of smoke that signalled the revolutionary nature of 2016, the global extent of its reverberations, the still limited nature of their shocks and the likelihood of more to come, it was a clash over a word. Towards the end of May, as the UK referendum campaign entered its final weeks, the *Financial Times* went head to head with the International Monetary Fund. The IMF published a report by a team of three economists from its research department, including its deputy director. They said that there was 'much to cheer in the neoliberal agenda' – millions had been brought out of poverty around the world, inefficient state industries had been privatised – but there were also problems. Removing capital restrictions and insisting on austerity to balance budgets, deregulation and, increasingly, competition had not achieved very much: 'The benefits in terms of increased growth seem fairly difficult to establish when looking at a broad group of countries.' The neoliberal agenda had increased inequality in a way that 'hurts the level and sustainability of growth'. The movement of money that accompanied opening financial markets also led to damaging instability.

The authors showed graphs that tracked how deregulation and competition led to an increased probability of an economic crisis, by tracking 149 'episodes' across 53 countries, and to a growth in inequality, examining 165 countries over 224 'episodes'. One of their conclusions: 'The pervasiveness of booms and busts gives credence to the claim by Harvard economist Dani Rodrik that these "are hardly a sideshow or a minor blemish in international capital flows; they are the main story"'.[1]

The *Financial Times* was beside itself. It was not angry to discover how little growth there had been, and at what cost. It was certainly not grateful for the huge amount of research that had gone into the IMF team's summary of their wide investigation. The inequality driven deep into societies throughout the world, that the IMF tried to measure, was not a problem for the pink broadsheet. Something much, much graver had taken place. Something that had to be stopped. The IMF team had betrayed the *omertà* of the financial universe. They had used the word 'neoliberalism' to describe what is happening. The *FT*'s news item on the report regarded this as the main story: 'the use of the term "neoliberalism" is provocative'. Then it explained to its readers that the word 'is normally used by critics of free market economics'.[2] To prove this it quoted the *Socialist Worker* (so now we know who reads it). A report on the investigation of a major failure across numerous countries of a huge global policy was not news. It was of little interest that the IMF's well-presented research showed that the UK government should abandon its policy of austerity. The big story was the 'provocative' use of a term that dates back to the 1930s and has been embraced by many distinguished economists since then. Four days later the paper's leader writers got to work. Their editorial was calculated and ferocious: its aim was to intimidate the IMF, and anyone else for that matter, from ever doing it again. 'Neoliberalism', the *Financial Times* declared with all its authority, is 'an all-purpose insult'. One, however, it assured its readers, that 'has lost any meaning'. A 'sorry spectacle befell the International Monetary Fund', it continued, in allowing itself to publish a report that claims, 'instead of delivering growth, some neoliberal policies have increased inequality, in turn jeopardising durable expansion'. This was 'navel-gazing', 'childish rhetoric', and the IMF had 'taken its eye off the ball'. Puffing itself up to its full might, the *FT* sought to contrive the most damming insult it could imagine to put a stop to such behaviour. The IMF, the paper declared, 'looks as out of date as a middle-aged man wearing a baseball cap backwards'.[3]

If this is the best its editors can do, the *FT*'s new owners, Nikkei, may have overpaid. But the paper's rage is understandable. The myth of the free press is that the great institutions that govern us try to keep their methods and failures private from the public, and that the role of the press is to expose reality and reveal what they are up to. All of a sudden, the roles were reversed. The *Financial Times* was shown to be part of the order of things, while the Fund had blown a small whistle that named the policy framework that governs the global economy – and pointed to some disastrous consequences.

If there is one general world condition that provoked Brexit and Trump, it is 'neoliberalism'. This is the word that names the dominant political-economic order often described as 'globalisation'. Neoliberalism drives the insecurity of employment, the privatisation of the NHS if you are in Britain, the inflation of asset prices that makes housing so costly in the cities and their catchment areas around the world; it is permissive of immigration, scornful of loyalties, encourages booms and busts, and has generated acute inequality and grotesque speculative fortunes. Part of its success is that although it has been legislated and regulated into existence, it has avoided being named. Whenever there is an outrage, like Macavity, the master criminal of T. S. Eliot's *Cats*, neoliberalism is not there.

When Donald Trump's 62 million supporters, cheer on his denunciation of 'globalism' and 17 million Brits vote to 'take back control', they are responding to the failure of neoliberalism to satisfy their sense of self-government while it increases their insecurity. This is linked to neoliberalism's unequal economic outcomes, mapped by the IMF report. Its authors may use the word because without it they can't salvage their domination. The *FT* fears that by acknowledging its name they draw back the curtain to reveal it as a ruling order, the essential first step to its replacement.

At the start of the book I described four breaches of trust. Two concerned military domination: the deceit of the 2003 invasion of Iraq, and its continued, drawn out military failure. The second two were products of neoliberalism: the financial crash of 2008, and the way the system was saved. The crash was caused by unregulated financial speculation, permitted because 'the market knows best'; the lame recovery since shows it is *not* 'the market' that decides, but its high priests: the banks, funds and politicians who ran things, albeit incompetently, for their own benefit. Thus austerity in the UK was used to impose savage cuts on local government services. This was justified in the name of reducing the budget deficit. But there are other ways to achieve this than cutting benefits to the poorest (a modest wealth tax, for example). A study from University of Warwick of 380 local authority areas concluded there was a direct link between austerity driven cuts and the vote for Leave.[4]

From the *Financial Times* downwards, public discourse is filled with gatekeepers forbidding the use of the name of the god that rules. It is essential to break the taboo if we are to recover from Brexit and Trump. 'We live in a neoliberal world' should be on every bumper-sticker. The cause behind the crisis cannot be removed until it can be named and described. This is what I will attempt to do here in order to sketch the economic background whose neoliberal system led to the demands for an end to the way Britain and America are governed that came to a head in 2016.

Neoliberalism is not globalisation. Globalisation can take many forms. In a great book, *Globalization in Question*, first published in 1996 when early Clintonism was just making the idea fashionable, Paul Hirst and Grahame Thompson warned those tempted by its bandwagon. Globalisation is not new, they argued and they showed that there had been intense internationalisation of the world economy between 1870 and 1914. The new supranational structures being created might meet a similar fate, they presciently warned.

After 1945, the British, led by John Maynard Keynes, assisted the creation of an American global financial order at Bretton Woods, with fixed exchange rates centred on the dollar. So there have been at least two major and different kinds of international systems of 'globalisation'. One preceded the First World War, the next followed the Second. The form it took after 1945, initiated by the Bretton Woods Agreement, is known as Keynesianism. Its core concept is that societies could and should ensure near-full employment through demand management, while using taxation to provide a welfare state. Keynesianism was an explicit ideology of government of the market, to try and ensure that the economy worked for all. Keynes was a liberal and it was not socialism. Social democrats, Christian democrats and conservatives could all adopt a Keynesian approach, which changed through time.

Keynesianism started to run out of steam and then fail from the end of the sixties into the seventies, and was replaced by the advent of neoliberalism with the elections of Reagan and Thatcher, although President Carter and Prime Minister Callaghan had started a turn towards it. Its approach had been given its name in Paris in 1938, and it was developed as a critique of Keynesianism and socialism through the fifties.[5] But when it became influential and replaced Keynesianism in the 1970s and 1980s, those who carried it forward dropped its name. The adoption of neoliberalism coincided with its apparent disappearance. This became part of its power and effectiveness. It projected itself as a natural expression of human economic activity, summed up by Margaret Thatcher as 'There is no alternative'.

The world is complicated and we need terms and language to describe and understand it, capable of containing complexity. Keynesianism, which is not so hard to understand, at least in my simplistic description, is sophisticated and had many variants. The formulation of neoliberalism was developed by several economists and political philosophers, and like Keynesianism has developed as it influenced government. It is not a doctrine. It is a broad ideology with various schools and tendencies within it. While lots of scholars write about it, it has a peculiar quality when it enters the public realm and influences policy, which it does a lot. It denies it is an ideology. Instead, as an ideology it claims that it is merely advancing natural activities which are best not governed or directed. It is as if it claims to be a finger pointing at realities while not in any way constructing or directing realities. In fact it dictates economic policies with real-life effects. It is possible therefore to describe what neoliberalism does even though its perpetrators want us to believe that it is not responsible for anything. The following is a sketch of what follows from the governing political-economic theory of our time.

Its core belief is that individual competition is the primary quality of human nature and this should be given expression by encouraging market values to dominate everything. While I will emphasise its negative consequences, it is not all bad. Since the 1980s it has accompanied the greatest movement out of extreme poverty in history, the transformation of humanity from a predominantly rural to an urban species and the digital revolution. Today, its denial of the intrinsic value of government, its privatisation of the commons and lionising of profit is set to blight the world. To prevent this it must be openly recognised for what it is: the supremacy of money over meaning. The following set of contrasts simplify the principles of the neoliberal order:

**Competition (not markets)** Neoliberalism as a policy seeks to marketise as much of life as possible. It privatises state-owned resources, including prisons, and brings private companies in to manage and profit from public work. But it is not the case that the market lies at its heart. The driving idea of neoliberalism is the need for competition. As Will Davies puts it, 'the market is a space of equivalence in that two people come together and perform an act of exchange ... For neoliberals, the market is something which produces inequality between people'. This is because it claims that value comes from competition.[6] The distinction is especially important because defenders of the current order, especially on the left, dismiss critics of neoliberalism for being against 'the market', which need not be true. In a market exchange between a producer and a consumer, both parties benefit in a transaction of mutual gain. In competition between producers, there can be overall gain but the primary aim is supremacy. Neoliberalism fetishises competition. It contrives competitive mechanisms and pushes them into state and society, via quasi-markets such as league tables, undermining the ethos and vocations on which professionalism and care depend. Neoliberalism is above all an ideology of 'competition' that dehumanises and controls.

**Profit (not customers)** In a famous 1970 article in the *New York Times*, Milton Friedman, one of the founders of neoliberalism, concluded by quoting from his *Capitalism and Freedom*: 'there is one and only one social responsibility of business – to use its resources and engage in activities designed to increase its profits ...'[7]

Many objected, because it is not true. Companies make things or supply services to customers. This is their purpose. Profit should be a consequence, not the aim, and for all good businesses this is the case. But value for neoliberalism is measured only by money in the form of profit. And there is a twist: profits from rental incomes from rights and services and rising asset values are more important than traditional 'making and trading' profits.

**Maximisation (not optimisation)** If the measure of success and virtue for neoliberalism is profit, then the more the better. It regards profit as something to be maximised. But this is an extreme approach that led critics like George Soros to criticise neoliberalism for being a 'market fundamentalism'. Firms and enterprises of all kinds should seek to *optimise* their returns, balancing local employment, the satisfaction of the workforce, the quality of the goods or services and, above all, sustainability, not simply maximise their profit to give the highest rate of return to shareholders, who in turn seek maximum returns on the stock exchange. As optimisation involves making local judgements that cannot be quantified and compared, it falls outside the framework of competition and neoliberalism.

**Individual (not society)** The dehumanisation of society is embedded in the notion of maximisation. In the same *NYT* article, Friedman wrote: 'There are no values, no "social" responsibilities in any sense other than the shared values and responsibilities of individuals. Society is a collection of individuals and of the various groups they voluntarily form.' This is the source of Margaret Thatcher's claim that 'There is no such thing as society'. The atomisation of society is an important attribute of neoliberalism: it privatises people and families. Trade unions become a restraint on the very nature of life, mutuality is nixed. Individual choice, investment, speculation is rational and good; state expenditure, support and collective decision-making is bad – inherently wasteful and oppressive. Tax is always a 'burden'.

**Financialisation (not investment)** Maximising profits by skimming other people's money through speculation is the most competitive way possible to generate large returns. Neoliberalism has become a vehicle for global financial manipulation that hugely intensifies inequality. All barriers to the reach and speed of speculation are regarded as impediments. This extends to the use of labour, seen as a commodity on an international scale. The dissolution of borders follows. Because it is monetised, neoliberal cosmopolitanism does not delight in difference or pluralism; it values plush, commercialised uniformity everywhere, brightened by passing celebrity extremism and local colour.

**Market competition (not government service)** The greatest flow of wealth is via the tax base of the state. It becomes a lucrative target to be levered open for corporate profit. The overall role of the state is to assist neoliberalism in creating profit, which is the only form of value. 'A proper functioning state was obviously necessary to do what only governments could do, as was a thriving and competitive private sector to generate the nation's wealth. Together, each in their proper sphere, they determined prosperity.'[8] The author is Tony Blair. The error here is simple, devastating and the acme of neoliberalism. The description denies the possibility of the *public* sector creating wealth and makes it the whole aim of government to assist the private sector that alone 'generates the nation's wealth'. The state is conceived as a specialist, instrumental function. Implicitly, the aim of the nation is to service its capitalist class. I say that the error is simple and devastating. In the UK, for example, part of the BBC's *value* is that it is *not* part of the private sector. There is value in taking some utilities such as water out of the market. This is even more true of the Health Service, which generates huge money efficiencies, saving Britain from a vastly expensive and often counterproductive medical insurance system, while relieving people of the anxiety of paying for a major illness which itself is of unquantifiable value. That a Labour politician should be unaware of this is an indictment. Associated with neoliberalism's resistance to government is a preference for rights that impose market values irrespective of party politics.

**Disruption (not continuity)** In order to impose its preferences, keep governments on the run, break up traditional companies and institutions, neoliberalism thrives on shock and disruption. Booms and busts transfer wealth to those who manage financial operations, extend precariousness and thus start new rounds of competition.

**Concentration (not openness)** We are told we live in a free society of open markets, but its neoliberal nature ensures the concentration of power, especially financial, and now platform power (Google, Amazon, Facebook). While it projects an ethos of liberty and freedom, the underlying force of neoliberalism is corporate power reinforced by surveillance through which individual choice is shaped to maximise returns for platforms and corporations.

**Women (not feminism)** Neoliberalism has played a part in the most important political transformation of our epoch, equality for women. The market welcomes them as individual consumers, especially of competitive fashions, and has helped break down barriers of entry for women everywhere. At the same time it undermines their organisation as women, and it is the enemy of the values of feminism, solidarity, humanism and human equality.

**A small state (not a strong one)** Because it seeks competition the neoliberal state is ideally small and minimal. Whereas, to get the benefits of world trade large, active states are needed. For example if you want to make the best of globalisation, you need life-long learning – not a budget cut of 40 per cent for those teaching adults.

**Depoliticisation (not engagement)** By turning individuals into competitive consumers and insisting that the market rules as a force of nature not a policy of responsible government, neoliberalism encourages fatalism and political powerlessness. Abstention from voting, disbelief that anything can change, acceptance that there is no alternative, resignation and addiction are neoliberalism's form of serfdom: self-subordination and political abstention.

**Economics (not political economy)** With so much money around and so many policy issues posed by the need to understand the world economy, there has to be a profession. As much as possible this has been turned into an arcane mathematical specialism serving unquestioned competitive values. The real responsibility of economists, to ensure that the production of the marketplace benefits humankind, needs politics as well as economics.

**The Macavity Syndrome (Macavity's not there)** The distinctive public feature of neoliberalism is that you are forbidden to mention its existence in regular language. Nor is 'it' responsible. No one is. The rule of competition and the laws of the market are facts of nature not the consequences of government, and the public must understand that there is no alternative. Wherever the scene of the crime, Macavity is not there, politicians are not responsible, no one is, except for the supra-human market that provides the law of the financial universe.

If you take these attributes of neoliberalism together there are four sets of outcomes: planetary, national, corporate and individual.

At the planetary level, it means treating workers as a commodity everywhere and maximising returns by internationalising investment and acquisition. This is now putting the planet at risk. The fundamental need to challenge neoliberalism stems from the urgent priority to govern the global environment and protect its ecosphere.

At the national level, neoliberalism means a strange kind of hyper-regulation and austerity driving obsessive audits into parts that should be free to breathe. It seeks to shrink the state and welfare costs, supposedly to improve the prospects for growth, defined as increasing the value created by the private sector. Austerity does not work for whole countries, as the IMF analysis showed, but it does enrich the rich. At the same time it regulates and audits all areas of life, especially those public services that remain as it seeks to 'marketise' their ethos – from universities to financial service providers. Behind this is neoliberalism's anti-national ideology of globalisation as, through its mantra of competition, it serves up the national marketplace to transnational corporations.

Corporations are the greatest beneficiaries of neoliberalism, as the bodies best able to benefit from competition that crushes, or takes over, rivals. This is where the competitive, winner-takes-all nature of neoliberalism trumps its lauding of the marketplace. It is particularly evident in the capture of government by banking and financial services – from 1998 to 2008, 'the financial sector spent

$1.7 billion on US campaign contributions and $3.4 billion lobbying the government.'[9]

For individuals, the ideology of neoliberalism is delightful as the more successful you are in monetary terms, the more you think you inherently deserve it. Fail, and you deserve your insecurity, your foreclosed home, your zero hours, your lifetime of debt ... the crucial thing to understand about the experience of neoliberalism is that it is not responsible for its outcomes, *you are*.

It is evident, therefore, that neoliberalism is an inhuman and depraved way to try to run global affairs and national economies. No decent capitalist trying to run a good company for the long term would dream of endorsing its attributes. Worse, it is a kind of 'economic imperialism', in that neoliberals refuse to recognise non-economic forms of value – which shows why it is fundamentally wrong. How, then, has neoliberalism succeeded in conquering the Western world?

It grew and developed – it was never a 'doctrine' or a conspiracy – assisted by four broad reasons. First, it presented itself back in the 1980s with energetic answers to the stultification of Keynesian paternalism. The success of neoliberalism was partly due to genuine improvement. It is better to be treated as a customer by local and national state and public services than as a slave, even if we should still better be treated as citizens with a vocation for democracy. Accountability has increased, closed hierarchies have been opened up, paternalism and its special forms of privilege and cronyism have diminished, minorities have been protected from discrimination. These advances may need to be defended from the protectionist, economic nationalism of Trumpeteers and Brexiteers.

Second, it was turbocharged by the Chinese communist party's embrace of capitalism, triggering the largest, fastest industrialisation and urbanisation in history; as well as by rapid growth in other developing countries. Branko Milanović's well-known 'elephant graph' gives a picture of what happened on a world scale. The poorer half of the world experienced tremendous increase in income over the twenty years to 2008, and so did the 1 per cent. Those on lower and middle incomes of the developed world had a relatively grim time. The lowest tenth saw a significant improvement in the UK and the EU (though not the USA) before 2008, but not since.[10] Brexit and Trump are the sounds from the dip in the curve, the bottom of the valley. But the neoliberal economic order boomed overall.

Third, neoliberalism integrated itself into and then boldly rode the tiger of the transformation of our lives by the digital revolution, which created new platforms and technologies for production, distribution and communication globally (while accelerating financial markets). More people in more countries saw a greater improvement in their lives in less time than ever before. Its era is one of unprecedented inequality for the super-rich that has also made different societies and nations around the world more equal. It was a period of emancipating growth, with a huge increase in air travel, migration and knowledge of other places. Neoliberalism is a scar disfiguring a process of beauty. Nowhere is this clearer than with climate change – as the means to prevent the burning of the planet become readily available, big oil bought Washington.

Fourth, neoliberalism is an ideology that denies that it is an ideology. This denial has been vital to its success. It insists that it expresses an emanation of nature and 'the market', even while it imposes relationships on us with an absolutist and unnatural fatalism. It hollows out government by demanding that as many rules as possible, when there must be rules, are 'non-political' and uphold the market. It turns the essential administrative functions of the state into a bureaucratic nightmare of form-filling, seeking to emulate competition through targets. It seeks to turn government into regulation, politics into a service industry of competition, as illustrated by Blair's description of the role of the state. It exercises its hegemony, its influence over ruling values and shared presumptions, by claiming to be 'how things are' in a way that puts it beyond challenge. This is its first and most powerful line of defence: to deny critics, or even partial advocates, the use of its name or of any term that might stand in for it. We know that Keynesianism was dominant as a way of governing the economy. We know it was replaced. What replaced it? Answer 'neoliberalism' and the gatekeepers swoop: it means 'nothing', it is just an 'all-purpose insult', 'the *mot du jour* of every bluffing teenage radical' (Janan Ganesh again in the *Financial Times* in August 2015)[11]. Dare to use it *in public* (where it might excite people's interest: academic journals do not matter), then, like the dogged researchers of the IMF, you had better watch your step: you will be called a maverick, a leftist, a baseball-cap wearer, you will even be compared to Naomi Klein. Most damaging of all, the term is one that regular people 'cannot understand', and therefore you are an 'elitist' because you have called the spade a spade. What is strangely absent from all the attacks on the use of the term neoliberalism is the offer of an alternative name for what is clearly a world system. Because it isn't the name that is being objected to, but the act of naming – the bringing into consciousness of what is being done to us.

We all know the folk tale of the emperor who had no clothes. How tricksters persuaded him they would weave magnificent cloth with the magical power of being invisible to those who were stupid or unfit for office. The King paraded in them. As no one, included himself, wanted to admit they could not see them, all admired his finery while the thieves escaped. It took a child to tell the truth: 'The King has no clothes'. Neoliberalism has pulled the opposite trick. It has persuaded us that we are governed by the naked. The thieves steal our lives away and we say how natural this is, how without any clothes of intent or self-interest our government is. 'Its anonymity is both a symptom and cause of its power', as George Monbiot says in his short, sharp account.[12]

After all this abstraction, a moment to show what it means in terms of one policy and a reflection on the personal consequences of neoliberal culture. New Labour policy towards higher education is a demonstration of the penetration of neoliberal thinking into the public realm. When Peter Mandelson (the same) became Secretary of State for Business, Enterprise and Regulatory Reform in 2008 under Gordon Brown, he body-snatched the Department for Innovation,

Universities and Skills to become overlord of the Department of State for Business, Innovation and Skills. Thus, the UK's universities became part of his fiefdom. He wanted to expand higher education for all and increase income from fees. In the preface to his strategic overview, Mandelson wrote:

> We will enable universities to *compete* for funds ... Universities will need to ... be more efficient ... withdrawing from activities of lower priority and value ... students and employers will be enabled to make informed choices that increase *competition* between institutions. No student should ever be misled into believing that a course will deliver employment outcomes that it will not. [12] (my emphasis)

Mandelson commissioned a review on how to implement this approach from a colleague in the House of Lords, John Browne. Browne had run BP for twelve years until 2007 and resigned under a cloud. Tom Bower argues that Browne changed BP's company culture from oil engineering to financial engineering with, he implies, dire consequences in the Gulf of Mexico.[13] Financial engineering was clearly the approach Browne adopted towards the UK's universities. Published on 12 October 2010, his report states that no 'objective metric of quality' could be identified with respect to higher education to decide how to 'distribute funding' to it. In other words, values such as access to culture, breadth of knowledge, preparation for life, ensuring a familiarity with arts, science and technology, could not be measured and therefore were worthless – beyond justification – with respect to public funding. The government, being unable to value higher education 'outputs', should not pay universities anything (except for science). Instead, universities should charge whatever they wished and compete for students. All funds must be routed through student loans. The students will decide how best to enhance their employment prospects. The only objective measure of quality for them is a 'single online portal' that will:

allow students to compare courses on the proportion of students in employment after one year of completing the course; and average salary after one year. Employment outcomes will also make a difference to the charges set by institutions ... students will only pay higher charges if there is a proven path to higher earnings ... Courses that deliver improved employability will prosper; those that make false promises will disappear.[14]

This is neoliberalism taken to its logical conclusion – absurdity. It exposes the gap between competitive marketisation and real life. The government capped fees, torpedoing the logic, but retained the pernicious culture. A year later, as the new government implemented the measures, English students rioted.[15]

Finally, a salute to the late Mark Fisher, whose influential essay of 2009, *Capitalist Realism*, communicated the psychological impact of neoliberal culture. Younger people, he wrote, become 'resigned to their fate ... not out of apathy, nor of cynicism, but of reflexive impotence. They know things are bad, but more than that they know they can't do anything about it.'[16] Using a wide variety of sources, he shows how 'There is no alternative' can become an all-encompassing experience of a market society in which we are obliged to turn ourselves into commodities to survive, and within which there seems to be no credible fulcrum on which to lever resistance to it. The consequences of experiencing futility are extremely painful. The solutions on offer are stimulants presented as a freedom of choice, yet the only way of achieving them is through forms of debt and rental contracts that enslave. Every way out leads deeper into the maze. Fisher vividly conceptualises what it is like to live in an age of neoliberalism, where the capacity to shape and effect society has been sucked out of politics – and a society of stimulants offers only its own forms of closure in lethargy interrupted by outbreaks of futile rage. He does not extend his analysis to the old who can feel just as frustrated by a sense of closure, redundancy and pointlessness, as the society they knew is sold off around them.

The cultural nature of neoliberalism that Fisher writes about in depth is a vital part of its influence. It is not just an all-embracing policy of government, like Keynesianism. Wendy Brown has shown how it projects itself as a way of life.[17] It enters into the language of relationships; Doreen Massey, in *After Neoliberalism? The Kilburn Manifesto*, points to how teacher/student or doctor/patient relations become 'customer relationships'.[18] Tax is always described as a 'burden', yet this is only so if all value is created in the market, which it isn't. The metaphor of the market spreads to become the only way to describe reality. We talk of 'democratic deficits', for example, when democracy is a non-market relationship, not a profit-and-loss account. Jeremy Gilbert argues:

> Neoliberal hegemony is dependent on constant work to make sure that popular media stay on-message with a culture of competitive individualism and political apathy ... to make sure that working class communities do not re-discover their own capacities – which they threaten to do constantly.

Perhaps the greatest success of neoliberalism in this respect was its recruitment of social democratic parties into becoming its co-creator as globalisation kicked off at the end of the 1980s. Blair and Mandelson's manipulative corporate populism then recruited able young Tories such as Cameron and Osborne. They did as much to break the influence of trade unions as Margaret Thatcher. Their high point was 8 August 2007. The next morning inter-bank lending froze and signalled the coming of the financial crash a year later. The political crash took much longer. Mandelson did his best to ensure that both schools and universities in England were captured by corporate realism. When Cameron and Osborne took over in the UK, they imposed a neoliberal policy of austerity without naming it as such, confident that the financial press would not do so either. As the *FT* leader shows, the mention of neoliberalism is still regarded as a threat should it venture outside circles of radical scholarship into the mainstream.

But Brexit and Trump have challenged a fundamental aspect of neoliberalism in an unexpected way: from the right. Both attacked neoliberalism's Macavity syndrome, its black art of denying responsibility and blaming the world market. Both demand borders, intervention, control of markets, an end to free movement. Trump declared the system was rigged, globalist, and had to be brought back under the control of America's government. The Brexiteers assailed the unaccountable procedures of Brussels and demanded the return of control to Britain. Both countries now are represented by governments that must take responsibility for economic outcomes and thus breach the covenant of neoliberalism. At the same time both are creatures of neoliberalism's post-crash breakdown, in the absence of an alternative. Trump is a bizarre acolyte of neoliberalism's loathing of politics, the personification of its manipulative corporate populism and anti-politics. The rhetoric of Brexit rings out with calls to embrace the global market. Each can be seen as an attempt to engineer consent to ultra-capitalism when capitalism's greatest success was to persuade people that it was a force of nature beyond the need for consent.

Whether or not neoliberalism can preserve itself by admitting its existence, it cannot be displaced until it has been named in public discourse. Inchoate opposition to it roused many to join the causes of Trump and Brexit. For them to become allies of a better globalisation, neoliberalism's current domination of it needs to be challenged by speaking its name. The same applies to its sway within the European Union, including the European Court of Justice – where opposition needs continental solidarity as only a pan-European movement will be able to challenge neoliberalism across its multifaceted efforts to marketise life.

# 27

# The Legitimacy of the European Union

Something is not happening. We are Europeans on the ground. We are Europeans in our stomachs, as a succession of food crises has shown, but we are not Europeans in our heads.
Reinhard Hesse, speech writer for Gerhardt Schroeder
– *openDemocracy*, May 2001[1]

The European Union has been a Petri dish for neoliberalism. It has built stringent deficit targets into its members' budgets. It has imposed open-market verdicts against trade unions via the European Court of Justice in Luxembourg (not to be confused with the European Court of Human Rights in The Hague). It organised a 'loan' to Greece that went straight into the European banks that had foolishly lent into the country, saving the banks but not Greece, in a classic neoliberal operation. The failure in Greece has been well documented. The 'success' of austerity in Ireland which is in the eurozone and growing again, came at an extraordinary price thanks to lack of solidarity, especially from Germany. In Ireland:

The economic costs of the Great Recession saw median disposable income falling by over 16% between 2008 and 2013 ... just over a quarter of the population was lacking two or more basic necessities, such as heating, the ability to buy meals or to have proper clothing in 2012; and the country witnessed significant increases in relation to basic deprivation and consistent poverty.[2]

The undemocratic character of the euro is neoliberal because both the launch of the new currency and likewise its management through the financial crisis were treated as technical matters when they were political. Responsibility for the consequences was shifted onto market criteria to mask the reality of the policy-makers – with the German finance minister telling his counterparts, when confronted by Greek resistance: 'elections cannot be allowed to change an economic programme of a member state'.[3] These flaws are beginning to be recognised. There is also a larger context. The lack of democratic accountability within the Eurozone was embedded in the framework of the European Union itself, in whose creation the UK was an active member.

The profoundly undemocratic character of *today's* EU was not inevitable or built into its nature sixty years ago when it began life with the Treaty of Rome. The treaty has been upgraded, deepened and expanded since then, with a series of treaties, each of which replaces and displaces the previous one. The current treaty is the Lisbon Treaty of December 2007 that came into force in 2009. It sets out the nature and power of the currently existing European Union, and will continue to do so until it is replaced.

The importance of Lisbon goes back to the beginning of the century. The euro (brought about by the Treaty of Maastricht) was to be launched on 1 January 2002, along with rules for the accession of ten countries (eight former communist ones plus Malta and Cyprus) scheduled to become members in May 2004. A Constitutional Convention on the Future of Europe was initiated, a move strongly supported by the Blair government. After a sixteen-month process, a four-part, 200-page draft constitution was adopted in June 2004 for ratification by the member states.[4] It set out how the EU would become an autonomous legal entity in its own right, and no longer just the creature of its member states. It proposed a fully functioning supreme court to adjudicate over it; a foreign minister; expanded control of the continent's domestic policies by majority vote over justice, law enforcement and migration; and a new president for the council of the heads of state, alongside the president of the commission.

While Spain supported it in a referendum, France did not. Every household in France was sent a copy of the final document. On 29 May 2005, voters across France rejected it by 55 to 45 per cent on a turnout of 69 per cent. Three days later, the Netherlands, the most European of all European countries, was even more decisive, and gave the proposed constitution a thumbs down by 61 to 39 per cent.

These two votes in heartland countries of the EU were the moment of truth for the whole European project. The financial crash was still to come. The euro was proving a success. The expansion of the EU was taking place, confirming the successful replacement of Soviet communism. Politically and economically, Europe was on a roll; the conditions could not have been more auspicious for the European project to become a transnational entity with global influence.

But by clear, decisive majorities the creation of a such a superior apparatus over Europe's nation states, with weak, indirect democratic accountability, was turned down. A referendum had also been scheduled in the UK. It was called off because it was redundant. It would almost certainly have been lost too. The German constitution does not allow for referendums, but in all likelihood a majority would have joined its French and Dutch fellows. No one suggested that the votes of those two countries did not represent the considered views of the publics across most of the Union. The Spanish, who had joined twenty years previously in 1986 and were still enjoying the end of fascism, were seen as the exception.

At this point, then, the leaders of Europe faced the most important decision of their lives, that would reshape the continent for a generation, if not two. How would they respond to their own people after such a clear popular rejection? Were they going to reconsider, to learn from the rebuff, to rethink? Were they, hell. Tony Blair's special assistant Robert Cooper had been made the EU's director-general for External and Politico-Military Affairs. He wrote anonymously expressing the Brussels view: it was really 'an intergovernmental document', it should not have been called a constitution, this was excessive European rhetoric 'that obscures rather than illuminates, and threatens when what is needed is reassurance'. He made the case that what was proposed did not undermine the nation state and argued that the new arrangements needed to exist before they could be accepted.[5] Later, he looked back on Blair's decade and gave him relatively high marks for the normalisation of the UK's presence in the EU's capital. He referred to referendums as 'vermin'.[6]

This was the approach the mandarins of Brussels and the leaders of Europe used to persuade themselves that they should pursue the course their people had rejected. They recycled the proposed constitution into a 'non-constitution' that could come about through intergovernmental treaty change alone. If the peoples of the nations of Europe did not wish to alter the way they were governed, then they would get used to its being altered without their permission. The result was the Treaty of Lisbon, signed in the Portuguese capital at the end of 2007.

Giscard d'Estaing, the former French president who had headed the Constitutional Convention, could not resist winding up the English by gloating in *The Independent*:

> The difference between the original Constitution and the present Lisbon Treaty is one of approach, rather than content ... In terms of content, the proposed institutional reforms are all to be found in the Treaty of Lisbon ... There are, however, some differences. Firstly, the noun 'constitution' and the adjective 'constitutional' have been banished from the text.[7]

Angela Merkel told the EU Parliament: 'The substance of the constitution is preserved. That is a fact'.[8] Jean-Claude Juncker was his usual refreshing self: before the French vote he said: 'If it's a Yes, we will say "on we go", and if it's a No we will say "we continue."'[9] They continued.

Although the proceedings up to Lisbon took place under Blair, by the time of the signing ceremony Gordon Brown had succeeded him. In a manoeuvre typical of Brown, who wanted to avoid the adverse publicity of being photographed sharing sovereignty with his European colleagues, he did not attend the summit, claiming that he was obliged to appear before a House of Commons select committee. His newly appointed foreign secretary, David Miliband, stood in for him. According to the BBC, 'UK Independence Party leader Nigel Farage said he spoke to Foreign Secretary David Miliband in Lisbon just moments before he signed the treaty and repeated his demand for a referendum, receiving only "a hollow laugh" in reply.' Later, Brown flew to Lisbon to sign it on his own. He said: 'If this was a constitutional treaty, we would hold a referendum. If there was a vote on a euro, we would hold a referendum. But the constitutional concept was abandoned.'[1]

It was not. What was abandoned was the democratic legitimacy of the European Union as a whole. There is a revealing account of the process that led to this outcome, written and published very early on by the Labour MP Gisela Stuart, when the constitution was still a proposal. To prove the British government's strong support of the EU's constitutional convention, Blair sent her to be a key UK representative. At the time one of the Labour Party's most pro-European MPs, she is German-born and represents Neville Chamberlain's old constituency in Birmingham, and thus personified Labour's openness to Europe. Writing in the *Guardian* in December 2003, she recounts:

> I entered the process with enthusiasm ... The most frequently cited justifications for a written constitution for Europe have been the need to make the treaties more understandable to European voters and streamline the decision-making ... I support both of these aims. But ... it is clear that the real reason for the constitution is the political deepening of the union ... The convention [has] brought together a self-selected group of the European political elite ... who see national governments and national parliaments as an obstacle. Not once in the 16 months I spent on the convention did representatives question whether deeper integration is

what the people of Europe want, whether it serves their best interests or whether it provides the best basis for a sustainable structure for an expanding union ... This Treaty establishing a constitution ... will be difficult to amend and will be subject to interpretation by the European court of justice. And if it remains in its current form, the new constitution will be able to create powers for itself. It cannot be viewed piecemeal ... we have to look at the underlying spirit.[2]

Her warning that a Frankenstein was under construction was ignored. She was patronised and sidelined by the all-male Euro-elite. Twelve years later she became the co-chair of Britain's Vote Leave.

The British exit is a consequence of the EU's nature and the decisions taken then. It will cause grief for the United Kingdom and its peoples, especially its young people, as well as harm to the EU itself. Leaving is a mistake and should be reversed, preferably along with changes in the EU itself. But any European democrat, whether a citizen of the EU or not, needs to confront a bigger question: the fundamental legitimacy of the European Union.

When the EU was first launched it took down barriers to trade and commerce. In this historic if negative way, dismantling impediments between European countries and citizens, it became the most inspiring political attainment of my generation. It was experienced as an enhancement of people's freedom and, as Alan Milward showed in a famous, exhaustive study, it rescued the European nation states, and by doing so it created stronger civic national democracies living in peace and openness with each other in the aftermath of a savage war. It was an immense civilising achievement.

In this context the exceptional democratic achievements of the EU need to be saluted as well. Some of the strongest wildlife protections in the world; important digital laws designed to protect consumers from data mining; the social charter that outlines a maximum working week; the European arrest warrant; wonderful support for academic research and science. The EU has become a home for genuine international advance. But at the end of the 1980s, intoxicated by the prospects of globalisation, depoliticised by the nostrums of neoliberalism, emboldened by the historic expansion to the East, the masters of Europe believed themselves to be on the threshold of creating a new superpower. In Brussels, the would-be oligarchs absorbed the claret of federalism. They viewed the nations as if they were the equivalent of the feudal principalities that Italian unification melded, or the group of smaller German states swept up into Bismarck's audacious nation-building. This was an extraordinary error, as the EU was made up of modern nations, fully part of the advanced technological world: developed countries, home to self-conscious peoples, harbouring the precious beginnings of self-government. Why should they exchange this for a powerless role in someone else's inflated glory?

In an earlier section discussing the crisis of Britain's institutions, I set down what a constitution does and added that all constitutions are lived, and that how they are lived is more important than what is written. It seems a strange formulation: how are constitutions 'lived'? The Lisbon Treaty is the EU's constitution. A comparison shows how the 'life' in a constitution starts with the way it is created. In 1994, with the end of apartheid, a new South Africa was born. Since then it has been ruled by one party, the ANC. Yet it is not described as simply a one-party state, not just because it has an opposition and a vigorous legal system able to hold the president to account, but because it has a constitution people believe in. Part of the reason for this is that its constitution was created by a process that included an enormous amount of direct public participation in the convention and drafting process, with considerable attention paid to minority rights. For all its current horrors and abuses, South Africa's constitutional procedures and safeguards are themselves safeguarded by the identification with a memorable historic process. It is not perfect, but it is legitimate.

Contrast this to the miserable, secretive, sly and duplicitous imposition of the EU's constitution. Today's EU is a thief in the night, created *in defiance* of popular assent. The early EU was pre-democratic but limited, enlarged the capacities of Europeans and proved popular. The Lisbon Treaty is globally ambitious, calculatedly anti-democratic and unpopular. National parliaments and congresses are going through their own crises of legitimacy as they try to re-establish their democratic credentials after the long hollowing out of neoliberalism. The EU's constitution as a whole is unable to mount a similar effort – it was undemocratic from the start. The consequence can be seen in the steady decline of overall turnout for the elections to the one directly democratic component, the European parliament, from 62 per cent in 1979 to 42 per cent in 2014 – despite the huge expansion of its powers thanks to Lisbon.[3]

There is still an enormous historic goodwill towards the idea of Europe, and gratitude for surpassing the conflicts of the twentieth century across the continent. But this loyalty to peaceful collaboration is being exploited and abused by leaders who know that they dare not consult with their own people about its continuation in its present form – hard-faced, hard-drinking Eurocrats whose coldness towards mere electorates is a consequence of their rigid superiority complex.

The EU has betrayed itself. So profoundly that it cannot survive in its present form. The world is undertaking a wild democratic warming exploited by populists. If the EU simply defies this, it will be broken by its own stubbornness. It was one thing – mistaken perhaps, but honourable – to foresee the freely exchanged *replacement* of national nationalisms with a European patriotism, larger, more expansive, implicitly more civilised, in the long-term prospectus of the 'ever closer union' of Europe's peoples – the plural is in the treaty. This needed a European democracy not a male-dominated oligarchy. Without the energy and loyalty that comes from active assent, the EU cannot succeed if the idea is to compete with global powers such as the USA and China. Today this option has been foreclosed for the existing EU, thanks to the way with arrogant insouciance it overreached itself with its Lisbon constitution and set its face against its own publics. A form of rule created in plain defiance of popular judgement now confronts the need for a deep transformation to establish legitimacy.

How can this happen? One answer comes from the pan-European

organisation DiEM25, inspired by the most despised figure in the corridors of Brussels, Yanis Varoufakis, and his co-founder Srecko Horvat. It calls on Europe to democratise or it will destroy itself. A well-argued manifesto sets out its case.[4] Among other suggestions it demands real transparency of the key EU and Eurozone decision-making processes and a full-scale democratic constitutional convention. I have observed and participated in several efforts to democratise the EU, including the Swedish EU vice president Margot Wallström's Plan-D. They were futile, evaporating into fine sentiment. DiEM25 is different because it foresees a breakdown; whether from another a financial crisis, a default – or just Italy, garrotted by its inability to devalue. Brexit might provide a more positive context leading to an official opposition within the EU, without which there can be no democratic future, a modest but obvious point recently made by Luuk van Middelaar.[5]

Since Lisbon the Commission and its Eurocracy have sought to shield discussion about the nature of the 'European project' from the earthy localism of national legislatures and popular assent. However, if all goes according to intentions, in 2018 a draft of the EU and UK's divorce and future relationship must go to each of the EU's twenty-seven member states for ratification. An intense period of reflection might then take place to define how the EU relates to a Britain that is leaving. Nationally elected representatives will debate in their own parliaments what they think. Done well, this could start to repair the democratic damage of Lisbon, by building a relationship between the EU and European citizens through their elected assemblies, as they consider their relationship to what will probably be multi-speed union. For, in response to Brexit, the arch federalist himself, the German federal minister of finance Wolfgang Schäuble has already conceded in an interview with the *Financial Times*:

> The federal idea has not gone away but at the moment it has no chance of being realised ... there are no broad majorities to give additional shares of national sovereignty to Brussels ... we have to improve ... our intergovernmental methods.[6]

Just what the British asked for in the first place. Regular Pew surveys show that across the EU as a whole, people are happy for it to play a larger role in world affairs, but only around 20 per cent want more powers transferred from their nation states to Brussels.[7] There is no 'threat' of a superstate.

The sense that the EU has lost its way was reinforced by a feeble White Paper presenting *Reflections and Scenarios for 2015*, which the Commission prepared for the leaders' 60th anniversary summit.[8] It set out five options and in effect suspended closer union for the duration. In a concluding paragraph it says, 'We want a Union in which all citizens and all Member States are treated equally'. In the UK, the argument for Leave was that the EU was crushing the autonomy of its member states. Now we discover it aspires to treat all of them equally. This is why England should have been there: to urge on the change to law-based European democracy. For the dangerous lack of it threatens us too.

# 28

# Britain and the EU

The undemocratic, neoliberal nature of the EU provoked the UK into Brexit. But across the continent many who also oppose it are not seeking to leave. Why did it not occur to the British to arouse European opinion in solidarity with their demands, rather than scoffing at their fellow Europeans? Why, after forty years in which it enjoyed considerable influence, did the UK continue to regard the EU as an 'other' that played no part in its conception of itself in the world? Why were Europe's faults used as an excuse to bash it rather than mend them and the UK's lack of democracy?

The way Britain related to the problems of Europe was itself a problem in the UK. This is a difficult matter to unravel. I don't want to use it as an excuse for the EU's failings. Without doubt these failings were a major reason for Brexit – which was, after all, a vote on continued membership. If the European Union had not embraced neoliberalism and had been growing strongly economically, without imposing austerity on Greece and Spain, then, despite the undemocratic nature of the Lisbon 'constitution', the UK would have voted to Remain. Had the EU rid itself of the undemocratic features of Lisbon, then, even if it remained stuck in its post-crash economic downturn, the UK would also have voted Remain. The killer combination was an EU that was indefensibly undemocratic and economically sclerotic.

The problem for the UK is that Europe is our home and living room. Not just because it takes 44 per cent of the country's trade, although this too is a major link, but because we are not Americans. However Americanised our culture may seem, the way in which we relate to America is in a European fashion. Why didn't we stay and fight for what is ours?

The immediate answer is that David Cameron insisted that the Remain campaign treat the EU as a means, not an end. He then ran on fear, saying that the country could not afford to leave in terms of a business proposition. If your sole argument is limited to saying that the EU works for Britain, it can only be less than convincing if the EU is itself working badly.

Which poses the question of why the positive case for Europe had such little traction. Years of tabloid anti-EU propaganda fed into the 2016 campaign, and could not be turned around overnight. But its torrent of sludge was never opposed effectively across four decades. The reason for this, as I have tried to set out, was a proud English nationalism that sublimated itself into something greater than itself – Britain. All the main political parties were formed within and committed to the British Union, something that is intrinsically threatened by EU membership in terms of its constitution, its institutions and its supposed governing principle, 'the absolute sovereignty of parliament'. While Brits could be very pro-European personally, the parties, government and the state were unable to achieve this politically.

In other European countries the EU can be regarded as an enhancing not competing form of identity. It can be seen as a way of bringing some control over international forces and their crooked penetration of your society and a protection against globalisation. With good reason, those with a strong sense of place in, say, Italy, might regard the EU as a support for their local culture, heritage and habitats, and identify with it because they feel it protects their nation. Forms of adaptation to this attitude could have developed in Britain as well. I want to look briefly at why this did not happen: why the UK, which energetically renewed itself economically after 1979, became stuck in a time warp politically. Any examination of the referendum's outcome has to try and take a measure of this.

When the UK first attempted to join the EU in 1960, the Establishment refused to see this as a challenge to reform itself. Before I started writing this book, I thought this remained the fundamental reason why the UK never wholeheartedly became part of the EU in good faith. I threaded it back to two maiden speeches by ex-grammar-school boys in the House of Commons, made within weeks of each other in 1950. The first, by Enoch Powell, called for 'the defence of this worldwide Empire'; the second, a few weeks later by Edward Heath, called on the Attlee government (then in its last year) to engage with the Schuman Plan that was to prefigure the EU. Twenty years later Heath was to become prime minister and take the UK into Europe; Powell was to be his nemesis in 1974, in revenge.[1] But the early arguments, which once seemed formative, I now think only appear to be so in retrospect, like back-projected myths.

Margaret Thatcher was a member of Edward Heath's 1970 Cabinet. In her memoir, published much later in 1995, she says she took little interest in the issue of sovereignty at the time. With the advantage of hindsight, she quotes from the 1971 White Paper that set the government's case for joining:

> There is no question of any erosion of essential national
> sovereignty; what is proposed is a sharing and an enlargement
> of individual national sovereignties in the general interest.[2]

Thatcher comments that this is 'an extraordinary example of artful confusion to conceal fundamental issues'. A neat description. There are many other examples. What they show is that those who governed Britain and decided on EU membership understood its explosive consequences for the constitution. They decided to work around the problem. They 'artfully' acknowledged it so as to ensure that the gelignite was separated from a detonator. They knew that to *really* join the EU, Britain had to change, but the whole point of joining for them was *not* to change. Their aim was always to preserve as much great-power status as they could. But Washington decreed that for the UK to remain a serious ally, it could not be isolated from the growing influence of Europe.

The core project, therefore, was to conserve the influence of British sovereignty. When Enoch Powell deployed the cadence of his voice to tell them that the logic of sovereignty would not allow such cohabitation, they shrugged, said life is not logical and hoped for the best. It was not a 'betrayal', it was a judgement about the country's interests. The crucial point is that, from 1960 to 1988, no one on London's side of the Channel called for the British to become Europeans and embark on the necessary constitutional revolution. They simply hoped that EU membership would reverse an otherwise inevitable decline.

Nonetheless, a process of Europeanisation was set in train. It might have worked. Britain could have made it to becoming a European country through a process of cultural and political assimilation but for three developments: Thatcher's election, the Falklands war that clinched her domination, and the unification of Germany that ensured her fall.

The original domestic intention behind joining what was to become the EU was to reverse the UK's decline by adopting the European economic model, while making Europe the focus of the UK's diplomacy. Thatcher's election, followed by Reagan's in 1979, saw a return to a primary alliance with Washington. Her economic policy was a 'monetarist', early neoliberal approach, not a European Christian Democratic one. Her election thus reversed the two main motivations behind the turn to Europe.

Even this would not have locked the UK into an irreversibly divergent path from Europe. Geoffrey Howe, Thatcher's chancellor, implemented the ruthless monetarist assault on the economy, but he was also committed to membership of Europe, and in 1990, in a Commons speech that destroyed her premiership, he set out the classic statement of the need to remain within the European project.

Thatcher and Howe's economic policy was very unpopular. They were saved by Argentina's invasion of the Falklands. For the larger public the war was a brief and rousing episode now largely forgotten. For the nascent political-media caste, it was a formative moment. It entered their dreams as a perfect political intervention and defined the joy of power in the late-British psyche. It also revived a specific, degenerate form of Churchillism. Not the post-war Churchillism of consensus, but a mythic one that the country could take on the world and win on its own. The emotional attraction of the Second World War was passing into history. In 1982, it arose from the near-dead thanks to cardiopulmonary resuscitation in the South Atlantic. And although the wider population has moved on, thirty-five years later the ghosts of Falklands triumphant yomped through minds of those leading the Brexit campaign.

It was the third episode, however, that ensured the fateful divergence between England and the EU. The Berlin Wall came down. In 1989, the prospect of German reunification completely freaked the Iron Lady. She was unable to regard it as anything other than the threat of the rise of a new Reich, keeping maps of German expansion in her handbag. For almost everyone else, the end of Germany's hideous division was a cause for joy, but Thatcher was appalled by the prospect of a united Germany and tried to prevent it. Charles Moore's official biography has yet to reach 1989, but he writes that her thoughts on it were 'unprintable'.[3] Ken Clarke relates how he was aghast to be told by an aide of Germany's chancellor Kohl that Thatcher was blocking unification. He raised the issue in the Cabinet to ask if it was true (as ministers could still do before Blair). There was a 'heated and one sided' discussion. Other senior members were also ignorant of Thatcher's efforts and rounded on her. She found herself completely isolated, realised that her position was hopeless and stopped trying to prevent the inevitable.[4]

But the damage had been done. What she could not prevent she did not support. While President Bush (father), who had been elected in 1988, Chancellor Kohl and President Mitterrand treated Thatcher with respect, she was rightly sidelined as a slightly demented hangover from the Blitz. Bush gave the positive go-ahead for unification. Most accounts focus on the deal that followed between Mitterrand and Kohl that led to the creation of the euro, which the French insisted on to bind a united Germany to Europe. There is also a might-have-been. Had Thatcher stood hand in hand with Chancellor Kohl and the French president Mitterrand at the Brandenburg Gate with the Union Jack and the Tricolore joining the *Bundesdienstflagge*, they would have given Europe's flag a different meaning. Mitterrand, too, who had been a German prisoner-of-war, found the German triumph excruciatingly hard to bear. But he rightly turned down Thatcher's offer of an Anglo-French alliance against the German Republic. The French were left to deal with Kohl on their own.

The end of the division of Germany was a historic turning point far more important and more lastingly significant than the Falklands. It created an opportunity for Britain to share possession of the moment of European restitution. The triumph and relief of the unification of Germany could and should have belonged to us in Britain, as well as to Germany itself. It was the final liberation from Nazism, the end of that country's punishment, a time to welcome a great culture fully back into our arms. Britain bore a responsibility for sending the continent to war with appeasement in 1938. It had then fought at huge cost to end the fascist scourge until 1945. The British prime minister had every right to claim credit for the unification of our continent. Especially in Thatcher's case, as she had identified Gorbachev as a Soviet leader the West could work with. With different leadership, the unification of Europe and Germany could have been 'ours', rather than something done without us and against her wishes. Thatcher's pitiful and inexcusable response locked Westminster into its historical regression. Europe moved on from the Second World War and Britain didn't.

The fact that Thatcher clearly 'lost it' over Germany contributed to her colleagues' loss of confidence in her. Her downfall came a year later. Jacques Delors, who headed the EU's commission, felt history going to his head and said that the EU would turn into a superstate with its parliament, commission and council becoming its legislature, executive and senate. Delors's claim was absurd. Mitterrand shouted at the television when he heard it, saying, 'But that's ridiculous! What's he up to? No one in Europe will ever want that.'[5] He was right. But Thatcher, deranged by her bogies, exploited Delors to caricature the European process. She denounced his ridiculous scenario in the Commons, calling out: 'No, No, No.' Her escalation drove Geoffrey Howe to resign, and he made the now famous speech. Today, after the Brexit vote, it is worth quoting from it at length, as nothing of its quality was bequeathed by the Remain campaign:

> We have done best when we have seen the Community not as a static entity to be resisted and contained, but as an active process which we can shape, often decisively, provided we allow ourselves to be fully engaged in it, with confidence, with enthusiasm and in good faith. We must at all costs avoid presenting ourselves yet again with an over-simplified choice, a false antithesis, a bogus dilemma, between one alternative, starkly labelled 'co-operation between independent sovereign states', and a second, equally crudely labelled alternative, 'centralised, federal super-state', as if there were no middle way in between.
>
> We commit a serious error if we think always in terms of 'surrendering' sovereignty ... The European enterprise is not and should not be seen like that as some kind of zero sum game ... my right hon. Friend, seems sometimes to look out upon a continent that is positively teeming with ill-intentioned people, scheming, in her words, to 'extinguish democracy', to 'dissolve our national identities' and to lead us 'through the back-door into a federal Europe'. What kind of vision is that for our business people, who trade there each day, for our financiers, who seek to make London the money capital of Europe or for all the young people of today? ... the Prime Minister's perceived attitude towards Europe is running increasingly serious risks for the future of our nation. It risks minimising our influence and maximising our chances of being once again shut out. We have paid heavily in the past for late starts and squandered opportunities in Europe. We dare not let that happen again. If we detach ourselves completely, as a party or a nation, from the middle ground of Europe, the effects will be incalculable and very hard ever to correct.[6]

This devastating indictment was to have the opposite outcome of its intended effect. It led at once to Michael Heseltine challenging

Thatcher for the leadership. It was a disaster. Thatcher's removal should have been left to the electorate. She fell, but ensured that she was replaced by John Major, not the pro-European Heseltine. The coup saw a weeping Thatcher expelled from Downing Street. The injustice made her a martyr. She became the figurehead of a cult. A besotted, anti-European right pledged itself to revenge the fall of Thatcher; its followers renewed their vitality for the next quarter century, even through their darkest hours, by incanting 'No, No. No'. The country is now in their hands. Howe's warning should be nailed to their door.

True to their lonely Franco-German deal, the EU plunged ahead with the euro at the Maastricht treaty in 1992. John Major ensured that the British opted out, just as Howe asserted it could in another part of his speech. Two divergent momentums were established between the EU and UK from that point on.

Yet that was twenty-five years ago. Tabloid veneration of the martyrdom of Margaret Thatcher kept her anti-Europeanism alive. This was only part of the reason for its survival. Another was the way New Labour vaulted into power. The Blair government witnessed Europe at its most popular across the UK, as it was associated with growth at home and liberation from the homophobic atmosphere of Thatcher and her aftermath. But Blair himself was evanescent rather than institution-building. I referred in chapter 24 to his claim:

> I had a vision for Britain. All the way I had believed I could and would persuade the country it was the right choice, the modern way, New Britain going along with New Labour. It was ... bigger than any one thing; a complete vision of where we should be in the early 21st century; about how we finally overcome the greatness of our history to discover the full potential of our future.[7]

The mere 'greatness of our history' was not enough for Tony Blair. All that history, and all that greatness, was something to be 'overcome', thanks to his leadership, as we set out on the full potential of our future. His vision was of a Galactic Britain. In the introduction to the paperback edition of *A Journey*, he sets out his view on Europe from his extra-terrestrial perspective. 'For Europe, the challenge is strength'. He explains the problem: 'the trouble is that Europe is a collection of proud independent nations'. He briefly describes the consequence and concludes: 'the danger for Europe today is not war; it is weakness'. The debate must become 'one about how to project European power'. Expanding the authority of its parliament and other such reforms 'is a 20th century agenda'. Instead, Europe should concentrate on 'projecting power'.[8] I'm quoting Blair's own words so as not to be accused of prejudice or exaggeration. As prime minister, he assisted specific European processes such as the proposed constitution, but his soaring ambition, and the primacy that he gave to the United States, meant that he failed to embed in the UK any institutional relationships with the EU to replace Thatcherite Europhobia. This was far too small a matter for his 'complete vision' of a future beyond greatness.

As the Blair balloon deflated, his true successor, David Cameron, was left with a country that had no emotional investment in European collaboration or institutions to express this. Everything that happened with Europe was seen as a one-way street interfering with our way of life. It was accused of generating over half of UK laws, which was absurd, as you can see by visiting the web page of Full Fact's 'UK law: What proportion is influenced by the EU?'

> In agriculture, fisheries, external trade, and the environment, it's fair to say that EU legislation and policy is indeed the main driver of UK law and policy, although the UK retains some freedom of action in these areas. In other important areas – for example, welfare and social security, education, criminal law, family law and the NHS – the direct influence of the EU is far more limited.[9]

There was significant criticism of the European Court of Justice expanding its powers in ways that are unacceptable, for example by

Marina Wheeler QC, who argues, convincingly, that it is creating new rights when it was claimed it would not.[10] The principle is important but the substance narrow and public understanding zero. Nothing was done *with* the European Union. Everything was done by it to us. Unable in post-crash times to summon up a Blairite vision to leap over the constant grumpiness, Cameron declared that for Britain the EU was just a means to an end. He reduced it to an uninspiring, instrumental vehicle that nonetheless the UK needed for its own benefit. Tragically, by being so negative, his Remain campaign severed the last bonds of solidarity and mutual advantage the English should have felt for their European Union. When it came to a vote the country shrugged it aside. Only now are the sentiments that should have been part of any argument about our membership being painfully brought to life.

# 29

# No Left to Turn to

On a warm summer night Sherlock Holmes and Dr Watson decided to sleep rough on the Moors rather than head for the local inn still some miles away. In the middle of the night Holmes shook Dr Watson by the shoulder and woke him. 'Look up there, Watson', he said, pointing to the stars, 'what do you make of the significance of *that*?' 'I'm not sure', said the sleepy Watson, 'it shows the night sky of the northern hemisphere'. 'No, no, my dear Watson, what *else*?' 'Well, Holmes, it is a dark, clear moonless summer night and Orion is in the ascendant'. 'No, no, something more important than that, Watson.' 'Oh, I don't know, Holmes', Dr Watson replied, now wide awake, 'what *does* it show?' Nothing stirred across the bleak, windless moors. After a silence Sherlock Holmes replied, 'It means, my dear Watson, that someone has stolen our tent'.

What did it mean that the whole population of Britain could watch the strange movement of the stars in the constellation of the Conservative Party so clearly, as they fell upon one other in the night sky of the country's referendum? It meant that the British Labour Party had been stolen away. The Conservatives had no need to hide their differences, because there was no threat to their heavenly supremacy. Just as the absence of a thrusting, profitable, democratic European Union made Leave a credible option, so the absence of a viable, popular Labour Party, threatening to win the next election, meant that the Tories felt no need to stick together.

How to explain the ongoing importance of an absence? It is no idle question. The only hope for England-Britain to return to Europe over the coming decade depends on an alliance of the left and centre left. Whether Labour can become a credible English

Party, or, if it can't be, how to replace it, are critical questions. By a significant majority, most Labour voters supported Remain (65 per cent overall), while Conservatives voted down their prime minister's recommendation and were 60 per cent for Brexit.[1] With Remain and Leave both presented as right-wing causes, it is understandable that Labour voters split and the party was muted in its views. But what was a form of embarrassment has become feebleness and threatens to turn into irrelevance. To follow what has happened – and why – we must track the extraordinary rocket of Corbynism that whooshed into the right-wing night sky over Britain and then attempted to go into orbit.

Jeremy Corbyn became Labour leader in September 2015, because of the first mass movement in Britain to expressly oppose neoliberalism – in the form of his opposition to austerity. This was very refreshing. Support for budget cuts fell away across the spectrum. Within six months, however, the EU referendum put his leadership to the test. Although he spoke frequently at public meetings, which he enjoys, Corbyn's support for EU membership had always been tepid. He said, 'We, the Labour Party, are overwhelmingly for staying in, because we believe the European Union has brought investment, jobs and protection for workers, consumers and the environment', and he added the need to work together on twenty-first-century challenges, such as climate change and restraining global corporations.[2] Labour was unable to project a picture of how Britain and Europe should relate as country and continent. When asked on a comedy show what he thought about the EU, two weeks before the referendum, he said he would give it 'seven to seven and a half' out of ten.[3]

Such a low-key, zero-rhetoric honesty may have suited the moment, when the transactional value of the EU was the only approach sanctioned by the official campaign. Apparently, Corbyn refused to be on the same platform as Blair. He thus blocked a proposal that all the previous prime ministers appear together with current leaders to demonstrate their shared views of the danger of Brexit. If this was seriously considered, it shows how out of touch the Remain campaign was – nothing could have been more likely to provoke voters into a fury of Brexiteering, than the sight of 'the whole lot of them' lined up together, trousering millions and telling the country to carry on as we are. If Corbyn kept Blair off the Remain platform, he might have done the larger cause some good. He did his own none.

No Labour figure made any lasting impression during the referendum or proposed a memorable overview as to why the country should remain part of the EU. David Miliband flew in from New York and gave a long speech on the international order and how Britain should continue to be a 'firefighter not an arsonist', saying it was 'project fantasy' to think that the UK would be more influential outside the EU than in.[4] He displayed the fluent qualities of a Blairite world-view – and did not address what people were feeling on the ground, let alone address the English. Across the UK, voters were thinking about what was being done to them by the EU, not what Britain could do for the world. His speech turned out to be the best Labour could do and was irrelevant. There were and are able, intelligent and ambitious Labour politicians keen to make an impression. There is an array of reformist think tanks and campaigns with high-calibre policy advisers and researchers. Yet none was drawn upon by a Labour figure to help address the United Kingdom at a historic moment, when the country's place in the world and future development was clearly at stake. Such a failure cannot be blamed on a single low-key leader. When voters chose Leave, the party's half-hearted opposition turned into a call for a better Brexit. The move from opposing Brexit weakly to supporting it badly, left voters baffled as to what Labour *really* thinks – at a moment when authentic voice is valued above all. This applies across almost the whole party. Clive Lewis, resigned from the Shadow Cabinet, along with Tulip Siddiq and Jo Stevens, apparently believing that there can be no progressive future within a Brexit Britain, as indeed, there can't. But they have yet to make an impact.

Labour is participating in a worldwide collapse of the social democratic left. This is especially striking in Europe, with its cluster of historic working-class parties that no longer share any feeling of continental solidarity. The central reason: they, including Labour's Tony Blair, were co-architects of the EU's neoliberalism in the first place. They participated in the depoliticisation of economic decision-making. Europe's traditional social democratic parties helped to stir the bureaucratic miasma of the EU and most are drowning in its quicksands. They took advantage of the positive, material gains generated by capitalism since the 1980s to modernise welfare. New Labour's thirteen years in power were a measure of its capacity to make far-reaching, positive domestic reforms that distinguished it from the lacklustre administrations of the Wilson and Callaghan Labour governments. At the same time, they melded their urge to govern into the measurement of competition and helped dream up centralised audits and league tables, sidelined trade unions, encouraged financialisation and backed the structural reforms that deepened marketisation across the EU. When the crash came in 2008, its neoliberal culture undermined the traditional left's capacity to lead a political response.

One telling example reveals how this worked within the UK – and played a direct role in preventing Labour from renewing itself. The financial crash led to a humongous increase in the UK's public debt, as the banks were saved. When George Osborne became Tory chancellor in 2010, he blamed the Labour Party for overspending during the boom. He used this to justify the imposition of austerity to balance the budget. The accusation was false and the policy of austerity misguided. Labour had not badly overspent and austerity was a disguise for an ideologically driven attack on the public sector which, as the IMF report shows, was no way to restore growth. Osborne's falsehood that Labour had overspent, however, which he used to justify austerity, did have some truth to it. Labour *was* deeply implicated in the crash, not because it was profligate in its spending but because it had gambled on getting government revenues from the boom. Nick Pearce sums it up. Labour, he says:

mistook the buoyancy of revenues from the housing market and the City for a secure, sustainable tax base. When the accumulated asset and debt bubbles finally burst, revenues from these sectors collapsed. Fully a quarter of all corporation tax derived from financial services before the crash, and this revenue fell from £10.3bn in 2007/2008 to £4.6bn in 2009/2010. Stamp and share duties fell from £14.1bn to £7.9bn ... [this] explains the size of its deficit relative to other countries that experienced a similar loss of economic output ... In Germany, the general government deficit reached just 4.3 per cent of GDP, whereas in Britain it rose to nearly 12 per cent at its peak, even though Germany's fiscal stimulus was larger.[5]

As the party of government, Labour was therefore responsible for the ballooning of the national debt and the enormous deficit that followed the banking collapse. But even in the leadership campaign that followed the party's defeat in 2015 (which Corbyn won), all the candidates agreed that the crash had been 'made in Wall Street not Downing Street'. After five years in opposition to reflect, and eight years on from the crash itself, none of the candidates could confront the nature of their party's complicity in the disaster – that stemmed from their government's embrace of neoliberalism. They had a good case when they justified the need to save the financial system, to prevent a far worse downturn. But the scale of the UK deficit that resulted was due to the way Labour had supported deregulation and made its revenues dependent on the boom. Voters, while far from having Nick Pearce's grasp of the details, knew that Labour shared responsibility for the crash, showed no remorse, made no reckoning and therefore probably had not changed.

Jeremy Corbyn's election was an attempt to draw the line, emotionally if not intellectually – and emotion is at least as important. His triumph was a pre-Brexit shock. It marked the end of New Labour but not its replacement, as he attacked the tangible consequences of austerity from food poverty to the undermining of the NHS, without knowing how to get a measure of the intangible financial networks that generate modern inequality.

The origins of Labour's 2015 heart attack go back to 2010. After Gordon Brown's Labour government lost power, five candidates pitched for the leadership and the contest came down to the two Miliband brothers: David, the older, a Blairite and a supporter of the Iraq war; Ed, the younger, who opposed the war and was closer to Gordon Brown. Ed won by a whisker thanks to the support of the trade unions and lost heavily among MPs, a sign of the widening breach between MPs and the party. A loser in all but votes, yet convinced the party had to appear united, Ed Miliband encompassed the MPs who had rejected him and carried Labour forward 'like a Ming vase'. A brilliant operator, he prevented any split and ensured the vase and its contents stayed intact for five years. He left one transformative legacy. His love of American democracy led him to mimic the primary system, to break the party away from charges of trade union control that followed his own election in 2010. He created a category of registered supporters who for a small fee could participate in leadership elections.

When Miliband lost the 2015 election, he stood down and dropped the vase. Three leadership candidates staggered out. After five suffocating years, they were reduced to shallow automata of the Brown and Blair era and had hardly an idea in their heads. Desperate for some vitality, Jeremy Corbyn was added as a candidate. A loner, he had been safely outside the vase ever since he was elected to parliament in 1983 – and had not changed his views since then. The hope was that his ancient principles might stimulate a bit of thinking. He was so obviously unsuited, modest and earnest that he presented no left-wing danger. Only his preternatural stubbornness had ensured his survival. Corbyn was a living mummy excavated from its Bennite sarcophagus (he had been a close young colleague, when Tony Benn led the Labour left in the seventies). It was impossible to imagine a less-likely leader of any party.

The effect was electrifying. Corbyn said what he thought and meant what he said on the headline issues of the economy and equality. The populist effect kicked in immediately. Then he denounced austerity and voted against government welfare cuts in parliament, that the interim Labour leaders had decided were unfortunate but necessary. Support exploded. 185,000 people joined the Labour Party, doubling its size to nearly 400,000 in four months, and nearly 350,000 of them voted – with just over a quarter of a million backing Corbyn. The impulse within the Corbyn wave had the same character as the mass support for Brexit: a willed, defiant refusal to carry on being confined and manipulated and a sugar-rush to support an offer of change however improbable. Jeremy Corbyn and Boris Johnson are more dissimilar than chalk and cheese, but the way they were seized upon was the same: as refreshing, different, authentic individuals who did not play the game.

In Corbyn's case the hopeful energy condensed upon a figure who refused to be altered – despite being projected to the forefront of his country's history. He responded to a period of intense change with a steady-as-you-go approach to both the referendum and its outcome. Rather than let public and party witness how inappropriate this was for a leader at the cusp of a redefinition of British destiny, most of his Shadow Cabinet colleagues resigned immediately after the Brexit vote. In a pre-emptive strike, they organised for Labour MPs to pass a vote of no confidence in Corbyn by 172 to 40, to force a new leadership election within a year of his initial election. Thousands more joined the party in disgust at the way Corbyn was being treated. In September, after he had withstood the full might of being hung, drawn and quartered by the political-media caste, *half a million voted*, 313,000 of them for Jeremy – 61 per cent. The extraordinary numbers have locked Labour into his leadership, while the cult-like intensity of the supporters who surround him, made it hard for him to step down.

The eruption that created Corbyn matters more than the man. In 2015, he was a deserved and refreshing rebuke from Labour's past to Labour's present – and the force of the rebuke raised hopes. But he himself provided no forward movement and put his party into suspended animation. Corbyn represents a form of regressive radicalism. Many who supported him are genuinely radical: young, open and thinking differently. Momentum, a creation of the Corbyn wave, initiated the 'World Transformed' conferences that have been full of significance, in a way that Labour events have never been before. Momentum freaked Labour MPs. They reckoned new members could refresh local parties, and be made politically safe by being sucked into constituency routines. The idea of a network that would exchange ideas horizontally, and could use social media to turn Labour into more of a movement and less of a parliamentary party, distressed them. They feared it would transmit sectarian politics determined on inner division and purification. But they also sought to control the political narrative and the party's appeal. By turning on Momentum rather than working with it, they savaged Labour's future.

One telling example shows how the Corbyn approach is mired in the tangible, unable to engage with the all-important intangible that shapes how people vote and how financial power and democracy work. He gave a keynote Westminster leader's speech to the Scottish Labour Party conference in February 2017 and attacked the Scottish Nationalists who have been in government for ten years and were polling nearly 50 per cent support at the time, with Scottish Labour down to 14 per cent, and the Green Party, that supports independence, on 12 per cent – only 2 points behind Labour. In a country with such a wide-ranging, popular civic nationalism rooted in Scotland's 'Democratic Intellect', Corbyn told the delegates, 'You can't eat a flag.'[6] In that nation and circumstance, there could hardly be a more crass and inappropriate pitch to win back support. His whole speech was equally revealing of Corbyn's political dissonance. He listed the seventeen things Labour is 'committed to', such as education for all, and the eight things it will 'stand up for', such as workers and businesses. He called this 'a plan'.

When issues of self-government and popular control are the order of Brexit, Corbyn's approach stuck to the mannerisms that appear radical only in the mirror of self-deception. A plan consists of at least three things: a description of the overall balance of forces so realistic that the wider public recognise its validity, for credibility; a vision of what you want to achieve to alter the balance of forces, for inspiration; and immediate steps to get from here to there, for recruitment. The vision these days must include how politics is done. We do, most of us eat and want something more as well: to fly the flags of being self-governing humans. To join the argument over the *best* flag to fly is one thing, as Theresa May has done. To say flags are less important than haggis is to submit to the status quo. Incongruous as it may seem, this is what Corbyn has done. He has an old-fashioned belief in the British state and refuses negotiations with the SNP. He is a Labour tribalist, opposed to electoral pacts even in by-elections. He abhors coalition politics. He supports winner-takes-all voting and rejects proportional representation.

Corbyn is a product of what used to be called 'Labourism'. This is a term for the way Labour politics integrated itself into the fundamentals of Westminster, rather than challenge them. The concept was first developed by Ralph Miliband (father of the two brothers) in *Parliamentary Socialism*, published in 1961. Ironically, Tony Blair read it and learnt from it the need to spring the Westminster trap, if not in the way the author intended. Now, in rejecting Blair, Corbyn has returned Labour to Labourism. It does not matter that his is a left-wing version. The framework is a confinement.

The consequence proved fatal for Corbyn in the aftermath of the referendum. Labour's position should have been simple and clear. As it voted in favour of the referendum, it had to obey the outcome. At the same time, while seeking the least damaging form of separation, it should have set its heart on persuading voters to change their minds. Of course, this would have meant saying *why* it wanted to be in the EU, what is *wrong* about the UK going it alone, its view of *sovereignty*, why sovereignty needs to be *shared,* and *how* it thinks we should be governed. Labourism buries all such questions in its devotion to the Westminster parliamentary system. Accordingly, Corbyn and his team adopted the course of loyal opposition and demanded a better Brexit. This was politics as usual – which was a personal disaster for Labour's unusual leader. Not just because he lacks the necessary skills to be a traditional politician but because the source of his distinction and popularity was that he was not one.

The tenacity of Corbynism had two causes. Its asphyxiation in the leather benches of Westminster was due to its Labourism, rooted in Corbyn's own antique origins. Just as important, Labour as a whole is being pulled apart on the rack of England's division between its cities and its towns. The 'city-based' are more liberal in lifestyle, open and cosmopolitan. Even when working under conditions of precarity, they are 'middle-class' in the way that nurses are categorised as middle-class. Generally, they are pro-immigrant. The 'town-based' long for steady jobs, a traditional lifestyle, and dislike immigrants. Labour voters in the cities were largely for Remain. They are not 'citizens of nowhere', on the contrary they identify strongly as Mancunians, Liverpudlians or Londoners – cities that know themselves as part of the world. The Labour towns, as we have seen in Cartwright's Black Country, feel that this process is extracting their lifeforce, want protection from it and were for 'Out'.

While this social division runs right through its English voters, Labour has experienced the national disintegration of its support in Scotland. The two together mean it is undergoing a form of breakdown. What kind of recovery can Labour seek, if one is possible at all? Going back to the 1980s Corbyn-style has clearly failed. But the restoration of Blair-style globalisation politics is implausible in terms of its new membership and defies voters' newly expressed democratic intransigence. The alternative to the hospice is for Labour to undertake another form of renewal. It needs to commit itself to a fundamental change of character – and work with other parties.

A devastating, mordant philippic by Jeremy Gilbert shows why Labour must seek a form of what he calls a progressive alliance.[7] It is published by Compass which was born in the Labour Party but now includes Greens and holds out its hand to the Lib Dems – so it practises the change it advocates. Frankly and patiently, Gilbert shows that, given the SNPs hold on Scotland, Labour can never win power on its own again, even with an electoral miracle. Every rule has its exception, and now the rule of 'Never say never' has to bow its head and admit defeat. Written from the left, for the left, Gilbert carefully answers every possible objection. When you get to the end, it is clear that anyone who wants a Labour-led government must support a version of an electoral alliance. Why then, do Labour politicians refuse to adopt this course? What possible force could resist so overwhelming a reality and such a forensic demonstration of it? There is only one emotion deep and irrational enough to defy such an obvious necessity. Only love. Labour's unrequited adoration of Great Britain is the love affair its supporters cannot relinquish. I've seen it at first hand. Gilbert's completely irrefutable argument is met with a duck of the head, an inward smile, a gentle shrug. It's love. The dream is to be Her Majesty's Government of Great Britain and Northern Ireland. To seek to pollute such a prize with an alliance with the Lib Dems, the Greens or the SNP is out the question, it would betray the sweetheart of one's life.

Can the lively environment of think tanks, campaigns, policy analysts, advisers, Momentums, trade unionists, feminists, the Green party and the Liberal Democrats do anything with such an apparently hopeless case? All that is needed is to open the door marked 'English Europeans' and push Labour through. Instead of being filled with inspiration, whether of this or any other kind, the Corbyn wave into the Labour Party fell back by 40,000 in early 2017, taking membership down to 483,000. More may drop away, without arguments for effective change and resistance to Brexit to sustain them, while being told 'You can't eat a flag' as if they are idiots. The potential remains to engage with the causes of Brexit that lie in the appalling way the UK has been abused rather than well-governed. Without this, the tent will not be re-pitched. Then, either the public will have to lie back and watch the movements of Tory stars and planets indefinitely, or the 48 per cent will create a different political force to shape the fight back.

*A note:* What *should* Labour have done after the Brexit vote? DiEM25 also opposed it. Inspired by Yanis Varoufakis, it offered a brilliant way forward. In three stages. First, trigger Article 50 straight away. Second, join the EEA, the European Economic Area, immediately, for a period of five years until 2021. Dues must be paid and free movement continue until then, but it ends all political integration; gives agriculture and fishing back to the UK; allows the UK to make trade agreements with non-EU countries; means staying in the single market and gives business, trade and universities plenty of time to plan. Third, work out what the options are and use the 2022 election to allow the population to choose the option they want via their choice of MPs. This approach would have democratised the discussion about what Brexit can mean, without denying the Leave vote. Why did no one take any notice of the suggestion, surely not because it came from abroad? The deaf ear of Labourism struck again.

# 30

# Where the 48 Per Cent
# Go Next

Should Labour's disabling partition continue, energetic pro-Europeans will leave it to join the Greens or Lib Dems while those for Brexit will shift to May's Conservatives. Unless a different kind of rising occurs that displaces them all in their current form. Many among the 48 per cent who voted to Remain will not give up their European birthright without resistance, especially if Brexit threatens to turn into a chauvinist, ultra-neoliberal deregulation of the UK. Jeremy Gilbert's progressive alliance is proposed as an argument to salvage Labour influence. The alliance needed to turn England back towards its continent has a different, over-lapping purpose. Local and national experiments are taking place to work out how to achieve this and on 25 March 2017 an impressive demonstration of more than 100,000 pro-Europeans stretched from Hyde Park to Parliament Square in London, as the government finalised its letter to trigger Article 50.

The Liberal Democrats, the Greens and the paper *New European* helped make the march happen. The spirit of the demonstration was novel but the organisers run the danger of attempting to wind back the clock. As is always the case with a historic turn, we have to look back to origins to assess how to move forward; a rush to reverse the outcome only deepens the quandary. One of the first speakers to address the demonstration in Parliament Square was Blair's original spin-doctor, Alistair Campbell. Fluent in the cause he may be, but when he opens his mouth the souls of Iraqi innocents roll from his tongue. The European cause cannot succeed if it is turned into the restoration of Blair and company as they are so implicated in the causes of Brexit. For the Greens, by contrast, the EU's environmental record provides a basis for a multinational European politics, even if the EU often supports corporate power as well. The story of the Lib Dems provides a miniature version of the issues that the 48 per cent face as they regroup.

After being nearly wiped out in the 2015 election that reduced fifty-one MPs to their current nine, the Lib Dems could be forgiven for thinking they have already had their breakdown and can only grow. A serious party with a national organisation, a committed membership and experienced in local government, they are likely to play a crucial role in any effort to persuade England of its European calling. But like the Labour Party they will have to make a double reckoning with their past: with the national question, where in their own way they share Labour's evasions, and with chronic self-righteousness.

Take the most important human transformation of our time, feminism. Liberal support for women's rights goes back to John Stuart Mill, the conscience of the Victorians. Liberals were ahead of everyone on equality for women. Yet they seem untouched by the spirit of contemporary feminism. There is little sense of the struggle for solidarity or the exploration of change and learning in the Lib Dems, an absence that gives them a pre-sixties feel. Their attitude seems to be that they were first and everyone else needs to catch up with them. Or take the constitution on which I have worked with them since the 1980s. With one great exception, Trevor Smith, who is now a Lib Dem peer, their attitude has been that they own constitutional reform and anyone else is a blow-in. It was a mindset handed on to Clegg's generation. When he became deputy prime minister after 2010, he was responsible for the reform of the House of Lords. I tried to warn him that he was heading for a car crash. The Lib Dem mindset that everyone else is out of step with them kicked in. I was brushed aside as someone who didn't understand how things worked. The crash and total write-off followed.

'If a democracy cannot change its mind, it ceases to be a

democracy,' said Nick Clegg on BBC *Question Time*, quoting the London Labour MP David Lammy's speech to the demonstration two days before.[1] True enough, but Clegg makes it seem like a consumer choice (as in 'I selected Brexit but now, thank you, I've changed my mind'). It's an attitude that entails a mistake many Remainers have made, to regard Brexit voters as being transactional in their approach. Some were, and were taken in by the deceit of £350 million a week for the NHS. Most were not. Unlike Remain supporters, who reported economic reasons for staying in the EU and therefore looked forward and made a calculated judgement about what was best for their future, most Leave voters made a judgement on the past. Some felt there had to be self-government, others there had been too much immigration. Some desired a sense of agency now it was being offered to them, after decades of democracy that felt like a form of confinement.

Support for the EU may grow if May's government proves to be authoritarian, turns Brexit into oppressive centralisation and wasteful deregulation, and leaves most people feeling more marginalised rather than in control. This will not justify Lib Dems congratulating themselves for being right all along, as they are so prone to do. The Remain side were in power continuously the whole of this century, the Lib Dems included in the last crucial five years. They too bear a responsibility for England turning against everything they stand for. How will they reassess and change in the light of this?

When Nick Clegg took over the party leadership in 2006, he was a contributor to the Orange Book crowd. They replaced the party's mix of nineteenth-century humanism and twentieth-century Keynesianism with twenty-first-century, inhuman neoliberalism. They led the party to embrace the free market of free competitive individuals rather than a free society. It was a baffling change for outsiders and an inner integrity was broken. There were always free-market advocates in the liberal tradition, but this did not stop them seeing the market from the perspective of society as a whole. The Beveridge group of MPs was founded in 2001 to defend this tradition, and to resist the rising influence of neoliberal globalisers taking place under the influence of the New Labour government – and lost. With Clegg's victory in the leadership contest in 2006, the party became the 'Neo-Liberal Democrats', as one ex-member said. Economic liberalism and its necessities were separated from the political and social, and given priority over them – a classic neoliberal move of depoliticisation.

The most infamous example was the way in the run-up to the 2010 election, Lib Dem candidates personally signed an electoral oath not to support an increase in university tuition fees should their party go into a coalition. They then broke their bond. The party's pride – that it was different and could be trusted – evaporated. Neoliberalism functions to undermine politics. They became its plaything. In power-sharing mode Clegg then unforgivably supported the marketisation of the NHS, when his party could have stopped it. One incident that may seem remote demonstrates the dire consequences: the fate of the Child Trust Fund.

Practical social democrats within the Labour government created the fund, which became law in 2005. It gave every child £250 at birth in an account they could not access until they are 18 (£500 for families on low incomes). Relatives, parents and grandparents could add to it and were encouraged to. The aim was to ensure that everyone starts their adult life with an asset. It was extraordinary successful at getting poorer families to save, mainly via grandparents; 30 per cent of families that had children with an income of less than £19,000 a year, saw the child's fund topped up. One mutual saving fund reported, 'In terms of changing people's behaviour, this is the most successful product there's ever been.'[2] It was also, you might have thought, the most purely liberal policy there could be, bar none. For it enabled all individuals to have their own stake and learn how money works. But the Orange Book Lib Dems opposed it and when they got into the Coalition government, they agreed to its abolition. The Child Trust Fund may have been old-fashioned liberal but it was not neoliberal. It involved an act of government not the market: it was egalitarian not competitive.

What does this have to do with Brexit? In so far as the anti-EU outcome was caused by millions of voters from poorer families feeling the state is against them, and that their interests are not represented in the way the country is run, the abolition of the Child Trust Fund confirmed their view. The plan had been for the government to add a further £250 when each child was seven. The Lib Dems prevented the scheme from reaching that age. To live on an estate (such as one of Cameron's 'dumps'), to learn from a neighbour that the child trust fund had been created as a universal right, hear about children who benefited, to look forward to your own doing so, then to have this small but significant policy of togetherness taken away – is to be taunted by the well-off. Poor working people felt the state was playing with them. It was not the straw that broke the back of voter allegiance to their rulers, but it was a straw.

Lib Dems' responsibility for this, however partial, indicates why they need to make a self-reckoning, to get to a place where they can appeal to the country to agree with them. This will not come easily to a minority party that has survived for half a century on its own self-confidence. They also have 102 members of the House of Lords, which cannot help.

Just as the EU needs to tame its oligarchs to become a union of democratic collaboration, so England will at some point have to return to the EU. Following the example of Scotland this will be powered from the centre and the left. What is unclear is how long this process will take and how it will come about. To succeed it needs to confront and partly absorb the strange energies of Brexit. Writing in 2008 about the popularity of the 1963 movie *The Great Escape*, Paul Gilroy observed:

'There is something about the idea of escape itself that has become deeply pleasurable. The mythology of that thwarted wartime breakout and the peculiar mixture of failure and triumph that it articulates provides ways to make the nation's painful geo-political and economic transition psychologically bearable to many who experience its unhappy consequences without appreciating their underlying cause. There is also something else at stake. It can be interpreted as a repressed desire to be able to escape from the grip in which the invented memory of that anti-Nazi war has held us. Somewhere, against the odds and in opposition to the logic of our national melancholia, many people do want to work through the past. Half the country is desperate to move on.'[3]

More than half the people across the UK are desperate to move on, today. The referendum showed this, but also divided them. The irony is well observed by Gilroy with respect to those across England-Britain who wanted to escape the feeling of needing to escape – and hoped an exit from the EU would provide this relief. For them, Europe represented the confinement that had to be set aside, to make a fresh start in the world. Others felt that only a commitment to the EU provided a route to freedom from the claustrophobia of British self-righteousness. What kind of escape does Brexit provide? The problem with seeing it as a getaway is that the EU was never a serious trap for the UK but rather a privilege. The Eurozone *is* an imprisonment but Britain is not a member of it. The rulings of the European Court could become a serious infringement of national democracy, but given the public mood across the continent it would not survive a political fight over its powers. Britain's problem was an English problem and England's problem was with itself and its confinement in 'Great Britain', its Westminster institutions and mentality. Now England will learn that flight preserves the inner condition it seeks to escape. The only effective escape route from one's troubles, such as lack of good government, is to confront the causes.

The more honest Brexiteers have even welcomed this, saying that it means 'we won't be able to blame the EU for our problems any more'. A sharp, personal version of this was uttered by Niall Ferguson, who has been described by the *Daily Mail* with unusual generosity as 'Britain's most influential historian'. He supported Remain and recanted after the vote, blaming his friendship with David Cameron and George Osborne. Proclaiming himself a Thatcherite he said he was wrong and Brexit was right. Now, beamed into a conference in

London from Stanford California, he compared Brexit to a divorce in which you realise that 'many of the things you blamed on your ex... are your own problems'.

Not only are they our own problems, Europe was not preventing the nations of the UK from solving them. This is the uncomfortable truth the country will have to face. The gung-ho Brexiteers advocate a way out through maximum globalisation and deregulation: the off-shore island strategy. There are three drawbacks to it. The success of a Hong Kong or Singapore model depends on a lot of immigration, as you would expect. Second, the EU will not permit de-regulation by making sure that access to its markets is conditional on the UK retaining the standards of the EU. Third, it is London-centred, benefitting the City and finance whose privileges the Leave vote was directed against.

The route left for Theresa May as she 'gets on with the job' will be to develop industrial policies, regional authorities, training programmes, decent schools and... well, all the forms of government that are the mark of countries that are members of the EU. To put it another way, 'our own problems' that Ferguson refers to, are the problems of not being European enough. This is the bitter irony for Brexit Britain. However 'global' her rhetoric might be, the task for holy Theresa will be to impose the responsibilities of European Christian democracy on a heathen land.

Initially she is likely to scoop up the traditionally Methodist older Labour support along with the UKIP inclined. What can the 48ers possibly achieve against such an extraordinary alliance? Especially when its leading voices are still largely Blairite and Cameroon, representatives of a deceitful, undemocratic past clinging to the hope of restitution. The answer is that this is the wrong way of looking at post-Brexit Britain.

The fruits of Brexit cannot satisfy the contradictory passions of its rag-bag of supporters. Their alliance will hold together while May's firm commitment to ensure that 'Brexit means Brexit' remains just that. While she demands unity and promises delivery, opposition is helpless. But there will come a point at which the promise hits reality. When Brexit is no longer a debate about what May means by it, but what it has become as she makes her call in the face of what the EU offers – for it will set the terms for the UK's exit from the Union.

Then the outcome will be taken to Europe's parliaments. As the UK's fate is debated in the democratic assemblies across the continent, the English will realise that they are a European country after all. At that point we need to be prepared to make common cause with our fellow Europeans as democrats. For they too are face-to-face with the hypocritical monstrosity of neoliberalism and its even more rigid German form of *ordoliberalism*. To prepare for this those of us who voted Remain need to prepare for the break-up of our alliance, which is at least as shaky as those who supported Leave, to reach out to the democratic anger behind the Brexit vote. While this must take a national form its purpose is to address the wider, international political economy that undermined democracy in the first place. This is the challenge for creative organisation and inventive thinking that can link up with and learn from the movement against Trump gathering across the United States.

# 31
# People Flow

In 2003, when I was editing *openDemocracy*, I was approached by Tom Bentley, then the director of Demos, to co-publish a debate. He was working with a senior Dutch civil servant Theo Veenkamp, then head of strategy in Holland's Ministry of Justice, who earlier had been in charge of his country's asylum programme. Having witnessed migration policy and its problems, he had developed a strategy in response called People Flow. The research was based on two years of careful efforts after Veenkamp realised the need to think through the issues from first principles.

He'd made a Copernican breakthrough with respect to immigration. After much staring through telescopes and calculation, Copernicus understood that the sun did not go round the earth, nor did the planets: the earth and the planets go round the sun. Veenkamp's research had done something equivalent in challenging the orthodoxy of our day. The debate *openDemocracy* carried about his thesis and its implications was huge in numbers of contributors, high in quality, thoughtful in content, international in scope, and even included a contribution signed by David Blunkett, then New Labour's home secretary. A selection was then edited and published by Rosemary Bechler. The established powers across Europe did not torture or denounce Veenkamp, or force him to retract. They applied the first line of defence used to repress an enemy these days, they ignored him.

Nonetheless, he was right then and has been proved right since, repeatedly, over a decade and a half. What he realised, as he researched the material and saw the steady numbers arriving, was that every time there was an incident in poorer countries, more and more refugees and immigrants turned up in the EU, and every time a cluster of them were identified in a European city, a 'crisis' was declared. Whereupon politicians scrambled to deal with opinion inflamed by alarmist stories that sold newspapers. He looked at the pattern over time, and estimated future trends. It was clear that something is happening which is not a crisis. This was his Copernican moment as a policymaker. *Immigration is normal.* Immigration may rise and fall in numbers. Its geographical pattern alters. It will always remain: it is an ongoing fact about the nature of humanity in our time.

The notion of an immigration 'crisis' stems from an official and public refusal to accept immigration as normal. This is the equivalent of believing that the sun goes round the earth. Officials cannot plan for it. Governments hope it will shrink to such low numbers that it will effectively cease to be noticeable. To *prepare* for immigration is regarded as politically unacceptable: it is 'inviting them in', or providing a 'pull factor', and is close to incitement. Thus, the normal becomes the unthinkable, and we stagger on from crisis to crisis. This then wears down the fabric of our democracy and public life.

Because migration is normal and continues, it goes underground. Individuals and even entire villages raise large sums of money and pay smugglers. International networks of criminals establish lucrative routes, bribing officials and ensuring a steady movement of illegals across long and hazardous routes. Increasingly costly policing measures have to be created to try and prevent entry. After people get through, processing is costly. Local people get angry that immigrants who arrive can immediately 'claim benefits'. Most don't, but because those who do come are not regarded as normal, no policies are broadcast to show what is happening. Nothing is admitted and therefore nothing can be denied as rumours spread.

You cannot put a stop to this destructive cycle until you realise that you can no more prevent migration than prohibition could prevent the consumption of alcohol. It is normal. It will continue. It cannot be prevented. Therefore it is essential to *govern migration as something that is normal.*

The principle on which it should be governed is mutual benefit. First, you must start from the point of view of immigrants. Given the numbers and the inequality, there will be so many enterprising individuals who want to migrate that they cannot all be stopped. Accept the fact that this is normal and inevitable. On this basis, for example, decide there will be 1,000 migrants a year from Indonesia. Run a lottery for all communities that wish to apply. Those who win a place have to pay a sum of money, say, around 75 per cent of the charge that people smugglers demand. This goes to the community of the country the immigrant arrives in. A safe journey is assured, a training scheme will make sure that the immigrant has skills, there can be a language qualification. With a cheaper, safer route available, smuggling will die away, and should be hit very hard if it occurs. Migrants, Veenkamp observes, are usually energetic and hard-working, and do not make the journey to get welfare. Have a period of, say, four years, when they must pay into the welfare system in order to qualify for it.

I've crudely summarised some aspects of a very detailed and researched set of policy proposals that distinguishes between self-funded immigrants and forcibly displaced asylum seekers and suggests how to handle rights, legal processes, families and organising sponsorship. It has the aim of:

> positively managing the flow of people, rather than controlling it. This approach seeks to manage movement of people by taking their needs and purposes as a starting point, matching them as closely as possible with the system they encounter, and channelling their energies and potentials.[1]

I like the integrity of the People Flow concept. It is humanist. It establishes mutual benefit. Instead of immigrants paying large sums to smugglers, with People Flow funds go to the host society and the immigrants work their way into the benefit system. It extends rights to the migrants and ensures their well-being. It normalises reality. Above all, everyone takes responsibility for what is happening.

Behind the rhetoric policies of normalisation are being developed. *Der Spiegel* has recently published a survey by Hein de Haas that shows migration has remained at a steady three per cent of the global population since 1960, growing in numbers along with the world population, accompanying and assisting economic liberalisation. While border controls against illegal migration and asylum speakers have got tougher, policies on migration have tended to become less not more restrictive.

The problem is not migration but the politics of migration and tabloid coverage. Two years after *openDemocracy* published People Flow, there was a migration panic in the build-up to the UK's 2005 election. The Tories demanded stricter controls. Blair announced he would act. The *Sun* ran a screaming headline: 'Finally Blair acts. No skills. No English. NO ENTRY'. Tom Bentley wrote:

> Here we go again ... 'Tough' approaches that mean greater 'control' of the flow of migrants, with all the racist overtones, is proving popular across Europe ... What is especially pathetic, not to say disappointing, about this, is that we saw it coming, we laid out the argument about what to do, and it seems to have had less impact than blowing in the wind.[2]

A decade later and, in the UK, it has been déjà vu year after year.

Veenkamp was not writing about freedom of movement within the EU, and published before the Eastern European countries became full members. But when considering migration it is essential to start from principle and at a planetary level. People Flow is invaluable because it establishes the joint perspectives of the migrants and the host countries. Guy Aitchison, whose work on how human rights can reinforce rather than undermine politics is becoming influential, set out what the alternative to People Flow would look like, namely a fundamental human right to cross borders.[3] Clearly there must be an individual right to leave a community or nation. But the right to arrive, settle and work must be a matter for the society of destination, in terms of accepting a new citizen. The right of asylum is different: it states that every country must be willing to offer refuge to someone driven from their homeland against their will. Economic migration is the migration of people made by choice, not under duress. It is perfectly principled for this to be dealt with at the level of government as a political matter.

The politics can be lethal because of the 'othering' of migrants, always exacerbated by economic stress and military conflict – or terrorism. In the United States, Trump's demagogy used Mexican migration as a fascistic mobilising device, while knowing that more Mexicans had been leaving the US than arriving since 2005 (see the Pew Report[4]). I just want to look at the role that the issue of migration played in the British referendum. In the UK, farcical diagrams of Turks descending on Britain circulated by the Leave campaign in the name of apparently civilised figures like Johnson, Gove and Gisela Stuart are destined to be some of the more shameful exhibits in the museum of chauvinism. What their caricature illustrated was a huge European Union penetrated by uncontrolled movement. The principle of free movement within it was used to scare people into thinking there might be uncontrolled movement across it from *outside.* The confusions and vulnerability that permitted the Brexiteers their propaganda coup was, however, the creation of the British government, and especially of then Prime Minister Cameron after 2010.

The void between what David Cameron said and did was shocking when it came to migration. I have already looked at the way he pledged to get net migration down to tens of thousands in his 2010 election manifesto and turned this into a continued 'ambition' in 2015, knowing that he could not deliver. The actual numbers of net migration over the period were: 2010: 256,000; 2011: 205,000; 2012: 177,000; 2013: 209,000; 2014: 313,000; 2015: 333,000.[5] These figures are the net outcome. The overall *flow* of people is much larger than the net figures. Over 500,000 arrived every year and 200,000 or more emigrated annually. Less than half the inflows came from the EU, although the EU proportion has been rising significantly. Over 150,000 a year come as students – that is they pay to study in Britain and then leave – yet the government persists in defining them as migrants because they stay longer than a year.

I want to emphasise that Cameron and his colleagues knew they could not achieve the low net figures they 'pledged'. For them it may have been mere words but their pernicious consequences were to lead towards Brexit. Because it was government policy that the problem would not persist, no measures were put in place to manage what was happening. Instead, the government's endorsement that numbers were much too high made people who were already frightened and vulnerable more anxious. The state agreed that net migration was a big problem, promised to reduce the numbers and was unable to do so – the country was out of control – who knows what the numbers might be next year!

To get a sense of policy failure, overall the UK has about 13 per cent foreign-born residents, divided approximately into 5 per cent from the EU and 8 per cent from outside the EU. France, Germany, Spain and the US also have the same overall proportion of migrants in their countries.[6] Germany has far more from within than from outside the EU (before it took around a million refugees from Syria). The largest numbers of EU citizens in the UK are from Poland (831,000), Ireland (382,000) and Germany (286,000). In terms of total numbers rather than per capita proportion, in 2014 the UK had the second-highest total in the EU after Germany. It was only the eighth-highest in terms of immigrants per head of the population.[7] In terms of the larger context, across the EU as a whole, the official Eurostat website states that for 2014, the latest year it has full records:

A total of 3.8 million people immigrated to one of the EU-28 Member States while at least 2.8 million emigrants were reported to have left an EU Member State .... among these 3.8 million immigrants during 2014, there were an estimated 1.6 million citizens of non-member countries, 1.3 million people with citizenship of a different EU Member State from the one to which they immigrated, around 870 thousand people who migrated to an EU Member State of which they had the citizenship (for example, returning nationals or nationals born abroad), and some 12.4 thousand stateless people.[8]

There are over 500 million people in the EU as a whole.

This was the context for Cameron demanding a renegotiation of the EU's principle of the free movement of its citizens, urged on by tabloid press claims that it undermines the integrity of British society and placed intolerable economic burdens upon it. There is a fantastic, painfully honest account of negotiations by Daniel Korski, who was deputy director of David Cameron's policy unit and a loyal member of his team. Despite his attempt to justify their efforts, Korski's honesty reveals the strategic vacuum of Cameron's administration. His European colleagues took the prime minister and his team seriously, as you would expect, when he demanded to renegotiate the UK's relationship. Immigration was an important political issue for Cameron. Korski's account needs to be quoted in full:

> As we tried to argue that the U.K. faced a unique set of circumstances, which required a fundamental redraft of the relevant European rules, we struggled to provide evidence to support our case.
>
> We tried using absolute numbers: three million migrants likely to come over the next 10 years, 6 percent of Lithuania's population living in the U.K. already. We highlighted the pressure on public services like schools and hospitals. And we appealed to European leaders to consider the impact of migratory flows on their own economies.
>
> These arguments were quickly shot down. Our European counterparts pointed out that the number of immigrants moving to the U.K. was relatively limited, compared to, for example, Germany. Or they called attention to the fact that European migrants paid more tax and used fewer public services than British citizens, which was true.
>
> They noted that our economy was growing, that we were almost at full employment, and thus that migration was more

or less inevitable. *They showed us how our rate of financial distribution to the areas under pressure was much lower than, say, Germany's, and concluded that we should just spend a lot more money addressing the challenges there.*

We were never able to counter these arguments. To be honest, we failed to find any evidence of communities under pressure that would satisfy the European Commission. At one point we even asked the help of Andrew Green at Migration Watch an organization that has been critical of migration. But all he could provide was an article in the *Daily Telegraph* about a hospital maternity ward in Corby. There was no hard evidence.[9] (my emphasis)

How about that? I have emphasised the passage on investing financial support 'to the areas under pressure' in this jaw-dropping account. The Europeans said: Show us an area that is really suffering as you claim. The response that came back was: Sorry, we can't. The Europeans asked: Where there is a problem, what are you doing about it as a government? The answer was: Nothing.

If you get the impression that the Europeans think the Brits are unserious and incompetent, it is not Boris Johnson's bluster that is at fault. Cameron's government was unserious and incompetent in the way it governed Britain. They went along with the press when it blamed Europe for problems that Whitehall was largely responsible for. Then they blamed the EU for not conceding enough in negotiations, when they could not substantiate the reasons for their demands. When they told the public to vote Remain, they simply refused to say anything about immigration. Looking back, it is unbelievable. Having shot themselves in the foot on the most dramatically important issue, the one that most crystallised fears, they then shot themselves in the head.

Immigration played a specific role in Brexit, greater and different from its influence in the Trump campaign and the rise of right-wing nativist movements across the EU. Across the board, it is a real issue, not just a symptom. As Eric Kaufman and Zack Beauchamp have shown, it is not the case that economic improvements are the 'answer' to anti-immigrant sentiment.[10] Those of us who want a society that is open to immigrants, welcomes the gifts they bring, and feels that anyway the numbers are relatively small and the benefits in terms of change are positive, have to start by making the argument in principle. People flow is a fact of life, it must be and ought to be managed. This means the arguments as to how it is governed need to be won politically, not diverted into regulations. Buried, the issue will detonate. Migration is part of every living community. No existing community is a given, defined only by its past, nor are those who welcome migration part of some dissolving globalist blob dislocated from patriotism by higher education.

The fact that migration is normal makes the argument winnable. One of the areas I have not seen any research into are the very large numbers who are anyway leaving the UK, and how many Brits are returning. The total flow of people both leaving and coming to live in the UK in 2014 and 2015 was approaching a million. The numbers leaving will rise with Brexit. The mass experience of migration within families, as well as its frequently temporary nature, is part of a massive, shared experience. Yet this does not get fed into the political story of 'dangerous incomers stealing our welfare'. The 'othering' of migrants needs to be counterbalanced by its normalisation.

This is why I argue that migration is an excuse running through Brexit and Trump, not a cause. There are a significant number of racists and bigots. *They* are a problem. There is the question of control, of how migration is governed and managed. *That* is a problem. There is the question within the UK of a country that does not know how to believe in itself and feels threatened – England. *It* is a problem. Finally, there are the callous masters of neoliberalism turning people into a competitive workforce of individual profit seekers and *this* is a problem. But migrants and migration – they are a normal, three per cent of life on earth.

# 32

# Combined Determination

When President Kennedy gave his inaugural address on 20 January 1961, he told his compatriots, 'my fellow Americans: ask not what your country can do for you; ask what you can do for your country'. Three days later, a B-52 bomber on a routine flight went into a tailspin and lost two 4-megaton hydrogen bombs over North Carolina. The nation's capital was within fallout range. The parachute of one bomb opened as it was supposed to if released on purpose. Three of its four trigger mechanisms, designed to prevent accidental ignition, engaged. It is not clear whether they did so in sequence or because of the aircraft's mid-air catastrophe. At any rate, they worked. When the bomb hit the ground, 'a firing signal was sent to the nuclear core'. The remaining trigger, a low-voltage switch, held. It could easily have shorted. Had it done so, an investigator concluded, 'It would have been bad news – in spades'.[1] Certainly it would have given a different meaning to the words, 'ask not what your country can do for you'.

When looking at surprising political explosions like Brexit and Trump – they are not revolutions but nor are they mere rebellions – it is useful to bear this incident in mind, both as an event and a metaphor. Take the event. History would have been very different if North Carolina had gone up in a mushroom cloud, as it very nearly did, and made America's capital uninhabitable. You could say, it would have been 'just an accident'. But the Cold War had spawned what the outgoing President Eisenhower criticised as a 'military-industrial complex', which contrived a 'missile gap' to ensure funding for its own overkill capacity, along with contracts, self-importance and sending B-52s on routine flights loaded with armed holocaust devices. So, yes, it would have been an accident;

at the same time there was a systemic vulnerability – you could say that it was an accident waiting to happen.

Were Brexit and Trump explosions of this kind, ignited by a series of mishaps as safety catches failed? This might be called the Andrew Marr defence of not having to think. Marr is a leading BBC presenter, the anchor of a Sunday morning programme. He seems to believe that everything would be the same were it not for an accident, or in the case of Brexit four accidents. 'Had we not had poor financial regulation just before the globalisation of the money markets, leading to the financial collapse of 2008, public hostility to the top class of financiers would be nothing like as strong as it is now'; and, second, had not, 'parliament ... approved the Blair government's armed intervention in Iraq in 2003'; and, third, 'had this not been followed by the relatively minor local scandal of MPs' expenses'; and finally, 'if David Cameron hadn't decided to hold the referendum in the first place'; well then, everything would have stayed as it was. Marr concludes: 'In short, the Brexit rebellion arose less from the vast forces of modern globalisation than from the awkward decisions, wrong turnings and mistakes of specific British politicians from the early 1980s onwards'.[2] This is an outstanding example of Anglo-Saxon empiricism – of history being just one damn thing after another with no need to talk about 'vast forces' or 'globalisation'. Brexit happened thanks to a few wrong turnings and mistaken decisions taken by political chumps who should have known better. End of story.

The Marr defence sounds convincing but does not stand up. Hostility to financiers is not due to the financial crash but to the way those responsible responded – paying themselves astronomic fortunes to rescue the system while regular incomes were frozen. The problem with Iraq was not just the lies that led to it but the fact that no one paid a price for them afterwards. Would they have done so in the UK if Parliament had refused to vote for war? The parliamentary expenses scandal was minor only in terms of the amount spent on duck ponds; the permissiveness it displayed was endemic, voters know that if you catch a canny thief cheating just a little he is nonetheless a thief. Had Cameron not agreed to put a referendum in his 2015 party manifesto, the Conservatives would have needed UKIP support to form a government; because more than two Tory MPs would have defected and UKIP got nearly four million votes despite Cameron's pledge. Brexit was not the result of four or five slips and mishaps. It was an explosive protest against continuing with the system, which could not stop the deceptions, incompetence and greed even after they were accidently exposed.

Marr's resistance to the existence of underlying forces helps to identify what needs to be explained. The initial issue with respect to both Brexit and Trump is why the publics of the USA and the UK in their millions lost trust and confidence in the existing political order. The second question is why they then embraced Brexit and Trump as a response to this loss. This in turn calls for a third explanation as to why these were the only alternatives on offer.

The first question needs to be answered at the global level in terms of the economic and military-political systems America created and the UK adopted, including what they achieved as well as failed to achieve.

The second question needs to be answered in terms of national institutions, old but backward forms of democracy, media and attempts at management of opinion, embedded in two proud national histories – that led voters to gamble on Brexit and Trump.

A third set of answers are needed because Trump and Brexit are pseudo-solutions. They will make matters worse for their nations and their publics. Not because they are 'wrong' in the simple sense, as there were very good reasons not to support Hillary Clinton or David Cameron. But because Trump and Brexit represent exacerbated forms of continuity of the system they apparently condemned when they offered voters the chance to reject it. Trump won't make America great for voters, Brexit will not bring back control to voters, in ways that matter. Why have such doomed enterprises gripped their respective countries?

The reason for events like Brexit and Trump is multi-layered.

I call it *combined determination*. Different levels of active causality are involved. It is their combination, not one single cause or determinant that explains the explosions. Each level includes unpredictable elements of *conscious human agency*. We slide, we catch our footing, we are on a man-made slope, if we have good fortune there is a helping hand.

Take the causes of the 1961 incident. First, there is the Cold War between the USA and the Soviet Union as they challenge each other fundamentally, yet are also joined by its rules which they make up is it proceeds. Then, there is America's corporate-political military machine, lobbying for influence and generating its profitable weapon systems. There is the military system itself, in this case the air force with its training, pilots, airfields, planes and routine operations, planning daily for alerts. There is the actual bomb, its manufacture, upkeep and the design of its mechanisms. All four are complex processes – taken together they set that particular B-52 and its crew, with their potential for errors, into the sky over North Carolina with an H-Bomb. When, as it parachuted to the ground and the firing signal was sent to the nuclear core, its systems could be said to have both worked and failed. Systems are alive with danger but they also have discipline and predictability. Yet the military systems of that 1961 moment, a wire away from catastrophe, were the outcome of a simpler set of processes than the ones we are living under.

The answer to the first two questions is that two great political-economic forces can be identified as the determining contexts for the actual explosions of Brexit and Trump. First, the frustrated military supremacy of the United States even after it won the Cold War. Its might and firepower need not have led it to the staggering stupidity of the invasion and occupation of Mesopotamia in 2003. If Al Gore had won Florida in 2000, they would not have. But a defeat followed, which is still under way and has undermined the standing of America, with the UK tagging along in its shadow. Both had been supremely successful empires and with the new century they pitched for an even greater Anglo-Saxon world supremacy on the back of an ongoing financial globalisation. If then, as Bush and Blair hoped in their pathetic dreams, the masses of Bagdad had cheered them and the Stars and Stripes and the Union Jack for their liberation, angry, rancorous resentment would not now be suffocating Congress and Westminster in the same way, even with the crash and economic stagnation. There would have been no need for the lure of greatness – the two countries would be 'great'. Today, Trump would like to reverse the verdict. The Brexiteers dream of another Falklands.

More important than the context of military frustration is the impact of neoliberal globalisation, initiated and theorised in the United States and kicked into action by the City of London and Thatcher's massive pioneering privatisations. It was not a doctrine or a policy but an approach that placed the market above government by acts of government. Thirty years on, the extraordinary 'free market' system it created has become the victim of its success. Depoliticising the economies of the two countries and locking them into planetary competition went along with undermining the strength and autonomy of established institutions, parties, trade unions, churches, local governments, professional associations and universities. Even schools were stripped of their self-organisation, privileges and linkages into their local networks, economies and communities. Society was pulverised to open it up for competition. This prepared the way for neoliberalism's political downfall. For the defensive ramparts of institutional loyalties and fealties that the old establishments erected to defend their hegemony were now little more than tourist attractions.

There were new freedoms, opportunities and benefits – until the crash they worked and were transformative. Thanks to the distribution of government largesse, the crash did not lead to a great depression which would have been truly catastrophic. But this essential intervention exposed neoliberalism as a form of government not nature. Growing inequality became *a regime of the 1 per cent* and not, as it had been presented, as being due to a-lot-of-rich-people-who-happened-to-make-it-by-their-own-individual-efforts-who-we-could-join-if-we-worked-hard. Many began to feel the system was shamelessly fixed. For all the honest companies working within it, there was a permissiveness towards the financial sector that undermined the responsibility of government, hence democracy itself.

Neoliberalism taunts us as it intensifies competition, makes lives insecure, forces us into debt, encourages immigrants to come, while claiming government is powerless and the market knows best, and *at the same time* the government fixes the rules to help the rich. In 1940 Karl Polyani warned that the depoliticised marketisation of humanity proposed by early theories of neoliberalism in opposition to a planned society, was a 'utopia'. If attempted, he predicted it would result in a return to fascism – what was called for was democratic government.[3] In which case 2016 may be seen as a dry run in the wake of neoliberalism's failed utopia: a popular rejection of the powerlessness overseen by the representatives of what I have called the CBCs – the Anglo-American leaders from Clinton (Bill) to Cameron and Clinton (Hilary) via Bush, Blair and Brown – who defined the arc of power over the last quarter century.

This was not a story of the screwed and impoverished rising in anger. On the whole, the true underdogs voted for Clinton in America and abstained in the referendum. But those who did have something to lose if not much, millions of whom were so disenchanted they had ceased to vote, seized the opportunity. They rallied against 'a rigged system' to quote the demagogue Donald Trump and 'The EU, they say – it's crap' to quote the lesser demagogue, Boris Johnson, who, typically, got away with his expletive by stuffing the word into his opponent's mouth. Both offered an opportunity to turn resentment into more than another impotent protest, which is what the experience of voting had become – thanks to the way neoliberalism had evacuated any real influence from politics.

Neoliberalism's duplicitous marketisation of the whole of society with its privatisation, asset bubbles, disaggregation and irresponsibility created the context that caused the rebellions. But why did they take the specific form they did? Before answering this, it is vital to note that the votes were very close. Both the UK and USA split evenly. Any theory that suggests neoliberalism lay behind the votes for Brexit and Trump has to explain its impact on those who were for Europe and Clinton. The answer is that its fruits were manifold. If the negative side of neoliberalism was its marketisation, its positive side was the globalisation it brought with it: its liberalism; its open, often lively culture; its embrace of hi-tech communications; its permissiveness and sexual equality, toleration of difference; and for many its material rewards (see a recent lyrical account by Sam Bowman[4]). This contrast was and is especially acute with the European Union. The Eurogroup is an expression of its cartel nature, enforcing despicable policies on Greece and Italy, yet the EU is also an arena of human rights and emancipation from intolerance.

Alan Finlayson suggests a division to explain how this played out in terms of parallel impacts, economic and cultural.[5] Economically, globalisation draws people into its new planetary supply chains. Socially, it creates a liberal, open culture. The combination generates four groups: 1) Those who benefit from globalisation both economic and social; 2) those who don't benefit economically but gain from its social emancipation; 3) those who do benefit from it economically but are alienated by its liberal culture (a Trump, rich, old and philistine, would fit here); 4) those who do not participate in globalisation either economically or culturally. The cultural divide was critical, he suggests. If it is right, it suggests that groups 3 and 4, the ones most distant from the high values of cosmopolitanism, were those who embraced the call for democracy and self-government even if they were bombastic. It gave them a crucial political advantage and now sets a challenge for those of us who value international collaboration to ground our politics in ways that empower everyone.

Finlayson adds a fifth group. Those who benefit economically and socially from globalisation and want much more of both. They want even less restriction, correctness and regulation, and look forward to globalisation and competition squared. Finlayson suggests that Dominic Cummings (who ran Vote Leave) and Steve Hilton, (an early Cameron adviser now in California, who backed both Brexit and Trump) come into this group. Hilton wrote 'We are the radicals now, breaking apart the old system' into Cameron's first speech to the Conservative Party as premier in 2010.[6] Trump's adviser Steve Bannon said, 'I want to bring everything crashing down, and destroy all of today's establishment'.[7] Only if you are privileged, does this intensification of dissolving certainties attract. But it explains the dangerous alliance between the ultra-capitalists and hedge-fund neoliberals and those at the bottom of the globalisation heap, who do not benefit from the neoliberal system at all. Dangerous, because if the winning sides in the referendum and Trump's campaign find themselves frustrated, they have the class alliance and skilful demagogues.

This was the general framework that caused the explosions. Now for the second question. How come they detonated in the US and in Britain's England, but not, say, in Scotland or Canada? First, because the two old states suffered a legitimacy crisis brought on by the defeat of their world ambitions in the sands and mountains of Iraq and Afghanistan. In the United States Trump won thanks to a conventional presidential campaign even if he was an unconventional celebrity candidate. Clinton was a very poor opponent who had no story to tell about America except that she would be its first woman president, and this triggered a vile degree of misogyny as well as support. The deeper question about Trump's triumph lies in why the Republican Party could not prevent him from becoming its candidate. Part of the answer is that its own establishment backed its own CBC candidate, Bush (Jeb), as if dynastic familiarity was the most reassuring way to control the presidency. A key early moment in his doomed bid was when Bush (Jeb), challenged on the Iraq invasion, was unable to distance himself from his brother and gave four different answers over four days.[8]

In the UK, Brexit was the outcome of an exceptional referendum which came about thanks to a long-drawn-out constitutional and national impasse. It was not a consequence of decline but of failed renewal. Had Thatcher's support for the European single market been topped out with a shared claim on the unification of Germany,

British identification with post-Cold War Europe could have followed, to permit popular and, of course, critical engagement with the EU. Instead, she created a Falklands version of modern Britishness, an 'island story'. As history, it was removed from the realities of empire and engagement. As myth, it slotted in nicely with the City of London's neoliberal take-off.

When the Murdoch-backed political-media caste picked up Thatcher's baton under the headship of Tony Blair, it espoused personal liberalism and ruined the old constitution without replacing it. An incoherent union emerged that inflamed an English nation unable to speak or represent itself except through its 300-year-old imperial carapace of 'Great Britain'. This uncodified, multinational entity was incompatible with the European Union. The contradiction generated growing support for exit from it. An impulse that was reinforced by the EU's own embrace of neoliberalism. Because the EU and the Eurozone are rule-based, they made neoliberalism's opposition to democracy explicit. This was underlined by pro-market rulings of the European Court in Luxembourg which is beyond appeal. A grudge based on nationalist, melancholic regret was galvanised by a modern, legitimate grievance. In the referendum, this combination overwhelmed the narrow transactional arguments of the CBC campaign to stay in Europe, which dared not even confront the principles of immigration and democracy. The outcome, however, is an attempt to solve the UK's constitutional and national crisis by rolling back as far as possible the reforms of the Blair years and even reversing 300 years of Scottish autonomy to unify the UK into a single 'nation'. Prime Minister Theresa May explained that her Plan for Britain 'has at its heart one over-arching goal: to build a more united nation'.[9]

Support for Trump and Brexit drew on the democratic discontent bred by the neoliberal project of turning society into a pure marketplace, and then transformed it into a regressive turn towards a familiar identification with regimes of past global power. Instead of using the pent-up energy to mount a democratic challenge built on the international solidarity that modern globalisation makes possible, they fell back on imperial stereotypes.

The third question is, why did such doomed enterprises seize the thrones of the White House and Downing Street? The answer is that there was not an effective alternative on offer that engaged with the issues of democracy, control and world roles that Trump and Brexit addressed. In America, there could have been. Bernie Sanders tried to provide this and was blocked by his party's machine. While Trump with his millions can leap over the established parties, Sanders's movement in the Democratic Party needs to build resilient support. Without the state legislatures and Congress behind him or her, a popular reforming Democratic presidential candidate will not be able to deliver.

In England (but not Scotland) no opposition to Brexit has escaped the margins, so far, despite promising attempts. The reason is clear: any pro-European movement will have to do what Cameron and Mandelson's Remain campaign could not, and express a positive identification with the EU while also defying its neoliberal embrace. England needs to face up to its own national question, work with Scots who want an independent relationship with the EU and link up with Europeans opposed to the EU's own lack of democracy. You merely have to set down what must be done to sense how long the journey will be.

Trump's triumph and Brexit's victory were close-run and not inevitable. But nor were they accidents. They were the chosen outcomes of millions of voters responding to three sets of circumstances. First, there was a shared rejection of the globalist forces of neoliberalism: its economic inequity and insecurity, its manipulative, corporate populism, its political hypocrisy as the financial crash revealed it as a rigged not a 'natural' market system – as it failed to deliver growth. The rejection was narrow, as many benefited from the positives of the international achievements that accompanied the neoliberal decades. But the less educated, with less to lose, voted it down, for good reasons. Second, there were different but parallel national stories. Both the main Anglo-Saxon countries suffered from a historic loss of 'greatness' and a more recent, ongoing failure to rectify it in the wars of the Middle East they started in Iraq. Their ruling cross-party order of the CBCs, Democrat and Republican, Conservative and Labour, was jointly responsible for the financial ineptitude, the cynical depoliticisation, and then the reckless military frustration. They provoked their own overthrow.

Why, then, was it not overwhelming? Because, thirdly, the solutions on offer were led by demagogues and braggarts as much an expression of the worst aspects of neoliberal manipulation as a replacement of it. As yet there is no substitute for an unacceptably unequal global system with its national governments serving an undemocratic international order. But there is a desire for change that exploded in the form of Trump and Brexit: a desire to become more fully human agents implicit in the repudiation of neoliberal callousness. This too was a cause of 2016. A ballot-box repudiation of both patronising welfare controls and a rigged economy. Brexit and Trump were the outcome of *votes*. They are the result of judgements made: to take a risk, to roll the dice, to test what might come next, to refuse to carry on as before. This impulse was imprisoned by right-wing, demagogic politicians and media but remains the greatest, if long-run threat to their supremacy. It is called democracy.

# PART V
# CONCLUSION

Rock the win i the clear day's dawin
(A rough wind blows, a clear day dawns)
Hamish Henderson,
*Freedom Come A'Ye*, 1960

# 33

# Peace or War

Donald Trump has a habit of praising himself. A lot. In his first speech as president, he told the Central Intelligence Agency: 'Trust me, I'm like a smart persona.'[1] When he invited the police chiefs of the major cities to the White House, he shared with them his objection to the judges who had suspended his executive order banning Muslims from seven countries, saying: 'I understand things. I comprehend very well, okay? Better than I think almost anybody.'[2] When he and Prime Minister Theresa May held their joint press conference in Washington on 27 May 2017, Trump was asked about Brexit. He began with more ritual self-praise, saying: 'I happened to be in Scotland at Turnberry cutting a ribbon when Brexit happened and we had a vast amount of press there. And I said Brexit – this was the day before, you probably remember, I said Brexit is going to happen and I was scorned in the press for making that prediction. I was scorned.'

As a point of mere fact, Trump arrived in Scotland the day *after* the Brexit vote.[3] The British media did not remember this. The president was not publicly embarrassed in their reporting. However, he rubbed in his prescience: 'I said I believe it's going to happen because people want to know who is coming into their country and they want to control their own trade and various other things, and lo and behold, the following day it happened.' Lo and behold, it had already happened. He continued: 'the odds weren't looking good for me when I made that statement because, as you know, everybody thought it was not going to happen.'

Perhaps he was forgiven this rewriting of his own history, a constant for narcissists, because he had the nerve to set out for Scotland before the result of the referendum, and later, on 18 August, he tweeted: 'They will soon be calling me MR. BREXIT', as he forecast his success in the USA.[4] His Brexiphilia was on full display for the British prime minister: 'Brexit's going to be a wonderful thing for your country ... it will end up being a fantastic thing for the United Kingdom. I think in the end, it will be a tremendous asset, not a tremendous liability. OK?'

Trump and Brexit are twin discharges of the related right-wing upsurges of 2016. But Trump is a Brexiteer of the Nigel Farage UKIP variety and Theresa May is not. An initial remainer, she has embraced a Conservative Party vision of Brexit, whose master theoretician, the Conservative MEP Daniel Hannan, thought (how wrong can you be?) that Trump was the Jeremy Corbyn of US politics.[5] Trump is a Brexiteer, not all Brexiteers are Trumpeteers. The American may have predicted and he certainly welcomed Brexit. A similar constellation of forces brought him and it success. Will the similarity continue into his presidency and the UK government's exit from the EU?

Both Brexit and Trump seek to restore greatness to their respective countries. However, the USA is still the greatest world power. The purpose of Trump's administration is to put America first, reverse its relative economic slowdown and embrace 'Americanism not globalism', which Trump proclaimed to be 'my credo'.[6] The UK was a great power, it is no longer. Unhappy with a European alliance that made this evident, the conservative wing of its political class is seeking a self-governed role in the world within an open, expanding international system for trade and services. To use Trump's language, 'Globalism not Europeanism' is their credo as they pursue latter-day Great-Britishism. Before her meeting with the president, the prime minister told the Republicans gathered in Philadelphia that Brexit means the UK will 'become even more global and internationalist in action and in spirit' – a philosophy that is anathema to the Trumpeteers.

This difference alarms the British. Unable to hide it, they want instead to overcome it, mounting a great effort to ensure immediate access to the president and his team in order to separate Trump from the influence of Farage. May sent her joint chiefs-of-staff to meet confidentially with the president-elect's team in New York before he took office. They were followed by Boris Johnson. They secured an early official summit. The prime minister had three objectives. The first and most obvious, to get a commitment to a trade agreement as soon as the UK left the EU, to assuage business fears in Britain and strengthen London's hand in the negotiations with Brussels. The other two aims were just as urgent. The British need a united and friendly EU for Brexit to work. May's government cannot afford to initiate the fragmentation of Europe or its economic disintegration. Trump and some of his advisers see its destruction as advantageous. Just as alarming a prospect is the possibility of a breakdown of the Atlantic security alliance, where the UK prides itself on its pivotal role. Trump's sensible regard for an alliance with Russia against fundamentalism in the Middle East, and his virulent hostility to Germany for its economic surplus and peaceful inclinations, not to speak of his attraction to Putin, led him to denounce NATO as obsolete. If it is, then so is the British state. The UK's role as the fulcrum between the USA and Europe depends on the NATO alliance. Its unravelling would spell disaster, not least for British self-esteem.

It became an immediate priority for the May government to ensure that Trump renewed America's commitment to the treaty. She aims to make the combination of her Brexit and his election a way of renewing the continuation of the security alliance. To achieve this, the prime minister could hardly have gone more wildly over the top:

> As we rediscover our confidence together – as you renew your nation just as we renew ours – we have the opportunity – indeed the responsibility – to renew the special relationship for this new age. We have the opportunity to lead, together, again. Because the world is passing through a period of change ... we can take the opportunity once more to lead. And to lead together.[7]

May preceded this appeal, resonant of Blair's hallucinations, with the essential reference to Churchill. It was a blatant pitch to recreate the wartime and post-war Anglo-American alliance, so that the vows between Washington and London would be born again. Without this regressive perspective, the British government feared it could find itself in conflict with both its American cousins and its European neighbours – the greatest diplomatic catastrophe imaginable.

In their joint press conference the prime minister went out of her way in her opening statement to say how relieved she was that all would be fine. She was glad to inform the world that they both backed NATO, and added: 'Mr President, I think you said, you confirmed that you're one hundred per cent behind NATO.' Trump revels in saying that he is 100 per cent this or that. He said nothing. Everyone in the room knew that he had described the alliance as 'obsolete'. Her words, 'I think you said, you confirmed ...' betray a pertinent ongoing nervousness.

I'm writing in the early period of the Trump presidency. The spectacular bluster and branding could prove to be no more than that, except for the efforts to gerrymander the voting system to keep the right in power. It could be that the blatant leveraging of the presidency to advertise Trump's resorts and promote his family turns out to be a decoy, permitting Gary Cohn, a Democrat who was for ten years director and CEO of Goldman Sachs, to blast forth a fountain of growth behind the smokescreen of Trump's tweets. That is as may be. I am just going to look at contrasting inner logics of the politics of Trump and Brexit, to ask whether they might clash fundamentally. While of little concern to Trump, this could be disastrous for the British Brexit. To investigate the possibility we need to look at the relationship between the inner, domestic drives of the two governments and how these shape their external ambitions, starting with the UK.

Success for Theresa May means completing the negotiation to leave the EU in the two years allotted by Article 50, ensuring that there is an acceptable transition, not a cliff edge, and then winning the 2022 general election, as a grateful country embraces what she describes as its 'self-determination'. To achieve this, as it heads into the Brexit rapids, May set out a well-strategised pitch: a *Daily Mail* vision of a hard-working, increasingly skilled, well-remunerated workforce, with communities secure, security threats diminished, enterprises growing, exports rising, and the country's freedom and independence rewarded by national pride and international respect.

I have shown how difficult this will be to achieve, given that May inherits a constitutional settlement now on its last legs, kept upright thanks to the hip replacements of the deep state. In terms of its all-important constitutional patriotism, May's Brexit is a regressive conservatism. She is hostile to the legal standing of human rights and has called for the UK to leave the International Convention on Human Rights. Already, she is rolling back freedom of information, threatening to jail reporters who receive leaked information. The entire raft of New Labour's constitutional changes that unwound the old regime is not to her liking, and she would wind them back as far as she can. Given that she is seeking to restore the authority of an unwritten constitution, her role is necessarily personalised. It is as if she is what the Queen would be like, were she to become prime minister. Stiff, practical, no-nonsense, leaving her courtiers to do the hard work, staying on top of the memos, keen on details and showing a flash of her sex in her choice of shoes. But above all, keeping the old show on the road and strengthening the existing British institutions.

Rallying the whole of the UK to such a bleak prospectus will be challenging enough, especially because May needs compliance and submission, while the shock of Brexit has galvanised everyone into realising that change is possible. Two significant obstacles stand out.

She needs the support of the City of London and its financial networks, although she has gone out of her way to scorn its globalism and speculative values, and is insisting on greatly reducing the number of immigrants. Her stated aim is an industrial renaissance of Britain as a modern manufacturing society. But financial and other services are now an exceptionally large part of the UK's economy. Without their highly educated and skilled workforce, the economy would tank completely. Since her Falklands victory in 1982, Britain has always had a deficit in manufactured goods. It has become a buyer, not a maker. Currently the UK runs a chronic balance of payments deficit of around 5 per cent of its gross domestic product.[8] One result is a highly vulnerable economy, despite the Thatcherite success of creating a huge centre for financial services.

In addition, May needs a world that is at peace for Britain to trade at its best. As if securing a conservative unity at home, and the support of a financial and service sector reliant on people flow, were not enough, international conditions need to be benign. Once, war was excellent for business, consuming vast quantities of material over long periods of time. But this is the age of drones. Embargoes, stand-offs and catastrophic destruction draw on specialist industries employing few. Brexit needs peace and plenty to encourage global free trade.

The first signs of Trumpism suggest that a very different scenario is unfolding in America. Like the UK, the United States has a chronic deficit, but one of only 2–3% of GDP. It has huge internal resources, a massive need for infrastructure investment, and is far more self-sufficient. It could well grow while buying less from abroad, while putting a brake on immigration and deporting millions of technically illegal immigrants, as it seeks to increase its relative advantage over its competitors. This would indeed assault the multinational, multiracial nature of America – everything Obama represented.

Far from being a constitutional conservative like Theresa May in Britain, Trump belongs to a tradition that was confined and kept at a distance by the founders of the republic and has chafed ever since. The United States was unique in having a radical, constitutional separation of powers, drawn up specifically to prevent dictatorship once independence from colonial subordination was achieved. For the ex-colonies needed a standing army, not just to defend themselves but to deploy as the United States expanded across the American plains, genociding the Indians, defeating Mexico, denoting South America as its sphere of influence in 1823. They needed a conquering force to expand outwards, while ensuring its generals were under civilian command and could not subjugate them domestically. Ever since, the USA has reproduced its two-sided character: pledging allegiance to a constitution, being exceptionally procedural and legalistic, defending liberty of speech, separation of powers and states' rights, and at the same time being lawless and aggressive externally and towards slaves and their descendants. The Civil War turned lawlessness inwards, especially with Sherman's march to the sea after his destruction of Atlanta, with his orders to 'enforce a devastation more or less relentless'. Yet this was the action of a soldier under orders from Lincoln, in a war that established the Constitution's supremacy.

Remarkably, when the US achieved world domination in 1945 thanks to its staggering productive capacities, it preserved its old-fashioned democratic constitution. After concentrating its genocidal capacity into Little Boy and Fat Man and dropping them on Hiroshima and Nagasaki, Washington supported the legal re-creation of Europe, put the Nazis on trial for war crimes and laid the basis for a rule-based world order alongside its lawless reach. This was challenged domestically by McCarthyism during the Cold War, but when he attacked the army as well as the state department McCarthy was brought down. Then came the Vietnam War to stop the spread of communism. It was popular when it first escalated, quite unlike Iraq. Only as the casualties grew, the barbarity became clear, and the draft penetrated working-class communities did the opposition escalate into the tumult of the late 1960s. In response, Nixon and Kissinger attempted a deliberate creation of an imperial presidency to win in Vietnam, but the constitutional checks proved too strong. It was a crucial test.

The attacks of 9/11, coming literally out of the blue, provided the old and still unrequited Vietnam-hand, Vice President Cheney the opportunity to avenge defeat in Southeast Asia. While the military under the command of George W. Bush swept aside the Iraqi army as if they were the Iroquois, he preserved the processes inherited from his father. The elder President Bush, having headed the CIA, was a creature of the American state and its procedures. He may have overseen post-truth, but George W. Bush was far from post-Washington. He, like his successor Obama, was tidy and constitutional at home, even while struggling with the ongoing defeat of Cheney's self-inflicted murderous folly. It was only the arrival of the financial crash that finally broke their weakened hegemony.

At which point the monster began to emerge from the depths of American power: the rule-free zone of genocide, racism, conquest and supremacism that always lurked below the libraries and their fine law books.

Trump and his band of extremists are the spawn of McCarthy and Nixon. They have shocked the world because they are so American. Their ease with the dark side of the American spirit makes them appear somehow legitimate, even when they are shredding the principles of American legitimacy. Unlike McCarthy, Trump's denunciations of Washington and its bureaucracies as the home of traitors to the American dream has led him to the White House. Unlike Nixon, he has not inherited a war that needs a mixture of negotiations and bombing. Hopes that Trump would therefore default to the mores of the established separation of powers were confounded. Without drawing breath, he has abused the judiciary directly and called their procedures political, which is quite different from disagreeing with their judgements. He has denounced the press as 'the opposition', an extraordinary contempt for a pillar of American freedom. The trope of 'Fake News' prepares the way for his crushing the media if he is given the time. He has rallied the police and promised to arm them even more. He has turned the White House into an extension of his property developments. A polarisation of the USA that reveals its truely beastly side is under way. Trump is the American Mr Hyde whose vicious persona is bursting out of its Dr Jekyll.

There is a rational kernel to Trump's foul behaviour: to replace globalism with Americanism economically. He has turned to Goldman Sachs and Wall Street to ensure delivery, having excoriated their influence over Hillary Clinton in the campaign. To ram through the transformation that he needs, Trump is likely to ramp up his assault on his country's constitutional framework. In contrast to Theresa May's Brexit conservatism, he is embarking on a radical, not a conservative, shift of the way his country is governed. Far from seeking a historic restoration, he has thrown down the gauntlet and challenges the long tradition of constitutional patriotism, with its norms and procedures, insisting upon executive supremacy. In place of what he calls 'politics', he will run America like a business, as he promised, the ultimate corporate populist.

Both Trump and May are seeking executive centralisation to drive through their dangerous and domestically transformative programmes. For May, this means pushing back the reforms of the past twenty years, with their human rights, freedom of information and national parliaments, to restore the full powers of Britain's elective dictatorship. For Trump, it means dismantling the core features of a US constitution designed to prevent elective dictatorship and letting his supporters rip.

Whereas Theresa May needs a conservative unity, Trump needs populist disunity, to release the forces of the state that can crush his opposition – institutional, legal and regulatory. A neat way to achieve this is through international conflict, as his close adviser Bannon seems to have advocated. Given his team's administrative incompetence, his personal petulance and the degree of resistance he has already generated, a president who lost the popular vote by a record near-three million votes has still to establish his sway. The Trump team may calculate that a successful foreign adventure would be ideal, to provide the rallying cry for the domestic regimentation and adulation that Trump himself and his followers crave. Both McCarthy and Nixon tried to bring their wars home: the Cold War and the Vietnam War respectively. Trump, having arrived in the White House complaining of his country's lack of victories, can be expected to seek one. To sustain his bellicose contempt for the media-judiciary-university-immigrant-loving-and-immigrants-in-fact-pink-hatted-women-democrats who outnumber his supporters, he is going to need a means of imposing his will. As he escalates against those who he claims are dangerous to America, and rolls out the military-style expulsions of 'drug-dealing, illegal criminals' already in America, a foreign conflict will help him overcome popular resistance. His first target of choice is likely to be North

Korea; his second, Iran as it links to his domestic mobilisation against immigrants and terrorism. He may strike the monstrous Asian dictatorship's nuclear facilities to trademark a willingness to use force and send a warning to China. But he has already Twitter-denounced Iran as '#1 in terror'.

Trump and his advisers may desire shock and foreign confrontations to assist their protectionist aims. These are the last thing Brexit Britain needs. On the Iran nuclear deal, they have diametrically opposed views; May has praised it in firm terms. Britain needs trade with Iran and a growing, peaceful Persian Gulf with its plentiful investments (Boris Johnson flattered its sultans of the seven United Arab Emirates by telling them that London is the 'eighth Emirate'). Washington's bellicosity and hostility to globalism could be particularly serious for Brexit even without open war. To gain a reasonable deal from the EU, the UK must befriend, not provoke, Europe's leaders and parliament. It does not want a euro collapse that will make any strategising about Brexit irrelevant. In 2019, when Brexit is scheduled to finally happen, positive relations are essential, hopefully with a growing EU able to make generous terms. Ironically, Brexit means that for the first time since 1945, the fate of Europe is more important to the UK than the relationship with the United States. Trump's strategy, however, is to cut Germany's surplus down to size. He would be delighted to see the break-up of the Eurozone and EU itself, which he regards as a 'consortium' designed against American economic interests.

Dani Rodrik's trilemma is a way to measure the divergence of Brexit and Trump. If you take the three elements of national independence, democracy and integration with globalisation, any country can increase two of these but not all three. Thus, the main EU countries are attempting deep international integration and can grow European democracy but their nation states will lose out. Both Trump and Brexit are projects to increase national independence. May wants Britain to be more globalised. Therefore she will have to subordinate British democracy to achieve this. Trump desires the US to be less globalised. By withdrawing from international integration, he will be able to build up his populist democracy. The two are likely to clash over globalisation, where their direction of travel is in conflict.

Britain is a vulnerable country made weaker by Brexit. America is the pre-eminent power with intact institutions that may not tolerate their bumptious would-be dictator. Trump needs to rally his forces within the USA and ponders the provocations that could stimulate and legitimise his supremacy with democratic support. The question is war or peace. The likely answer will be one that encourages the disruption of his economic enemies, China and Germany in the European Union. The fate of England's gamble rests on the outcome.

# 34
# Citizens, Reimagine

What steps can be taken to learn the lessons of Brexit and Trump? This is a different question from seeking to limit the damage that the Trump administration appears to be set upon, or a disastrous form of Brexit.

Trump is capable of winning a war against North Korea and triggering a short-term boom that will see him, or a chosen successor, elected in 2020. His administration might also implode. Brexit could all go horribly wrong. But if the euro collapses, it might seem a brilliant pre-emptive escape from the continent. The City of London could reward the May government accordingly and she could storm home to an impressive majority in a 2022 election. My question assumes that both Washington and London will witness twin triumphs of Trump and Brexit. This will make 2016 an even more remarkable year than it seems at present, when many still hope that both will nosedive.

The greatest danger at this point is to cling to the belief that there should be a return to the status quo. We know where the set-up prior to Trump and Brexit leads – it leads to Trump and Brexit. It will do so again in a new and probably worse form. Meanwhile, as I have tried to spell out, Theresa May's rigorous definition of Brexit is designed to return Britain to its traditional, centralised and authoritarian past. She is not intent on encouraging the spirit of self-government and anti-elitism expressed in the referendum. In his trademark fashion, Trump will betray the hopes of many who backed him. He is a demagogue manipulating his capacity to voice the frustrations of his supporters to secure a system that will screw them even further. His final dramatic TV advert singled out Goldman Sachs as a sinister influence behind the Clinton aim to restore the rule of Wall Street. With five appointments from the firm, Trump has now handed the economy over to them more completely than any traditional politician could dare. The certain failure of Brexit and Trump as democratic movements should not fill anyone's hearts with joy. Even the hedge funds will find themselves crushed as the doors close.

But the system *was* rigged. It continues to be so under its new masters. Those of us who opposed Brexit and Trump must work with the forces that exploded with rage in 2016 to this extent: we must accept the historic rebuke they delivered to the structures that excluded them. How can such an argument be joined? In a spirit of tenderness. There is a tremendous amount of hurt and the more this is deepened the better it is for demagogues and the tabloid press and TV. The ogre himself is a master at tweeting his opponents into a fury, as he lives off polarisation.

To break the stratagems of a diversionary polarisation, we need to address the way that democracy is carried out. Both Trump and May are likely to exploit their advantage to intensify their countries' unfair electoral systems. It is important for those who oppose them to reach across to their supporters who felt empowered by the events of 2016. One modest reform could start this off, on both sides of the Atlantic. The change would be simple enough: a three-headed alteration to the way we vote. 1) Voting should be compulsory. 2) All ballot papers to include 'none of the above'. 3) If 30 per cent of voters chose 'none of the above', all candidates must step down for a new election to take place.

One of the disastrous effects of neoliberalism was to drive people away from voting, as political choice was eviscerated thanks to money corrupting the system. It generated a culture where people said voting won't change anything. Their abstention served only to reinforce a depoliticisation that safeguarded neoliberalism. Its form of globalisation was blown out of the water by non-voters returning to the ballot box in 2016, drawn by the smell of cordite – the real change offered by Trump and Brexit, at least in terms of defying the status quo and rolling the dice. Right now, the triumph of Trump and

Brexit has shown that voting can change things. We need to ensure there is no reversion to low-turnout voting. Just as we now seek to hold politicians to account, so citizens need to be held to account: they must vote. Compulsory voting exists in Australia, Belgium and Brazil. There is no technical difficulty to prevent its introduction.

What consequences follow? First, the justified complaint that many do not count will start to be addressed. Politicians will have to attend to the needs of everybody, as everybody will be voting. Second, many of the various efforts and techniques of physical disenfranchisement deployed in the UK as well as the US will be frustrated. It will no longer be up to voters to make sure that they are registered; it will become the duty of local government to ensure that all citizens can cast their choice.

Third, the need to register 'none of the above' makes it possible to overcome Anglo-Saxon resistance to compulsion. Voters will not be required to choose between the candidates on offer; they have the freedom to reject them all and the right to have their overall rejection of the choice they have been offered counted. This is an essential condition to resist populist fake outrage at bureaucrats forcing people to act against their will.

Finally, taken together candidates must win the support of a sufficient number of voters for the outcome to be declared valid. It should not be possible for a small minority who are alienated and disaffected to force the entire population to go through the whole exercise again. But the number of 'none of the above' must be set low enough for a re-run to be an achievable threat. After watching two of the Clinton–Trump debates on television in California, I sympathised with the many Americans who felt ashamed that this was the choice they had to make. It made me ask, is there a way that voters could prevent a recurrence of 2016. It seemed to me that 30 per cent would have said, 'Sorry, this is not an acceptable choice'. Had they been able to do so under this proposal both Clinton and Trump would have had to withdraw and a new choice put to the American voter.

Such a reform would have an immediate impact on the role of money in both America and the UK. By saying the candidates together have to be able to get 70 per cent of voters to choose them, the party machines will need to ensure they are credible and attractive: the interests of voters as a whole will be built into elections. The parties will have to look to what kind of choice the whole electorate wants, not just their funders.

In the face of a profoundly undemocratic globalised order, millions voted for Brexit and Trump out of the sheer thrill of agency in order to make a difference. A widespread response among many who are appalled at the outcomes and have suffered their first profound political defeat, is a revulsion from democracy, as if enlightened elitism stood any chance whatsoever of 'taking back control'. Demagogy, hostility to internationalism, nativism, scorn for culture and all round reaction are winners of 2016. They threaten what democracy we already have. In the face of this, only two responses are possible. You can either push back against the democratic spirit of Brexit and Trump and demand better elite rule, less exposed to populist mobilisation. Or you can call for more and much better democracy: thoughtful, honest, safeguarded as much as possible from manipulation, including referendums that are rule-based and not arbitrary. Many of those who supported Brexit and Trump are fully aware of the dangers to democracy entailed, only they gave greater weight to the threat from the EU's oligarchy or Clinton's culture of entitlement. There has to be an alliance for planetary humanism that crosses the voting divide of 2016. It must be grounded on good republican principles of self-government, liberty and accountability that celebrate people's desire to vote with effect.

Even to advocate voting reform on these lines could have a positive impact on the political systems in the US and UK. In the former it demands a constitutional amendment; in my own country a constitutional convention process. A constitutional amendment; in the US requires winning two-thirds of the state legislatures, a considerable obstacle. But any movement against Trump needs to confront the control that Republicans exercise outside Washington, for unless this is undone autocratic presidents will become the norm not an anomaly. Republican funders have spent well to secure local state power, while Democratic Party funders, being more fashion-conscious and enchanted with the glamour of the presidency, do not invest in mere local politics – where the national outcome is decided over the long run. This effort is left to grassroots Democrats. But they too need a national story to inspire them through the long days of dealing with city and state politics. Perhaps the need to capture the legislatures one by one to ensure they can reshape the constitution can provide a way of networking their local efforts with a 'grand narrative'.

For the UK, I have set out the argument as to why England-Britain needs to abandon the political shell of Britain. The country supposedly proclaiming its independence from the EU – the 'precious union' and 'united, Global Britain' of Theresa May and the *Daily Mail* – will colonialise England and London. England can free itself to become a European country and Britishness can belong to all those who have benefited culturally and socially from its history. The moment you try to imagine this, however, you realise that one thing stands in the way of England joining the world to become contemporary: the buildings of the Palace of Westminster. For, as Scotland, Northern Ireland and, hopefully, Wales find their own place in the international order, the House of Commons will become the parliament of England. In its present establishment it will be unable to abandon the imaginative grip of past greatness. Built as the Victorian epoch neared its apogee, the building's architecture, its decor, its paintings, its procedures, reproduce imperial Britishness. Round the corner, the Treasury was modernised. A new entry was opened at the back so that the heavy influence of its looming spaces was reduced. The same thing cannot be achieved with the Houses of Parliament. The enervating weight of the Palace of Westminster forecloses the chances of open reform; its architecture speaks of subjecthood and ruling natives, its routines are carved into its parody of the Gothic. Proudly of its time, it can be no other.

Could there be an alternative? The warren of decrepit ancient tunnels below it need repairs, at humongous cost. Seal the cellars and turn Pugin's parliament-palace into a museum of democracy. Just up the road stands one of the least interesting and dullest architectural monuments of the eighteenth or any other century, Buckingham Palace. It is far too large for a modern monarchy, which anyway has Windsor Castle on the edge of London and controls fine dwellings in nearby St James. Dismantle Buckingham Palace, railings, throne room and all, keeping only the royal collection of drawings; perhaps sell it to a buyer who would like to reassemble it as a spectacular attraction. Then pull down the walls around its huge gardens. Join these to St James's Park and Green Park to create a stunning green public space, with, at its centre, a new parliament building for England.

OK. There is not a political force in sight that could offer this prospect to the public. The same goes for my suggested reform of the voting system. I propose neither as 'demands' or even suggestions, but simply to assist a necessary process. Speaking in Berlin, where she was being honoured with the 2016 World Literature prize, just after the election of President Trump, Zadie Smith said: 'progress is never permanent, will always be threatened, must be redoubled, restated, and *reimagined* if it is to survive. I don't claim that it's easy. I do not have the answers.'[1] Amen to that. Unlike her, I have lived a political life, although not one attached to any party. Like her, I do not have answers. Only some suggestions. If I have been firm about saying the British state needs to bow out, it is not because this is 'an answer', but because we English need to cast aside the now mangy British comfort blanket, so that we can become ourselves. What answers will then be forthcoming, I await with interest.

Smith is right about the need to *reimagine* progress (her emphasis). It is pointless to seek a return to what may have seemed like progress before 2016. The post-war 'American Dream' that celebrated itself with Presidents Kennedy and Reagan, and that Obama attempted to revive, has been irreparably torn by Trump. Vietnam also tore it, but the US redeemed itself by impeaching Nixon. We are still living with Bush's Iraq catastrophe, but Obama denounced it as a 'dumb war' before it was even launched, and sought to manage the retreat. Now Trump has exposed the inner forces of bigotry, demagogy and resentment that generated those external monstrosities. He is a response to failure. Not just on the battlefields of the Middle East, but of the world project to dominate the globe militarily and politically as the new century began, spelt out in the private exchanges between Bush and Blair. The daring and scale of transporting a modern army halfway around the world to impose its will was a project to make America greater still. Its failure is now disabling the pale colossus. Trump cannot make America great again in the way that it once was. Nothing can do that. China is becoming its economic equal, the European Union seeks to be so too. In these truly dangerous circumstances, the promise of globalisation, that it could save us from world wars, must not be lost – even while its neoliberal dismantling of democracy must be reversed.

How we go about the latter needs imagination. This is the point. The astonishing Brazilian political philosopher Roberto Unger has complained that while business and commerce and the media innovate restlessly, our political forms of representation and decision-making are regarded as taboo and stuck in inappropriate routines. We need experimentation, political daring, new forms of representation – such as the ability of voters to declare the choice of candidates they are offered invalid. This is especially important with respect to the use of data and metadata and the transformative rise of global internet platforms. Change is needed most of all in the ways we conduct politics. My suggestions have only one purpose here, to help stimulate *reimagination*.

This puts me head to head with the least imaginative prime minister I can remember, since the fourteenth Earl of Hume was dragged from the Lords for a brief period in 10 Downing Street in the early 1960s. (Perhaps I am being unfair to him, as I can only recall his tenure dimly as an object of satire.) When she opened her set-piece speech to her first Conservative Party conference as its leader, Theresa May said: 'people want me to answer. What's my vision for Britain? My philosophy? My approach? Today I want to answer that question very directly. I want to set out my vision for Britain after Brexit. I want to lay out my approach – the things I believe.' One of the things she valued, she declared, is 'the spirit of citizenship'. (In

Britain we can only enjoy the spirit, without a written constitution.) May rightly goes on to say this means: 'you respect the bonds and obligations that make our society work. That means a commitment to the men and women who live around you.' Then she adds: 'Today, too many people in positions of power behave as though they have more in common with international elites than with the people down the road.' This brought her to her punchline: 'If you believe you're a citizen of the world, you're a citizen of nowhere. You don't understand what the very word "citizenship" means.' Just in case you thought you could get away with this, Mrs Brexit continued: 'I'm putting you on warning. This can't go on anymore.'[2]

In 1969, for the first time, a human being watched the Earth rise as a shining blue-and-white orb over the horizon of the moon. The moment the image was shared, we saw our home as a vulnerable planet. We all knew then that we are citizens of the world. Citizens, meaning not just the inhabitants of this planet at this time, but people with a direct responsibility for its fate and well-being.

It took forty years for scientists to formally recognise and give a name to our ongoing responsibility. In August 2016, between the Brexit vote and the PM's speech to her party conference, the official International Geological Congress recommended that the 'Anthropocene' be recognised as a new geological epoch. Beginning about 1950, it succeeds the Holocene, the approximately twelve thousand years of stable climate since the last ice age. The acceleration of the impact of human ingenuity and emissions has transformed the planet itself; we live in the age of the human planet.

The result is that the world and all who are in it are our responsibility, 'ours' meaning all of us who are humans – especially our leaders. It is our *duty* to be citizens of the world.

I am entirely with Theresa May in her condemnation of those who feel they are *only* citizens of the world, with no sense of any responsibility to country of residence, or residences. Theirs is a planetary inhumanity – a refusal of the granularity of life and responsibility to others – and there is indeed an international elite for whom concern about their environment means complaining about the quality of air conditioning in first-class cabins. If she had them in her sights, that would be fine with me. But there is an ideological sleight of hand involved in her singling out these overpaid villains. Her main aim is to confine the rest of us to only a single somewhere. And anyone who is British, whatever the nationality, to being *only* British, a citizen of one country with one loyalty.

We all have multiple loyalties, and it is far from being traitorous to say so: to our nation, our state, our religion, our continent if we are Europeans, to the world and possibly to other countries too. Many of these have institutions that make claims. Increasingly, as individualism is being fuelled by the market, we ourselves have new kinds of claims as citizens. It is profoundly wrong to suggest that citizenship is a matter just of loyalty and then *only* to one's country. Nor is its pluralism a matter of overlapping layers either, like Stephen Dedalus writing out his full address until he gets to the universe, in *Portrait of the Artist as a Young Man*. Citizenship is dangerous because it is a claim and a becoming – something that is growing, a relationship that is reciprocal and on the move, not a given. Especially important is the nature of its reciprocity: most famously that my liberty as a citizen entails my defending the liberty of others – and in the days of the internet of all around the world.

This is not an argument about the nature of identity. There is a politics to May's approach, similar to the politics of Trump. She told the Scots, and not just the Scots, that she has 'one over-arching goal', the building of a single, 'more united nation'. Indeed, as we have seen, she insists that we in the UK are 'one people' and that this unity overrides even the constitution. Her message to all four nations of the UK: 'when we work together and set our sights on a task, we really are an unstoppable force'. Her words echo Donald Trump in his inauguration address: 'When America is united, America is totally unstoppable.' Both use the language of internal closure and regimentation. Trump: 'a new vision will govern our land ... total allegiance to the United States of America'. May: 'we will put the preservation of our precious Union at the heart of everything we do'. From their imagined fortresses, Trump and May both aim to rejuvenate their domestic greatness. In Trump's case to keep on 'winning' militarily as well. Both are captives of outdated nationalisms, defined by the singular, lured by dreams of yesterday. It may take years, but neither will succeed. The question is how they are going to fail.

# 35
# Conclusion

Three empires, as much of the mind as reality – mixtures of hope, intent, nostalgia, greed and self-importance – were exploded by the revolutions celebrated on the gilded staircase of London's Ritz Hotel and the golden elevator of New York's Trump Towers. The American vision of irresistible globalisation decorated by multicultural enlightenment; a European project of Brussels becoming the equal of Washington and Beijing; and Cameron's British fantasy of leveraging inflated real-estate values, US finance and London's network of tax havens into world influence: all were cast aside by contemptuous voters. The trouble is that what has replaced them will prove worse.

Only perhaps in the European Union is there an immediate chance of a better outcome. For the most obvious victim of Brexit and Trump was something that only existed as a potential: the forging of a single continental power of Europe that would become a world player equal to America, China and Russia. The development of the European Union was woven from several different dreams. One of them was to overcome the belligerent hostilities of its nation states, so that its peoples could live and trade in peace with one another. In this it triumphed, building institutions that embody the greatest political improvement of the latter half of the twentieth century in the developed world. Another was to protect and consolidate its internal economy to ensure cartel advantages. The third, to create a power that would project its interests across the globe. The success of the second was supposed to underpin the third – and in so doing inspire the peoples of its old nations to cast aside their mere local democracies for the greater identity of Europe.

If this was a plan, the moment that the deepening of the cartel was supposed to swivel into the start of global power was the creation of a single currency. Any such economic scheme must have the capacity to withstand, indeed to make good use of, crashes and busts. The enormous property bubbles in Ireland and Spain, the corrupt loans to Greece, the deflation of Italy, were all caused by the architecture of the euro and were therefore the shared responsibility of its builders. Instead of accepting this, Germany, with the strongest economy, blamed the victims. Perhaps German voters, having taken the hit of paying for the unification of their own East, felt they had made a sufficient contribution to the cause. If so, this shows that in the heartland countries of the EU, just as much as the more peripheral, national democracy remains a vital experience and will not be cast aside by the peoples. The euro became an instrument that exacerbated the inequality between its member states, which deepened fissures within them. Italy is the ongoing problem if the challenge of the French far-right is beaten back. The EU must now accept the ongoing reality of national democracy, not defy the European peoples.

Because the result at the moment is a fractured, troubled set of institutions, with flashy buildings, high salaries, a coldly undemocratic commitment to marketisation and endless words. In 2015, the EU issued a report on the prospectus for future union. It was published over the names of the President of the Commission, the President of the Council, the President of the Parliament, the President of the Eurogroup and the President of the Central Bank and is known as 'The Five Presidents Report'. In an omen of the failure of their union when they tried to get together for their official photo call on 15 June 2015, one of them could only be present by 'conference call'.[1] At the same time as this inflated ensemble failed even to meet in person, innocents drawn to their economy or fleeing war and famine, drowned off the coasts of Europe to its lasting shame. Two years later the Commission had to present another report, to a summit of the member states gathered to mark the 60th anniversary of the EU's founding. It did so not with five presidents but with five enfeebled 'scenarios'.[2] It was already under pressure from the rise of antagonistic parties, such as Le Pen in France and the Five Star movement in Italy, which threaten the euro most of all. Then, the British from outside the Eurozone although big contributors to the EU, broke the spell.

Brexit helped to shatter the dream of a Great EU that was never going to be realised. Today, for all of us who live in the United Kingdom, whether for or against Leave, the most important priority is to ensure Brexit does not damage what the EU has achieved. We must work with our fellow Europeans to help protect the Union's core achievement: the transcontinental solidarity of its peoples. This is not just a matter of trade and travel but also free movement within a space shared by responsible democracies in a common continent of intense nations, regions and cities. England too is a part of this and if a reformed EU survives, it will eventually return to Europe. For now, the more the Le Pens rise, the more the fight against them is ours too – because the fate of Europe is our fate.

The British called a halt to the fantastical hopes of a single European power, not out of wisdom but jealousy. Like a star turning into a supernova before it collapses, Brexit burned brightly, flashing out the last pulses of the one-time greatness of a world empire before finally folding in towards the decomposition of the British state. The aim of the UK's EU membership was always to preserve its separate, British global influence. The long-run incompatibility of the two multinational purposes of the UK and the EU – Great Britain fundamentally conservative while seeking to renew itself, Europe profoundly forward looking but moving with collective deliberation – ensured there was not a shared belief between the political elites on the two sides of the Channel/*la Manche*. This could have been overcome by a European patriotism had Thatcher supported the unification of Germany and claimed it as a UK success. Perhaps Blair had the best chance to build a European democracy in the UK with New Labour's unprecedented constitutional reforms. What could have been transformative become disintegrative. As we have seen, Blair preferred to 'Finally overcome the greatness of our history to discover the full potential of our future'. His 'complete vision', as he described it, 'bigger than Iraq, bigger than the American alliance',[3] separated Britain from Europe. While his combination of unprecedented executive power, Scottish and Welsh national parliaments, a supreme court, and incorporating human rights, left England voiceless but seething.

The result was Cameron, a shallow EU-loathing prime minister quite unsuited to the renegotiation he pledged before a referendum called for reasons of party not country. The Brits had the advantage of seeing that the EU should not *replace* the nation states whose modern, post-war revival had been assisted by the creation of the European Union. But Cameron was unable to propose a positive reason why his 'world-shaping' vision needed to share power with the continent. An even more philistine and ignorant section of the Tory Party encouraged those (mainly Conservative but also working-class Labour) who were fed up to the back teeth with Cameron and his kind, to seize on the opportunity of the referendum. They assured voters that the UK could swashbuckle and buccaneer its way into becoming a Global Britain that will anchor a world Anglosphere. They won the Leave vote, if for other reasons than their deceptive rhetoric, thanks to England-without-London. This will precipitate the end of the empire state. For they are attempting an impossible solution to what was for them an unendurable liaison.

The leadership of Brexit has been seized by Theresa May. Originally, she had backed Remain out of good economic sense, but also saying that Leave would threaten the Union of the United Kingdom of Great Britain and Northern Ireland. In her heart, like a good *Daily Mail* reader, she wanted Out. When that is what English voters decided, she put herself at the head of Brexit means Brexit – and made it her priority to save the Union. The manner of her insistence has already inflamed many in Scotland, as she demands the subordination of its 'devolved' government to her own. The result of her hard line on leaving the single market and preventing EU immigration means a painful Brexit. It will take the form that all change does in our era. There will be no cliff drop. Too much is at stake for the corporate economy to allow that. At first everything will seem much the same and the borders will hold. An enormous investment in time, energy, policies and media campaigns will be committed to shoring up the status quo. Gradually everything will change. A new generation in Scotland and Northern Ireland will tire of the bullying and split away. Investment will follow the money and shift to Europe. The best of British research will also home onto the EU to benefit from its arena of international collaboration. Brexiteers will say they did not mean to end shared scholarly and scientific investment. But Europe will say if you are not in you are out. The government, under pressure from within and without, will demand more control when the need is for less if Brexit is to mean popular self-government. Eventually Brexit will collapse. The sooner, the less excruciatingly drawn-out the pain will be. Then Britain's separate nations, England especially, can recover as themselves, to put their admirable qualities and pugnaciousness to good use in collaboration with their neighbours – for the road back to our European identity lies through England gaining its independence and therefore the confidence to share power without feeling shame.

Behind the downfall of Great Britain masquerading as would-be Global Britain, and an EU itching to become a 'Great EU', was the economic achievement and political hollowness of neoliberal globalisation. Alongside the glorious improvements of liberated human relationships, material well-being and the lifting of a majority of humankind from extreme poverty that was achieved across the thirty-year transformation from 1980 to 2010, a poisonous, inhuman ideology was promulgated. This put competition in the marketplace above government, in an extraordinary anti-democratic exercise that confined liberty to commerce, and turned freedom into competition. Above all it undermined government responsibility for the welfare of all, made possible by economic and productive advance, as it enthroned finance and its ethos of maximisation as the new overlord. Its embrace of marketisation outside the reach of politics undid the European Union. It permitted the elite to camouflage their pretentions behind claims that the market rules. A very convenient way of denying responsibility when things were good, their neoliberalism disabled them from having any way of rallying support when the downturn came. In Britain it was worse. In a cruel and unforgivable onslaught on the country's local governments, welfare and public health services, the UK's government unfurled the colours of high-neoliberal austerity to claim it was only carrying out what market reality demanded. By so doing it severed the loyalty of millions of UK citizens to their government and laid the basis for the poetic justice of Brexit as it decapitated the perpetrators.

It also helped inspire the victory of Trump. But his is not the sign of an empire imploding, but a contest of genuine world importance over how its form of superiority should change. What was experienced as a period of defeat domestically by white communities across the South and middle America may prove to be the time a new type of domination was developed. Trump's cry that the USA must start winning again looks back to an outdated suzerainty. Despite America's global share of world output steadily declining to less than a quarter, its grip on the global economy increased as Obama deliberately disentangled America's military overextension. The country's influence remains overwhelming. First, thanks especially to the reach of its corporations. Through them as well as directly via the stock exchanges of lesser nations, American citizens 'continue to own the dominant share of global wealth at 40% or more.'[4] Second, the pre-eminence of its electronic platforms is becoming more intrusive with the penetration of social media. Within less than a month of Trump settling into the White House to establish his new parochialism, Mark Zuckerberg published his five principles for building a global community that 'We at Facebook' will follow. Their aim to: 'develop the social infrastructure to give people the power to build a global community that works for all of us'.[5] With two billion users sharing their Facebook pages, his priorities seem more credible than the EU's five options for its five presidents.

Trump represents the acme of neoliberal obsession with winners and losers and hence enemies (and limited wars to keep the public bellicose). The race is on to make us selfish, angry, isolated, fearful and despairing before we discover the other route. There is however one positive that can be gained from the wreckage. It explains the paradox of Trump being everything that is worst about corporate manipulative populism and its obsession with competition. For if he is the ultimate product of neoliberalism, why is he so dangerous for it? The answer is in the naming of the brand. The skyscrapers of neoliberalism are anonymous commodities, bought and sold by funds to house the staff of other funds. Soaring achievements whose architecture functions by its sheer physical presence to intimidate by cruel indifference. Towering palaces of the rule of market forces, their awesome engineering proclaims: we are the inevitable. Then Trump puts his name at the top of his. Even as he builds them out of financial manipulation, he claims his constructions to be his own work. He takes responsibility for his success. He fuses celebrity, business and now political purpose. He strips the mystification from the anonymity of neoliberalism to show us that its edifices and policies are the work of man. The system is rigged, Trump tells us, and then he adds, he should know because he 'was' the system. Is, Mr Trump, is. But thank you for the warning, let's hope no one forgets.

Taken together Brexit and Trump should put relationships rather than policies to the forefront of our minds. What kind of relationship do the members of the EU want to have with each other? What relationship should the nations of Britain have with each other? What relationship do Americans wish to have with one another? And with the world? For the world has a stake in this and will help shape the answers. Embedded in this question is what relationship do we have to the economy? Does it set the rules or do humans set its rules? Consequences and outcomes can never be known in an era of rapid change, but how we seek to govern them and distribute the fruits of production not only can be, but are, the result of government as the financial crash proved. The rule of the market is the rule of the rich hiding behind forces they declare to be blind. Implicitly, Brexit and Trump challenged this. They recruited the dream of defying it to their causes, by calling for 'Take Back Control' and 'Make America Great Again'. By proclaiming he is their voice, Trump claimed to speak for the underdogs. As it highlighted £350 million a week for an NHS that everyone uses, the Leave campaign presented Brexit as enabling voters to take control of their priorities. Instead, Theresa May insists on an unforgiving presidential power, while Trump seeks to turn the presidency into a dictatorship. Both will turn the jailbreak that propelled them to power into a lockdown. The challenge for all of us is to build a democracy and an economy with a culture that is wiser, more thoughtful, open and honest, especially about who is doing what to whom as well as noisy and argumentative. In this way we can upturn the course Trump proclaims for America and May has decreed for Brexit UK.

## Post-conclusion

In the age of post-truth, my publishers have kindly agreed to a post-conclusion. When Donald Trump's election transformed the significance of Brexit I switched from a book on just the UK referendum to *The Lure of Greatness*. It was written between December 2016 and March 2017. After it went to page Theresa May called her snap general election in Britain. As I write this addition to the final proof, Marine Le Pen and Emmanuel Macron have qualified for the French presidency and Trump has concluded his first 100 days. But the British parties have yet to publish their manifestos, the far more important French presidency has yet to be decided and Trump is still preparing – or pretending he is preparing – for the war I suggest he needs to bolster his popularity.

Meanwhile the EU's twenty-seven countries are deciding how to ensure that Brexit does not threaten their union and to minimise the damage that the UK decision has inflicted on them. It was their initial response to Theresa May's letter triggering Article 50 that forced her to go back on her pledge not to call an election. Her strategy had been to achieve a clean Brexit and then win five years of power in 2020. But the EU made it clear this scenario is not possible: there will need to be a transitional period, the European Court will oversee this, dues will be paid through this period in addition to the bill to discharge the UK's obligations. Except for the final amount of the bill, these conditions were laid down as non-negotiable. Therefore, May faced the prospect of a 2020 election with the UK still under the sway of the EU. In such circumstances UKIP could make a comeback. Backed by hedge-fund ultras it could eat back into Conservative electoral support while extreme anti-Europeans in her own party could divide it with calls for a summary rupture from the EU.

To escape this fate she gambled on giving herself another two years to 2022 based on a large parliamentary majority. The risk seemed small. The temptation of a sweeping victory over Jeremy Corbyn and gaining her own mandate was considerable. The key prize: nearly 4 million UKIP voters likely to rally to her side. They alone should ensure a crushing victory delivered by first-past-the-post elections. An enlarged parliamentary majority will allow May to accept the EU's conditions and ensure her Brexit, while her manifesto will provide a chance to pitch her appeal to Labour's English and Welsh historic heartlands.

Assuming May succeeds in being re-elected according to her plan how do my arguments stand up to this immediate, unexpected test? I identified May's project as an attempt to impose an authoritarian unity on the UK and this has been confirmed. The *Daily Mail* captured the spirit of the age of May as it backed her election decision with the headline 'Crush the Saboteurs'. The 'saboteurs' were MPs doing their duty but of course they were also any of us thinking of challenging her supremacy. She justified her reluctant change of mind saying, 'The country is coming together but Westminster is not.' This is hardly convincing. A mere nine Lib Dem MPs could hardly 'grind the business of government to a standstill,' as she claimed. The whole point of a parliament is that it provides a cockpit for disagreement and argument. Just as she excluded the Cabinet from her drafting of the government's historic letter withdrawing from the EU, May now aims to subordinate parliament and the UK as a whole to her will.

At the start of a sudden election it is foolish to predict how things will turn out. Even with possible criminal charges hanging over the Conservative Party for its corrupt practices in the 2015 election, its victory seems certain given the apparent unelectability of the opposition. But it seems to me that May's aura as Brexit

Britain's saviour will be chipped despite her likely election gain – as voters start to judge her by the cut of her politics. In seeking to win power with a call for strength and toughness in the face of European opposition she is positioning herself as a recycled version of Margaret Thatcher, egged on by the tabloids. Yet, as I pointed out, she has few of her predecessor's qualities apart from stubbornness. Nor is it just ideas that she lacks. Thatcher battled enemies she sought to defeat. However defiantly May talks on Europe, the EU is not and cannot be an enemy: it is not the Argentinians or the miners or the establishment 'wets'; it is an essential ally and partner – nor did it initiate hostilities. Crushing a weak and divided Labour opposition is not brave; reaching agreement with the EU, as she surely must, is not audacious. Why is she calling for battle stations when Britain needs peace not war? If indeed she emerges as contrived and opportunistic, it may not take long for her popularity to deflate.

The most worrying aspect to the election is the way it has been accepted as legitimate. To this degree May has succeeded in normalising her domination. Brexit was a breakdown. She has used the election to turn it into normality.

The costs of Leaving the EU are cultural and political more than economic. The tragedy is that for it to succeed politically, France needs to go fascist or, apparently more likely, Italy needs to crash out of the euro. But any such disaster for the European 'project' will undermine it and with it the hope of an advantageous settlement in terms of trade and growth, which the UK as a vulnerable economy badly needs. In terms of British life and politics, as 'leaving' goes on and on, the underlying pathology of Brexit will become more intense: England's displaced frustration with the ill-fitting carapace of Britishness, seeking enemies it can 'slay'.

My argument that Corbyn's Labour disqualified itself from office because of its approach to Brexit also seems to be confirmed. Britain as a whole, although not Scotland, is deprived of an opposition. Hopefully, the termination of 'Labourism' – a fixation on one-party, Great British rule based on first-past-the-post elections and Westminster government – will be accelerated. But it has to be replaced, as it will never die of its own accord. Three days after May called the election I attended a crowded, pop-up 'progressive alliance' meeting in a Tory marginal where the Lib Dem came second in 2015. For the first time I heard experienced Labour activists saying they would vote Lib Dem. They did not want to agree a statement of 'progressive values' or a call for fair votes, they just wanted to prevent the prime minister from 'crushing democracy'. It was a healthy, vigorous response. But to win over the wider electorate a larger, strategic purpose will be needed.

One of the sources for any such renewal in the UK and across Europe will be the epochal transformation of American politics initiated by Trump's defeat of the Democrats after eight years of Obama. It is now clear that a hugely important argument has been joined between those who want the Democratic party to confront the issues the American demagogue tapped into, however abusively, on the way to the presidency, and members of the party machine looking forward to his failure, to confirm that they were right all along. This conflict will be fought out through the exercise of internet enhanced organisation based on decentralised, networked methods. The USA is leading a cultural transformation of democratic politics in this respect, thanks to the much greater integration of the women's movement and the harsh challenge of racial equality across America.

The quickening of events, and the sharpening of divisions *within* established machines confirms a larger disintegration is underway. What is the best way to see this? At the beginning of the book I compared 2016 to 1968. Looking back we can see that the revolt that began in 1968 led to a renewal not of socialism but of capitalism. Between 1968 and 1979 there was a decade of turmoil and tumult that resulted in the replacement of paternalistic Keynesianism by neoliberalism. Even in the last month or two, the term has become more widely used and its background influence on the rise of right-wing populism accepted. I tried to set out how neoliberalism is an ideology that denies it is an ideology, as it instigated an across-the-board attempt to depoliticise society in general and electoral politics in particular, in the name of the global market, profit, competition and individualism. In 2016, this aspect of its dominant economic order was challenged by electoral insurgencies of Trump and Brexit. Although products of it, they have defied the core assertion of neoliberalism: that state and government must be subordinated to the priorities of globalism and can do nothing to constrain the movement of people and capital. The paradox of President Trump and Prime Minister May is that they are products of revolts against a system that they also represent. Their role now, which is becoming clearer by the day, is to check the spirit of the force that has delivered them into office. To do so, both of them seek to restore the old order: May by calling an election; Trump by tweeting his own exercise in deflation. In the short term she is likely to gain and he will not.

But this is just the beginning of a likely decade or more of conflict over how neoliberalism will be replaced. The immediate threat is a 'Chinese model' in which the state pre-empts opposition and suppresses criticism – crushes saboteurs. A different outcome that assures liberty for people and society will rely upon politics being seen once again as a core human activity. Feminism, the greatest positive achievement to emerge from the sixties, will be a vital source for any such challenge. Despite Theresa May becoming the personification of Brexit, she has snatched its definition from the jaws of men. Trump, UKIP, Murdoch, the UK's tabloid media, Fox News and Brexit itself are an extraordinarily patriarchal phenomenon. Despite their ranting against the global order, they reassert its underlying authority in a crude form. Against them the opposition to Brexit and Trump will need to draw upon the fundamental equalities of women and men if it is to grow into a movement for a democratic economy.

28 April 2017

# Notes

These notes, with live links, can be found at www.unbound.com

## New Walls

1   Greg Palast published an early investigation and warning, in August 2016, http://www.rollingstone.com/politics/features/the-gops-stealth-war-against-voters-w435890

2   http://civilrightsdocs.info/pdf/reports/2016/poll-closure-report-web.pdf

3   http://www.cbsnews.com/news/cbs-news-exit-polls-how-donald-trump-won-the-us-presidency/

## 1  Jailbreak

1   http://news.sky.com/story/ukips-nigel-farage-hails-year-of-big-political-revolution-at-party-10669453

2   https://www.theguardian.com/music/2017/jan/23/brian-eno-not-interested-in-talking-about-me-reflection

3   http://blogs.spectator.co.uk/2016/10/full-text-theresa-mays-conference-speech/

4   https://reaganlibrary.archives.gov/archives/speeches/1989/011189i.htm

5   The passage comes from *Hold Everything Dear*, London, 2008, and is included in *Landscapes*, London, 2016, edited by Tom Overton.

6   https://www.oxfam.org/en/pressroom/pressreleases/2016-01-18/62-people-own-same-half-world-reveals-oxfam-davos-report

7   The title of Nick Davis's book, *Flat Earth News*, London, 2008.

8   https://www.adamtooze.com/2017/02/09/americas-political-economy-leaving-50-behind-latest-piketty-saez-co/

9   http://lithub.com/a-90-year-old-john-berger-is-not-surprised-by-president-trump/

10  http://blog.samaltman.com/what-i-heard-from-trump-supporters

11  https://www.facebook.com/brianenomusic/posts/1543156529031866

## 2  The Four Breaches of Trust

1   https://www.opendemocracy.net/conflict/article_1624.jsp

2   Iraq Body Count measures fatalities in Iraq, https://www.iraqbodycount.org

3   https://www.opendemocracy.net/conflict/article_1127.jsp

4   https://www.democracynow.org/2010/9/20/john_le_carr_the_united_states

5   http://www.nytimes.com/2004/10/17/magazine/faith-certainty-and-the-presidency-of-george-w-bush.html

6   https://web.archive.org/web/20100130144134/http://www.fco.gov.uk/resources/en/pdf/pdf3/fco_iraqdossier

7   https://en.wikipedia.org/wiki/Opinion_polls_about_9/11_conspiracy_theories

8   http://www.motherjones.com/politics/2004/01/lie-factory

9   http://www.iraqinquiry.org.uk/media/244166/2003-03-26-note-blair-to-bush-26-march-2003-note-the-fundamental-goal.pdf

10  http://www.npr.org/templates/story/story.php?storyId=99591469

11  http://edition.cnn.com/2003/US/07/17/blair.transcript/

12  http://news.bbc.co.uk/1/hi/uk_politics/4287370.stm

13  http://webarchive.nationalarchives.gov.uk/+/http://www.hm-treasury.gov.uk/2014.htm

14  https://www.ft.com/content/7e82da50-c184-11e6-9bca-2b93a6856354

15  http://www.theatlantic.com/politics/archive/2016/10/how-democrats-killed-their-populist-soul/504710/

16  https://www.theguardian.com/us-news/2017/apr/01/stephen-king-on-donald-trump-fictional-voters-truth-about-us-election

17  http://blogs.spectator.co.uk/2016/10/full-text-theresa-mays-conference-speech/

18  http://archive.defense.gov/Transcripts/Transcript.aspx?TranscriptID=2594

19  https://www.nytimes.com/2016/11/14/opinion/the-incendiary-appeal-of-demagoguery-in-our-time.html?_r=0

## 3  Roll the Dice

1   https://yougov.co.uk/news/2015/11/16/why-uk-might-end-voting-brexit/

2   http://lordashcroftpolls.com/2016/06/how-the-united-kingdom-voted-and-why/

3   Craig Oliver, *Unleashing Demons*, London, 2016, pp. 398–9.

4   https://www.youtube.com/watch?v=KG5jvQyF5bA

5   http://lordashcroftpolls.com/2016/11/the-unexpected-way-donald-trump-is-like-barack-obama/

6   https://mainlymacro.blogspot.co.uk/2016/08/a-divided-nation.html

7   http://www.vox.com/policy-and-politics/2016/11/30/13631532/everything-mattered-2016-presidential-election

8   http://lordashcroftpolls.com/2016/06/how-the-united-kingdom-voted-and-why/

9   https://dominiccummings.wordpress.com/2017/01/09/on-the-referendum-21-branching-histories-of-the-2016-referendum-and-the-frogs-before-the-storm-2/

10  http://www.mirror.co.uk/news/uk-news/nigel-farage-calls-barack-obama-9233130

11  http://www.telegraph.co.uk/news/2016/06/10/dont-let-david-cameron-and-george-osborne-fool-you-heres-what-my/

12  https://www.theguardian.com/politics/2016/dec/09/7-local-voters-on-the-sleaford-and-north-hykeham-byelection

13  https://assets.donaldjtrump.com/DJT_Acceptance_Speech.pdf

14  http://www.usatoday.com/wlna/news/politics/elections/2016/06/28/donald-trump-globalization-trade-pennsylvania-ohio/86431376/

## 4  Explaining the Disruption

1   https://www.washingtonpost.com/news/the-fix/wp/2016/12/02/yes-you-can-blame-millennials-for-hillary-clintons-loss/?utm_term=.7fec31769119

2   http://www.theneweuropean.co.uk/articles/the_reply_a_c_grayling_got_when_he_wrote_to_parliament_and_how_he_reacted_1_4789695

3   http://www.nytimes.com/2016/11/07/opinion/how-to-rig-an-election.html

4   https://fullfact.org/europe/our-eu-membership-fee-55-million/

5   https://dominiccummings.wordpress.com/2017/01/09/on-the-referendum-21-branching-histories-of-the-2016-referendum-and-the-frogs-before-the-storm-2/

6   http://www.resolutionfoundation.org/wp-content/uploads/2016/11/In-the-swing-of-things-FINAL.pdf compares the two votes; the link in the next note provides coverage of the personality type that voted for Brexit.

7   http://fivethirtyeight.com/features/even-among-the-wealthy-education-predicts-trump-support

8   http://blogs.lse.ac.uk/politicsandpolicy/brexit-and-the-left-behind-thesis/?utm_content=buffer26af3&utm

9   James Curran and Jean Seaton, *Power Without Responsibility*, London, 2010, p. 297.

10  Tim Shipman, *All Out War*, London, 2016, p. 587.

11  http://www.perc.org.uk/project_posts/trump-and-the-charisma-of-unreason/

12  http://www.perc.org.uk/project_posts/thoughts-on-the-sociology-of-brexit/

13  http://www.bbc.co.uk/news/business-37005457

14 http://www.independent.co.uk/news/uk/politics/brexit-salford-vote-european-union-latest-updates-polls-a7103521.html

15 Michael Ashcroft, *Hopes and Fears*, London, 2017, p. 68.

16 https://www.adamtooze.com/2017/03/02/notes-global-condition-mapping-debate-around-left-behind-white-working-class/

## 5 The Authenticity of Leave and Trump

1 http://www.cjr.org/covering_trump/trump_brand_america_media.php

2 https://www.jacobinmag.com/2017/02/the-great-god-trump-and-the-white-working-class/.

3 https://www.ft.com/content/97b44f88-4509-11e6-9b66-0712b3873ae1

4 https://www.opendemocracy.net/ourkingdom/anthony-barnett/party-memberships-in-uk-some-context-tory-termination

5 http://www.independent.co.uk/news/uk/politics/eu-referendum-michael-goves-full-statement-on-why-he-is-backing-brexit-a6886221.html

6 Tim Shipman, *All Out War*, London, 2016, p. 609.

7 http://www.thetimes.co.uk/tto/opinion/leaders/article4700662.ece

8 Tim Shipman, as above, p. 152.

9 https://www.ft.com/content/3482b434-c37d-11e6-81c2-f57d90f6741a

10 http://www.telegraph.co.uk/opinion/2016/06/17/we-face-a-very-serious-decision-next-week-but-not-a-terribly-di/

11 http://www.telegraph.co.uk/business/2016/06/12/brexit-vote-is-about-the-supremacy-of-parliament-and-nothing-els/

12 http://rodrik.typepad.com/dani_rodriks_weblog/2016/06/brexit-and-the-globalization-trilemma.html

13 https://opendemocracy.net/uk/oliver-huitson/eu-piece

14 http://www.thetimes.co.uk/edition/focus/beefy-and-i-will-whack-the-pm-for-six-ngnzrgk7x

15 http://www.independent.co.uk/news/uk/politics/eu-referendum-michael-goves-full-statement-on-why-he-is-backing-brexit-a6886221.html

16 https://www.theguardian.com/business/2016/nov/04/wetherspoons-boss-tim-martin-interview

17 https://www.theguardian.com/politics/blog/live/2016/apr/13/labour-says-whittingdale-should-lose-control-of-press-regulation-after-sex-worker-revelation-politics-live?page=with:block-570e5c6ae4b083e7edf07044#block-570e5c6ae4b083e7edf07044

18 http://www.telegraph.co.uk/news/2016/10/14/the-norman-conquest-was-a-disaster-for-england-we-should-celebra/

19 https://dominiccummings.wordpress.com/2017/01/09/on-the-referendum-21-branching-histories-of-the-2016-referendum-and-the-frogs-before-the-storm-2/

20   https://dominiccummings.files.wordpress.com/2017/01/20170130-referendum-22-numbers.pdf

21   https://www.opendemocracy.net/uk/anthony-barnett/referendum-in-doncaster-and-labours-disappearing-trick

22   https://opendemocracy.net/uk/anthony-barnett/would-you-believe-it-boris-and-gove-defy-corporate-fatalism

23   Tim Shipman, as above, p. 613.

## 6  The Artificiality of Remain and Clinton

1    https://assets.donaldjtrump.com/DJT_Acceptance_Speech.pdf

2    http://www.politico.com/story/2016/07/full-text-hillary-clintons-dnc-speech-226410

3    https://medium.com/@lessig/on-trumps-final-argument-for-america-corruption-72570a8d36bf#.5dpfszfil

4    http://www.bbc.co.uk/news/uk-politics-36872264

5    Tim Shipman, as above, p. 54.

6    https://wikileaks.org/podesta-emails/emailid/20454

7    https://www.washingtonpost.com/news/the-fix/wp/2016/10/19/hillary-clintons-84-proposed-campaign-slogans-ranked/?utm_term=.e18abe492854

8    http://www.bsgco.com/

9    Tony Blair, *A Journey*, London, 2011, p. 344.

10   Tim Shipman, as above, pp. 234–6.

11   http://www.telegraph.co.uk/women/politics/not-even-samcam-can-stop-women-voting-for-brexit/

12   Craig Oliver, as above, p. 310.

## 7  A Man of Means, Not Ends

1    Anthony Seldon & Peter Snowdon, *Cameron at 10: The Verdict*, London, 2016, p. 547.

2    Seldon & Snowden, as above, pp. 261–5.

3    Private email from Douglas Carswell.

4    http://www.talkcarswell.com/home/its-time-for-change/2801

5    http://www.britishpoliticalspeech.org/speech-archive.htm?speech=314

6    Speech to Chatham House, 10 November 2015, http://blogs.spectator.co.uk/2015/11/full-text-david-camerons-chatham-house-speech-on-europe/

7    Craig Oliver, as above, p. 42.

## 8  Words Pop Out of His Mouth

1    https://www.ft.com/content/6044d4e8-3a03-11e6-a780-b48ed7b6126f

2   http://www.dailymail.co.uk/news/article-3367352/David-Cameron-s-handwritten-note-reveals-fear-losing-s-election.html

3   https://www.opendemocracy.net/ourkingdom/adam-ramsay-oliver-huitson-others/ourkingdom-rolling-election-blog

4   http://www.bbc.co.uk/news/mobile/world-africa-14934352

5   http://www.theatlantic.com/magazine/archive/2016/04/the-obama-doctrine/471525/

6   https://www.statisticsauthority.gov.uk/archive/reports---correspondence/correspondence/letter-from-sir-andrew-dilnot-to-chris-leslie-mp-031014.pdf

7   http://www.independent.co.uk/voices/comment/is-cameron-a-liar-now-for-the-official-verdict-8475851.html

8   https://www.opendemocracy.net/uk/anthony-barnett/chapter-two-dodgy-daves-referendum-deal

9   https://www.theguardian.com/environment/2013/nov/21/david-cameron-green-crap-comments-storm

10  https://www.theguardian.com/politics/2015/mar/30/a-z-britains-first-coalition-government

11  David Laws, *Coalition*, London, 2016, p. 73.

12  http://news.bbc.co.uk/1/hi/uk_politics/5403798.stm

13  https://www.kingsfund.org.uk/blog/2016/01/how-does-nhs-spending-compare-health-spending-internationally

14  https://www.politicshome.com/news/uk/political-parties/labour-party/house/82718/jamie-reed-what-12-years-parliament-taught-me?

15  https://www.youtube.com/watch?v=iTuXFue03L4

16  https://www.theguardian.com/commentisfree/2016/jul/13/bullingdon-set-politics-david-cameron-new-era

17  http://www.dailymail.co.uk/news/article-3174689/Lord-Snorty-Blair-crony-responsible-behaviour-peers-filmed-taking-cocaine-200-night-prostitute-s-breasts-romp-two-escorts-discounted-flat.html

18  https://www.thesun.co.uk/archives/news/104057/sneer-of-the-realm/

19  http://www.independent.co.uk/news/uk/politics/what-lord-sewel-said-about-david-cameron-boris-johnson-tony-blair-george-bush-alex-salmond-andy-10418315.html

20  https://www.theguardian.com/politics/2010/feb/20/david-cameron-the-pr-years

21  All quotes in this paragraph are from a two-chapter account of Cameron's time with Carlton TV, in Francis Elliot & James Hanning, *Cameron: The Rise of the New Conservative*, London, 2009, pp. 156–94.

22  Elliot & Hanning, as above, pp. 172–3, 185.

23  http://www.thetimes.co.uk/tto/news/politics/article2026991.ece

## 10 It Was England's Brexit

1   http://www.huffingtonpost.co.uk/lisa-nandy/lisa-nandy-ippr-speech_b_15216124.html

2   Anthony Barnett, *Iron Britannia*, London, 2012, preface to the new edition, pp. xxiv–xxv.

3   https://wiltshirecf.org.uk/sites/default/files/0210_WCF_MainReport_FINAL%20PDF%20SP.pdf

4   http://www.devizes.org.uk/

5   http://www.somersetlive.co.uk/trowbridge-wetherspoons-eyewitness-describes-shocking-scenes-in-100-man-bar-brawl/story-30132796-detail/story.html

6   http://truevisiontv.com/wiltshire-voices-pewsey

7   http://www.thesundaytimes.co.uk/sto/comment/columns/jeremyclarkson/article1677071.ece

8   Laura Barton, *Guardian*, 25 October 2011, https://www.theguardian.com/stage/theatreblog/2011/oct/25/why-i-love-butterworths-jerusalem

9   http://www.knutsfordguardian.co.uk/news/10089886.End_of_an_era_for_town_as_Conservative_club_shuts_for_good/

10  http://www.vanityfair.com/magazine/photos/2015/11/annabel-astor-british-noble-ginge-manor

11  http://www.telegraph.co.uk/news/politics/david-cameron/5245604/David-Camerons-mother-in-law-Lady-Astor-on-the-pain-of-losing-Ivan.html

12  http://www.knutsfordguardian.co.uk/news/14442590.Sam_Cam_s_mum_s_firm_sparks_row_after_taking_down_Union_flag/?ref=mr&lp=1

13  https://granta.com/black-country/

## 11 Anglo-Britain, the Hybrid Nationalism

1   http://uk.businessinsider.com/full-text-theresa-mays-speech-to-the-republican-congress-of-tomorrow-conference-2017-1

2   http://www.telegraph.co.uk/news/2016/10/05/theresa-mays-conference-speech-in-full/

3   http://www.dailymail.co.uk/debate/article-3430870/DAILY-MAIL-COMMENT-speak-England.html

4   The words are Fred Halliday's, I quote them in my *Iron Britannia*, as above.

5   https://www.parliament.uk/about/how/laws/bills/public/english-votes-for-english-laws/

6   https://www.publications.parliament.uk/pa/cm201516/cmhansrd/cm160204/debtext/160204-0002.htm

7   Michael Kenny, *The Politics of English Nationhood*, Oxford, 2014.

8    https://www.ons.gov.uk/peoplepopulationandcommunity/
     culturalidentity/ethnicity/articles/ethnicityandnationalidentityinengl
     andandwales/2012-12-11#national-identity-in-england-and-wales

9    http://www.centreonconstitutionalchange.ac.uk/sites/default/files/
     news/Taking%20England%20Seriously_The%20New%20English
     %20Politics.pdf and http://www.ippr.org/files/images/media/files/
     publication/2013/07/england-two-unions_Jul2013_11003.pdf

10   http://www.thetimes.co.uk/tto/opinion/columnists/article3775800.ece

11   https://www.theguardian.com/uk-news/2014/oct/19/immigration-
     policy-ukip-restrictions-european-union

12   http://www.conservativehome.com/thecolumnists/2016/04/nick-
     timothy-port-talbot-should-make-us-question-the-unthinking-
     liberalism-of-our-governing-classes.html

## 12  I'm Not English. Oh Yes You Are!

1    https://www.theguardian.com/commentisfree/2015/may/10/snp-
     english-national-identity-class-cultural-divide

2    https://www.theguardian.com/books/2006/nov/11/society.politics

3    Liah Greenfeld, *Nationalism: Five Roads to Modernity*, Cambridge, MA,
     1993; Ernest Gellner, *Nations and Nationalism*, Ithaca, NY, 1983; Ben
     Anderson, *Imagined Communities*, London, 1983, revised 2006.

4    Tom Nairn, *The Left Against Europe*, Middlesex, 1983.

## 13  Big Britishness

1    http://www.politico.eu/article/why-we-lost-the-brexit-vote-former-uk-
     prime-minister-david-cameron/

2    http://www.independent.co.uk/news/uk/politics/david-cameron-
     interview-prime-minister-urges-people-to-vote-in-eu-referendum-
     or-youll-find-were-out-a6941436.html

3    http://www.bbc.co.uk/news/uk-politics-eu-referendum-36484357

4    https://www.ft.com/content/4c3b9c90-0422-11e7-ace0-1ce02ef0def9

5    http://www.dailymail.co.uk/news/article-4157848/Osborne-met-
     investment-firm-FIVE-times-Chancellor.html

6    http://www.dailymail.co.uk/news/article-4162438/Heads-roll-Osborne-
     storm.html

7    https://www.theguardian.com/politics/2016/dec/02/george-osborne-
     defends-earning-320k-on-speaking-tour

8    https://www.theyworkforyou.com/peer/10153/lord_darling_of_
     roulanish

9    https://www.ft.com/content/3cae4d6e-9cfd-11e5-b45d-4812f209f861

10   https://www.ons.gov.uk/economy/investmentspensionsandtrusts/
     bulletins/ownershipofukquotedshares/2015-09-02

11 http://www.thisismoney.co.uk/money/comment/article-3791704/ALEX-BRUMMER-Britain-s-sale-two-decades-takeovers-face-high-bar.html

## 14  English European, a Modern Nationalism

1 Interview with Robert Gordon, *Juncture*, Winter 2016, p. 174.

2 https://www.theguardian.com/politics/commentisfree/2016/jun/24/lifelong-english-european-the-biggest-defeat-of-my-political-life-timothy-garton-ash-brexit

## 15  Why the Right Wins and the Left Loses

1 Samuel Taylor Coleridge, *On the Constitution of the Church and State* (1830), edited and introduced by John Barrell, London, 1972.

2 Asa Briggs, *Victorian People*, London, 1954, p. 234.

3 Ferdinand Mount, *The British Constitution*, London, 1992, pp. 62–92.

4 http://www.nybooks.com/articles/2017/03/23/what-trump-could-do/?

5 http://www.thesundaytimes.co.uk/sto/newsreview/features/article1524824.ece

6 http://www.constitutionreformgroup.co.uk/publications/

7 https://reaction.life/use-brexit-reform-lords-overhaul-uks-constitution/

## 16  The Discombobulated Constitution

1 Walter Bagehot, *The English Constitution*, London, 1909, pp. 10–11.

2 Tom Bower, *Broken Vows*, London, 2016, pp. 13–14.

3 Tom Bower, as above.

4 http://news.bbc.co.uk/nol/shared/bsp/hi/pdfs/14_07_04_butler.pdf

5 https://www.theguardian.com/politics/2005/feb/28/iraq.iraq

6 Christopher Foster, *British Government in Crisis*, Oxford, 2005, p. 242.

7 Andrew Rawnsley, *Servants of the People*, London, 2000, p. 27.

8 David Owen, *Cabinet's Finest Hour*, London, 2017, pp. 255–70.

9 http://www.conservativehome.com/thetorydiary/2012/02/ten-things-you-need-to-know-about-the-group-of-four-that-runs-the-coalition.html

10 https://www.theguardian.com/uk/2012/dec/18/queen-attends-cabinet-meeting1

11 http://www.telegraph.co.uk/news/2017/04/01/revealed-cabinet-plotted-exploit-eus-defence-fears/

12 Caroline Lucas, *Honourable Friends*, London, 2015, p. 206.

13 Anthony Trollope, *An Autobiography*, Oxford, 1923, ch. 16, p. 264.

14 David Marquand, *Mammon's Kingdom*, London, 2014.

15 http://www.telegraph.co.uk/news/investigations/11428077/Ex-ministers-Jack-Straw-and-Sir-Malcolm-Rifkind-brag-to-business-about-their-political-contacts.html

16 http://socialinvestigations.blogspot.co.uk/2012/02/nhs-privatisation-compilation-of.html

17 Martin Williams, *Parliament Ltd, A Journey to the Dark Heart of British Politics*, London, 2017.

18 Richard Brooks, *The Great Tax Robbery*, London, 2013; Owen Jones, *The Establishment, and How They Get Away With It*, London, 2015; David Whyte, *How Corrupt is Britain?*, London, 2015; James Meek, *Private Island*, London, 2014.

19 David Rogers, *By Royal Appointment: Tales from the Privy Council – the Unknown Arm of Government*, London, 2015, p. 1.

20 Robert Tombs, *The English and Their History*, London, 2014, p. 888.

21 https://www.gov.uk/government/uploads/system/uploads/attachment_data/file/268021/oathofallegiance.pdf

22 http://www.democraticaudit.com/our-work/the-2017-audit-of-uk-democracy/

# 17  The Sovereignty of Parliament

1 A. V. Dicey, *Law of the Constitution*, London, 1885, p. 141.

2 https://www.gov.uk/government/speeches/the-governments-negotiating-objectives-for-exiting-the-eu-pm-speech

3 https://www.judiciary.gov.uk/wp-content/uploads/2016/11/summary-r-miller-v-secretary-of-state-for-exiting-the-eu-20161103.pdf

4 http://www.legislation.gov.uk/ukpga/2005/4

5 Stephen Sedley, *Lions Under the Throne*, Cambridge, 2015, p. 148.

6 Tom Bingham, *The Rule of Law*, London, 2010, pp. 166–170.

7 https://www.publications.parliament.uk/pa/ld201516/ldselect/ldconst/59/5903.htm#n37 (Clause 36).

# 18  The Monarchy and 'The People'

1 This I did with a convention organised by Charter 88 and sponsored by *The Times*, published as *Power and the Throne*, edited and introduced by Anthony Barnett, London, 1994.

2 http://www.thesundaytimes.co.uk/sto/news/uk_news/People/article1594307.ece?CMP=OTH-gnws-standard-2015_08_15 and https://www.buzzfeed.com/andrewkaczynski/donald-trump-said-a-lot-of-gross-things-about-women-on-howar#.btRnjazaL

3 http://www.bbc.co.uk/news/special/politics97/diana/panorama.html

## 19  The Blair Coup

1   Anthony Barnett, *Blimey, It Could Be Brexit!*, p. 93. https://drive.google.com/file/d/0B6iE9UndVXNKSlVfMkZ0RGNuN1k/view

2   http://www.prospectmagazine.co.uk/features/corporatecontrol

## 20  Manipulative Corporate Populism

1   Tony Blair, *A Journey*, London, 2011, p. xxvii.

2   Colin Crouch, *Post-Democracy*, Cambridge, 2004.

3   http://news.bbc.co.uk/nol/shared/vote2005/html/england.stm

## 21  From Churchillism to Thatcherism

1   David Edgerton, *Britain's War Machine*, London, 2011.

2   Barnett, *Iron Britannia*, as above, pp. xii–xvi and 32–48.

3   Ibid, p. 147.

4   http://europa.eu/european-union/about-eu/symbols/europe-day/schuman-declaration_en

5   Edmund Dell, *The Schuman Plan and the British Abdication of Leadership in Europe*, London, 1995, p. 227.

6   http://www.margaretthatcher.org/document/103485

7   Stuart Hall, 'Gramsci and Us', *Marxism Today*, June 1987, http://www.hegemonics.co.uk/docs/Gramsci-and-us.pdf

8   http://www.margaretthatcher.org/document/104475

## 22  From the Establishment to the Political-Media Caste

1   http://webarchive.nationalarchives.gov.uk/+/www.number10.gov.uk/Page1297

2   Published by the Thatcher Institute, http://fc95d419f4478b3b6e5f-3f71d0fe2b653c4f00f32175760e96e7.r87.cf1.rackcdn.com/FA5DB3D8544A461DACEDF181801765AE.pdf

3   https://www.theguardian.com/media/2012/mar/17/rupert-murdoch-margaret-thatcher

4   Curran and Seaton, as above, p. 73.

5   https://www.theguardian.com/politics/1999/feb/04/uk.politicalnews6

6   http://www.bbc.co.uk/news/uk-18405629

7   http://www.standard.co.uk/comment/comment/anthony-hilton-stay-or-go-the-lack-of-solid-facts-means-it-s-all-a-leap-of-faith-a3189151.html

8   https://www.theguardian.com/media/2003/feb/17/mondaymediasection.iraq

9   http://leveson.sayit.mysociety.org/hearing-6-february-2012/mr-paul-dacre#s41188

10  https://www.theguardian.com/politics/2016/jun/29/michael-goves-wife-doubts-boris-johnson-email-sarah-vine-dacre-murdoch

11  http://www.newstatesman.com/media/2013/12/man-who-hates-liberal-britain

12  http://www.dailymail.co.uk/news/article-360866/Why-Tories-choose-right-leader.html

13  http://image.guardian.co.uk/sys-files/Politics/documents/2007/06/12/BlairReustersSpeech.pdf

14  https://www.theguardian.com/commentisfree/2010/apr/04/david-cameron-andy-coulson-election

15  https://www.theguardian.com/media/2011/jul/20/andy-coulson-security-clearance-checks

16  https://www.opendemocracy.net/ourkingdom/anthony-barnett/murdoch-and-big-lie

17  https://www.opendemocracy.net/ourkingdom/anthony-barnett/after-murdoch

18  https://www.theguardian.com/politics/2013/oct/01/miliband-furious-daily-mail-father

19  http://reutersinstitute.politics.ox.ac.uk/publication/uk-press-coverage-eu-referendum

20  Peter Mair, *Ruling the Void*, London, 2013.

21  https://capx.co/triumphant-theresa-is-reshaping-british-politics/?omhide=true

## 23 The *Daily Mail* Takes Power

1  http://www.dailymail.co.uk/news/article-3665146/SARAH-VINE-Victory-vitriol-craziest-days-life.html

2  http://www.conservativehome.com/platform/2016/02/david-davis-britain-would-be-better-off-out-of-the-eu-and-heres-why.html

3  http://www.conservativehome.com/platform/2016/07/david-davis-trade-deals-tax-cuts-and-taking-time-before-triggering-article-50-a-brexit-economic-strategy-for-britain.html

4  https://www.theguardian.com/politics/2016/oct/25/exclusive-leaked-recording-shows-what-theresa-may-really-thinks-about-brexit

5  http://www.dailymail.co.uk/debate/article-3668924/DAILY-MAIL-COMMENT-party-flames-Theresa-leader.html

6  http://www.dailymail.co.uk/news/article-3669017/The-vicar-s-daughter-met-husband-Conservative-disco-Deadly-Utterly-steely-Etonians-grammar-school-girl-grandmothers-service-just-Britain-needs.html

7  Robert Tombs, as above, p. 810.

8  Charles Moore, *Margaret Thatcher, Vol. 1: Not for Turning*, London, 2013, p. 351.

9  https://www.ft.com/content/db6dd3c2-f849-11e6-9516-2d969e0d3b65

10  https://www.totalpolitics.com/articles/news/theresa-may-turns-daily-mail-new-comms-chief

11  https://www.lrb.co.uk/v38/n21/william-davies/home-office-rules

12  http://www.legislation.gov.uk/ukpga/2016/25/contents/enacted

13  Theresa May and Nicholas Timothy, *Restoring Parliamentary Authority: EU Laws and British Scrutiny*, Politeia, London, 2007.

14  https://www.gov.uk/government/speeches/the-governments-negotiating-objectives-for-exiting-the-eu-pm-speech

15  Ibid.

16  https://www.politicshome.com/news/uk/political-parties/conservative-party/theresa-may/news/83696/theresa-may-tells-scottish?

17  http://www.scottishconservatives.com/2017/03/theresa-may-speech-to-scottish-conservative-conference/

18  http://www.newstatesman.com/2017/02/-theresa-may-method-interview-jason-cowley

19  Ron Davies, *Devolution: A Process Not an Event*, Institute for Welsh Affairs, Cardiff, 1999.

20  https://d25d2506sfb94s.cloudfront.net/cumulus_uploads/document/oxmidrr5wh/EUFinalCall_Reweighted.pdf

## 24  The BBC

1  https://www.theguardian.com/books/2009/mar/07/politics-biography-chris-mullin

2  http://www.currybet.net/cbet_blog/2004/01/bbc-staff-advert-in-the-daily.php

3  https://www.opendemocracy.net/100ideasforthebbc/

4  https://www.versobooks.com/books/1106-the-return-of-the-public

5  https://www.opendemocracy.net/ourbeeb/david-elstein/bbc-and-media-plurality-ofcom-strikes-back-with-damp-cloth

6  https://life.spectator.co.uk/2016/11/many-many-millions-mogg/

7  http://www.bbc.co.uk/programmes/b07nsx8g

8  BBC Radio 4, *Today* Programme, 13 September 2016.

9  https://www.opendemocracy.net/ourbeeb/mike-berry/british-are-dangerously-ill-informed-about-eu-referendum

## 25  What Kind of Country Do We Want to Be?

1  https://www.gov.uk/government/speeches/pms-statement-following-cabinet-meeting-on-eu-settlement-20-february-2016

2  http://press.conservatives.com/

3  Blair, *A Journey*, London, 2012, p. 570.

4  https://www.planforbritain.gov.uk/

5   http://www.thetimes.co.uk/edition/news/we-can-build-a-stronger-fairer-britain-2dtf6b03r?CMP=TNLEmail_118918_1484205

6   http://www.telegraph.co.uk/news/2017/01/25/theresa-may-america-britain-will-lead-together-brexit-election/

## 26 Neoliberalism: Just Say the Word

1   https://www.imf.org/external/pubs/ft/fandd/2016/06/pdf/ostry.pdf

2   https://www.ft.com/content/4b98c052-238a-11e6-9d4d-c11776a5124d

3   https://www.ft.com/content/ae448fcc-23fa-11e6-9d4d-c11776a5124d

4   http://www2.warwick.ac.uk/fac/soc/economics/research/centres/cage/manage/publications/305-2016_becker_fetzer_novy.pdf

5   Daniel Stedman Jones, *Masters of the Universe*, Princeton, 2012.

6   http://staffblogs.le.ac.uk/management/2015/04/15/the-limits-of-neoliberalism-an-interview-with-will-davies/

7   http://www.colorado.edu/studentgroups/libertarians/issues/friedman-soc-resp-business.html

8   Blair, *A Journey*, London, 2011, p. 119.

9   Raoul Martinez, *Creating Freedom*, London, 2017, p. 138.

10  https://reaction.life/in-defence-of-neoliberalism/

11  https://www.ft.com/content/454cb11a-3f45-11e5-b98b-87c7270955cf

12  https://www.theguardian.com/books/2016/apr/15/neoliberalism-ideology-problem-george-monbiot

13  http://webarchive.nationalarchives.gov.uk/+/http:/www.bis.gov.uk/wp-content/uploads/publications/Higher-Ambitions.pdf

14  http://www.spectator.co.uk/2010/06/the-real-villain-of-bp/

15  https://www.gov.uk/government/uploads/system/uploads/attachment_data/file/422565/bis-10-1208-securing-sustainable-higher-education-browne-report.pdf

16  https://www.opendemocracy.net/ourkingdom/ourkingdom/fight-back-reader-on-winter-of-protest

17  http://www.zero-books.net/books/capitalist-realism

18  Wendy Brown, *Undoing the Demos: Neoliberalism's Stealth Revolution*, Boston, 2015.

19  https://www.lwbooks.co.uk/soundings/kilburn-manifesto

## 27 The Legitimacy of the European Union

1   https://www.opendemocracy.net/democracy-europefuture/article_337.jsp

2   https://www.socialeurope.eu/2017/03/beautiful-freak-poster-child-irelands-dramatic-rebound/

3   https://www.theguardian.com/world/2016/apr/05/yanis-varoufakis-why-we-must-save-the-eu

4    http://www.hrcr.org/hottopics/EuropeanC.html

5    https://www.opendemocracy.net/democracy-europe_constitution/
     union_2623.jsp

6    https://www.opendemocracy.net/tony_blair_and_europe.jsp

7    http://www.independent.co.uk/voices/commentators/valeacutery-
     giscard-destaing-the-eu-treaty-is-the-same-as-the-constitution-
     398286.html

8    http://news.bbc.co.uk/1/hi/world/europe/8282241.stm

9    https://en.wikiquote.org/wiki/Jean-Claude_Juncker

10   http://news.bbc.co.uk/1/hi/world/europe/8282241.stm

11   https://www.theguardian.com/world/2003/dec/08/eu.politics2

12   http://www.europarl.europa.eu/elections2014-results/en/turnout.html

13   https://diem25.org/wp-content/uploads/2016/02/diem25_english_long.
     pdf

14   https://www.theguardian.com/commentisfree/2017/mar/25/three-
     things-the-eu-must-do-to-survive

15   https://www.ft.com/content/b7018d6c-0fc8-11e7-b030-768954394623

16   http://www.pewglobal.org/2016/06/13/europeans-face-the-world-
     divided/

17   https://ec.europa.eu/commission/sites/beta-political/files/white_
     paper_on_the_future_of_europe_en.pdf

## 28  Britain and the EU

1    Barnett, *Blimey, It Could Be Brexit!*, p. 30. https://www.opendemocracy.
     net/uk/jamie-mackay/blimey-it-could-be-brexit-book-so-far

2    Margaret Thatcher, *The Path to Power*, London, 1995, p. 209.

3    Charles Moore, *Margaret Thatcher, Vol. 2: Everything She Wants*,
     London, 2015, p. 396.

4    Ken Clarke, *Kind of Blue*, London, 2016, pp. 163–5.

5    Luuk van Middelaar, *The Passage to Europe*, New Haven and London,
     2014, p. 187.

6    http://www.britpolitics.co.uk/speeches-sir-geoffrey-howe-resignation

7    Tony Blair, as above, p. 570.

8    Tony Blair, as above, pp. xxxiv–xxxviii.

9    https://fullfact.org/europe/uk-law-what-proportion-influenced-eu/

10   https://ukhumanrightsblog.com/2016/02/09/cavalier-with-our-
     constitution-a-charter-too-far/

## 29  No Left to Turn to

1    https://yougov.co.uk/news/2016/06/27/how-britain-voted/ & http://
     lordashcroftpolls.com/2016/06/how-the-united-kingdom-voted-and-
     why/

2    http://www.bbc.co.uk/news/uk-politics-eu-referendum-36430606

3   http://www.bbc.co.uk/news/uk-politics-eu-referendum-36506163

4   http://labourlist.org/2016/04/britain-needs-europe-and-europe-needs-britain-full-text-of-david-milibands-pro-eu-speech/

5   http://www.newstatesman.com/uk-politics/2012/03/new-times-new-thinking

6   http://labourlist.org/2017/02/jeremy-corbyn-labour-fights-for-scottish-communities-whilst-the-snp-fail/

7   http://www.compassonline.org.uk/wp-content/uploads/2017/03/Labour-the-PA.pdf

## 30  Where the 48 Per Cent Go Next

1   BBC Question Time, 27 March 2017, and https://www.theguardian.com/politics/2017/mar/25/nick-clegg-tells-eu-march-there-is-a-perpetual-sense-of-anger-over-brexit

2   https://en.wikipedia.org/wiki/Child_Trust_Fund

3   Paul Gilroy, 'The Great Escape', in Mark Perryman, ed, *Imagined Nation*, London, 2008, p. 194.

## 31  People Flow

1   https://www.opendemocracy.net/theo-veenkamp-tom-bentley-alessandra-buonfino-anthony-barnett/people-flow-migration-and-europe

2   Ibid.

3   https://www.newsdeeply.com/refugees/community/2017/01/04/we-all-have-a-fundamental-right-to-cross-borders

4   http://www.pewhispanic.org/2015/11/19/more-mexicans-leaving-than-coming-to-the-u-s/

5   http://www.migrationobservatory.ox.ac.uk/resources/briefings/long-term-international-migration-flows-to-and-from-the-uk/

6   http://www.libdems.org.uk/brexit-challenge-movement-paper

7   http://ec.europa.eu/eurostat/statistics-explained/index.php/File:Immigrants,_2014_(per_1_000_inhabitants)_YB16.png

8   http://ec.europa.eu/eurostat/statistics-explained/index.php/Migration_and_migrant_population_statistics

9   http://www.politico.eu/article/why-we-lost-the-brexit-vote-former-uk-prime-minister-david-cameron/

10  http://blogs.lse.ac.uk/politicsandpolicy/trump-and-brexit-why-its-again-not-the-economy-stupid/ and http://www.vox.com/world/2017/3/13/14698812/bernie-trump-corbyn-left-wing-populism

## 32  Combined Determination

1   https://www.theguardian.com/world/2013/sep/20/usaf-atomic-bomb-north-carolina-1961

2   http://www.newstatesman.com/politics/uk/2017/03/anywheres-vs-somewheres-split-made-brexit-inevitable

3    https://static1.squarespace.com/static/541ff5f5e4b02b7c37f31ed6/t/
     58a45f5a414fb58912c01995/1487167328959/Polanyi+final
     +5+lectures+Publication+15+Feb+final+final+pdf.pdf

4    https://reaction.life/in-defence-of-neoliberalism/

5    https://www.opendemocracy.net/uk/alan-finlayson/who-won-referendum

6    https://www.theguardian.com/politics/2010/oct/06/david-cameron-
     speech-tory-conference

7    http://www.thedailybeast.com/articles/2016/08/22/steve-bannon-
     trump-s-top-guy-told-me-he-was-a-leninist.html

8    https://www.theguardian.com/us-news/2015/may/15/jeb-bush-iraq-
     war-ivy-zietrich-isis-george-w-bush

9    https://www.gov.uk/government/speeches/pm-speech-to-department-
     for-international-development-staff

## 33  Peace or War

1    http://www.politico.com/story/2017/01/full-text-trump-pence-
     remarks-cia-headquarters-233978

2    http://thehill.com/blogs/pundits-blog/the-administration/318525-
     transcript-of-president-donald-trumps-speech-to-the

3    http://www.bbc.co.uk/news/uk-scotland-glasgow-west-36606184

4    https://twitter.com/realdonaldtrump/status/766246213079498752

5    http://www.conservativehome.com/thecolumnists/2016/01/daniel-
     hannan-has-the-rise-of-trump-proved-me-wrong-on-open-
     primaries.html

6    https://assets.donaldjtrump.com/DJT_Acceptance_Speech.pdf

7    https://www.gov.uk/government/speeches/prime-ministers-speech-to-
     the-republican-party-conference-2017

8    https://www.ons.gov.uk/economy/nationalaccounts/
     balanceofpayments/timeseries/aa6h/ukea

## 34  Citizens, Reimagine

1    http://www.nybooks.com/articles/2016/12/22/on-optimism-and-
     despair/

2    http://press.conservatives.com/

## 35  Conclusion

1    https://ec.europa.eu/commission/five-presidents-report_en

2    http://europa.eu/rapid/press-release_IP-17-385_en.htm

3    Tony Blair, as above, p. 570

4    https://www.adamtooze.com/2017/03/30/notes-global-condition-
     americanization-global-capital/

5    facebook.com/notes/mark-zuckerberg/building-global-community

# Acknowledgements

If you enjoy reading *Lure of Greatness* the pleasure is due to Judith Herrin, who transforms duty into delight. Her unstinting provision, along with tremendous support from our daughters Tamara and Portia, made it possible to write under the time pressure. *My turn now.*

Jamie Mackay identified the slogan that would have won the referendum for Remain. His assistance, ideas and outstanding judgements have been a vital contribution throughout the writing and rewriting.

*Lure of Greatness* would not exist but for the encouragement of Felicity Bryan – who is a star – and James Curran and Tony Tabatznik, and most important, a big thank you to all those who subscribed so patiently to the Unbound model that has made publication possible.

A special thanks to subscribers who voted for Brexit knowing I backed Remain. I want to emphasise that all those who subscribed in advance have shown a generous interest in a good argument and nothing more. Neither they, nor anyone who has helped the book, has in any way signalled their agreement with any of my claims or analysis.

Two teams made *Lure* possible. I am tremendously grateful to *openDemocracy*. Its Editor-in-Chief, Mary Fitzgerald, Rosemary Bechler and Adam Ramsay have helped me consistently since they started to publish *Blimey, it could be Brexit!* every week during the referendum campaign. I also worked closely with and learned greatly from Benjamin Ramm, Cathy Runciman, En Khong and Ralph Pritchard.

Unbound came to my rescue and I cannot thank them enough for their patience and backing. Their new model of publishing deserves to be a great success. Special thanks to my publisher, John Mitchison (also for his incredible honey), to Anna Simpson, Lauren Fulbright and Alex Eccles. To cover designer Mark Ecob, copyeditor Steve Best, proofreader Lin Vasey and indexer David Atkinson.

Judith Herrin, Nick Pearce, Stuart White and Rosemary Bechler read an early draft very fast and helped me a lot with their wisdom. James Curran, Tamara Barnett Herrin, Will Davis, Todd Gitlin, Tom Nairn and Richard Parker read sections at my request and helped more than they realise.

The following assisted in different ways, small and large and sometimes quite unwittingly. While I thank them all, they bear no responsibility whatever for the use to which I have put their help: Hugh Brody, Douglas Carswell, Anthony Cartwright, Colin Crouch, Tony Curzon Price, Mike Davis, Pavlos Eleftheriadis, David Elstein, Jeremy Fox, Gerry Hassan, Caspar Henderson, Paul Hilder, Damien Hockney, Stephen Howe, Helena Kennedy, Roman Krznaric, Simon McBurney, John Mills, Suzanne Moore, Kalypso Nicolaidis, Ann Pettifor, Henry Porter, David Potter, Kate Raworth, Laura Sandys, Trevor Smith, Tim Stevenson, Robert Tombs, Yanis Varoufakis, Hilary Wainwright, James Walsh, Stuart Weir, Stephen Wetherill and Gareth Young.

The history of the present is necessarily an exploration in which the meaning of any particular excavation alters as more is uncovered. I have investigated the issues covered in *Lure of Greatness* since 1982 and have had to change my mind. *This Time*, for example, argued for a renewed British union. Here I have recycled many passages published across the years including most recently from *Blimey, it could be Brexit!* For those who find them familiar my excuse is that the context changes their significance.

# Index

# Supporters

Unbound is a new kind of publishing house. Our books are funded directly by readers. This was a very popular idea during the late eighteenth and early nineteenth centuries. Now we have revived it for the internet age. It allows authors to write the books they really want to write and readers to support the books they would most like to see published.

The names listed below are of readers who have pledged their support and made this book happen. If you'd like to join them, visit www.unbound.com.

Jan Adams
Terry Aduh
Richard Agnew
Guy Aitchison
Luc Alexander
Peter Allen
Beverly Anderson
Perry Anderson
Anuradha Vittachi Armstrong
Jake Arnold
Juliet Ash
Michael and
   Francesca Ashburner
Pauline Asher
Dean Ayotte
Michael Bailey
Sebastian Bain
Rona Baker
Ken Baldry
David Barker
Guinevere Barnes
Andrew Barnett

Tamara Barnett-Herrin
Logie Barrow
Aaron Bastani
Eleni Bastea
Ann Basu
Jay Basu
Laura Basu
Henrietta Batchelor
Mike Bates
Julian Batsleer
John Baxendale
Rosemary Bechler
Neil Belton
Paul Bennett
Wayne Bennett
Catherine Bent
Margaret Bent
Roy Berman
Lorna Berrett
Adrian Berry
Portia BH
Geoffrey Bindman

| | |
|---|---|
| Mike Birkin | Graham Chadwick |
| Fiona Blackburn | Charles Chadwyck-Healey |
| Owen Blacker | David Chandler |
| Danby Bloch | Jung Chang |
| Arthur Blue | Bruce Clark |
| Margaret Bluman | Christopher Clark |
| Susan Bly | Neil Clement |
| Bruce Bowie | John Clements |
| Tricia Boyd | Chloe Clemmons |
| Conall Boyle | Anthony Coates |
| Reuben Briggs | Clare Coatman |
| Jonathan Bright | Laurence Cockcroft |
| Ivan Briscoe | Andrew Collard |
| Victoria Brittain | Patti Collins |
| Sebastian Brock | Naomi Colvin |
| Hugh Brody | Steve Comer |
| James Brookes | Bim Cooper |
| Sally Brooks | Martin Cooper |
| Archie Brown | Anne Corbett |
| Felicity Bryan | P J Cornelissen |
| A BS | Adam Corner |
| Jeremy Burke | Ivor Cornish |
| Tom Burns | Dominique Courtois |
| Camilla Bustani | John Crawford |
| Daniel Butt | Lucy Crehan |
| David Cain | Elizabeth Cringle |
| Averil Cameron | Carol Croft |
| Neil Cameron | Jon Cruddas |
| Bob Campbell | James Curran |
| Chloe Campbell | Andrew Curry |
| Costa Carras | Tony Curzon Price |
| Peter Carty | Rishi Dastidar |
| Robert Cassen | Edward Davey |
| Brian Cathcart | Kevin Davey |
| Roger Cavanagh | Brian Davidson |

Geraint Talfan Davies

Kathryn Davies

Lynne Davies

Russell Davies

Valerie Davies

Will Davies

Madeleine Davis

Natalie Zemon Davis

Cathy Debenham

Anne Deighton

John Denham

Bradley Dodd

Rigas Doganis

Thomas Dowling

Andrew Duff

Max Duncan

Bill Dunlop

Gill Edmonds

Gavin Edwards

Michael Edwards

Brin Edwards

Isin Elicin

Jane Ellis

Joan Ellis

David Elstein

Bill Emmott

Brian Eno

Jan Erola

Martyn Evans

Sam Evans

Richard Eyre

Rachel Farebrother

Edmund Fawcett

Natalie Fenton

Alan Finlayson

Mary Fitzgerald

Mike Flood Page

Judith Flynn

Claire Fox

Jeremy Fox

Sean Fox

Peter Frankopan

David Freedberg

Des Freedman

Graham Fulcher

Laurence Fuller

Andrew Gamble

Mark Gamble

Peter Garland

Timothy Garton Ash

Robert Gee

Charlotte Gerada

Sue Gerhardt

Luke Gething

Tim Gibbons

Daniele Gibney

Bola Gibson

Jeremy Gilbert

Robert Gildea

Tom Giles

Paul Gilroy

Marcus Gilroy-Ware

David Gladstone

Jeff Gleisner

Misha Glenny

Miriam Glucksmann

Nigel Goddard

Eunice Goes

David Goldblatt

Martin Golding

Cathrine Gomani

Chris Goodall

Paul J. Goodison

Jane Gould

Michael Goulden

Peggotty Graham

Keith Griffin

Tom Griffin

Vincent Guiry

Peter Hain

Catherine Hall

Dan Hancox

Jeremy Hardie

Angela Hardy

David Hare

Pauline Harkness

Andrea Harman

Guy Harper

Hermione Harris

James Harvey

George Hawthorne

Anne Haynes

Richard Healey

John Healy

Jake Helliwell

Caspar Henderson

Griselda Heppel

Judith Herrin

Graham Hewitt

Katharine Hibbert

Kevin Hickman

Ronald Higgins

Paul Hilder

Elizabeth Hilliard Selka

Dougald Hine

Christopher Hird

Damian Hockney

Godfrey Hodgson

H V Holden Brown

John Holloway

Michael Holt

Janice Holve

Jane Howard

Stephen Howe

Annabel Howland

Nick Hubble

Patrick Hughes

Oliver Huitson

Gareth Humphreys

Rob Humphreys

Robin Hunt

Will Hutton

Joyce Hytner

Susie Ibbotson

Joanna Innes

Ian Irvine

Ben Jackson

Dan Jackson

Elizabeth Jackson

Thomas Jackson

Rafe Jaffrey

Tim James

Peter James

Naadir Jeewa

Nicholas Jeune

John, Nicola and Moana

Marjorie Johns

Mark Johnson

Emily Jones

Gareth Stedman Jones

Hywel Ceri Jones
Mark Jones
Frank Judd
Stella Kane
Mats Karlsson
Sunder Katwala
Hannah Kaye
Noel Kehoe
Niel Kenmuir
Helena Kennedy
Hugh Kennedy
Michael Kenny
Martin Kettle
Dan Kieran
Patrick Kincaid
Clico Kingsbury
Robin Kinross
Alex Kirby
Graham Knox
Jakub Korab
Helene Kreysa
Bernard Krichefski
David Krivanek
Roman Krznaric
Richard Kuper
Pierre L'Allier
Pierre Landell-Mills
Anne Lapping
Martin Large
Paul Lashmar
Steve Lawrence
Neal Lawson
Rick Le Coyte
Mark Le Fanu
Adam Lennox-Warburton

Lap Gong Leong
Katriina Lepanjuuri
Jeremy Lester
Henry Leveson-Gower
John Levett
Michael Levi
David Levy
Colin Leyden
Anatol Lieven
Alison Light
Toby Limbrick
Alistair Livingston
David Lloyd
James Loxley
Caroline Lucas
Diarmaid MacCulloch
Ann & Dougal Mackay
Bruce Mackay
Jamie Mackay
Lindsay Mackie
Mala Mahadevan
Colin Mair
Virginia Makins
Roger Manser
Fred Martenson
Kostas Mavrakakis
Jamie Maxwell
Andy May
Anne McDermid
Ian McEwan
Peter McLaverty
Tess McMahon
Martin McMillan
John McTernan
Jim Mehta

Sam Mendes

Valerie and Peter Mendes

Catriona Menzies

Anthony Michaels

Peter Milburn

Andrew Milliken

John Mills

John Milne

Michael Mitchell

John Mitchinson

Virginia Moffatt

George Monbiot

Richard Montagu

Charlie Moore

R I Moore

Edward Morgan

Leigh Morgan

Stephen Morris

John Morrison

Dianne Moyes

Matilda Munro

Turi Munthe

Robin Murray

Maurice Naftalin

Tom Nairn

Charles Nathan

Carlo Navato

Alan Neale

Jinty Nelson

Philip Nelson

Alex Newell

Donald Nicholson-Smith

Kalypso Nicolaidis

Sue Nieland

Niels Aagaard Nielsen

Grant Nightingale

Magnus Nome

Richard Norton-Taylor

Hilary Nunn

Jeremy O'Grady

Martin O'Keeffe

Peter Oborne

Mr D Occomore

Mrs T Occomore

Rachel Oldroyd

Don Osborne

John Osmond

Olivette Otele

Tom Overton

Leo Palmer

Graham Partridge &

    Jane Kilpatrick

Nick Pearce

Iain Pears

Ewan Pearson

Margaret Pennington

Sarah Perrigo

Tanya Peters

Julian Petley

Andrew Pettegree

Prof James Pettifer

Ann Pettifor

Drusilla Gabbott Pickthall

William Pike

Chris Pilley

John Pinto

Elizabeth Pisani

Andrea Pisauro

Stephen Pittam

Justin Pollard

Richard Pollitzer
Charlie Pope
Sue Pope
Jonathon Porritt
Henry Porter
Elaine and David Potter
Tom Pratt
Vivien Prendiville
Adam Price
Huw Price
Mari Prichard
Caroline Priday
Stuart Proffitt
Sophia Pugsley
Judith Pullman
Philip Pullman
Tom Quick
Geoffrey Rabe
Benjamin Ramm
Adam Ramsay
Louise Ramsay
Leonie Randall
Pamela Raspe
Ali Rattansi
Susan Richards
Chris Riddell
Mary Riddell
Liam Riley
Ivor Roberts
Mary Roberts
Pippa Robertson
Nick Robins
Matthew Robinson
Judy Robinson
Paul Rogers

Lorraine Rogerson
Lyndal Roper
Ed Ross
Cathy Runciman
Michael Rustin
Maddy Ryle
Michael Salander
Robert Salisbury
Laura Sandys
Billy Sawyers
Julian Sayarer
Bill Schwarz
Roger Scruton
Robert Seago
Matthew Searle
Jean Seaton
Lynne Segal
Niki Seth Smith
John Seymour
Michael Shackleton
Ben Shave
Martin Shaw
Avi Shlaim
Eleanor Shore
Emma Sinclair-Webb
Clifford Singer
Quentin Skinner
John Sloboda
Andrew Smith
Anthony Smith
Naomi Smith
Zadie Smith
Carolyn Smith
David Smith
Ali and Sarah Smith and Wood

Trevor Smith of Clifton

Hamish Soutar

Andrew Sparrow

Dionysios Stathakopoulos

Suzanne Stephenson

David Stevens

Dennis Stevenson

Tim Stevenson

Gordon Stokes

Ian Strathcarron

Keith Sutherland

Chris Swan

Derek Tatton

Chris Taylor

Stephen Taylor

Jessie Teggin

Danielle Texeira

Cameron Thibos

Lucy Moy Thomas

Bill Thompson

Grahame Thompson

Paul Thompson

Peter Thompson

Carol Tinegate

Henry Tinsley

Oscar To

Allan Todd

Robert Tombs

Camilla Toulmin

Robert Triggs

Daniel Trilling

Antzela Tsilikova

TuairimFánach

Nigel Tucker

Ruth Tudge

Miranda Tufnell

Christopher Tugendhat

Kate Tunstall

Andrew Vagg

Marianne Velmans

Jenny Vernon

John Vernon

Gabriel Vogt

Catherine von Heidenstam

Hilary Wainwright

H D Walmsley

David Walser

Frances Walsh

Francis Ware

Vron Ware

Caroline Warman

Felix Warre

Ruth Waterton

Johnny Webb

James Webber

Edwin Weber

Stuart Weir

Jody Wetton

Bernard Weyman

Francis Wheen

Hannah Whelan

Nick Whitaker

Stuart White

Andreas Whittam Smith

Merryn Williams

Richard Williams

Rosy Williams

Derek Wilson

Martin Wolf

Christian Wolmar

SUPPORTERS

Jim Wolton
Penelope Woolley
Peter Wragg
Anna Wright

Will Wyatt
Gareth Young
Martin Young